Lecture Notes in Artificial Intelligence 10413

Subseries of Lecture Notes in Computer Science

LNAI Series Editors

Randy Goebel
University of Alberta, Edmonton, Canada
Yuzuru Tanaka
Hokkaido University, Sapporo, Japan
Wolfgang Wahlster
DFKI and Saarland University, Saarbrücken, Germany

LNAI Founding Series Editor

Joerg Siekmann
DFKI and Saarland University, Saarbrücken, Germany

More information about this series at http://www.springer.com/series/1244

Jan Ole Berndt · Paolo Petta
Rainer Unland (Eds.)

Multiagent System Technologies

15th German Conference, MATES 2017
Leipzig, Germany, August 23–26, 2017
Proceedings

 Springer

Editors
Jan Ole Berndt
University of Trier
Trier
Germany

Paolo Petta
University of Vienna
Vienna
Austria

Rainer Unland
Institute for Computer Science and Business
 Information Systems (ICB)
University of Duisburg-Essen
Essen, Nordrhein-Westfalen
Germany

ISSN 0302-9743   ISSN 1611-3349   (electronic)
Lecture Notes in Artificial Intelligence
ISBN 978-3-319-64797-5   ISBN 978-3-319-64798-2   (eBook)
DOI 10.1007/978-3-319-64798-2

Library of Congress Control Number: 2017948182

LNCS Sublibrary: SL7 – Artificial Intelligence

Printed on acid-free paper

This Springer imprint is published by Springer Nature
The registered company is Springer International Publishing AG
The registered company address is: Gewerbestrasse 11, 6330 Cham, Switzerland

Preface

In 2017, MATES, the German Conference on Multiagent System Technologies, celebrated its 15th edition—a blessed age in a fast-changing and moving field like computer science. Over these 15 years, the MATES conference series has been aiming at the promotion of and the cross-fertilization between theory and application of intelligent agents and multi-agent systems. In all these years, numerous brilliant, renowned keynote speakers, Program Committee (PC) chairs, and honorary chairs helped to promote MATES and to lift it to an internationally highly respected and accepted conference level. This year was no exception as can easily be seen from the list of keynote speakers. Thus, it was no surprise that Springer decided to publish the proceedings ab initio in its *Lecture Notes in Artificial Intelligence* (LNAI) series. And of course, 2017 was no exception.

MATES celebrated its significant birthday during August 23–26, 2017, in Leipzig, Germany, in conjunction with the 2017 IEEE/WIC/ACM International Conference on Web Intelligence (WI 2017). This was seen as a dignified location and setting for this event given the fact that the Steering Committee (SC) of MATES had decided to end this conference series with this event. It was an affair of the heart for the SC to end this series as long as it is still going strong and the SC came to the conclusion that the 15th edition is the right time and location to execute this decision. Of course, now that MATES leaves the stage with its head held high we would like to thank all those who have contributed to the enormous success of MATES, especially Matthias Klusch, as one of the most active founding members of MATES, and Springer for their excellent support of this conference during all these years. We are very grateful to all those who did the work, the PC and honorary chairs, the keynote speakers, the many PC members, the even bigger number of authors. A toast to all.

This year, the combined event of MATES and Web Intelligence offered six excellent keynote talks by renowned scientists and expert practitioners. In particular, distinguished cognitive science scholar Cristiano Castelfranchi contributed his views on the problems of mixed reality and hybrid societies consisting of natural and artificial intelligences. Turing Award winner Raj Reddy extended this vision by discussing the benefits and potentials of computational social science. These positions were complemented by Amit Sheth's talk about the background and applications of semantic, cognitive, and perceptual computing. Frank Leymann bridged the gap between agent-based and Web technologies with his discussion of architectures for loose coupling of systems. Finally, both Christine Preisach and Matthias Klusch focused in their keynotes on the highly timely and exciting topics of the Internet of Things and Industry 4.0. They addressed these emerging technologies from a machine-learning as well as an agent-based computing perspective, respectively.

In addition, both MATES and WI conferences shared a doctoral consortium (DC) program, chaired by Alexander Pokahr and René Schumann. This program offered PhD students a platform to present and to discuss their work in an academic professional environment. Students presented their PhD projects, receiving feedback and suggestions from both their peers and experienced researchers. Moreover, each PhD student was assigned to an expert in the respective field as a mentor for individual interaction.

As conference chairs and on behalf of the MATES SC, we are very grateful to the authors and keynote speakers for contributing to the success of this conference. Moreover, we would like to express our thanks to the PC members and additional reviewers for their timely and helpful reviews of the submissions, as well as to the local organization team at the University of Leipzig. Besides, we are indebted to the Springer LNAI team for their kind and excellent support in publishing these proceedings.

Finally, we hope that all attendees enjoyed MATES 2017 and had interesting inspiration and exciting insights from attending the conference.

June 2017   Jan Ole Berndt
                                                                  Paolo Petta
                                                               Rainer Unland

Organization

General Chairs

Jan Ole Berndt	University of Trier, Germany
Paolo Petta	OFAI and University of Vienna, Austria
Rainer Unland	University of Duisburg-Essen, Germany

Honorary Chairs

Ana L.C. Bazzan	Federal University of Rio Grande do Sul, Brazil
Maria L. Gini	University of Minnesota, USA
Andrea Omicini	University of Bologna, Italy

Doctoral Consortium Chairs

Alexander Pokahr	University of Hamburg, Germany
René Schumann	HES-SO Western Switzerland, Switzerland

MATES Steering Committee

Matthias Klusch	German Research Center for AI (DFKI), Germany
Winfried Lamersdorf	University of Hamburg, Germany
Jörg P. Müller	Clausthal University of Technology, Germany
Sascha Ossowski	Rey Juan Carlos University, Spain
Paolo Petta	OFAI and University of Vienna, Austria
Ingo J. Timm	University of Trier, Germany
Rainer Unland	University of Duisburg-Essen, Germany

Program Committee

Karl Aberer	EPF Lausanne, Switzerland
Thomas Agotnes	University of Bergen, Norway
Sebastian Ahrndt	DAI Lab, Berlin University of Technology, Germany
Matteo Baldoni	University of Turin, Italy
Bernhard Bauer	University of Augsburg, Germany
Federico Bergenti	University of Parma, Italy
Jan Ole Berndt	University of Trier, Germany
Olivier Boissier	ENSM de Saint-Etienne, France
Vicent Botti	DSIC, Spain
Nils Bulling	Capgemini, Germany
Ricardo Büttner	Aalen University, Germany
Cristiano Castelfranchi	National Research Council, Italy

Liana Cipcigan	Cardiff University, UK
Massimo Cossentino	National Research Council, Italy
Paul Davidsson	University of Malmoe, Sweden
Jörg Denzinger	University of Calgary, Canada
Virginia Dignum	Delft University of Technology, The Netherlands
Frank Dignum	University of Utrecht, The Netherlands
Jürgen Dix	Clausthal University of Technology, Germany
Johannes Fähndrich	DAI Lab, Berlin University of Technology, Germany
Klaus Fischer	German Research Center for AI (DFKI), Germany
Giancarlo Fortino	University of Calabria, Italy
Maria Ganzha	Warsaw University of Technology, Poland
Paolo Giorgini	University of Trento, Italy
Vladimir Gorodetsky	Russian Academy of Sciences, Russia
Axel Hahn	University of Oldenburg, Germany
Koen Hindriks	Delft University of Technology, The Netherlands
Stamatis Karnouskos	SAP, Germany
Takahiro Kawamura	Japan Science and Technology Agency, Japan
Wolfgang Ketter	Rotterdam School of Management, The Netherlands
Yasuhiko Kitamura	Kwansei Gakuin University, Japan
Franziska Klügl	University of Örebro, Sweden
Matthias Klusch	German Research Center for AI (DFKI), Germany
Ryszard Kowalczyk	Swinburne University of Technology, Australia
Winfried Lamersdorf	University of Hamburg, Germany
Jiming Liu	Hong Kong Baptist University, SAR China
Arndt Lüder	Otto-von-Guericke University Magdeburg, Germany
John-Jules Meyer	University of Utrecht, The Netherlands
Lars Mönch	University of Hagen, Germany
Jörg P. Müller	Clausthal University of Technology, Germany
Ingrid Nunes	Federal University of Rio Grande do Sul, Brazil
Eugenio Oliveira	University of Porto, Portugal
Nir Oren	University of Aberdeen, UK
Sascha Ossowski	Rey Juan Carlos University, Spain
Peter Palensky	Delft University of Technology, The Netherlands
Marcin Paprzycki	IBS PAN and WSM, Poland
Terry Payne	University of Liverpool, UK
Paolo Petta	OFAI and University of Vienna, Austria
Alessandro Ricci	University of Bologna, Italy
Jordi Sabater Mir	IIIA-CSIC, Spain
David Sarne	Bar-Ilan University, Israel
David Sislak	Czech Technical University, Czech Republic
Michael Sonnenschein	University of Oldenburg, Germany
Andreas Symeonidis	Aristotle University of Thessaloniki, Greece
Huaglory Tianfield	Glasgow Caledonian University, UK
Ingo J. Timm	University of Trier, Germany
Adelinde Uhrmacher	University of Rostock, Germany
Rainer Unland	University of Duisburg-Essen, Germany

Giuseppe Vizzari	University of Milano-Bicocca, Italy
George Vouros	University of Piraeus, Greece
Georg Weichhart	PROFACTOR, Austria
Gerhard Weiss	University of Maastricht, The Netherlands
Michael Weyrich	University of Stuttgart, Germany
Michael Winikoff	University of Otago, New Zealand
Franco Zambonelli	University of Modena and Reggio Emilia, Italy
Ning Zhong	Maebashi Institute of Technology, Japan
Ingo Zinnikus	German Research Center for AI (DFKI), Germany

Additional Reviewers

João Guilherme Faccin
Kai Jander
Paulo Leitao

Claudio Savaglio
Bastin Tony Roy Savarimuthu

Keynotes Abstracts

Semantic, Cognitive, and Perceptual Computing – Three Intertwined Strands of A Golden Braid of Intelligent Computing

Amit Sheth

Wright State University
3640 Colonel Glenn Hwy, Dayton, OH 45435, USA
amit.sheth@wright.edu

Abstract. While Bill Gates, Stephen Hawking, Elon Musk, Peter Thiel, and others engage in OpenAI discussions of whether or not AI, robots, and machines will replace humans, proponents of human-centric computing continue to extend work in which humans and machine partner in contextualized and personalized processing of multimodal data to derive actionable information. In this talk, we discuss how maturing towards the emerging paradigms of semantic computing (SC), cognitive computing (CC), and perceptual computing (PC) provides a continuum through which to exploit the ever-increasing and growing diversity of data that could enhance people's daily lives. SC and CC sift through raw data to personalize it according to context and individual users, creating abstractions that move the data closer to what humans can readily understand and apply in decision-making. PC, which interacts with the surrounding environment to collect data that is relevant and useful in understanding the outside world, is characterized by interpretative and exploratory activities that are supported by the use of prior/background knowledge. Using the examples of personalized digital health and a smart city, we will demonstrate how the trio of these computing paradigms form complementary capabilities that will enable the development of the next generation of intelligent systems.

AI and Machine Learning in IoT

Christine Preisach

SAP Deutschland SE & Co. KG
Hasso-Plattner-Ring 7, 69190 Walldorf, Germany

Abstract. Machine Learning is a hot topic in general, but even more in the area of Internet of Things because of the huge amount of data collected and the necessity to extract insights from it. Example use cases are predictive quality in manufacturing, predictive maintenance for machines, smart buildings, smart cities, smart logistics and many more. In this talk we will discuss why Machine Learning is important and focus on how Machine Learning can be successfully integrated into IoT applications and provide an outlook in the future of AI and Machine Learning in the space of IoT.

Cognition and Self-organization in a Hybrid Society and Coupled Reality: The Role of AI

Cristiano Castelfranchi

Institute of Cognitive Sciences and Technologies
Via San Martino della Battaglia, 44, 00185, Roma, Italy
cristiano.castelfranchi@istc.cnr.it

Abstract. We are not just building a new technology but a new Socio-Cognitive-Technical System, a new form of society, an anthropological revolution. We are social engineers. Are we aware of? I will focus on some problems and dangers of the Digital and WEB Revolution and of the "mixed" (virtual and physical) reality and "hybrid" society (natural and artificial intelligences) we will live in. Not just Privacy, Security, War and Artificial soldiers/arms, Ethics inside Artificial creatures and algorithms and so on, but less discussed problems, like the need for a decentralized control, for a understanding and dealing with self-organization, for becoming aware of the interest behind the "invisible hand" and the "spontaneous" emerging "order". The possibility to improve human intelligence of social dynamics, an effective democracy, and reducing manipulation and alienation. The role of distributed intelligences and of computer modeling and social simulation, as a collective "imagination" power for planning, participation, and policies decisions. The need for dis-agreement technologies, defense of user's interests, supporting and managing conflicts. The role of Intelligent social "presences" in our life and home; guardian angels and tempting devils. The need for a tutelary non-manipulative role.

The Ultimate Web Intelligence: Computational Social Science

Raj Reddy

School of Computer Science, Carnegie Mellon University
Wean Hall 5325, Pittsburgh PA 15213, USA
rr@cmu.edu

Abstract. Computational Social Science (CSS) is the use of Web Intelligence and the tools and technology capable of monitoring, analyzing, diagnosing, and resolving day-to-day problems of society. CSS is the development of intelligent systems and solutions to address the critical problems of the society such as poverty and hunger, slavery and torture, disease and suffering, and create tools that enable an illiterate person to be as productive as a PhD. Computer Science and Artificial Intelligence must embrace CSS as the next frontier in Web intelligence and Web Intelligence and WIC need to be at the forefront of inventing that future.

Loose Coupling and Architectural Implications

Frank Leymann

Institut für Architektur von Anwendungssystemen
Universitätsstraße 38, 70569 Stuttgart, Germany
Leymann@iaas.uni-stuttgart.de

Abstract. Loose coupling is a key architectural principle for ensuring a range of non-functional properties. It is extensively and successfully used in message queuing since many decades. In this talk we will show that service computing (in both styles, i.e. SOA-based as well as REST-based) is enabling loose coupling too. Based on this, the talk will argue why microservices is nothing really new. Best practices (aka patterns) will be discussed that help building loosely coupled applications for the cloud. The use of patters in architecting applications will reveal some opportunities for future research.

Intelligent Agents and Semantic Technologies for Industry 4.0: Showcases and Challenges

Matthias Klusch

German Research Center for Artificial Intelligence (DFKI)
Agents and Simulated Reality Department
Stuhlsatzenhausweg 3, Campus D3.2/R+1.26 66123 Saarbruecken, Germany
matthias.klusch@dfki.de

Abstract. About a decade ago, the fourth industrial revolution, also known as Industry 4.0, has been ushered by the introduction of the Internet of Things and Services into the manufacturing environment. Industry 4.0 is focused on creating smart products and processes flexibly in dynamic, real-time optimised and self-organising value chains, and profitably even down to production lot size of one. To rise up to this challenge, Industry 4.0 applications basically operate on the principles and use of autonomous cyber-physical systems with self-* properties for integrated production across the entire value chain. In particular, the IP-networked and sensor-equipped machinery, systems, vehicles and devices of smart factories are vertically and horizontally integrated with service-based business processes both within a company and inter-company value networks. Besides, cyber-physical production systems are envisioned to not only cooperate with each other but also with humans on a new level of sociotechnical interaction. From a holistic perspective, Industry 4.0 connects smart production closely with the areas of smart transport and logistics, smart buildings, and smart energy, while keeping humans in the loop via smart multimodal assistance in modern working environments. In this context, agent-based and semantic computing both with deep roots in AI are considered as keys to implement intelligent cyber-physical systems for Industry 4.0 scenarios in the future Internet. In this talk, I will present selected showcases of leveraging intelligent agents and semantic technologies for different Industry 4.0 applications, and discuss related research and societal challenges.

Contents

Learning About Human Personalities

Sebastian Ahrndt$^{(\boxtimes)}$ and Sahin Albayrak

Faculty of Electrical Engineering and Computer Science, DAI-Laboratory of the
Technische Universität Berlin, Ernst-Reuter-Platz 7, 10587 Berlin, Germany
sebastian.ahrndt@dai-labor.de

Abstract. This work approaches the question whether or not agents
are able to learn the personality of a human during interaction. We
develop two agent-models to learn about the personality of humans during repeatedly played rounds in the Colored Trails Game. Human personality is described using a psychological theory of personality traits
known as the Five-Factor Model. The results show that some characteristics of a personality can be learned more accurately than others. The
work extends the state-of-the-art in that it does not follow a supervised
learning approach requiring existing data sets.

Keywords: User/machine systems · Human factors · Software psychology · Automatic Personality Recognition · Five-Factor Model · Colored
Trails Game

1 Introduction

Automatic Personality Recognition (APR) is the task of recognising the true personality of an individual [18]. Figure 1 illustrates the cognitive processes together
with this task and highlights the relations between externalised observable
behaviour on the one hand—named *distal cues*—and the perceptual process—
named *proximal cues*—on the other. Within this work, we develop two agent
models that infer the self-assessed personality traits from distal cues. In the context of human-agent interaction, distal cues are all forms of a humans' behaviour
an agent can observe, as most of these behaviours encode personality traces [18]
(e.g. loudness of voice, interaction patterns, appearance). We develop such agent
models, as the related work concentrates on learning personality traits using
supervised approaches, though, in several domains the requirement of having
labelled training data sets is not satisfied. This justifies to approach the question: *Can agents learn about the personality of a human during interaction with
this human?* As a side-question we want to make use of the learned information, and further approach the question: *Can we use the personality information
directly to make informed decisions about the potential behaviour of humans?*

The paper starts with background information in Sect. 2. After introducing
the applied personality theory and the used environment, the paper proceeds
with analysing the related work and classifying our own work in Sect. 3. The

© Springer International Publishing AG 2017
J.O. Berndt et al. (Eds.): MATES 2017, LNAI 10413, pp. 1–18, 2017.
DOI: 10.1007/978-3-319-64798-2_1

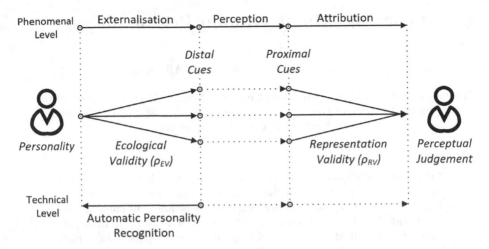

Fig. 1. Brunswick's Lens model and the technical task of Automatic Personality Recognition (APR). APR contributions are based on the idea that each action and in consequence each observable behaviour encodes personality traces. The ecological validity is used to measure the performance of APR solutions, in that it provides the covariation between personality traits and distal cues. This illustration is adopted from published work [18, p. 276].

agent models that are applied are introduced in Sect. 4. The experimental setup and the results are presented in Sect. 5. Finally, we will discuss the results in Sect. 6.

2   Background Information

Next, we give some background information about personality as affective phenomena and how it is defined by psychologist and the scientific game we use to develop and test our agent models.

2.1   Personality – The Five-Factor Model

Human factor psychology describes a human's personality as *". . . a pattern of relatively permanent traits and unique characteristics that give both consistency and individuality to a person's behavior"* [3, p. 4]. Although there are different theories about personality, we have shown [1] that the Five-Factor Model [9] (FFM) is suited for the integration of personality in agents. FFM introduces—as indicated by the name—five dimensions characterising an individual. These are *openness to experience*, which is related to a person's preference to act inventive, emotional and curious vs. acting consistent, conservative and cautious; *conscientiousness*, which is related to a person's preference to act efficient, planned and organised vs. acting easy-going, spontaneous and careless; *extraversion*, which is related to a person's preference to act outgoing, action-oriented and energetic vs.

acting solitary, inward and reserved; *agreeableness*, which is related to a person's preference to act friendly, cooperative and compassionate vs. acting analytical, antagonistic and detached; and *neuroticism* which is related to a person's preference to act sensitive, pessimistic and nervous vs. acting secure, emotionally stable and confident.

2.2 Environment – The Colored Trails Game

The Colored Trails Game [6] (CT) is a multi-agent testbed to investigate cooperative decision making within a chess-like setting.[1] The primal settings of the game are the following: The board is an $N \times M$ grid consisting of coloured squares with a previously defined set of available colours. Each player has a specific starting position and a set of coloured chips. The colours for the squares and chips are determined by the same palette. The player has to use chips that match the colour of an adjacent square to move to that square. The primary objective for each player is to reach one of the 'goal squares', which are marked with a 'G', as reaching it usually ends the game and provides the biggest reward for a player. Secondary objectives could be the amount of remaining chips or the number of rounds played. Having this competitive aspect on the one hand, players have to cooperate with each other during a communication phase on the other. During the communication they are allowed to negotiate the exchange of an arbitrary amount of chips. This phase usually consists of the proposal stage, the decision stage, and the actual exchange of the chips. Offered proposals can be accepted or refused, though, players are not enforced to hand-over the (amount, coloured) chips that have been proposed. Within each game the players act consecutively and alternate their roles as being the proposer or the responder. Finally, CT exchanges the chips and makes the best movement towards the goal square automatically using the Manhattan distance algorithm.

3 Classification and Related Work

In the following, we will concentrate on approaches that specifically focus on recognising personality as one of the phenomena that influence a humans' '... *disposition toward action, belief, and attitude formation.*' [11, p. 146], *i.e.* that focus on personality information as predictive of outcomes of interest [17]; introducing approaches where agents learn the personality of other agents (artificial and natural) in different scenarios.

Agent-based work on this topic originated from approaches that applied social preferences to enhance predictability. Here, [7] presents a work where agent use a weighted sum of the other agents expected outcomes as utility function. The examined behaviour is called socially rational decision-making and is

---

[1] Several groups have used CT to study different behavioural aspects. A list of related papers can be found here: https://goo.gl/BnsXof, last visit: 2017-14-06. We selected CT as it provides a relatively simple environment, which is complex enough to learn aspects of human behaviour as shown in existing work.

based on the idea of social welfare functions, where the individual agents have to balance their individual utilities and the social utilities with the intention to maximise the welfare of the group, making it possible to have selfish or selfless personalities. The authors applied Q-learning in a way that each agents learns which interaction with other agents (personalities) is beneficial. A comparable work is presented in [5] introducing social preferences in terms of the three dimensions self-interest, social welfare and inequity aversion. Agents build knowledge in these dimensions about the other agents and integrate this knowledge into their own decision-making process. [15] use the dimensions equality and selfishness to learn the behaviour of other agents during a repeatedly played trading game. In the experiments, groups of agents played the game and the composition of the group changes during the game, making it one of the early work that adds the requirement of life-long learning. [16] present a work that illustrates the use of a rather simple abstraction of personality types. Personalities of agents are determined through the two dimensions cooperation and reliability. The agents play the CT game and try to optimise a utility function incorporating whether or not the player reaches the goal, the distance to the goal, and the number of chips left. During repeatedly played games the agents reason about each others helpfulness along the two dimensions. Consequently, they try to respond more effectively by customising their behaviour appropriately for different personalities.

The introduced approaches have in common that they learn what can be identified as sub-traits of the Big-Five Factors, *i.e.* traits which cope with specific aspects of one of the five dimensions. However, the models are usually not grounded in psychological literature by the authors, e.g. it is not substantiated how the authors decided what is meant by selfish or selfless behaviour. Furthermore, the agent-models applied learn the behaviour of other artificial agents that simulate different personality aspects. In contrast, we focus on learning the personality of humans. In addition, our goal is not to produce optimal group behaviour but to prove if we can learn personality information in direct interaction with an individual human, and if we can use information about the personality of the human directly to make informed decisions. This work is partly comparable to the discussed related work as it also applies a multi-attributed utility function for the decision-making process. In fact, it is motivated by the work of *Talman et al.* [16] and transfers the presented ideas from agent-agent to human-agent cooperation.

[2] present a work, which examines if the interaction of humans with humans and agents depends on the humans' personality type according to the MBTI. The experiments done using the cake-cutting-game show that the different personalities act in different ways, but also show that there is only little clue, when trying to make predictions about possible behaviour based on information about personality. In any case, the work provides a ground truth, that even in scientific games, one can identify personality characteristics using the available distal cues. [18] presents an overview about 55 publications on automatic personality recognition (pp. 277–282). The authors classified the approaches w.r.t. the used data

sets; classifying it as text-based, based on nonverbal communication, using data sets collected via mobile and wearable devices, social media based, and computer game behaviour based. The majority of the described approaches[2] uses supervised machine learning techniques working on different data sets and distal cues reaching from linguistic features in speech and text to physical activities to social network activities and observations of gaming behaviour.

The majority of the work discussed here applied the FFM using all traits. Roughly half of the described approaches aim to determine the actual personality using the theories' continuous values. The other half aims to determine if a person is on one side of the traits' extremes or the other. This process is called binarization. This work differs from the ones listed in the survey as the agents learn about the personality in direct interaction with the human. In contrast, the other approaches use existing data-sets to learn classifiers using different machine learning techniques. Furthermore, the objective of this work is to learn the actual self-assessed personality characteristics of the human.

4   Modulating Agents That Learn Personality

Our approach is based on the idea to link the personality traits to the available actions by interpreting the meaning of the trait taking into consideration the effect of the action. In doing this, it can categorised as applying reverse factor analysis techniques. To achieve the goal we follow the Realistic Accuracy Model [4], that introduces the concepts of Relevance and Accuracy. These concepts advice one, to restrict the experiments to the relevant traits, i.e. the traits that can be expressed in a given environment, and the available traits, i.e. the traits that can be perceived by others [19]. Given the CT environment we have to restrict our agent models to three of the five dimension (conscientiousness, extraversion, agreeableness) of the FFM. The inclusion of the remaining traits (openness, neuroticism) is hard to accomplish as they cannot be expressed in the environment. That is because, CT does not provide the options to reward or punish creative or conservative behaviour to perceive information about the openness trait. Furthermore, as CT is a scientific game it is not constructed to evoke emotional reactions in its players. One might argue that repeatedly loosing in the game will lead to an emotional reaction; but this effect provides little indication about the emotional stability of a person and cannot be perceived observing the players' game actions. Thus, we do not expect users to show behaviours related to the neuroticism trait. On the other hand, we include conscientiousness due to the trading component and the possibility to cheat on other players, extraversion due to the communication component, and agreeableness due to the negotiation component of the game.

The agent models that will be described next have in common that they follow the same objectives:

---

[2] Only one publication described an unsupervised learning technique.

1. Building an estimate of a humans' personality observing the humans behaviour in the CT game, which is the task of APR that was introduced and will be used to answer the first research question; and
2. Using this estimate to make informed decisions while playing the game, which is the task of predicting the possible course of action of the human and will be used to answer the second research question.

To build an estimate about the personality traits of the human the agent i refers to a human k using the set $P_k = \{p_c^k, p_e^k, p_a^k\}$, where each $p \in P$ represents a personality trait (p_c – conscientiousness, p_e – extraversion, p_a – agreeableness). As the traits within the FFM are characterised using a continuous scale, the range of each p is $[0, 1]$ and the initial value is set to 0.5. This set is the main feature used by i to build the expected utility of taking an action $a \in A$ in the current state $s \in S$ playing against k, which we denote as $u : S \times A \times P$. To improve the estimate of the personality the agent adapts each p during the interaction. In favour of this task, we develop two different approaches that are described next. The first approach learns about the personality of the human online, *i.e.* using the observations directly to adapt the personality estimate. The second one applies a classical Naive Bayes (NB) classifier using relative sparse data to the very same environment and is used to compare the results of the first approach with the commonly used supervised learning techniques.

4.1   Adapting to Human Personality

The first, and arguably simpler model, uses different equations to build estimates from the observation of the humans actions within the game. In the following, we will describe the construction of the model and substantiate the design-decisions that have been made.

The distal cues available to both agent models are restricted to the actions taken by the human. The action-space comprises the action to do nothing, to make proposals to exchange chips, to accept or refuse proposals made by the other, the actual exchange of chips, and the movement of the player. All of these actions, except the latter which is automatically performed by CT, can be used to reason about different facets of the humans personality, e.g. how beneficial a proposal is for oneself or for the opponent or if the human sticks to reached trade agreements or frauds the agents.

In order to adapt the estimates for the individual personality traits we apply the one cue–one trait process [4], in which we use observations of single behaviours of a single cue to build knowledge about a single trait as follows:

– p_c—denotes the estimate of the conscientiousness of the human and is interpreted as how reliable a player is.

Therefore, fulfilling a trade agreement increases and not fulfilling it decreases this value. As failing to predict the reliability of a player can lead to significant score losses for the agent, this trait is of utmost importance. To update the estimate after each trading agreement, we compute the conscientiousness of a human by increasing/decreasing it with a constant factor $x_c \in [0,1]$ using the following equation:

$$p_c \leftarrow \begin{cases} p_c + x_c & \text{if successful exchange} \\ p_c - x_c & \text{if successful exchange but fraud} \\ p_c - 2 \cdot x_c & \text{if fraud} \end{cases}.$$

The first case applies when the proposed set of chips is equal to the one received. The second case applies when the set of proposed and received chips is not equal, but in the set of received chips exist some chips that are useful for the agent. The last case applies if the agent was fooled. This is when there is no exchange or when the agent only receives useless chips. Thus bailing out on an agreed trade is punished harder, as it is a greater break of trust and might critically damage the agent's chance to reach the goal square.

- p_e—denotes the estimate of the extraversion of the human and is interpreted as how contact friendly the player is.

Therefore it is increased when the player makes a proposal of exchanging chips, which is the most extroverted actions possible in the game. It is decreased when the player acts passively not proposing anything. To update the estimate after each round, we compute the extraversion of a human by increasing/decreasing it with a constant factor $x_e \in [0,1]$ using the following equation:

$$p_e \leftarrow \begin{cases} p_e + x_e & \text{if proposed and} \\ p_e - n \cdot x_e & \text{otherwise} \end{cases}$$

The first case applies when the player offers an proposal, the second case otherwise. The multiplicator n is growing until the player offers something and depicts the number of rounds played:

$$n \leftarrow \begin{cases} 0 & \text{if proposed} \\ n + 1 & \text{otherwise} \end{cases}.$$

- p_a—denotes the estimate of the agreeableness of the human and is interpreted as how friendly/altruistic a player is.

Therefore it increases when the player accepts offers and decreases when the player declines an offer. Furthermore, the reward for an acceptance is reinforced if the proposal is favourable to the agent, *i.e.* rewarding an altruistic action twice as much. On the other side, the estimate is decreased twice if the not accepted proposal was indeed favourable for the agent. To update the estimate after each active communication phase, we compute the agreeableness of a human by increasing/decreasing it with a constant factor $x_a \in [0,1]$ using the following equation:

$$p_a \leftarrow \begin{cases} p_a + 2 \cdot x_a & \text{if accepted and favourable} \\ p_a + x_a & \text{if accepted and not favourable} \\ p_a - x_a & \text{if not accepted} \\ p_a - 2 \cdot x_a & \text{if not accepted but favourable} \end{cases}.$$

This equation rewards generous offers and exchanges as they might be harmful to the player's own score. To analyse if the acceptance or non-acceptance was altruistic/favourable requires the CT environment to be fully observable. At the same time, the agreeableness estimate is decreased when the exchange of valuable chips were declined. Thus, the level of agreeableness is a kind of measure of the selfishness of the player.

The constants x_c, x_e and x_a were adjusted and determined in test-games played prior the experiment. For reasons of readability the edge-cases when the estimates reach the minimal/maximal value of the interval are omitted within the formulas. In these cases a positive/negative adjustment is no longer applied.

Using the Personality Estimates. The above-described part of the agent model is used to build the estimates about the humans personality. These personality estimates are used within the decision-making by calculating a utility for each action. The estimates p_e and p_a are utilised to calculate the expectation that a proposal will be accepted, as weighted sum $c^{acc} = p_e \cdot w_e + p_a \cdot w_a$. The weights are used to adjust the influence of the traits. In addition, $e^{exc} = p_c$ indicates the expectation if an agreed exchange indeed takes place.

The second feature to build the expected utility is the reachable score with the current set of coloured chips (r^c), the reachable score after a successful trade (r^t), and the reachable score when falling for a betrayal (r^f). Betrayal means accepting a trade and transferring own chips without getting the promised response. All three can be easily calculated when knowing (1) that CT controls the movement phase by applying the A* algorithm to move towards the goal square and (2) the scoring function of the game, which sums the following parameters: 100 points for reaching the goal square and ending the round as winner; 5 additional points for all coloured chips left; and 10 penalty points for each tile between the final position and the goal square calculated using the Manhattan distance.

Both features are used to calculate the expected value (reward) of executing action a given the current state of the game s using the following multi-attribute utility function when making a proposal:

$$u_a^i(s, P_k) = e^{acc} \cdot e^{exc} \cdot r^t + (1 - e^{acc}) \cdot r^c +$$
$$e^{acc} \cdot (1 - e^{exc}) \cdot r^f.$$

When the agent receives a proposal the likelihood that it will be accepted is not of relevance since the agent can choose its answer and only has to consider that the exchange truly takes place. Therefore we remove e^{acc} when building the utility for an action in this case.

Given this function the estimate of the personality of the human influences the policy of the agent, which tries to maximizes the utility. If equally valued actions exists, the one is selected that was found first. Indeed, in the implementation the agent has no knowledge that there exists more than one action that maximises the utility.

4.2   Bayesian-Based Estimation of Human Personality

The second model applies Bayesian techniques to the same task and environment. In order to receive estimates of the humans' personality the agent is interacting with, we again apply the one cue–one trait process, following the argumentation that a humans' behaviour depends on the personality and the rewards which can be received. Figure 2 depicts these assumptions using the notion of a MDP. It highlights the possible state transitions for the players, the starting state being the proposers position to create a proposal in a one-shot round of the CT game. The move actions and the next round of the game with swapped roles are started automatically, after the process of making a proposal or not $(s_0 \rightarrow s_1 \rightarrow \dots$ or $s_0 \rightarrow s_4)$, accepting the proposal or not $(s_1 \rightarrow s_2 \rightarrow \dots$ or $s_1 \rightarrow s_3)$, and trading the agreed chips (trade) $(s_2 \rightarrow s_5)$ or some other selection of chips (fraud) $(s_2 \rightarrow s_6)$ are finished. Several actions lead to a reward, though, the most beneficial policy is the one that leads to a successful exchange (either trade or fraud) as the scoring-function for the games played reads as follows: each player starts with 100 points; 50 points are granted for reaching the goal square and ending the round as winner; 10 additional points are granted for all coloured chips left; and 20 penalty points for each tile between the final position and the goal square calculated using the Manhattan distance.

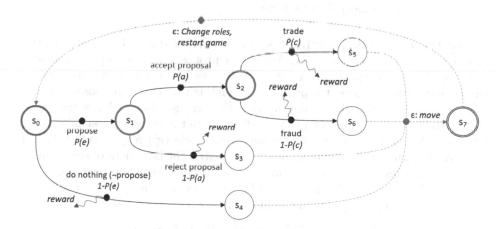

Fig. 2. Illustration of the CT environment using the notion of MDPs (transitions starting in green states are conducted by proposing players, transitions starting in blue states are conducted by responding players). Automatically performed actions are marked with an ϵ. Game restarts with swapped roles after each round. (Colour figure online)

The figure also highlights the linkage between the personality traits and the actions. Again using reverse factor-analysis techniques and interpreting the meaning of the trait taking into consideration the effect of the action. This is done as follows:

– $P(c)$, $1 - P(c)$—denotes the likelihood that a player acts reliable, which is indicated by the conscientiousness of the human. As discussed before, we interpret this trait as how likely an agreed trade will take place $P(trade \mid c)$ $\widehat{=} P(c) \widehat{=} c$ and how likely it is that the agents falls for a betrayal $P(fraud \mid c)$ $\widehat{=} 1 - P(c) \widehat{=} 1 - c$.

– $P(e)$, $1 - P(e)$—denotes the likelihood that a player is contact friendly, which is indicated by the extraversion of the human. As before, we interpret extraversion as how likely it is that a player offers a proposal $P(propose \mid e) \widehat{=}$ $P(e) \widehat{=} e$ or not $P(\neg propose \mid e) \widehat{=} 1 - P(e) \widehat{=} 1 - e$.

– $P(a)$, $1 - P(a)$—denotes the likelihood that a player acts friendly/altruistic, which is indicated by the agreeableness trait of the human. As before, we interpret agreeableness as how likely a player accepts an offer $P(accept \mid a)$ $\widehat{=} P(a) \widehat{=} a$ and how likely an offer is declined $P(reject \mid a) \widehat{=} 1 - P(a) \widehat{=}$ $1 - a$.

Given these links we conduct an experimental protocol where we first play 30 games against a human recording its behaviour and use the generated training data set to train a Naive Bayes (NB) classifier for each human. Thus we follow the assumption of NB, that the attributes we want to use are conditionally independent of each other, given the action space. To handle the relative small sample size for each game, we apply a maximum-likelihood method assuming that all traits are equally likely a priori.

Using the Personality Estimates. In the second stage, the agent uses the classifier to adapt its behaviour. We use a proposer and a responder utility function. For the proposing case, we have to take into account the cases where the human does not accept a proposal, the human accepts a proposal and the trade takes place, and the human accepts the proposal but it dupes the agent during the trade. Again we refer to these facets with the currently reachable score (r^c) and the reachable score after a successful trade (r^t) respectively betrayal (r^f). We introduce the weights w_0, w_1, w_2 to control the behaviour of the agent as acting more or less optimistic and more or less risky, balancing between proposals that are fair and acceptable for both sides vs. proposals that promise maximum score. For the proposing case the utility function reads as follows:

$$u_a^i(s, P_k) = \underbrace{(1 - P(a)) \cdot w_0 \cdot r^c}_{no\ trade} + \underbrace{P(a) \cdot P(c) \cdot w_1 \cdot r^t}_{accept,\ trade} +$$

$$\underbrace{P(a) \cdot (1 - P(c)) \cdot w_2 \cdot r^f}_{accept,\ fraud}.$$

For the responding case the agent only needs to take the likeliness into account that human frauds it during the trade, which shortens the utility function to the following:

$$u_a^i(s, P_k) = \underbrace{P(c) \cdot w_1 \cdot r^t}_{trade} + \underbrace{(1 - P(c)) \cdot w_2 \cdot r^f}_{fraud}.$$

Giving these utilities the personality estimate influences the policy of the agent trying to maximise the utilities. This means, that the agent selects the action with the highest utility, similar to the behaviour discussed in the other agent model.

5   Experimental Setup and Results

For the experiment we implemented the introduced agent models for the CT environment and invited under-graduated students to play against our agents. At the beginning, the participants were asked to self-assess their personality using established assessment questionnaires (as described in the next sections). Afterwards, the game environment was explained and each participant got a 10 min tutorial to get familiar with the environment, the game rules, and the control elements. We explained the rules, the scoring function and played the game in practice with the subjects. In this initial stage the participants played against an agent that did not adapt to the opponent. Afterwards, the attendees played 30 games in a row against the adapting agent and 40 games in a row against the Bayesian agent. The latter applied the learned personality estimates during the last 20 games and used the first 20 games to build the training data set used to train the classifier. The goal of the participants was to reach the maximum score as often as possible. The participant were not explicitly informed about our intention to learn about their personality, but were told that we develop an AI to play CT and want to test it.

5.1   Adapting Agent

In the experiment with the adapting agent 22 participants took part. To assess the personality of the participants we used a 100-Item questionnaire derived from the IPIP[3]. After collecting the data we compare the personality estimates that have been build by the agent and the estimates derived from the self-assessment. Table 1 lists the data. The scoring results listed in column 2 and 3 show the mean value of the points of all 30 games determined for each human player and the agent playing against the participant. It shows that the agent outperforms the human players in average, but the difference is fairly small. Setting up the CT environment we made the individual game rounds more comparable by distributing the same amount of chips to the opponents and centralising the goal square. Taking that and the total number of 660 games played into consideration the scoring difference could be interpreted as an indication that we actually can use the personality information to make informed decisions. However, a detailed discussion of the figures is required to come up with a comprehensive conclusion. To do so, we will discuss both research questions separately next.

---

[3] IPIP—International Personality Item Pool: A Scientific Collaboratory for the Development of Advanced Measures of Personality and Other Individual Differences—http://ipip.ori.org/. For the experiment the 100-Item Set of IPIP Big-Five Factor Markers has been used.

Table 1. Adapting agent – Listing of the average scores reached by the opponents (human and agent) and the average score (μ) and deviation (σ) over all games (column 2 and 3). Listing of the deviation between the agents personality estimates and the one derived from the questionnaire (column 4 to 6). At the bottom the Pearsons r and Spearmans ρ correlation coefficients between the reached scores and the deviation of the personality estimates.

#	Human	Agent	Extraversion	Agreeableness	Conscientiousness
1	111	99	0.18	0.225	0.265
2	107	154	0.09	0.09	0.12
3	98	113	0.02	0.28	0.245
4	121	127	0.075	0.025	0.215
5	118	140	0.035	0.06	0.4
6	105	113	0.05	0.19	0.175
7	132	134	0.03	0.235	0.09
8	100	107	0.14	0.335	0.24
9	88	154	0.015	0.05	0.425
10	142	102	0.045	0.225	0.11
11	104	106	0.055	0.195	0.075
12	105	112	0.07	0.295	0.37
13	99	144	0.06	0.17	0.425
14	121	120	0.065	0.19	0.12
15	126	111	0.16	0.095	0.215
16	145	137	0.04	0.05	0.22
17	86	141	0.025	0.215	0.065
18	102	107	0.015	0.06	0.13
19	138	132	0.145	0.075	0.47
20	154	110	0.05	0.21	0.275
21	101	124	0.02	0.165	0.215
22	97	138	0.125	0.285	0.23
μ	**113.64**	**123.86**	**0.07**	**0.17**	**0.23**
σ	**15.84**	**14.77**	**0.04**	**0.08**	**0.09**
Pearsons r			−0.23	−0.11	0.16
Spearmans ρ			−0.32	−0.06	0.09
			$p > 0.1$	$p > 0.1$	$p > 0.1$

Can agents use our model to learn about the personality of a human during the interaction with this human?

Table 1 lists the deviation between the agents estimate of the personality traits (column 4 to 6) of its opponents and the actual self-assessed personality characteristics derived from the questionnaire including the average deviation. It shows that least variety exists with the extraversion parameter, while agreeableness and conscientiousness are drifting apart stronger (Fig. 3a depicts the spreading of the values in a boxplot chart). A zero value here would mean that both characterisations are perfectly equivalent, which is only a theoretical option, that cannot be reached when comparing the results of different assessment instrument, e.g. self-assessment, questionnaire, professional assessments, or psychological interviews.

To get an indication about the accuracy of the reached results we have to calculate the ecological validity ρ_{EV}, which is the Spearmans ρ between the ranked values of the agents' personality estimate and the self-assessed personality [10,18]. The ecological validity shows to which extent the findings of an experiment could be generalised to real-life settings, *i.e.* it provides a measure that answers the questions whether or not we can use observations from artificial laboratory settings in more natural environments [14]. For the deviation between the self-assessed personality and the agents' estimate of the personality the ecological validity for the traits is $\rho_{EV}^e = 0.88$, $\rho_{EV}^a = 0.36$, and $\rho_{EV}^c = 0.3$. These values substantiate what is already visible in Fig. 3a, showing that the results for extraversion are promising whereas the results for the other traits have to be improved.

One way to improve the results for agreeableness and conscientiousness would be to change the adaptation of the estimation functions for the observed actions, *i.e.* our interpretation of the link between the actions and the agreeableness and conscientiousness trait is not accurate. An obvious solution would be to use the same adaptation mechanism then applied for extraversion. However, several researchers showed that individual mechanisms for each distal cue and each trait are more promising [18]; substantiating our design decisions to use individual mechanisms.

To conclude, the results show that we can learn about the personality of a human in direct interaction and that some characteristics of a personality can be learned more accurately than others. From the experience we gained during the development and substantiated by the related work, it can be concluded that one needs streamlined learning mechanisms for the distal cues that are observable in an environment.

Can we use the personality information directly to make informed decisions about the potential behaviour of the human?

The hypotheses to test our second objective read as follows:

- H_0 : *The agent does not perform differently, i.e. the agents score does not increase/decrease, if the personality estimates becomes more accurate.*
- H_1 : *The agent performs better, i.e. the agents score increases, if the personality estimates becomes more accurate.*

The last two rows of Table 1 show the Pearsons r and Spearmans ρ [10]. Due to the sample size, the Pearson's r is not that meaningful and can only be used to give an indication. This indication is substantiated with the Spearmans ρ, which is better suited for relative small sample sizes. Both values show that the agent performs the worse the more accurate the personality estimate becomes for extraversion and agreeableness (negative correlation). On the other hand, the agent performs better the more accurate the conscientiousness becomes (positive correlation). Here a zero value for either correlation score means that the scoring ranks do not correlate with the ranked personality estimates; in other words, as the scoring ranks increase, the deviation of the personality estimates do not increase (or decrease). As neither r nor ρ become zero for any of the traits we cautiously reject the null hypothesis H_0 as the coefficients show a weak correlation. We cautiously reject it as the significance level of 0.1 is not reached by any of the traits. Thus, for the adapting agent we have to conclude that the applied utility function does not use the personality information to predict the humans course of action in the way it was intended.

5.2   Bayesian Agent

Within the experiment with the Bayesian agent 10 other participants took part. For the personality assessment we used a 30-Item questionnaire provided by *Satow* [13]. We selected another questionnaire as the applied maximum-likelihood method requires prior knowledge about the distribution of the arguments. These values are given by *L. Satow* and read as follows: $p_e = 0.65$, $p_c = 0.65$, and $p_v = 0.75$.[4] These values are not available for the IPIP questionnaire used in the first experiment, neither was the requirement known while performing the first experiment. However, the results remain comparable, as both questionnaires assess the Big Five factors with reasonable reliability coefficients. The remaining setup stayed the same. Again, we will discuss both research questions separately next.

Can agents use our model to learn about the personality of a human during the interaction with this human?

Table 2 lists the data recorded for the Bayesian agent. In column 4 to 6 the deviations between the personality assessment and the personality estimate of the agent are listed. The least variety exists with the conscientiousness trait, though, extraversion shows a closely related value. The average difference and the spreading for the agreeableness trait is much bigger. Figure 3b visualises the results as a boxplot. Due to the fairly small sample size the ecological validity has to be interpreted quite carefully. For each trait it reads as follows: $\rho_{EV}^e = 0.83$, $\rho_{EV}^a = 0.63$, and $\rho_{EV}^c = 0.84$. This gives an indication that the Bayesian agent might work more accurate than the adapting agent, e.g. given another population or another environment. Given much bigger sample sizes, the related work shows several approaches that have applied the NB classifier successfully to the APR task [18]. In contrast to the adapting agent the Bayesian agent applied the same

---

[4] Values are derived from a sample size of 5520 with a Cronbachs Alpha between .76 and .87 [13, p. 20].

Table 2. Bayesian agent – Listing of the results reached for the Bayesian agent. Table show same structure than Table 1.

#	Human	Agent	Extraversion	Agreeableness	Conscientiousness
1	112	113	0.095	0.47	0.115
2	139	110	0.06	0.225	0.03
3	113	113	0.035	0.225	0.06
4	115	123	0.175	0.155	0.195
5	116	110	0.18	0.155	0.075
6	129	129	0.07	0.03	0.175
7	115	119	0.215	0.43	0.16
8	129	127	0.39	0.12	0.3
9	125	108	0.13	0.3	0.035
10	135	111	0.05	0.05	0.175
μ	**122.6**	**116.2**	**0.14**	**0.22**	**0.13**
σ	**9.28**	**7.29**	**0.08**	**0.11**	**0.07**
Pearsons r			0.38	0.21	0.41
Spearmans ρ			0.28	0.09	0.47
			$p > 0.1$	$p > 0.1$	$p > 0.1$

approach to each distal cue, eliminating one dynamic factor. Still, the figures reveal a difference between the individual traits. This substantiate the prior made statement, that one should use different techniques to recognise the effects of personality traits that are expressed within a distal cue that can be observed.

Can we use the personality information directly to make informed decisions about the potential behaviour of the human?

Column 2 and 3 of Table 2 list the scoring results including mean and deviation. In contrast to the adapting agent the human outperformed the Bayesian agent in more than half of the games. Indeed the humans were successful in 224 of the 400 played games. Taking the same hypotheses as above into account, we can again reject the null hypothesis H_0 as shown by the correlation coefficients. As they are positive for each of the traits, it seems promising to repeat the experiment with a stronger null hypothesis, which could be read as follows: The agent does not perform better, i.e. the agents score does not increase, if the personality estimates becomes more accurate, i.e. if the deviation of self-assessed personality and the agents estimates decreases. The strongest correlations exists for the conscientiousness trait, however, neither of the correlations reach an acceptable significance level and the number participants is fairly small. Thus, as well as for the adapting agent we conclude for the Bayesian agent that the applied utility function does not use the personality information to predict the humans course of action in the way it was intended.

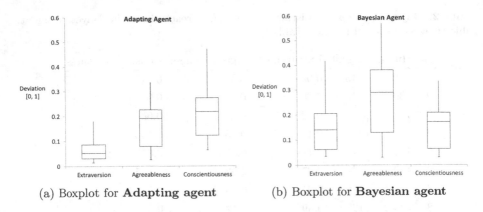

(a) Boxplot for **Adapting agent**   (b) Boxplot for **Bayesian agent**

Fig. 3. Deviation between questionnaire and the agents' personality estimate.

6 Discussion

The results that have been described are mixed. On the one hand, they show that we are able to learn about the personality in direct interaction with the human using a fairly simple approach or using only a few observations to train a classifier. On the other hand, we learned that the linkage between the observable actions and the expressible and interpretable distal cues is crucial. Furthermore, the results show that we were not able to use the learned personality estimates given the described utility functions.

Since the CT game has very limited action space available to evaluate and analyse the behaviour of the other player, it is complicated to associate these actions with factors of the FFM. Thus, the environment/action-space might have to be more complex. Another possible explanation for the estimates not depicting the assessment results is that a person might behave different to the interpretation we had while associating actions with traits. Since the goal of the game is to reach the best possible score, it might be beneficial to use a more generalised trait just indicating how cooperative the human is (*cf.* [16]). Despite these imaginable hindrances the outcome is still good, especially for the value of extraversion.

It can be concluded, that some of the traits can be estimated more accurately than others, at least in the CT environment. During the experiment we followed the relevance and accuracy features. Leading to the focus on three out of the five traits of the FFM. It was shown that we were able to more accurately learn the extraversion trait than the agreeableness and conscientiousness trait. There are multiple reason for that. One is based on the distal cues itself, *i.e.* are those cues observable and how well does the physical cue encode the characteristics of the personality traits. This is known as the good trait variable of accuracy [4, p. 662], which describes the possibility that some traits might be easier to estimate accurately than others as some behaviours might be easier to judge than others. To approach this problem, we provided and discussed justifications how and why we made design decisions in the agent model. It is just right, to assume that we made errors during this process coming up with an inaccurate agent model and that better results can be achieved with another one. One potential problem here is an oversimplification of the effects of the personality traits on the distal cues. Another reason can be found in the perception module, *i.e.* how we actually used observed behaviours to generate personality estimates. This is known as the good judge variable of accuracy [4, p. 660], which describes the possibility that different individuals are differently good in judging personality. Although [4] writes about human judgement, these variables apply for machine learning as well as shown by the different approaches and their reached accuracies on same data sets in [18]. To approach this problem, we applied two different approaches within the same setting. Both of them show the same tendency that in the selected environment using the identified distal cues, extraversion can be better estimated than agreeableness and agreeableness can be better estimated than conscientiousness.

The above-discussed points are directly related to the presented approach. Beside that, we can identify limitations w.r.t. the conducted experiments and result analysis. First of all, the sample size for both experiments is limited ($n_{adapting} = 22$, $n_{bayesian} = 10$) making it possible that the results are random, biased w.r.t. the sample, or related to other (non-human) factors [8]. Other common method biases such as the measurement and item context effects may induce further weaknesses [12]. Within the experimental design we addressed this by separating the measurement of the self-assessed personality and the agents' estimation using a cover story that disconnected both parts.

Overall, although the results are mixed, we argue that the presented findings provide interesting insights into the task of learning about personality traits in interaction with a human. That is because very little is known about this task as shown in the related work section. Thus, even imperfect information and approaches offer valuable insights at this stage.

Acknowledgement. Special thanks goes to Dr.-Ing. Frank Trollmann for his insightful comments and to the anonymous reviewers for their valuable critique, suggestions, and questions.

References

1. Ahrndt, S., Aria, A., Fähndrich, J., Albayrak, S.: Ants in the OCEAN: modulating agents with personality for planning with humans. In: Bulling, N. (ed.) EUMAS 2014. LNCS (LNAI), vol. 8953, pp. 3–18. Springer, Cham (2015). doi:10.1007/978-3-319-17130-2_1
2. Du, H., Huhns, M.N.: Determining the effect of personality types on human-agent interactions. In: 2013 IEEE/WIC/ACM International Joint Conference on Web Intelligence (WI) and Intelligent Agent Technologies (IAT), vol. 2, pp. 239–244. IEEE (2013)
3. Feist, J., Feist, G.J., Roberts, T.A.: Theories of Personality. McGraw-Hill Education, New York City (2012)

4. Funder, D.C.: On the accuracy of personality judgment: a realistic approach. Psychol. Rev. **102**(4), 652–670 (1995)
5. Gal, Y., Pfeffer, A., Marzo, F., Grosz, B.J.: Learning social preferences in games. In: Proceedings of the 19th National Conference on Artificial Intelligence, pp. 226–231. The AAAI Press (2004)
6. Grosz, B.J., Kraus, S., Talman, S., Stossel, B., Havlin, M.: The influence of social dependencies on decision-making: Initial investigations with a new game. In: Proceedings of the 3rd International Joint Conference on Autonomous Agents and Multiagent Systems (AAMAS 2004), pp. 782–789. ACM Press (2004)
7. Hoog, L.M., Jennings, N.R.: Socially intelligent reasoning for autonomous agents. IEEE Trans. Syst. Man Cybern. **31**(5), 381–393 (2001)
8. Hunter, J.E., Schmidt, F.L.: Methods of Meta-Analysis, 2nd edn. Sage Publications Inc., Thousand Oaks (2004)
9. McCrea, R.R., John, O.P.: An introduction to the five-factor model and its applications. J. Pers. **60**(2), 175–215 (1992)
10. McDonald, J.H.: Handbook of Biological Statistics, 3rd edn. Sparky House Publishing, Baltimore (2014)
11. Pianesi, F.: Seasearch for personality. IEEE Signal Process Mag. **1**(30), 146–158 (2013)
12. Podsakoff, P.M., MacKenzie, S.B., Lee, J.Y., Podsakoff, N.P.: Common method biases in behavioral research: a critical review of the literature and reommended remmedies. J. Appl. Psychol. **88**(5), 879–903 (2003)
13. Satow, L.: Big-Five-Persönlichkeitstest (B5T): Testmanual und Normen (2012). http://www.drsatow.de
14. Schmuckler, M.A.: What is ecological validity? A dimensional analysis. Infancy **2**(4), 419–436 (2001)
15. Sen, S., Dutta, P.S.: The evolution and stability of cooperative traits. In: Proceedings of the 1st International Joint Conference on Autonomous Agents and Multiagent Systems. ACM (2002)
16. Talman, S., Hadad, M., Gal, Y., Kraus, S.: Adapting to agents' personalities in negotiation. In: Pechoucek, M., Steiner, D., Thompson, S. (eds.) Proceedings of the 4th International Joint Conference on Autonomous Agents and Multiagent Systems (AAMAS), pp. 383–389. ACM (2005)
17. Vinciarelli, A.: More personality in personality computing. IEEE Trans. Affect. Comput. **5**, 297–300 (2014)
18. Vinciarelli, A., Mohammadi, G.: A survey of personality computing. IEEE Trans. Affect. Comput. **5**, 273–291 (2014)
19. Wright, A.G.: Current directions in personality science and the potential for advances through computing. IEEE Trans Affect Comput **5**(3), 292–296 (2014)

An Agent Architecture for Simulating Communication Dynamics in Social Media

Stephanie C. Rodermund, Fabian Lorig, Jan Ole Berndt$^{(\boxtimes)}$, and Ingo J. Timm

Business Informatics 1, Trier University, 54296 Trier, Germany
{s4strode,lorigf,berndt,itimm}@uni-trier.de

Abstract. Social media like Facebook, Twitter, or Google+ have become important communication channels. Nonetheless, the distribution and dynamics of that communication make it difficult to analyze and understand. To overcome this, we propose an agent architecture for modeling and simulating user behavior to analyze communication dynamics in social media. Our agent decision-making method utilizes sociological actor types to represent motivations of media users and their impact on communicative behavior. We apply this concept to a simulation of real world Twitter communication accompanying a German television program. Our evaluation shows that the agent architecture is capable of simulating communication dynamics in human media usage.

Keywords: Agent architecture · Social actor types · Social media communication · Agent-based social simulation

1 Introduction

Within the last decade, *social media* like Facebook, Twitter, or Google+ have become predominant means of communication for both private and professional users. They are used for purposes as various as casual smalltalk, commercial marketing campaigns, and the shaping of political opinion [19,23].

However, the inherent distribution of social media and the dynamics of user interactions therein make it difficult to analyze and comprehend that communication. Agent-based social simulations (ABSS) [11] are a promising technique for understanding complex dynamics of interrelated communication activities. For instance, viral dynamics of mass phenomena in social media like the *harlem shake* [6] can be reproduced by representing media users with artificial agents [21]. The interrelated activities of these agents within a simulation lead to emergent dynamics. Exploring various user populations and agent decisions in a controlled experiment helps understand these dynamics in real world social media [33].

Nevertheless, there is a discrepancy between the majority of agent-based models for social media analysis on the one hand and the available agent architectures based on sociological, philosophical, and psychological theories on the other. While the ABSS community has recognized these architectures for agent

© Springer International Publishing AG 2017
J.O. Berndt et al. (Eds.): MATES 2017, LNAI 10413, pp. 19–37, 2017.
DOI: 10.1007/978-3-319-64798-2_2

decision-making [1], agent-based social media simulation focuses largely on simple reactive agents (e.g., threshold models of information diffusion) without accounting for elaborate decision-making [10,18,36]. That is, these models only address the question, *whether or not* users communicate in a social network.

In this paper, we complement the aforementioned approaches with a sociologically inspired agent decision-making architecture for simulating user motivations and the resulting behaviors. In particular, we aim at modeling *when* and *why* users communicate in *which* way. This requires more differentiated models of agent decision contexts, their available activities, and their action selection mechanisms. Only if the agents in a social simulation experiment are complex enough in these respects, it is possible to reproduce realistic communication processes and to explain why and how these processes emerge.

The remainder of the paper is structured as follows. Section 2 provides an overview of social media communication, sociological and psychological models, as well as agent-based approaches to social simulation. Subsequently, Sect. 3 describes our agent decision-making concept for modeling communication dynamics. This concept covers the decision-making of individual social actors as well as populations of media users. Section 4 applies the concept to an example of communication processes on Twitter which accompany a German television program. In Sect. 5 we evaluate the agent architecture by simulating communication in that scenario and by comparing our results to a real world dataset. Finally, Sect. 6 provides a concluding summary and an outlook on future work.

2   Foundations

Agent-based social simulation models consist of three main components: The agents' decision-making *context*, their decision *mechanisms*, and their available *activity options* in a specific context. An agent observes a situation which provides the context for its decision. The decision itself is made by selecting an activity by means of its agent function (i.e., the decision mechanism). While context and activities depend on a particular application domain, there are domain independent theories and architectures for the actual decision-making. Thus, the following sections first introduce the application domain of social media communication to provide a scenario for agent-based social simulation. Subsequently, they discuss sociological and psychological theory and techniques for modeling decisions as well as the underlying motivations in such a setting.

2.1   Social Media Communication

Human communication can be considered as a sequence of actions by individuals, where the behavior of a sender influences the behavior of a receiver [3]. The sender uses a set of characters to encode a message, which is transmitted using an information medium. The receiver uses an own set of characters to decode and interpret the message and returns a feedback using the same mechanism [31]. The formulation and transmission of messages by the sender as well as the corresponding reaction by the receiver form the communicative activities available to users of social media.

Social media provide options to their users to connect and communicate with each other. In terms of graph theory, such a structure can be described by a set of users (nodes) and relationships between the users (edges) [35]. For instance, the online social network Twitter can be modeled as a directed graph. Twitter distinguishes between *followers* and *followees*. A user actively and voluntarily decides which other users to *follow* for receiving their status updates (Tweets). Being followed by another Twitter participant makes a user become a *followee*. However, the user being followed does not need to follow its *followers*.

When a user publishes a message on Twitter, all of that person's followers become notified. However, it is also possible to address other users directly in order to reply to a message and to forward messages to others. Using the @-symbol followed by the name of a user or putting the prefix *"RT"* (retweet) at the beginning of a Tweet establishes sequences of messages. These sequences form dialogs and conversations between two or more users [8]. In addition, Twitter provides another operator for classifying the content of a message. To that end, the #-symbol (hashtag) is used for categorizing messages and for marking keywords that describe the topic of a conversation.

Twitter has been widely used for conducting studies of certain subjects or events, e.g., spread of news and criticism [20,33], the activity of diseases [32], or political communication [23]. In an agent-based social simulation of such phenomena, the agents' activities comprise publishing messages. Their options among which to choose are given by the aforementioned operators. They can introduce new messages, retweet existing ones, address particular users, and cover specific topics. In addition, further content descriptors can cover the tonality and style of messages. This leads to a variety of possible agent activities.

Moreover, in a simulated conversation, an agent's previous messages as well as other agents' Tweets about the same topic form the context of the agent's decision-making. The agent observes the preceding sequence of messages and decides whether and how to react to it. Consequently, it requires a mechanism to process the conversational context and to select a response. In order to obtain a realistic simulation, it is desirable take sociological and psychological analyses into account for developing agent decision-making mechanisms. Such theory can provide deeper insights into the dynamics of communication processes and the underlying motivations of social actors from which they emerge.

2.2   Sociological and Psychological Models

Communication is inherently social. In fact, sociality can be considered to consist entirely of communication [22]. Social systems emerge from interconnected communicative activities being selected by social actors [15]. Those actors are influenced by an observed social situation and decide about their reactions to that situation which results in observable behaviors that lead to the emergence of a new situation (cf. Fig. 1). For example, a Twitter user can observe an ongoing conversation about a specific topic (1). She may decide to utter a controversial opinion about that topic (2) which becomes observable to other users in the form of her respective Tweet (3). This changes the conversation and provokes further reactions. Thus, the conversation on the macro-social level (4) both influences individual behaviors on the micro-social level and emerges from them.

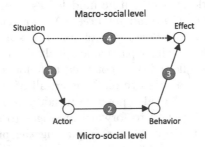

Fig. 1. Emergence of macro-social effects from micro-social behavior [15].

For explaining macro-level communication dynamics by means of the afore-mentioned model, it is necessary to understand the behaviors of participating actors on the micro-level. As discussed in the preceding section, in social media, the visibility of the situational context (1) is given by the social network platform. That platform also provides the activity options and publishes the selected action for other users to observe (3). However, given a specific situation, the user behavior (2) depends on various attributes and dispositions like static personal and demographic traits as well as dynamic motivations. Psychologically and sociologically grounded analyses identify these traits and motivations in order to derive their impact on the decision-making from empirical evidence.

There are several analyses of user behavior in social media available. For instance, activity frequencies on Twitter have been related to user attributes and traits such as gender, age, region, and political opinion [27]. While such an analysis reveals *how* social media users interact with each other, it cannot explain *why* they do it. To answer that question, other studies cover motivations for communication. These motivations can be categorized into groups like *smalltalk*, *entertainment*, or *information and news sharing* [17]. Additionally, they can be derived from psychological personality traits [21,34]. Such approaches provide insights into the decision-making of social actors in diverse situations ranging from casual comments on a television series [29] to crisis communication [16].

In addition to social media specific and psychologically founded motivations, there are also theoretical foundations for describing actor behaviors in sociology. Sociologists distinguish between four basic social actor types which differ in their behavior [12]. Firstly, a *homo economicus* is a rational decision-maker who strives to maximize her personal utility. Such an actor attempts to reach personal goals as efficiently as possible, whereas such a goal does not need to be monetary. Secondly, a *homo sociologicus* obeys social norms and obligations. This actor type tries to conform with expectations in order to avoid negative sanctions.

Thirdly, an *emotional man* is driven by uncontrollable emotions such as love, anger, respect, or disgust. This leads to affective behavior in response to, e.g., unfulfilled expectations [14]. Finally, an *identity keeper* tries to establish and maintain a desired social role. Such an actor seeks social acknowledgment by provoking positive reactions toward stereotypical behaviors. These basic types are theoretically well-founded and can be utilized to describe basic as well as mixed social motivations of humans [12].

2.3 Agent Architectures for Social Simulation

Communication processes in social media emerge from individual activities of the participating users. For experimentally analyzing such emergent phenomena, agent-based computer simulation has been established as a standard means. By modeling real world actors as software agents, individual behavior and antici- pation of behavior on the micro level can be simulated resulting in emergent effects on a macro level [4,7]. In terms of social sciences, this is referred to as agent-based modeling and agent-based social simulation [11].

The majority of agent-based models in social media analysis focuses on *infor- mation propagation*. These models aim at identifying the optimal group of users to spread information to as many others as possible [36]. The users are fre- quently modeled as reactive agents with behavioral rules that fire if an activation threshold is reached. The threshold denotes the required strength of influence (e.g., a number of received messages) on an agent until it becomes active itself. This method is particularly relevant for planning marketing campaigns in social media which make use of information propagation effects [10,18].

While threshold models are usually investigated by means of simulation stud- ies, there are also *analytical approaches* to agent-based modeling of opinion for- mation. These focus on the interactions among agents which lead to the diffusion and adoption of opinions in a process of compromising [25]. They model these interactions by means of thermodynamics [30] or the kinetic theory of gases [24]. These methods describe the emergence of macro-social phenomena from micro-social interactions using differential equations. This allows for analyzing the resulting opinion dynamics mathematically.

However, there is a discrepancy between threshold and analytical models on the one hand, and sociological perspectives on decision-making on the other. While these methods describe *how* opinion and communication dynamics occur in agent-based social simulations, they lack the descriptive power to analyze *why* this happens. That is, they focus on the dynamics between interacting agents and treat the agent population as a homogeneous mass. For instance, in kinetic theory, gas molecules behave solely according to their current states and their mutual influences without having individual habits. As a result, the discussed approaches largely leave the communication content as well as the participating users' underlying motivations out of account.

Thus, to understand human behavior, more elaborate agent decision approaches are necessary. In fact, a wide range of agent architectures based on philosophy, psychology and cognitive science is readily available [1]. The most prominent of those is the *belief-desire-intention* (BDI) architecture of practical reasoning [9, 28]. BDI agents are well-suited for modeling motivations in terms of *desires* and for deriving *intentional* behavior from them according to *beliefs* about the current situational context.

Nonetheless, BDI agents are more complicated to apply than reactive architectures. They are especially suitable for modeling strategic and goal-directed behavior. By contrast, social media communication is often governed by affective and spontaneous contributions [33]. Hence, there is no need for modeling persistent intentions to satisfy communicative desires in such a setting. Consequently, we propose to strike a balance between cognitive and reactive agents which utilizes the aforementioned sociological foundations for modeling complex agent behaviors based on social actor types.

Sociological theory and agent technology have been combined in the interdisciplinary field of *socionics* [13]. In that context, Dittrich and Kron model social characters by means of actor types and combinations between these types [12]. They simulate the "bystander dilemma" in which persons must decide whether or not to help a victim of physical violence. In their model, agents with the *homo sociologicus* and *identity keeper* roles feel obliged to help while *homo economicus* and *emotional man* flee the situation. Combining these dispositions on both the individual and population levels leads to complex macro-social behaviors.

As social actor types provide a simple method for modeling complex agent motivations, they are a promising concept for simulating other human interaction dynamics. However, it is unclear, how they can be transferred to other applications. Therefore, we provide an agent decision-making architecture based on these actor types and show its applicability for simulating communication dynamics in social media in the remainder of this paper.

3   Agent Decision-Making Concept

In this section, we adapt the agent decision-making approach by Dittrich and Kron [12] to modeling communicative user behavior in social media. In particular, we model the selection of messages about a specific topic to be published on a social media platform within a limited time frame [2].

Our modeling and simulation concept is structured as depicted in Fig. 2. Each decision-making situation receives an input of one or more keywords to

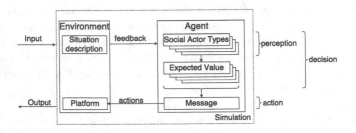

Fig. 2. Agent-environment interaction and agent decision-making concept.

describe that situation (e.g., a list of hashtags or abstract topic description). The respective output consists of messages being published at the social media platform by the population of agents. In order to produce that output, each agent observes the situation and calculates expected values for its potential reactions according to its respective social actor type and depending on the activities of other agents. It then selects its next message (or chooses not to publish any message) with respect to these expected values. The following sections describe the actor types, their combinations, and the resulting agent populations.

3.1   Social Actor Types and Decision-Making

According to Fig. 2, the agent decision-making maps a perceived situation description to a communicative action. Given a set S of possible situations and a set A of available actions, the agent function has the following structure.

$$action : S \rightarrow A$$

Besides the current situation $s \in S$, its social actor type determines an agent's decision-making. To that end, we model each type by means of a function EV that returns an expected value for each available activity option. For a *homo economicus* (HE), this amounts to a standard utility function. Contrastingly, a *homo sociologicus* (HS) prefers socially adequate behaviors over controversial actions. Such an agent makes its behavior dependent on contributions to a conversation by other agents. In addition, while the *identity keeper* (IK) has a genuine desire to further any kind of discussion, the *emotional man* (EM) only becomes active when being emotionally affected by the situation.

All of the expected value functions should cover the same range of values to make them comparable with each other. That range depends on the number of available activity options and their effects in a particular application scenario. Each option can either have a positive, neutral, or negative effect on an agent's motivations. For instance, a scenario with five possible messages can be encoded through the following set of values: $\{-1, 0, 1, 2, 3\}$. In this case, a message is either detrimental to an agent's goals (-1), it can be neutral towards them (0), or it furthers its motivations to different extents $(1-3)$. Then, the agent can select its next action $a \in A$ depending on the situation s as follows.

$$action_i(s) = \arg\max_a EV_i(s, a)$$

Each actor type $i \in \{HE, HS, EM, IK\}$ maximizes its expected value for all available actions a in the situation s. If there are several options with the same value, an agent decides randomly among them. This results in a specific message (i.e., Tweet) being selected and published at the simulated social network platform for all other agents to observe.

3.2   Actor Type Combinations and Populations

According to the preceding decision-making model, each agent can implement one of the four available actor types. However, these are only prototypical examples for categorizing motivations. In fact, an actor's motivational disposition will often be more adequately described by a mixture of several basic motivations [12]. Consequently, we allow for combinations of actor types within individual agents to represent that phenomenon.

For mixing several actor types, each agent is defined by four weights w_i, one for each actor type i, with $\sum_i w_i = 1$. Those weights denote the ratio with which those types contribute to its decision-making. Then, an agent with mixed types selects its activities by maximizing the weighted sum of the respective expected values (with a randomized selection in case of several maxima).

$$action(s) = \arg \max_a \sum_i EV_i(s, a)\, w_i$$

In addition to combining actor types within an individual agent, it is also possible to mix different agents within the overall agent population. That is, a population can either consist of homogeneous agents that all implement the same actor type combination, or it can comprise different agents. Homogeneous populations are particularly useful for model validation and calibration. They make the effects of different value functions easily observable and adjustable. Contrastingly, heterogeneous populations are more realistic. They lead to complex interaction dynamics which are necessary for replicating and explaining user behaviors in social media as described in the following sections.

4   Application to Social Media Communication

The preceding section has outlined the general agent decision-making behavior without specifying the application-dependent expected value functions for the four actor types. In this section, we complement that description by applying our modeling concept to an analysis of user behavior in communication processes on Twitter. In particular, we model live-tweeting behavior during an episode of the German television series "Tatort" (meaning *crime scene*). Running since 1970, "Tatort" is the most popular German TV series which attracts a broad audience across all social groups, genders, and ages. We use a dataset of Tweets about the episode "Alle meine Jungs" (*all my boys*), of May 18, 2014. The dataset has been obtained through the Twitter-API and contains 7448 Tweets. Out of these, 192 original Tweets (excluding Retweets) form eight distinct phases of Twitter activity which correspond to specific scenes of the episode. These scenes provide the situation for the agents in our model to react to. Each of them is described by one or more out of five attributional categories as shown in Table 1. The categories are described by

$$C = \{\text{thrilling, funny, music-related, emotional, judgmental}\}.$$

Each scene in this model is represented by a subset of C. Hence, $S = 2^C$ is the set of all possible scene descriptors.

The agents can act repeatedly during each scene. At the beginning of a scene, they base their actions only on the respective description; subsequently, they

Table 1. Situation descriptions.

Scene	Description
0	Thrilling
1	Funny, music-related
2	Funny, music-related
3	Funny, music-related
4	Funny
5	Thrilling, emotional
6	Thrilling
7	Judgmental

can also react to other agents' Tweets. Thus, a dynamic communication system emerges from these interrelated activities. In the following, we particularize the available actions and the decision-making of the four actor types.

4.1 Agent Activity Options and Auxiliary Functions

The Tweets in our data set can be classified by their sentiment and tonality along two different dimensions. They are either positive or negative and they are either joking or not joking (i.e., serious). The possible combinations of these categories result in four different message types available to the agents. However, since not all users reply to every message, an agent also has the option not to tweet. Nevertheless, it can still decide to participate in the conversation about the current scene at a later time after observing Tweets by other agents. This results in the following set A of five activity options.

$$A = \{\text{No tweet, Tweet}-\text{positive}-\text{joking, Tweet}-\text{positive}-\text{not joking,}$$
$$\text{Tweet}-\text{negative}-\text{joking, Tweet}-\text{negative}-\text{not joking}\}$$

Which option $a \in A$ an agent selects at what time depends on its underlying combination of actor types as well as on the activities of other agents. To include the latter into the decision-making, we define two auxiliary functions φ_s and $tweets_s$ which count published messages in the original data set as well as in the simulated communication process, respectively. The function $\varphi_s : A_{s \in S} \to \mathbb{N}$ returns the absolute number of each action a in scene $s \in S$ as contained in the data set. Analogously, the numbers of different Tweets being published at the time of decision in the agent-based simulation is given by $tweets_s : A_{s \in S} \to \mathbb{N}$. Those functions are necessary to take the activities of other agents into account in the agent decision-making process.

4.2 Agent Decision-Making

In our application example, the four actor types represent typical behavioral roles and motivations in social media communication. These include the maximization of publicity, a desire for serious discussion, the expression of anger, as well as genuine content production. These motivations are represented by the *homo economicus*, *homo sociologicus*, *emotional man*, and *identity keeper*, respectively. For all actor types, we evaluate the available activity options with respect to those motivations in each situation in order to identify expected values for the agents' decisions. Table 2 summarizes the criteria and values for that evaluation.

Table 2. Agent decision-making by social actor types (expected values).

Homo economicus	Homo sociologicus	Emotional man	Identity keeper
No tweet (0)	Must (3)	Unchanged (0)	Strengthened (3)
Utility function	Should (2)	Increased (−1)	Weakened (−1)
(0 to 3)	Can (1)	Decreased (2)	
Conversation size	Should not (−1)	Strongly	
Threshold (−1)		Decreased (3)	

In social media communication, a *homo economicus* agent tries to maximize the impact of its contributions on the conversation. Such an agent gains the highest utility by reaching agreement with as many others as possible. Thus, its underlying utility function anticipates probable majority opinions. Actions supporting these are rated higher than less popular or controversial contributions according to the ratio of actions in the original dataset. This agent type will maintain its ratings during a conversation regardless of other agents' behaviors. In addition, we use a threshold of a minimal number of Tweets by other agents for the agent to become active itself. The threshold is the mean number of Tweets across all scenes. Until this threshold is reached, an agent will not participate in the conversation which leaves its utility unchanged. Thus, the *homo economicus* represents a casual media user who only joins ongoing conversations to represent common sense opinions shared by the expected majority of recipients.

The corresponding expected value function depends on the Tweets published in the current scene s so far as given by $tweets_s$. If the overall number of Tweets in $\sum_{a' \in A} tweets_s(a')$ does not exceed the threshold, the *homo economicus* has a value of -1 for all other actions than the no Tweet option. The threshold $\frac{1}{|A|} \sum_{a' \in A} \varphi_s(a')$ is the arithmetic mean of all Tweets throughout the scenes in the entire original data set. Otherwise, the agent selects its actions according to their share in the real world data set given by $\varphi_s(a)$ The prevalent action is yielded by the term $\max_{a' \in A}(\varphi_s(a'))$ which iterates over all possible actions in the respective scene. Moreover, the utility values for a *homo economicus* are normalized and rounded to natural numbers between 0 and 3.

$$EV_{HE}(s,a) = \begin{cases} -1 & \text{, if } \sum_{a' \in A} tweets_s(a') < \frac{1}{|A|} \sum_{a' \in A} \varphi_s(a') \\ \left\lfloor 3 \frac{\varphi_s(a)}{\max_{a' \in A}(\varphi_s(a'))} \right\rfloor & \text{, otherwise} \end{cases}$$

Contrastingly, a *homo sociologicus* agent rates the available actions according to both general social norms as well as other agents' behaviors. Its expected value function evaluates these options by their perceived strength of obligation. For instance, an agent *should not* joke about an emotional scene. However, if the majority of other agents has deviated from such norms before, the *homo sociologicus* will mimic these previously observed activities in order to gain acceptance by other agents. Hence, that type of agent represents a both morally concerned and opportunistic user who joins the dominant group as soon as one emerges. This behavior is typical, e.g., in massive online protests [33].

The expected value of a *homo sociologicus* agent depends on the norm for the current situation and the predominant action so far. The function $norm(c, a)$ returns a value of -1 for an action it *should not* select, 1 if the agent *can* execute an activity, 2 if it *should* do it, and 3 if it *must* choose the respective action. Table 3 shows the norms that affect an agent for each attributional category in the current scene description.

$$EV_{HS}(s, a) = \begin{cases} 3 & \text{, if a } = \arg max_{a' \in A}(tweets_s(a')) \\ \sum_{c \in s} norm(c, a) & \text{, otherwise} \end{cases}$$
$$\text{with } norm : \ C \times A \rightarrow \{-1, 0, 1, 2, 3\}$$

The *emotional man*, on the other hand, represents an outright dissatisfied and angry user. Such an agent strives to express that anger which leads to predominantly negative and sometimes sarcastic (i.e., joking) contributions. By publishing negative Tweets, the agent decreases its anger until it no longer feels the need to communicate. Consequently, that behavior produces isolated criticism without any intention of engaging in an actual discussion.

The expected value for the *emotional man* depends on the output of an *anger*-function. That function evaluates the current attributional categories of the situation description according to their emotional implications for the agent. If an action *decreases* the agent's anger, its expected value is 2. If the agent can even *strongly decrease* it, the value is 3. In case an action would *increase* its anger instead, the *anger*-function returns -1 and if an action does not affect the anger at all, the yielded value is 0. Table 3 shows the results of the *anger*-function.

$$EV_{EM}(s, a) = \sum_{c \in s} anger(c, a), \text{ with } \ anger : \ C \times A \rightarrow \{-1, 0, 1, 2, 3\}$$

Finally, the *identity keeper* is a genuine content producer. This type of agent has the goal of bringing forward any kind of discussion in order to maintain its participation in it. That is, the agent can strengthen its identity by providing arguments for other agents to react to. For that purpose, any kind of Tweet can be appropriate, especially controversial ones if they provoke reactions. Only remaining inactive weakens that identity. As a result, the *identity keeper* represents a user who enjoys a conversation for the sake of the conversation and

Table 3. Values of $anger(c, a)$ and $norm(c, a)$ for categories and actions.

Category $c \in C$	Action $a \in A$	$norm(c, a)$	$anger(c, a)$
Thrilling	No tweet	1	0
	Tweet - positive - joking	2	−1
	Tweet - positive - not joking	2	−1
	Tweet - negative - joking	−1	3
	Tweet - negative - not joking	1	2
Funny	No tweet	1	0
	Tweet - positive - joking	2	−1
	Tweet - positive - not joking	3	−1
	Tweet - negative - joking	−1	2
	Tweet - negative - not joking	−1	3
Music-related	No tweet	1	0
	Tweet - positive - joking	2	−1
	Tweet - positive - not joking	3	−1
	Tweet - negative - joking	−1	2
	Tweet - negative - not joking	1	2
Emotional	No tweet	2	0
	Tweet - positive - joking	−1	−1
	Tweet - positive - not joking	1	−1
	Tweet - negative - joking	−1	0
	Tweet - negative - not joking	1	0
Judgmental	No tweet	−1	0
	Tweet - positive - joking	1	−1
	Tweet - positive - not joking	3	−1
	Tweet - negative - joking	−1	3
	Tweet - negative - not joking	2	2

who ensures a certain diversity of perspectives on the discussed topic. Thus, the expected value for the *identity keeper* is expressed as follows.

$$EV_{IK}(s, a) = \begin{cases} -1 \text{ , if } a = \text{no tweet} \\ 3 \quad \text{ , otherwise} \end{cases}$$

The described actor types explain different motivations that cause particular behaviors in decision-making. Combining these actor type models within individual agents creates complex agent behaviors. In the following section we evaluate this modeling approach by reproducing the behavior recorded in the real world data set in an agent-based simulation experiment.

5   Evaluation: Simulation of Social Media Usage

In this section, we evaluate the capability of our agent decision-making approach to reproduce realistic communication dynamics in social media. From a previous experiment [5], we know that the composition of the agent population in this kind of model has a large impact on the overall communication dynamics in the simulation. In that experiment, we evaluated two different settings to analyze the interplay of several actor types on the individual level and the population level. The first setting examined a homogeneous agent poulation ofpopulationll four actor types in equal shares. The second setting consisted of a heterogeneous agent population in which every agent implemented one of the four basic actor types. These experiments gave us an impression of the interplay of different actor types both within and between agents. In the following, we complement these findings with an analysis of whether the agent architecture is also capable of producing realistic simulation results.

5.1   Experiment Setup and Results

We implemented the four agent types in a *JAVA* program to imitate the behavior of 165 human Twitter users as represented in the aforementioned data set in a simulation experiment. Consequently, our experiment confronts a population of 165 agents with each of the eight scene descriptions shown in Table 1. This population comprises equal numbers of three different actor type combinations, each of which contains all four basic types to various extents. In particular, each agent includes all motivational descriptions for at least 10% and at most 70% to add up to a total of 100%. In our simulation, we vary the ratios of these combinations in steps of 10% in order to evaluate whether the resulting simulated communication accurately replicates the original conversation.

Iterating the percentages of the motivational descriptions results in 80 different actor type combinations. As the overall agent population consists of three of these combinations, our experiment covers 512 thousand different populations (80 × 80 × 80). Each of these populations is simulated 100 times to account for stochastic decisions. The arithmetic mean of those repetitions is used to evaluate the accuracy of the simulated data. To that end, the communication in each scene of the experiment is compared to that of the matching scene of the real world data set.

Throughout the experiment, the population of interacting agents does not have to remain stable across all scenes. In fact, in real world social media communication, users enter and leave the conversation. Furthermore, the composition of the four actor types within an agent is perceived as a current set of motivations. These motivations can vary depending on the situational context or other external or internal stimulations. Therefore, we treat each scene seperately in our search for a fitting agent population to reproduce real world communication dynamics. Table 4 presents the actor type combinations which lead to the most accurate simulation results for each scene.

Table 4. Agent population (actor type combinations) for the different scenes.

Scene	Combination 1				Combination 2				Combination 3			
	HE	HS	EM	IK	HE	HS	EM	IK	HE	HS	EM	IK
0	10	50	20	20	20	30	20	30	10	20	30	40
1	20	10	10	60	20	20	20	40	10	50	20	20
2	70	10	10	10	30	20	20	30	30	20	20	30
3	40	10	40	10	50	30	10	10	10	60	10	20
4	20	30	30	20	30	20	10	40	10	30	40	20
5	20	30	40	10	40	10	30	20	30	50	10	10
6	10	20	30	40	30	10	20	40	20	20	50	10
7	30	10	10	50	20	50	20	10	10	10	60	20

Figure 3 shows the outcomes of the expriment (except for the "No Tweet" option) for the populations listed in Table 4. The upper barplot represents the total numbers of Tweets taken by the different agents in the eight scenes. The numbers show the arithmetic mean of all 100 iterations of the simulation (omitting the standard deviation which never exceeds a value of 0.2). The lower barplot shows the relative ratio of the actions executed by the agent-population. The error bars depict the distance of the simulation output to the original real world data. Due to the small absolute number of Tweets in some scenes, a slight distance in individual actions leads to a more pronounced error bar in the relative ratio.

We define the distance $dist_{a,z}$ as the absolute difference between the numbers of occurrences of action a in the simulation and the real world data for any

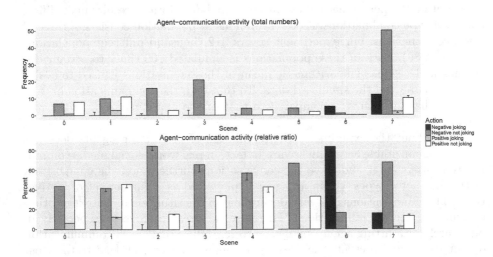

Fig. 3. Agent-communication activity.

scene $z \in \{0, \ldots, 7\}$. To calculate that distance, we count the occurrences of each particular action: $count_{sim,r}(a, z)$ in simulation run r and $count_{real}(a, z)$ in the data set. Then, we use the arithmetic mean of $count_{sim}$ for the $n = 100$ simulation runs and subtract $count_{real}$ to obtain our distance measure.

$$dist_{a,z} = \left| \left(\frac{1}{n} \sum_{r=1}^{n} count_{sim,r}(a, z) \right) - count_{real}(a, z) \right|$$

True to the real world data set, the results show a majority of negative not joking Tweets. Responsible for this are the actor types of *homo economicus*, *identity keeper*, and *emotional man* that consider this action either as the best or as one of their favorite activities. Moreover, while a *homo sociologicus* generally prefers positive and serious (not joking) Tweets, it imitates the dominant behavior. Only scenes 1 and 2 produce a majority of positive outputs. Scene 2 is described as being funny and music-related and scene 1 is characterized as thrilling. This leads to positive not joking actions being favored by three of the actor types which outrival the negative option selected by the *emotional man*. Furthermore, thrilling scenes reduce the overall number of Tweets. In the simulation, this is accomplished by the *homo economicus* needing to reach a threshold of 24 existing contributions to join a conversation.

Due to those effects, the absolute number of agent activities in the simulation deviates only slightly from the original user behavior. The maximum distance (in scene 3) amounts to a total of four Tweets. Here, the two major options selected by the agents are negative not joking and positive not joking Tweets. The former message option is favored by the first actor type combination, predominantly consisting of *homo economicus* and *emotional man*. The second form of Tweet is mainly chosen by the *homo sociologicus* in third combination of actor types. These actions are balanced out by the second actor type combination which is dominated by the *homo economicus*. When the threshold is reached, those agents decide for a negative Tweet. Otherwise, they do not participate in the conversation which boosts the relative ratio of positive contributions.

5.2   Experiment Discussion

The presented results show that our agent architecture allows for simulating realistic dynamics of social media communication in an agent-based setting. However, there are still some minor inaccuracies in the emergent agent behavior. In particular, the small percentage of *identity keeper* behaviors in the agent population leads to a slight under-representation of positive joking Tweets in scene 3. In order to reproduce the real data behavior exactly, a fourth combination of actor types would be required. By extending the experiment design with more actor types in each experiment, a more diverse activity-pattern can be achieved. This would facilitate further minimizing the distance between the simulated and the original behavior. Nevertheless, our results show that even a population of only three different actor type combinations is able to approximate real world social media communication in an agent-based simulation.

In addition, our experiment has analyzed the model behavior on the macro-social level. We have concentrated on evaluating the aggregated effects of the agents'different decision making strategies. While this allows for concluding on the emergence of communication dynamics, further experiments will provide deeper insights into micro-social behaviors that bring about these results. In this context, both the capability of our agent architecture to simulate individual media users and the interplay between their activities over time are of interest.

Firstly, the behavior of individual agents within a population should be compared to the real world behavior of actual media users. This amounts to evaluating the simulated behavior on the micro-social level with respect to the frequency of activity and the tendencies to react to a scene description and other agents' communication. This will then allow for examining which agents in the simulation are more important than others for the emergence of specific communication dynamics. In other communication contexts (e.g., massive online criticism), the conversation is frequently driven by few particular users [33]. Therefore, an accurate representation of such users in the simulation will be useful for analyzing communication strategies in such a situation.

Secondly, the discourse dynamics between different agents within the frame of each scene is a relevant aspect to evaluate. For deriving the aforementioned strategies, it is necessary to observe the impact of possible interventions on the communication. To that end, the agents' mutual reactions to each other's communicative acts must be understood. Hence, a next step in our future experiments will include a detailed analysis of trajectories and their stability within the dynamic multiagent communication system.

6   Conclusions and Future Work

In this paper, we have developed an agent architecture for modeling user behavior in social media. Our model utilizes well-established sociological foundations for representing actors that communicate about a specific topic. In particular, we have presented a concept for representing and combining motivational causes for user behaviors by means of four different social actor types in agent-based simulations. We have applied this concept to model and analyze Twitter communication about a German television program. Our evaluation shows that even few combinations of different motivations within individual agents are sufficient for near accurate replications of real world user behavior. Thus, we conclude that our agent architecture provides a promising approach toward more elaborate agent-based simulation studies of social media usage than existing information propagation models [36]. Such a simulation can serve as a useful decision support tool for planning communication strategies in social media [33].

Nonetheless, there are several extensions of our agent architecture we consider for future work. Firstly, we are interested in comparing this method with existing information diffusion approaches. This will provide further insights into which level of complexity is necessary for simulating meaningful social media communication. Moreover, integrating both approaches will extend our architecture with a representation of the social network in which an agent is connected with others. This network restricts an agent's ability to perceive other agents' activities. In addition, such an integration will complement information propagation methods with motivational aspects of *why* information is spread within a social network.

Secondly, it will also be necessary to represent the activity options and situation descriptions for the agents in more detail. In order to simulate, e.g., the shaping of opinions in political discourses, a classification of communication contents and their impact on the interaction is required. To achieve this, we plan to utilize content modeling and annotation techniques from media and communication studies [26] for encoding discourses in agent-based social simulations.

Finally, a more detailed decision context and activity representation enables more strategic decision-making. As developing behavioral rules for an increasing number of options quickly becomes complicated, we plan to re-implement the four social actor types as BDI agents. How these types can influence the adoption of communicative intentions by such agents will be subject of our future research.

Acknowledgments. We thank Carla Schmidt, Christof Barth, and Hans-Jürgen Bucher for providing us with the data set and a media studies perspective on our application example.

References

1. Balke, T., Gilbert, N.: How do agents make decisions? a survey. J. Artif. Soc. Soc. Simul. **17**(4), 13 (2014)
2. Belkaroui, R., Faiz, R., Elkhlifi, A.: Conversation analysis on social networking sites. In: 2014 Tenth International Conference on Signal-Image Technology and Internet-Based Systems (SITIS), pp. 172–178. IEEE (2014)
3. Berger, C.R.: Interpersonal communication. The International Encyclopedia of Communication (2008)
4. Berndt, J.O., Herzog, O.: Anticipatory behavior of software agents in self-organizing negotiations. In: Nadin, M. (ed.) Anticipation Across Disciplines. CSM, vol. 29, pp. 231–253. Springer, Cham (2016). doi:10.1007/978-3-319-22599-9_15
5. Berndt, J.O., Rodermund, S.C., Lorig, F., Timm, I.J.: Modeling user behavior in social media with complex agents. In: Third International Conference on Human and Social Analytics (HUSO 2017). IARIA (2017, to appear)
6. Bollen, J., Mao, H., Pepe, A.: Modeling public mood and emotion: twitter sentiment and socio-economic phenomena. In: 5th International AAAI Conference on Weblogs and Social Media, pp. 450–453 (2011)
7. Bonabeau, E.: Agent-based modeling: methods and techniques for simulating human systems. Proc. Natl. Acad. Sci. **99**(3), 7280–7287 (2002)
8. Boyd, D., Golder, S., Lotan, G.: Tweet, tweet, retweet: conversational aspects of retweeting on twitter. In: 43rd Hawaii International Conference on System Sciences (HICSS), pp. 1–10. IEEE (2010)
9. Bratman, M.E.: Intention, Plans, and Practical Reason. Harvard University Press, Cambridge (1987)
10. Chen, W., Wang, Y., Yang, S.: Efficient influence maximization in social networks. In: 15th ACM SIGKDD International Conference on Knowledge Discovery and Data Mining, pp. 199–208. ACM (2009)

11. Davidsson, P.: Agent based social simulation: a computer science view. J. Artif. Soc. Soc. Simul. **5**(1) (2002)
12. Dittrich, P., Kron, T.: Complex reflexive agents as models of social actors. In: Proceedings of the SICE Workshop on Artificial Society/Organization/Economy, Meeting of Systems Engineering, Tokyo, vol. 25, pp. 79–88, (2002)
13. Fischer, K., Florian, M., Malsch, T.: Socionics: Scalability of Complex Social Systems. Springer, Berlin (2005)
14. Flam, H.: Emotional 'man': I. the emotionalman'and the problem of collective action. Int. Sociol. **5**(1), 39–56 (1990)
15. Hedström, P., Ylikoski, P.: Causal mechanisms in the social sciences. Annu. Rev. Sociol. **36**, 49–67 (2010)
16. Hoste, V., Van Hee, C., Poels, K.: Towards a framework for the automatic detection of crisis emotions on social media: a corpus analysis of the tweets posted after the crash of germanwings flight 9525. In: 2nd International Conference on Human and Social Analytics (HUSO 2016), pp. 29–32 (2016)
17. Java, A., Song, X., Finin, T., Tseng, B.: Why we twitter: understanding microblogging usage and communities. In: 9th WebKDD and 1st SNA-KDD 2007 Workshop on Web Mining and Social Network Analysis, pp. 56–65. ACM (2007)
18. Kempe, D., Kleinberg, J.M., Tardos, É.: Maximizing the spread of influence through a social network. Theory Comput. **11**(4), 105–147 (2015)
19. Kirby, J.: Connected Marketing: The Viral, Buzz and Word of Mouth Revolution. Butterworth-Heinemann, Amsterdam (2010)
20. Lerman, K., Ghosh, R.: Information contagion: an empirical study of the spread of news on digg and twitter social networks. ICWSM **10**, 90–97 (2010)
21. Lorig, F., Timm, I.J.: How to model the human factor for agent-based simulation in social media analysis? In: 2014 ADS Symposium (Part of SpringSim Multiconference), p. 12. SCS (2014)
22. Luhmann, N.: Social Systems. Stanford University Press, Stanford (1995)
23. Maireder, A., Schlögl, S.: 24 hours of an# outcry: the networked publics of a sociopolitical debate. Eur. J. Commun. **29**(6), 1–16 (2014)
24. Monica, S., Bergenti, F.: An analytic study of opinion dynamics in multi-agent systems with additive random noise. In: Adorni, G., Cagnoni, S., Gori, M., Maratea, M. (eds.) AI*IA 2016. LNCS, vol. 10037, pp. 105–117. Springer, Cham (2016). doi:10.1007/978-3-319-49130-1_9
25. Monica, S., Bergenti, F.: Opinion dynamics in multi-agent systems: selected analytic models and verifying simulations. Comput. Math. Organ. Theory **23**(87), 1–28 (2016)
26. Neuendorf, K.A.: The Content Analysis Guidebook. Sage, Thousand Oaks (2016)
27. Rao, D., Yarowsky, D., Shreevats, A., Gupta, M.: Classifying latent user attributes in twitter. In: 2nd International Workshop on Search and Mining User-Generated Contents, pp. 37–44. ACM (2010)
28. Rao, S., Georgeff, M.P.: BDI agents: from theory to practice. In: Lesser, V.R., Gasser, L. (eds.) Proceedings of the First International Conference on MultiAgent Systems (ICMAS 1995), pp. 312–319. The MIT Press, Boston (1995)
29. Schirra, S., Sun, H., Bentley, F.: Together alone: motivations for live-tweeting a television series. In: 32nd Annual ACM Conference on Human Factors in Computing Systems, pp. 2441–2450. ACM (2014)
30. Schweitzer, F., Hołyst, J.A.: Modelling collective opinion formation by means of active brownian particles. Eur. Phys. J. B-Condens. Matter Complex Syst. **15**(4), 723–732 (2000)

31. Shannon, C.E.: A mathematical theory of communication. ACM SIGMOBILE Mob. Comput. Commun. Rev. **5**(1), 3–55 (2001)
32. Signorini, A., Segre, A.M., Polgreen, P.M.: The use of twitter to track levels of disease activity and public concern in the us during the influenza a h1n1 pandemic. PLoS ONE **6**(5), e19467 (2011)
33. Timm, I., Berndt, J., Lorig, F., Barth, C., Bucher, H.J.: Dynamic analysis of communication processes using twitter data. In: 2nd International Conference on Human and Social Analytics (HUSO 2016), pp. 14–22. IARIA (2016)
34. Vandenhoven, S., De Clercq, O.: What does the bird say? exploring the link between personality and language use in dutch tweets. In: 2nd International Conference on Human and Social Analytics (HUSO 2016), pp. 38–42. IARIA (2016)
35. Vega-Redondo, F.: Complex Social Networks. Cambridge University Press, Cambridge (2007)
36. Zhang, C., Sun, J., Wang, K.: Information propagation in microblog networks. In: 2013 IEEE/ACM International Conference on Advances in Social Networks Analysis and Mining, pp. 190–196. ACM (2013)

Two Analytic Models of Compromise in Multi-Agent Systems

Stefania Monica$^{(\boxtimes)}$ and Federico Bergenti$^{(\boxtimes)}$

Dipartimento di Scienze Matematiche, Fisiche e Informatiche,
Università degli Studi di Parma, 43124 Parma, Italy
{stefania.monica,federico.bergenti}@unipr.it

Abstract. This paper studies compromise, which is the tendency of agents to move their opinions towards those of agents they interact with, trying to reach consensus. Compromise is one of the most important phenomena in the study of opinion dynamics, and this paper presents two analytic models to study it. First, agents are considered deterministic and a preliminary model of the effects of compromise is derived. Then, the model is generalized to give agents some level of autonomy by modelling their behaviour in terms of a stochastic process. Both models are analytic and they can be used to study collective properties of multi-agent systems starting from the details of single interactions among agents. Analytic results concerning the conservation of the average opinion for both models are verified by simulation in the last part of the paper.

1 Introduction

This paper discusses an analytic framework that can be used to study relevant collective and asymptotic properties of multi-agent systems, which are assumed to be completely decentralized and with no form of supervised coordination. According to the proposed framework, observable macroscopic properties of a multi-agent system can be derived analytically under proper assumptions from the description of the effects of microscopic interactions among agents. The term *interaction* is frequently used in the description of the discussed framework to denote a message exchange among two agents, and each interaction corresponds to a single time step. Time is modelled as a sequence of discrete steps, which may not have the same duration, and each step corresponds to a single interaction among two agents. No restriction is imposed on the topological properties of the multi-agent system, and each agent is free to interact with any other agent. The discussed framework assumes that each agent is associated with a scalar attribute, and since the application of the framework considered in this paper refers to the study of opinion dynamics, we assume that such an attribute represents the opinion of an agent regarding a fact. Note that the ideas behind the discussed framework are not limited to the study of opinion dynamics and the proposed approach can be fruitfully applied to describe other attributes and other collective properties.

© Springer International Publishing AG 2017
J.O. Berndt et al. (Eds.): MATES 2017, LNAI 10413, pp. 38–53, 2017.
DOI: 10.1007/978-3-319-64798-2_3

Most of the existing agent-based models used to study opinion dynamics are based on simulations (see, e.g., [13] and referenced literature) and, hence, the validity of obtained results depends on the specific type of multi-agent system that is simulated, and on the actual values of the parameters of simulations. In contrast, the framework discussed in this paper is analytic, and it leads to results that are valid when the hypotheses used to derive them are valid. Analytic models are typically simpler than simulative ones, but they can be preferred when no representative simulations can be identified or when models are built primarily to identify the values of characteristic parameters that explain interesting collective properties. Note that analytic models are commonly verified by simulation in interesting cases, as done in Sect. 5 for proposed models.

The study of opinion dynamics normally considers a number of sociological phenomena that can be used to model the behaviours of agents (see, e.g., [13]). Among considered phenomena, some of the most extensively studied are:

- *Compromise:* the tendency of agents to move their opinions towards those of agents they interact with, trying to reach consensus [1];
- *Diffusion:* the phenomenon according to which the opinion of each agent can be influenced by the social context [3];
- *Homophily:* the process according to which agents interact only with those with similar opinions [16];
- *Negative influence:* the idea according to which agents evaluate their peers, and they only interact with those with positive scores [6];
- *Opinion noise:* the process according to which a random additive variable may lead to arbitrary opinion changes with small probability [4]; and
- *Striving for uniqueness:* the phenomenon based on the idea that agents want to distinguish themselves from others and, hence, they decide to change their opinions if too many agents share the same opinion [7].

We have already proposed analytic models to study, under proper assumptions, all such phenomena [2,8–15], and the main contribution of this paper is to account for the autonomy of agents with respect to compromise by modelling compromise as a stochastic process. First, compromise is studied for deterministic agents, and results on the conservation of the average opinion are presented. Then, the deterministic model is generalized to include stochastic agents, and the conservation of the average opinion is studied also in this case. The proposed stochastic model can be enriched to incorporate all mentioned phenomena by adding specific contributions to the description of microscopic interactions among agents, but such a generalization is not discussed in this paper.

In detail, the analytic framework to study opinion dynamics discussed in this paper is inspired by the kinetic theory of gases, a branch of physics according to which macroscopic properties of gases can be explained starting from the details of microscopic interactions among molecules. The idea is not new because the similarities between the kinetic theory of gases and the study of opinion dynamics are evident, and other models of opinion dynamics, closely related to the discussed framework, have been already proposed (see, e.g., [17,18]). An obvious parallelism between molecules in gases and agents in a multi-agent systems can be drawn, and it can be used to study collective properties concerning the opinion of agents using the same techniques that are adopted to study the temperature or other macroscopic properties of gases. Note that only a few results of the kinetic theory of gases are directly applicable to the study of opinion dynamics because the details of collisions among molecules are intrinsically different from those of interactions among agents. This is evident when comparing interaction rules used to model collisions among molecules with interaction rules considered in the study of opinion dynamics.

This paper is organized as follows. Section 2 surveys the kinetic framework that we use to study the dynamics of the opinion and it fixes notation and nomenclature. Section 3 presents a preliminary deterministic model of compromise which assumes that agents are deterministic. Section 4 generalizes the deterministic model by describing compromise as a stochastic process, which accounts for some level of autonomy of agents. Section 5 shows simulations that confirm relevant results of both models. Finally, Sect. 6 concludes the paper and outlines future work.

2   A Kinetic Framework to Study Opinion Dynamics

Taking inspiration from the kinetic theory of gases, in this paper we aim at discussing an analytic framework that allows deriving macroscopic properties of multi-agent systems starting from the details of microscopic interactions among agents. The discussed framework has already been applied successfully to describe various phenomena that govern the dynamics of the opinion [2,8–15]. While in the kinetic theory of gases each molecule is associated with specific physical parameters, such as its position and velocity, in the context of opinion dynamics we assume that each agent is associated with a single scalar attribute which models its opinion. In order to treat the dynamics of the opinion mathematically, the opinion is typically modelled as variable that takes values from either a discrete set or a continuous set [5,19]. Discrete models, where the opinion takes value from discrete sets, apply, for instance, in the context of political elections, where a finite number of parties, and, hence, a finite number of possible values for the opinion, is present. In contrast, continuous models, where the opinion takes values from a continuous set, are used to represent different level of agreement with respect to a single issue, for example, from strongly disagree to completely agree. In this paper, we model opinion as a continuous variable v defined over a closed interval I_v and, without loss of generality, we consider

$$I_v = [-1, 1] \tag{1}$$

where values close to 0 represent moderate opinions while -1 and $+1$ represent extremal opinions.

Ordinary kinetic theory of gases studies the *distribution function* $f(\underline{x}, \underline{v}, t)$, which denotes the number of molecules whose position is in $(\underline{x}, \underline{x} + d\underline{x})$ and whose velocity is in $(\underline{v}, \underline{v} + d\underline{v})$ at time t. According to the kinetic theory of gases, the temporal evolution of such a function is described by the *Boltzmann equation*, which is an integro-differential equation that takes into account the effects of the collisions among molecules and that can be used to analyze macroscopic properties of gases. Analogously, the discussed framework studies the distribution function $f(v,t)$, which represents the number of agents with opinion in $(v, v + dv)$ at time t, and we assume that the distribution function $f(v,t)$ is governed by the *homogeneous Boltzmann equation*

$$\frac{\partial f}{\partial t}(v,t) = \mathcal{Q}(f)(v,t) \tag{2}$$

where $\mathcal{Q}(f)(v,t)$ is an integral operator that takes into account the effects of interactions among agents, and that it is normally called *collisional operator*. In Sects. 3 and 4 we study two different models that can be used to describe how the opinions of agents changes because of interactions. The first model is deterministic, while the second model involves stochastic parameters. In both cases, we derive explicit expressions of specific collisional operators and we use them to study analytically macroscopic properties of multi-agent systems. Note that such explicit expressions are very different from the expression of the collisional operator normally used in the kinetic theory of gases because the description of the collisions among molecules in gases is very different from the description of interactions among agents.

Before describing mentioned models, let us introduce a proper notation relative to the macroscopic characteristics of multi-agent systems. The number of agents at time t is denoted as $n(t)$ and it can be obtained by integrating $f(v,t)$ with respect to v

$$n(t) = \int_{I_v} f(v,t)dv. \tag{3}$$

The average opinion at time t is denoted as $u(t)$ and it is computed as follows: $f(v,t)$ is multiplied by v, it is integrated with respect to v, and it is divided by the total number of agents,

$$u(t) = \frac{1}{n(t)} \int_{I_v} vf(v,t)dv. \tag{4}$$

Finally, the variance at time t is denoted as $\sigma^2(t)$ and it can be computed as follows: $f(v,t)$ is multiplied by $(v - u(t))^2$, it is integrated with respect to v, and it is divided by the total number of agents,

$$\sigma^2(t) = \frac{1}{n(t)} \int_{I_v} (v - u(t))^2 f(v,t)\, dv. \tag{5}$$

In order to analyze the temporal evolution of $u(t)$ and of $\sigma(t)$, let us introduce the so called *weak form* of the Boltzmann equation, which is obtained from (2) by multiplying by a suitable *test function* and by integrating with respect to v. The weak form of the Boltzmann equation with respect to a generic test function $\phi(v)$ can be written as

$$\frac{d}{dt} \int_{I_v} f(v,t)\phi(v)dv = \int_{I_v} \mathcal{Q}(f)(v,t)\phi(v)dv \tag{6}$$

where the right-hand side is called weak form of the collisional operator Q with respect to test function $\phi(v)$. It can be observed that the choice of proper test functions in (6) allows studying the temporal evolution of macroscopic properties of multi-agent systems. In detail, from (3) it can be easily observed that the left-hand side of (6) with $\phi(v) = 1$ represents the derivative, with respect to time, of the number of agents $n(t)$. Similarly, from (4), the integral at the left-hand side of (6) with $\phi(v) = v$ can be written as $n(t)u(t)$. Hence, the left-hand side of the weak form of the Boltzmann equation relative to test function $\phi(v) = v$ is related to the time derivative of the average opinion. Finally, choosing test function $\phi(v) = (v - u(t))^2$ in (6) and recalling (5), it is possible to observe that the integral at the left-hand side of (6) can be written as $n(t)\sigma^2(t)$, so that the left-hand side of (6) is related to the time derivative of the variance of the opinion. In summary, the weak form of the Boltzmann equation (6) can be used to write differential equations whose unknowns are:

1. The number of agents $n(t)$, for $\phi(v) = 1$;
2. The average opinion $u(t)$, for $\phi(v) = v$; and
3. The variance of the opinion $\sigma^2(t)$, for $\phi(v) = (v - u(t))^2$.

The explicit derivation of analytic results relative to the macroscopic properties mentioned above is performed in next two sections, considering two different models, a deterministic model and a stochastic model.

3   A Deterministic Model of Compromise

In order to analyze the temporal evolution of the macroscopic properties of multi-agent systems introduced in (3), (4), and (5), it is necessary to analyze the weak form of the Boltzmann equation, and the explicit expression of the weak form of the collisional operator in (6). In order to derive the explicit expression of the weak form of the collisional operator, the details of the effects of interactions on the opinions of agents need to be described. As stated in Sect. 1, we assume that each agent can interact with any other agent in the system and that interactions are binary, which means that a single interaction comprises only two agents. Under such assumptions, we aim at studying compromise, which models the idea that the opinions of agents after an interaction become closer.

Let us denote as v and w the opinions of two agents that are about to have an interaction, and as v' and w' their respective opinions after the interaction. In order to study compromise, we assume that the post-interaction opinions of the two agents are related to their pre-interaction opinions according to the following rules

$$v' = v + \gamma(w - v)$$
$$w' = w + \gamma(v - w)$$
(7)

where γ is a deterministic parameter used to quantify the effects of compromise. A proper choice of the admissible values of γ must be adopted to properly model compromise. Recall that compromise is the tendency of agents to change their opinions towards those of agents they interact with, trying to reach consensus. Therefore, rules (7) represent a good model of compromise when $v \neq w$ (see, e.g., [18]) only if the absolute value of the difference between post-interaction opinions is smaller than the absolute value of the difference between pre-interaction opinions

$$|v' - w'| < |v - w|. \tag{8}$$

Note that the difference between post-interaction opinions equals

$$v' - w' = (1 - 2\gamma)(v - w), \tag{9}$$

and therefore (8) holds if and only if $|1 - 2\gamma| < 1$, which means that

$$0 < \gamma < 1. \tag{10}$$

In addition, in a good model of compromise when $v \neq w$ (see, e.g., [18]) the post-interaction opinion of an agent is closer to its pre-interaction opinion than to the pre-interaction opinion of the agent it interacts with, which means

$$|v' - v| < |v' - w| \qquad |w' - w| < |w' - v|. \tag{11}$$

But, from (7) and considering (10), it can be derived that

$$|v' - v| = \gamma|w - v| \qquad |v' - w| = (1 - \gamma)|w - v| \tag{12}$$

and, therefore, the first inequality in (11) is satisfied if and only if

$$0 < \gamma < \frac{1}{2}. \tag{13}$$

When considering the second inequality in (11), the same condition on γ is found. Hence, in order to provide the model with an accurate description of compromise, which includes the fact that the opinion of each agent after an interaction is closer to its pre-interaction opinion than to the pre-interaction opinion of the agent it interacts with, we restrict the domain of γ to

$$I_\gamma = \left(0, \frac{1}{2}\right), \tag{14}$$

and for the rest of this paper we assume that $\gamma \in I_\gamma$. Observe that for this choice of γ, rules (7) guarantee that post-interaction opinions still belong to interval I_v where the opinion is defined because

$$|v'| = |(1 - \gamma)v + \gamma w| \leq (1 - \gamma)|v| + \gamma|w| \leq \max\{|v|, |w|\} \leq 1$$
$$|w'| = |(1 - \gamma)w + \gamma v| \leq (1 - \gamma)|w| + \gamma|v| \leq \max\{|v|, |w|\} \leq 1 \tag{15}$$

and, therefore, $v' \in I_v$ and $w' \in I_v$. Also note that from (7) it can be easily observed that the sum of post-interaction opinions equals the sum of pre-interaction opinions

$$v' + w' = v + w + \gamma(w - v + v - w) = v + w. \tag{16}$$

It can then be concluded that the average opinion is conserved in each interaction. Finally, we remark that rules (7) are different from those used in kinetic theory of gases to update the velocities of two molecules after a collision. This difference results in a different explicit expression of the collisional operator, and, hence, in different properties of the system, as shown in the rest of this section.

Microscopic rules (7) can be used to describe how the opinions of two interacting agents are updated after an interaction, which allows deriving the explicit formulation of the weak form of the Boltzmann equation (6). According to [14], it can be shown that

$$\frac{d}{dt} \int_{I_v} f(v,t)\phi(v)dv = \int_{I_v}\int_{I_v} \beta(v,w)f(v_*,t)f(w_*,t)\phi(v_* + \gamma(w_* - v_*))dw_* \, dv_* -$$
$$\int_{I_v}\int_{I_v} \beta(v,w)f(v,t)f(w,t)\phi(v)dvdw$$

where $\beta(v,w)$ represents the probability that an agent, whose opinion is v, interacts with another agent, whose opinion is w. Under the broadly-applicable assumption that $\beta(v,w)$ is constant [18], i.e., that it does not depend on the opinions of the two interacting agents, and using a proper change of variable, the weak form of the Boltzmann equation can be written in a simpler way as

$$\frac{d}{dt} \int_{I_v} f(v,t)\phi(v)dv = \beta \int_{I_v}\int_{I_v} f(v,t)f(w,t)\left(\phi(v'(v,w)) - \phi(v)\right)dv\,dw. \quad (17)$$

where $v'(v,w) = v + \gamma(w - v)$ denotes the post-interaction opinion of the agent whose pre-interaction opinion is v, as in (7).

Given the weak form of the Boltzmann equation (17), which is based on microscopic rules (7), it is possible to analytically study relevant macroscopic properties of the system, as explained at the end of the previous section. In particular, proper choices of the test function in (17) allow deriving first order differential equations whose unknowns are the number of agents, the average opinion, and the variance of the opinion, respectively.

Proposition 1. *The number of agents $n(t)$ is conserved.*

Proof. Let us set $\phi(v) = 1$ in (17), so that the left-hand side can be written as

$$\frac{d}{dt} \int_{I_v} f(v,t)\phi(v)dv = \frac{d}{dt} \int_{I_v} f(v,t)dv = \frac{d}{dt}n(t). \quad (18)$$

Since, according to this choice, the test function is constant, in (17)

$$\phi(v') - \phi(v) = 0. \quad (19)$$

Therefore, from (18), it can be concluded that the weak form of the Boltzmann equation (17) with $\phi(v) = 1$ can be rewritten as

$$\frac{d}{dt}n(t) = 0, \quad (20)$$

which corresponds to the conservation of the number of agents $n(t)$ in the multi-agent system, and it proves the proposition. □

We remark that this property is analogous to mass conservation in gases. Since the number of agents is constant, in the rest of this paper we denote it as n, thus omitting its dependence on time.

Proposition 2. *The average opinion $u(t)$ is conserved.*

Proof. Let us set $\phi(v) = v$ in (17), so that the left-hand side can be written as

$$\frac{d}{dt} \int_{I_v} f(v,t)\phi(v)dv = \frac{d}{dt} \int_{I_v} vf(v,t)dv = n\frac{d}{dt}u(t). \tag{21}$$

According to this choice, and using (7), the difference $\phi(v') - \phi(v)$ inside the integral on the right-hand side of (17) can be written as $\gamma(w - v)$. Therefore, the weak form of the collisional operator with $\phi(v) = v$ can be rewritten as

$$\beta\gamma \int_{I_v} \int_{I_v} f(v,t)f(w,t)(w - v)dvdw \tag{22}$$

which equals 0 because

$$\int_{I_v} f(v,t)dv \int_{I_v} wf(w,t)dw - \int_{I_v} vf(v,t)dv \int_{I_v} f(w,t)dw = n^2u(t) - n^2u(t) = 0.$$

Finally, the weak form of the Boltzmann equation with $\phi(v) = v$ becomes

$$\frac{d}{dt}u(t) = 0, \tag{23}$$

which proves the proposition. $\square$

We remark that this property is analogous to the conservation of momentum in gases. Since the average opinion is constant, in the rest of this paper we denote it as u, thus omitting its dependence on time.

Proposition 3. *The variance of the opinion $\sigma^2(t)$ exponentially tends to 0 as t tends to $+\infty$.*

Proof. Let us set $\phi(v) = (v - u)^2$ in (17), so that its left-hand side becomes

$$\frac{d}{dt} \int_{I_v} f(v,t)\phi(v)dv = \frac{d}{dt} \int_{I_v} f(v,t)(v - u)^2dv = n\frac{d}{dt}\sigma^2(t). \tag{24}$$

According to the choice of $\phi(\cdot)$, and using (7), the weak form of the collisional operator can be rewritten as

$$\beta \int_{I_v} \int_{I_v} f(v,t)f(w,t)\{[v + \gamma(w - v) - u]^2 - (v - u)^2\}dvdw. \tag{25}$$

Simple algebraic manipulations show that the integral in (25) can be written as

$$\int_{I_v} \int_{I_v} f(v,t)f(w,t) \left[\gamma^2(w - v)^2 + 2\gamma(v - u)(w - v)\right] dvdw, \tag{26}$$

which can be rewritten to

$$\gamma^2 \int_{I_v} \int_{I_v} f(v,t)f(w,t)(w^2 - 2vw + v^2)dvdw +$$
$$2\gamma \int_{I_v} \int_{I_v} f(v,t)f(w,t)(v-u)(w-v)dvdw,$$

and proper application of (4) and (5) leads to

$$\int_{I_v} \int_{I_v} f(v,t)f(w,t)\left[\gamma^2(w-v)^2 + 2\gamma(v-u)(w-v)\right]dvdw = \tag{27}$$
$$2\gamma^2 n^2 \sigma^2(t) - 2\gamma n^2 \sigma^2(t).$$

Inserting this result in (17), and recalling (24), shows that the weak form of the Boltzmann equation with $\phi(v) = (v-u)^2$ can be written as the following differential equation for the variance of the opinion

$$\frac{d}{dt}\sigma^2(t) = 2\beta n\gamma(\gamma - 1)\sigma^2(t). \tag{28}$$

Solving the differential equation (28) shows that the variance $\sigma^2(t)$ of the opinion as a function of time can be written as

$$\sigma^2(t) = \sigma^2(0)e^{2\beta n\gamma(\gamma-1)t} \tag{29}$$

where $\sigma^2(0)$ denotes the initial variance of the opinion. Observe that, since β and n are positive, and since, according to previous assumptions, $\gamma \in I_\gamma = \left(0, \frac{1}{2}\right)$, the coefficient of t inside the exponential function is negative. Hence, it can be concluded that the variance $\sigma^2(t)$ of the opinion tends to 0 as time t, which represents the number of interactions, tends to $+\infty$. $\qquad \square$

We remark that this property is not found in the kinetic theory of gases, and it follows from the specific assumptions that we took to model the opinion.

4   A Stochastic Model of Compromise

In this section, we introduce a stochastic component in the rules used to model the post-interaction opinions of two interacting agents as functions of their pre-interaction opinions. This generalization is meant to drop the assumption of deterministic agents and it can be used to give agents some level of autonomy. In detail, we now consider the following rules for opinion updates

$$v' = v + \gamma_1(w-v)$$
$$w' = w + \gamma_2(v-w). \tag{30}$$

where γ_1 and γ_2 are independent random variables with the same probability distribution function $\Theta(\cdot)$. Observe that rules (30) are obtained from (7) by replacing the deterministic parameter γ with two random variables γ_1 and γ_2. In the following, we denote as $\bar{\gamma}$ and σ_γ^2 the average value and the variance of such random variables

$$\bar{\gamma} = \mathbb{E}[\gamma_1] = \mathbb{E}[\gamma_2] = \int_{-\infty}^{+\infty} \gamma \Theta(\gamma) d\gamma$$

$$\sigma_\gamma^2 = \mathbb{E}[(\gamma_1 - \bar{\gamma})^2] = \mathbb{E}[(\gamma_2 - \bar{\gamma})^2] = \int_{-\infty}^{+\infty} (\gamma - \bar{\gamma})^2 \Theta(\gamma) d\gamma. \tag{31}$$

Note that rules (30) represent a good model of compromise when $v \neq w$ only if the absolute value of the difference between post-interaction opinions is smaller than the absolute value of the difference between pre-interaction opinions. Moreover, in order to provide the model with an accurate description of compromise, which includes the fact that when $v \neq w$ the opinion of each agent after an interaction is closer to its pre-interaction opinion than to the pre-interaction opinion of the agent it interacts with, we need to restrict the distribution function $\Theta(\cdot)$ to a suitable domain. Let us compute the average value of the difference between post-interaction opinions. From (30), it can be obtained that

$$\mathbb{E}[v' - w'] = \mathbb{E}[v - w + \gamma_1(w - v) - \gamma_2(v - w)] = (1 - 2\bar{\gamma})(v - w). \tag{32}$$

In order to guarantee that the idea of compromise is respected, it is necessary that $|1 - 2\bar{\gamma}| < 1$. This condition is guaranteed if we restrict the support of $\Theta(\cdot)$ to the interval $(0,1)$. Observe that if the support of $\Theta(\cdot)$ is further restricted to $I_\gamma = (0, \frac{1}{2})$, then it is also possible to reproduce the phenomenon, expressed in (11), according to which the post-interaction opinion of an agent is closer to its pre-interaction opinion than to the pre-interaction opinion of the other agent. Finally, from (30) it can be easily derived that the expected value of the sum of post-interaction opinions equals the sum of pre-interaction opinions, since the following equality holds

$$\mathbb{E}[v' + w'] = \mathbb{E}[v + w + \gamma_1(w - v) + \gamma_2(v - w)] = v + w + (\bar{\gamma} - \bar{\gamma})(w - v) = v + w. \tag{33}$$

Observe that in (33) we used the fact that the two random variables γ_1 and γ_2 have the same distribution and, hence, the same average value $\bar{\gamma}$.

As when considering the deterministic model for the update of the opinions of two interacting agents, we now aim at deriving macroscopic properties of the considered multi-agent system. In particular, we are interested in deriving the temporal evolution of the number of agents, of the average opinion, and of the variance of the opinion. This can be done, as in the deterministic case, by analyzing the weak form of the Boltzmann equation, whose general definition is (6). However, in this case, a different explicit expression of the collisional operator must be considered in order to account for the fact that a stochastic component has been introduced in the microscopic rules used to update the opinions of agents. The explicit expression of the weak form of the collisional operator for test function $\phi(\cdot)$ when considering interaction rules (30) is discussed in [18]

$$\int_{I_\gamma}\int_{I_\gamma}\int_{I_v}\int_{I_v}\Theta(\gamma_1)\Theta(\gamma_2)f(v,t)f(w,t)\phi(v+\gamma_1(w-v))\mathrm{d}v\,\mathrm{d}w\mathrm{d}\gamma_1\mathrm{d}\gamma_2\,-$$

$$\int_{I_\gamma}\int_{I_\gamma}\int_{I_v}\int_{I_v}\Theta(\gamma_1)\Theta(\gamma_2)f(v,t)f(w,t)\phi(v)\mathrm{d}v\mathrm{d}w\mathrm{d}\gamma_1\mathrm{d}\gamma_2$$

where the two integrals on I_γ have been introduced to consider the presence of random variables in (30). Using a proper change of variable, the weak form of the collisional operator can be written as

$$\int_{I_\gamma}\int_{I_\gamma}\int_{I_v}\int_{I_v}\Theta(\gamma_1)\Theta(\gamma_2)f(v,t)f(w,t)\left(\phi(v'(v,w,\gamma_1))-\phi(v)\right)\mathrm{d}v\,\mathrm{d}w\mathrm{d}\gamma_1\mathrm{d}\gamma_2.$$

As when considering the deterministic model, $v'(v,w,\gamma_1) = v + \gamma_1(w-v)$ inside the integrals at the right-hand side of the previous equation is related to the post-interaction opinion of the agent whose pre-interaction opinion is v.

We now consider the same test functions considered in the deterministic case to study the same macroscopic properties, namely the number of agents, the average opinion, and the variance of the opinion. Propositions proved for the deterministic model are generalized to the stochastic model with similar results, as follows. Note that the presence of random variables influences only the number of interactions needed to reach consensus, as detailed in Proposition 6. Also note that such results are essentially caused by the symmetry introduced by the assumption that random variables in (30) have the same distribution.

Proposition 4. *The number of agents $n(t)$ is conserved.*

Proof. We start by considering $\phi(v) = 1$ in the weak form of the Boltzmann equation. As in the deterministic case, according to the definition of the number of agents (3), the left-hand side of the weak form of the Boltzmann equation can be written as

$$\frac{\mathrm{d}}{\mathrm{d}t}\int_{I_v}f(v,t)\phi(v)\mathrm{d}v = \frac{\mathrm{d}}{\mathrm{d}t}\int_{I_v}f(v,t)\mathrm{d}v = \frac{\mathrm{d}}{\mathrm{d}t}n(t). \tag{34}$$

Due to the presence of the difference $\phi(v')-\phi(v)$ inside the integrals of the weak form of the collisional operator, the choice of a constant test function leads to

$$\frac{\mathrm{d}}{\mathrm{d}t}n(t) = 0, \tag{35}$$

which is the same equality found in the deterministic case. This implies that the number of agents $n(t)$ is conserved, and proves the proposition.   □

As in the deterministic case, this property is analogous to mass conservation in gases. In the rest of this paper we denote the number of agents as n, thus omitting its dependence on time.

Proposition 5. *The average opinion u(t) is conserved.*

Proof. Let us consider test function $\phi(v) = v$ in the weak form of the Boltzmann equation. According to this choice, its left-hand side can be written as

$$\frac{\mathrm{d}}{\mathrm{d}t}\int_{I_v} f(v,t)\phi(v)\mathrm{d}v = \frac{\mathrm{d}}{\mathrm{d}t}\int_{I_v} f(v,t)v\mathrm{d}v = n\frac{\mathrm{d}}{\mathrm{d}t}u(t). \tag{36}$$

Recalling (30), the difference $\phi(v') - \phi(v)$ in the weak form of the collisional operator can be written as

$$\phi(v') - \phi(v) = \gamma_1(w - v). \tag{37}$$

Therefore, the weak form of the collisional operator with $\phi(v) = v$ can be rewritten as

$$\int_{I_\gamma} \gamma_1\Theta(\gamma_1)\mathrm{d}\gamma_1 \int_{I_\gamma} \Theta(\gamma_2)\mathrm{d}\gamma_2 \int_{I_v}\int_{I_v} f(v,t)f(w,t)(w-v)\mathrm{d}v\,\mathrm{d}w. \tag{38}$$

Observe that the two integrals with respect to v and w are the same that appear in (22), and it has already been shown that they equal 0. Finally, from (36) it can be concluded that the weak form of the Boltzmann equation with $\phi(v) = v$ can be written as

$$\frac{\mathrm{d}}{\mathrm{d}t}u(t) = 0, \tag{39}$$

which proves the proposition because it ensures that the average opinion $u(t)$ is constant. $\qquad\square$

We remark that this property is analogous to the conservation of momentum in gases. Since the average opinion is constant, in the rest of this paper we denote it as u, thus omitting its dependence on time.

Proposition 6. *The variance of the opinion $\sigma^2(t)$ exponentially tends to 0 as t tends to $+\infty$.*

Proof. Let us set $\phi(v) = (v - u)^2$ in the weak form of the Boltzmann equation, so that its left-hand side becomes

$$\frac{\mathrm{d}}{\mathrm{d}t}\int_{I_v} f(v,t)\phi(v)\mathrm{d}v = \frac{\mathrm{d}}{\mathrm{d}t}\int_{I_v} f(v,t)(v-u)^2\mathrm{d}v = n\frac{\mathrm{d}}{\mathrm{d}t}\sigma^2(t). \tag{40}$$

According to this choice and using the first equation in (30), the weak form of the collisional operator can be rewritten as

$$\int_{I_\gamma}\int_{I_\gamma}\int_{I_v}\int_{I_v} \Theta(\gamma_1)\Theta(\gamma_2)f(v,t)f(w,t)\cdot$$
$$\left[(v + \gamma_1(w - v) - u)^2 - (v - u)^2\right]\mathrm{d}v\,\mathrm{d}w\mathrm{d}\gamma_1\mathrm{d}\gamma_2. \tag{41}$$

Simple algebraic manipulations show that (41) can be written as follows

$$\int_{I_\gamma} \Theta(\gamma_1)\gamma_1^2 d\gamma_1 \int_{I_v}\int_{I_v} f(v)f(w)(w^2 - 2vw + v^2)dvdw +$$
$$2\int_{I_\gamma} \Theta(\gamma_1)\gamma_1 d\gamma_1 \int_{I_v}\int_{I_v} f(v)f(w)(v - u)(w - v)dvdw \qquad (42)$$

where we used the fact that

$$\int_{I_\gamma} \Theta(\gamma_2)d\gamma_2 = 1. \qquad (43)$$

Straightforward calculation leads to simplify (41) to

$$2n^2(\sigma_\gamma^2 + \bar{\gamma}^2 - \bar{\gamma})\sigma^2(t). \qquad (44)$$

Inserting this result in the weak form of the collisional operator, and recalling (40), it can be easily observed that the weak form of the Boltzmann equation with $\phi(v) = (v - u)^2$ can be written as the following differential equation for the variance of the opinion

$$\frac{d}{dt}\sigma^2(t) = 2n(\sigma_\gamma^2 + \bar{\gamma}^2 - \bar{\gamma})\sigma^2(t). \qquad (45)$$

The explicit solution of the differential equation (45) shows that the variance $\sigma^2(t)$ of the opinion as a function of time can be written as

$$\sigma^2(t) = \sigma^2(0)\, e^{2n(\sigma_\gamma^2 + \bar{\gamma}^2 - \bar{\gamma})t} \qquad (46)$$

where $\sigma^2(0)$ denotes the initial variance of the opinion. Hence, it can be concluded that the variance $\sigma^2(t)$ of the opinion tends to 0 as t, which represents the number of interactions, tends to $+\infty$. □

We remark that this property is not found in ordinary kinetic theory of gases, and it follows from the specific choices adopted to model the opinion.

5   Verifying Simulations

Analytic models of compromise developed in Sects. 3 and 4 proved, for multi-agent systems where the hypotheses of models hold, that the average opinion is conserved, and that consensus is reached (exponentially) after a sufficiently large number of interactions. The simulations reported in this sections are meant to verify such results in a multi-agent system made of 10^3 agents that freely interact using binary interactions. Agents are initialized with random opinions uniformly distributed in $I_v = (-1, 1)$, with $u = 0$ and $\sigma^2(0) = \frac{1}{3}$. At each iteration of the simulation, two agents are randomly chosen and their opinions are updated according to the adopted interaction rules: (7) for the deterministic model, and (30) for the stochastic model. Note that described simulations are

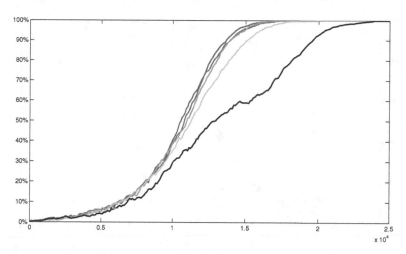

Fig. 1. Fraction of agents in the multi-agent system whose opinion falls in interval $(-10^{-2}, +10^2)$ as a function of the number of interactions: for deterministic agents (blue), and for stochastic agents with random variables γ_1 and γ_2 uniformly distributed in intervals $(1/4 - 1/32, 1/4 + 1/32)$ (red), in $(1/4 - 1/16, 1/4 + 1/16)$ (green), in $(1/4 - 1/8, 1/4 + 1/8)$ (cyan), and in $(0, 1/2)$ (black). (Colour figure online)

completely independent from the results of analytic models, and they are simple implementations of chosen interactions rules.

Figure 1 shows the results of simulations for the deterministic model and for the stochastic model with three different parameters. The figure shows for each iteration of the simulation the fraction of agents whose opinion falls in interval $(-10^{-2}, 10^2)$ for deterministic agents (blue), and for stochastic agents with random variables γ_1 and γ_2 uniformly distributed in $(1/4-1/32, 1/4+1/32)$ (red), in $(1/4 - 1/16, 1/4 + 1/16)$ (green), in $(1/4 - 1/8, 1/4 + 1/8)$ (cyan), and in $(0, 1/2)$ (black). Note that an increased level of autonomy of agents, which is modelled as an increased contribution of random variables, tends to slow the convergence to consensus.

Similarly, Fig. 2 shows the results of simulations for the deterministic model and for the stochastic model with three different parameters. In detail, the figure shows for each iteration of the simulation the fraction of agents whose opinion falls in interval $(-10^{-2}, 10^2)$ for deterministic agents (blue), and for stochastic agents with random variables γ_1 and γ_2 uniformly distributed in $(1/8-1/32, 1/8+1/32)$ (red), in $(1/8-1/16, 1/8+1/16)$ (green), and in $(0, 1/4)$ (cyan). As expected, also in this case, compromise makes agents tend to the same opinion, which is the average of initial opinions. The level of autonomy introduced in the model of compromise by means of the two random variables in (30) contributes to increase the number of iterations needed to reach consensus, but it cannot prevent the multi-agent system from reaching consensus.

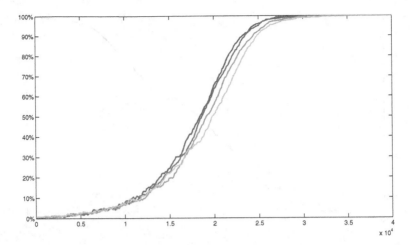

Fig. 2. Fraction of agents whose opinion is in interval $(-10^{-2}, 10^2)$ as a function of the number of interactions: for deterministic agents (blue), and for stochastic agents with random variables γ_1 and γ_2 uniformly distributed in $(1/8 - 1/32, 1/8 + 1/32)$ (red), in $(1/8 - 1/16, 1/8 + 1/16)$ (green), and in $(0, 1/4)$ (cyan). (Colour figure online)

6   Conclusions

This paper presented two analytic models of compromise. The first assumes that agents are deterministic and it can be considered preliminary. The second accounts for the autonomy of agents by modelling compromise as a stochastic process. Both models have similar properties and, in particular, in both models the average opinion of the multi-agent system is conserved and the variance of the opinion exponentially tends to 0 as the number of interactions tends to $+\infty$. Simulations reported in Sect. 5 confirm such properties and emphasize that the introduction of random variables in the stochastic model contributes to slow the convergence of the opinions. Even if the value of γ used to quantify the effects of compromise is the same as that of $\bar{\gamma}$, the number of interactions needed to reach consensus in the stochastic model is always greater than that of the deterministic model because of the effects of random variables. This property is coherent with the fact random variables are used to give some level of autonomy to agents.

References

1. Abelson, R.P.: Mathematical models of the distribution of attitudes under controversy. In: Frederiksen, N., Gulliksen, H. (eds.) Contributions to Mathematical Psychology, pp. 141–160. Holt, Rinehart and Winston, New York (1964)
2. Bergenti, F., Monica, S.: Analytic study of opinion dynamics in multi-agent systems with two classes of agents. In: Proceedings of 17th Workshop Dagli Oggetti agli Agenti (WOA 2016). CEUR Workshop Proceedings, vol. 1664, pp. 17–22. RWTH Aachen (2016)

3. Bonabeau, E.: Agent-based modeling: methods and techniques for simulating human systems. Proc. Natl. Acad. Sci. **3**, 7280–7287 (2002)
4. Galam, S., Gefen, Y., Shapir, Y.: Sociophysics: a new approach of sociological collective behavior. J. Math. Sociol. **9**, 1–13 (2009)
5. Hegselmann, R., Krause, U.: Opinion dynamics and bounded confidence models, analysis, and simulation. J. Artif. Soc. Soc. Simul. **5**(3), 1–33 (2002)
6. Mäs, M., Flache, A.: Differentiation without distancing. explaining bi-polarization of opinions without negative influence. PLOS One **8**(11), 1–17 (2013)
7. Mäs, M., Flache, A., Helbing, D.: Individualisazion as driving force of clustering phenomena in humans. PLOS One **6**(10), 1–8 (2010)
8. Monica, S., Bergenti, F.: A stochastic model of self-stabilizing cellular automata for consensus formation. In: Proceedings of the 15th Workshop Dagli Oggetti agli Agenti (WOA 2014). CEUR Workshop Proceedings, vol. 1260. RWTH Aachen (2014)
9. Monica, S., Bergenti, F.: A kinetic study of opinion dynamics in multi-agent systems. In: Gavanelli, M., Lamma, E., Riguzzi, F. (eds.) AI*IA 2015. LNCS, vol. 9336, pp. 116–127. Springer, Cham (2015). doi:10.1007/978-3-319-24309-2_9
10. Monica, S., Bergenti, F.: Kinetic description of opinion evolution in multi-agent systems: analytic model and simulations. In: Chen, Q., Torroni, P., Villata, S., Hsu, J., Omicini, A. (eds.) PRIMA 2015. LNCS (LNAI), vol. 9387, pp. 483–491. Springer, Cham (2015). doi:10.1007/978-3-319-25524-8_30
11. Monica, S., Bergenti, F.: Simulations of opinion formation in multi-agent systems using kinetic theory. In: Proceedings of 16th Workshop "Dagli Oggetti agli Agenti" (WOA 2015). CEUR Workshop Proceedings, vol. 1382, pp. 97–102. RWTH Aachen (2015)
12. Monica, S., Bergenti, F.: An analytic study of opinion dynamics in multi-agent systems with additive random noise. In: Adorni, G., Cagnoni, S., Gori, M., Maratea, M. (eds.) AI*IA 2016. LNCS, vol. 10037, pp. 105–117. Springer, Cham (2016). doi:10.1007/978-3-319-49130-1_9
13. Monica, S., Bergenti, F.: Opinion dynamics in multi-agent systems: selected analytic models and verifying simulations. Comput. Math. Organ. Theory, 1–28 (2016). doi:10.1007/s10588-016-9235-z
14. Monica, S., Bergenti, F.: A study of consensus formation using kinetic theory. In: Proceedings of the 13th International Conference on Distributed Computing and Artificial Intelligence (DCAI 2016), pp. 213–221. Sevilla, Spain, June 2016
15. Monica, S., Bergenti, F.: An analytic study of opinion dynamics in multi-agent systems. Comput. Math. Appl. **73**(10), 2272–2284 (2017)
16. Nowak, A., Szamrej, J., Latan, B.: From private attitude to public opinion: a dynamic theory of social impact. Psycol. Rev. **97**, 362–376 (1990)
17. Pareschi, L., Toscani, G.: Interacting Multiagent Systems: Kinetic Equations and Montecarlo Methods. Oxford University Press, Oxford (2013)
18. Toscani, G.: Kinetic models of opinion formation. Commun. Math. Sci. **4**, 481–496 (2006)
19. Yildiz, E., Ozdaglar, A., Acemoglu, D., Saberi, A., Scaglione, A.: Noisy continuous opinion dynamics. J. Stat. Mech. **9**, 1–13 (1982)

Team Formation Through Preference-Based Behavior Composition

Masoud Barati and Richard St-Denis[✉]

Département d'informatique, Université de Sherbrooke,
Sherbrooke (Québec) J1K 2R1, Canada
{Masoud.Barati,Richard.St-Denis}@USherbrooke.ca

Abstract. A team formation problem consists in finding an effective group of experts in a social network to accomplish a job with a minimum expenditure of energy and time. This problem has been transposed into the domain of multiagent systems to form a team of autonomous agents whose mission is to achieve a given goal. There is a wide range of such problems. This paper generalizes one of them by assigning explicit behaviors to agents whose tasks are equipped with multiple attributes. Their values are compared with preferences attached to the desired tasks of the goal. A synthesized controller realizes the goal by invoking tasks of a subset of the available agents, called a composition in this paper. Furthermore, utility values are assigned to compositions and robustness is considered to be an important property of a team to prevent its deterioration when one or more of its agents fail. Finding a robust team that satisfies the goal's preferences with better utility values for compositions constitutes a difficult optimization problem. The proposed method to solve this problem consists in three phases: controller synthesis with filtering on tasks with respect to some qualitative preferences, composition ranking based on their fitness, and multiobjective mathematical optimization.

Keywords: Multiagent system · Team formation · Preference modeling · Control · Planning · Multiobjective optimization

1 Introduction

Automated team formation plays a central role in multiagent systems [20]. It is a prerequisite to coordination and cooperation of agents, since a team specifies roles, relationships, and authority structures [16]. The latter control agent's behaviors. In the context of explicit control, they determine control laws and apply them to act on a group of agents, so that they collaborate to achieve a goal. The control actions need to be adjusted or recalculated due to failures or unfortunate situations, even if agents are assumed to be not malicious. This brief

The research described in this paper was supported, in part, by the Natural Sciences and Engineering Research Council of Canada (NSERC).

© Springer International Publishing AG 2017
J.O. Berndt et al. (Eds.): MATES 2017, LNAI 10413, pp. 54–71, 2017.
DOI: 10.1007/978-3-319-64798-2_4

description conceals a great deal of work done in many directions on this subject in the past [7,15,16]. Significant research efforts are still, however, required due to the fact that relatively few studies have paid attention to both behaviors inherent to agents and attributes associated with tasks. Behaviors are intrinsic to agents. They are abstraction of their reasoning capacities and interactions. Attributes are nonfunctional properties associated with the tasks that an agent can perform. Adding such features leads to a richer model of multiagent systems over which control policies can be synthesized.

A typical team formation problem includes a set of agents $A = \{a_1, \ldots, a_n\}$; a set of tasks $T = \{t_1, \ldots, t_m\}$; a function $\tau : A \rightarrow 2^T$, which assigns to every agent a subset of tasks that it can perform; and a goal $G \subseteq T$, which represents functional requirements [21]. In its simplest form, it corresponds to the set cover problem, which consists in identifying a subset C of A, with the smallest cardinality, such that C is an *effective team*, that is, $G \subseteq \cup_{a_i \in C} \tau(a_i)$ [7]. Such a team formation problem involves cooperation of agents according to the first condition stated in [10] (i.e., agents have a goal in common and their tasks tend to achieve that goal).

Various variants of this problem have been proposed in the past. For instance, the addition of a cost function $\kappa : A \rightarrow \mathbb{R}^+$, which assigns a cost to every agent, changes the objective to the minimization problem in order to determine an effective team with the minimal cost.[1] In an unpredictable environment or a hazardous system, a team must remain effective even if any k agents are removed from the original team. When a team satisfies this property, it is then said to be k *robust* [21]. A bi objective constraint-optimization problem then arises, because the cost must be minimized while k must be maximized. This variant adds an additional objective and intends to identify the Pareto-optimal front as illustrated in Example 1.1. More specifically, every team is such that there exists no other team with better cost and k value. More complex team formation problems can be defined when replacing the sets of tasks associated with agents by multisets of tasks [17] and considering more objectives. A common characteristic of all these variants is that most of them can be formulated as multiple-objective optimization problems [21] or linear integer programming problems [7].

Various algorithm strategies have been used to conceive exact algorithms and heuristics for solving team formation problems: from greedy algorithms to evolutionary approximation algorithms, including planning, branch-and-bound and dynamic programming algorithms [7]. All these problems find immediate application in the domain of cloud computing, where agents are virtual machines and tasks are microservices [11].

Example 1.1. In Fig. 1, $A = \{a_1, a_2, a_3, a_4, a_5\}$, $T = \{t_1, t_2, t_3, t_4, t_5, t_6, t_7, t_8\}$, and $G = \{t_2, t_3, t_5\}$. The set of tasks of agent a_1 is $\tau(a_1) = \{t_1, t_2, t_4, t_5\}$ and its cost is $\kappa(a_1) = 8$. The following table gives some effective teams with their cost and degree of robustness.

---

[1] If $\kappa(a_i) = 1$ for all i, the optimization problem reduces to the set cover problem.

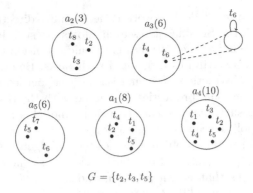

$$G = \{t_2, t_3, t_5\}$$

Fig. 1. An instance of a team formation problem

Team	Cost	k-robust
$\{a_4\}$	10	0-robust
$\{a_1, a_2\}$	11	0-robust
$\{a_2, a_5\}$	9	0-robust
$\{a_1, a_2, a_4\}$	21	1-robust
$\{a_2, a_4, a_5\}$	19	1-robust

The Pareto-optimal front is $\{\{a_2, a_5\}, \{a_2, a_4, a_5\}\}$.   ∎

In the aforementioned problems, there are strong implicit assumptions about the tasks that an agent can perform:

– they can be invoked anytime and in any order;
– they are plain tasks, that is, without attributes or properties.

The contribution of this paper is the tightening of the two above assumptions by combining a framework for behavior composition [8] (described in Sect. 2) with a preference model [18] (described in Sect. 3). This leads to a variant of the team formation problem, which has, however, consequential impacts with regards to the solutions already proposed, since mathematical regularity is lost. The benefit of such an approach lies in increasing the expressiveness of a goal with a better satisfaction level through control exercised on agents. The composition method implements a particular planning technique to synthesize plans, called controllers, which delegate the tasks of a goal to agents for execution, based on their current states [8]. The preference model includes constructors used to specify composite preferences from atomic ones, classified as qualitative or quantitative. Constructors and atomic preferences can be interpreted with respect to a well-defined semantics [18]. This combination is not, however, sufficient in itself to reach a team. According to their semantics, some preferences cannot be taken into consideration by the synthesis procedure, in the sense that only the candidate compositions that do not satisfy some strict preferences specified in the goal are discarded (described in Sect. 4). The other candidates must be compared with each other in order to determine their rank. On the one hand, the degree of robustness of a team can be determined from the compositions in the first rank or having a rank above a given threshold. This is possible because the synthesis procedure ensures that each composition forms an effective team. On the other hand, a bi-objective constraint-optimization problem can be formulated and solved by using usual approaches. The variables represent choices of compositions and the objective functions are defined by considering utility factors such as cost and degree of robustness (described in Sect. 5). This paper investigates all these aspects, including the obstacles that need to be overcome for an eventual deployment in real applications.

2   Preliminaries—A Behavior Composition Framework

In the basic team formation problem as stated in the introduction, the order in which the tasks are executed is irrelevant, both in the agents and the goal. Otherwise, behaviors arise and the behavior composition framework can be applied [8]. A basic issue in this framework is the synthesis of a universal controller, called controller generator. It determines a set of agents that are able to carry out each task conveyed by the goal based on the system's current state. In fact, a target behavior acts as a substitute for the goal. It forces an order in the execution of its tasks. The available agents have also behaviors. The selected agents are such that their behaviors coincide with that order. The universal controller encompasses all the possible compositions, where a composition is a narrow controller with the underlying set of agents realizing together the target behavior. The synthesis of the universal controller relies on the notion of *largest nondeterministic (ND) simulation* whose calculation involves a strict match between the tasks of the goal and those offered by the available agents, because they have neither semantics nor attributes.

Formally, each agent (behavior) is represented by a finite-state transition system $\beta_i = \langle B_i, T_i, \delta_i, b_{i0}, F_i \rangle$, where B_i is a finite set of states, T_i is a finite set of tasks (called actions in the original framework), $\delta_i \subseteq B_i \times T_i \times B_i$ is the transition relation, $b_{i0} \in B_i$ is the initial state, and $F_i \subseteq B_i$ is the set of final states. It should be noted that δ_i involves nondeterminism. Likewise, the target behavior is $\beta_t = \langle B_t, T_t, \delta_t, b_{t0}, F_t \rangle$. The original framework assumes that β_t is deterministic. It also includes the notion of environment (represented by $\mathcal{E}$). It is useful when one wants to impose local conditions on the triggering of behavior's transitions. In that case, the state transition systems are augmented with guards on transitions.

Example 2.1. Figure 2 shows the behavior of three agents available on the web which offer traveling services, namely β_1, β_2, and β_3. The goal is to realize an agent-based travel agency with behavior β_t. A transition labeled with more than one task is just a more compact notation to represent multiple transitions. There is no environment in this example to simplify the presentation.   ■

Let I_n be the set $\{1, \ldots, n\}$, where n is the number of available agents. The original behavior composition problem is formulated as follows [8]:

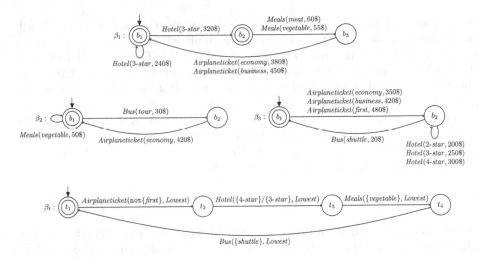

Fig. 2. Available agents and a goal for an agent-based travel agency

Given a system $\mathcal{S} = \langle \beta_1, \ldots, \beta_n, \mathcal{E} \rangle$ and a deterministic target behavior β_t over $\mathcal{E}$, synthesize a controller P (i.e., a plan) that realizes β_t.

The computation of a controller involves the five steps:

1. The asynchronous product of behaviors $\beta_1, \ldots, \beta_n$ synchronized with the environment to obtain the *enacted system behavior* $\mathcal{T}_{\mathcal{S}} = \langle S_{\mathcal{S}}, T, I_n, \delta_{\mathcal{S}}, s_{\mathcal{S}0}, F_{\mathcal{S}} \rangle$.
2. The synchronous product of the target behavior β_t and environment $\mathcal{E}$ to obtain the *enacted target behavior* $\mathcal{T}_T = \langle S_T, T, \delta_T, s_{T0}, F_T \rangle$.
3. The calculation of the largest ND-simulation of $\mathcal{T}_T$ by $\mathcal{T}_{\mathcal{S}}$. If $s_{\mathcal{S}0}$ simulates s_{T0} then there exists a controller that realizes β_t.
4. The construction of a *controller generator* from the simulation relation (i.e., a transition structure like a Mealy machine).
5. The inference of a (narrow) *controller* P from the controller generator.

Every transition of $\mathcal{T}_{\mathcal{S}}$ is labeled by a task and an index that belongs to I_n, which indicates the agent that can perform the task. Steps 3 and 4 may be replaced by the calculation of a winning strategy of a corresponding two-player safety game by using the model checker TLV/SMV [8].

Example 2.2. Figure 3 shows the controller generator calculated by TLV/SMV from β_1, β_2, β_3, and β_t introduced in Example 2.1. It takes into account the preferences of the goal (later explained in Sect. 4).   ∎

   In this paper a controller P is a subtransition system of the controller generator with the following restrictions. There is at most one transition from each state on a given task (while preserving nondeterminism) and this task is delegated to only one agent. The realization of a goal by a controller, together with the subset of agents $\{a_{i_1}, \ldots, a_{i_l}\} \subseteq A$ ($l \leq n$), defines a *composition* denoted by

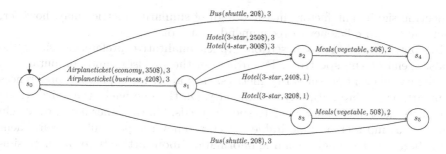

Fig. 3. The universal controller

C. Formally, $C = \langle P, \{a_{i_1}, \ldots, a_{i_l}\} \rangle$. This definition is quite different from the one introduced in the original framework, which is based on the notions of trace (infinite sequence of the form $\sigma^0 \langle t^1, i^1 \rangle \sigma^1 \langle t^2, i^2 \rangle \sigma^2 \ldots$, where $t^j \in T$, $i^j \in I_n$, and σ^j is a state of the controller generator), history (finite trace), and selection function ($S : \mathcal{H} \times T \rightarrow I_n$, where $\mathcal{H}$ is the set of histories of the controller generator, which means that the task t is delegated to β_i after the system has evolved according to h if $S(h, t) = i$). Then, the function $P : \mathcal{H}_S \times T \mapsto I_n$ represents a controller, where $\mathcal{H}_S$ is the set of histories of $\mathcal{T}_S$ obtained from those of the controller generator by projection. In that case, the choice of P is arbitrary. It does not depend on a requirements specification, more specifically, utility values attached to controllers such as cost or energy consumption.

3 Preliminaries—A Preference Model

The kind of control exercised in the behavior composition framework is a control by delegation. To make this model more flexible, it was suggested to introduce a compatibility relation $\ll \subseteq T \times T$ over the set of tasks [8]. It substitutes for the present equality between tasks in the definition of the ND-simulation relation and the underlying algorithm that computes it. A task t' can now be carried out by an agent, if it is compatible with the delegated task t, that is, $t \ll t'$. No more details were given by the authors. The use of the semantic-similarity metric sim constitutes a first appealing solution [2,23]. It evaluates the degree of similarity between any two tasks. Given a threshold $\epsilon \in (0, 1]$, two tasks are considered compatible (i.e., $t \ll t'$) if they satisfy the following similarity condition: $sim(t, t') \geq \epsilon$. Generally, such a metric fits with a domain ontology graph, usually in the form of a well-formed taxonomy of concepts and considers the multipaths connecting two concepts. The main effort must be concentrated on building ontologies [3]. Choice-relevant similarity metrics derived from aggregation of member preferences, based on their individual judgments, can be regarded as another approach [5]. They reflect a consensus between the members of a group. This approach is peculiar to intelligent recommendation tools, which match the most related artifacts with those supplied by a client agent, but when the latter is generally unaware of their functional or nonfunctional requirements.

Neglecting significant factors in the design of similarity metrics may, however, affect the overall efficiency of recommendation tools.

In contrast, techniques based on explicit qualitative preferences sit at the opposite end of the spectrum. Regardless of the precision and computational complexity inherent to similarity metrics, they allow for expressing preferences about artifacts more naturally and directly. On the one hand, they give strong control to client agents in regard to specific needs. On the other hand, they help alleviate the number of undesirable matches. They are particularly convenient when there is not enough semantic information about artifacts to calculate similarity ratings. Recent hybrid approaches aim at filling the gap between explicit qualitative preferences and similarity metrics required for the purpose of preference modeling [25]. These approaches are beyond the scope of this paper.

The preference model used hereafter has been defined to support complex database queries to match user preferences closely [18]. The principle behind a preference-based database search engine is query relaxation. Its adoption leads to reasoning about approximate-match query results, which is more appropriate, for instance, in real-world big-data applications. Later, a semantic ontology of user preferences, which largely rests on this work, has been proposed in the context of web-service discovery and ranking [13]. Basically, the authors follow the same mathematical formulation for preferences. Nevertheless, depending on the context in which the model is used, different interpretations can be adopted when the condition associated with a given preference is not satisfied. Given a set of available tasks T with their own attributes, the realization of a goal, through the synthesis of a decision maker, from functional and nonfunctional requirements expressed in terms of preferences among attribute values, is, in some sense, partly reminiscent of a complex preference query.

Let $Att = \{att_1, \ldots, att_l\}$ be the set of attributes. Each attribute att_i is associated with a domain of values $V_i = \mathrm{dom}(att_i)$. A valuation for a set of attributes Att is a function $\nu : Att \to V_1 \cup \cdots \cup V_l$, assigning a value $\nu(att_i) \in V_i$ to every attribute $att_i \in Att$. The term $\mathrm{val}(Att)$ denotes the set of all valuations over Att. The notion of valuation entails the idea of resource variability due to dynamic changes of task's attribute values.

The preference model distinguishes between atomic and composite preferences. The former are subdivided into qualitative and quantitative preferences.

3.1 Qualitative Atomic Preferences

A natural approach to specify qualitative preferences is to use sets of lexical terms instead of rating values. Given an attribute $att \in Att$, the disjoint sets *Fav*, *Alt*, and *Dis* included in $\mathrm{dom}(att)$ represent the favorite, alternative, and disliked values for attribute att, respectively. These sets or combinations of them induce strict partial orders over $\mathrm{dom}(att)$, which formally define some sorts of preferences:

$$x <^{Fav} y \text{ iff } y \in Fav \wedge x \notin Fav; \tag{1}$$

$$x <^{Dis} y \text{ iff } y \notin Dis \wedge x \in Dis; \tag{2}$$

$$x <^{Fav/Alt} y \text{ iff } (y \in Fav \wedge x \in Alt) \vee \tag{3}$$
$$(y \in Fav \cup Alt \wedge x \notin Fav \cup Alt);$$

$$x <^{Fav/Dis} y \text{ iff } (y \in Fav \wedge x \notin Fav) \vee \tag{4}$$
$$(y \notin Fav \cup Dis \wedge x \in Dis).$$

With respect to a favorite preference, the tasks with an attribute having a value that does not belong to Fav must be discarded. The notion of dislike preference is the opposite of favorite preference. The condition to discard a task is that the value belongs to Dis. A favorite/alternative preference gives an advantage to tasks with an attribute having a value that belongs to Fav, if they exist, without ignoring those for which the value belongs to Alt. The tasks for which the value of the attribute does not belong to Fav or Alt must be discarded. Finally, with respect to a favorite/dislike preference, a task should preferably have a value in Fav for the corresponding attribute. Otherwise, the value should not belong to Dis.[2] The condition to discard a task is the same as for the dislike preference.

3.2 Quantitative Atomic Preferences

Many preferences are often expressed by using numerical values rather than lexical terms. Typically, the attribute domain is $\mathbb{N}$, $\mathbb{Z}$, or $\mathbb{R}$ (equipped with a subtractive operation). Given an attribute $att \in Att$, typical preferences over $dom(att)$ are lowest, highest, around, and score. Let $f : dom(att) \to \mathbb{R}$, and $v \in dom(att)$. The induced strict orders are the following:

$$x <^{Lowest} y \text{ iff } x > y;$$
$$x <^{Highest} y \text{ iff } x < y;$$
$$x <^{Around(v)} y \text{ iff } |x - v| > |y - v|;$$
$$x <^{Score(f)} y \text{ iff } f(x) < f(y).$$

Contrary to qualitative preferences, none of these conditions allows for discarding tasks during controller synthesis.

3.3 Composite Preferences

Generally, a task has more than one attribute. Preferences must then be composed to relate two or more preferences. Constructors for balanced (or Pareto), prioritized, and numerical preferences have been introduced for that purpose. Using the third constructor can give rise to many specialized preferences. For instance, let $f_1 : dom(att_1) \to \mathbb{N}$ and $f_2 : dom(att_2) \to \mathbb{N}$ be two functions that

---

[2] The authors of [13, 18] give two different formulations of favorite/dislike. Both include an inconsistency. Equation (4) corrects these mistakes.

transform numerical values or lexical terms of two different domains into natural numbers. Let $F : \mathbb{N} \times \mathbb{N} \to \mathbb{R}$ such that $F(n_1, n_2) = 0.3n_1 + 0.7n_2$, then the following strict order defines a numerical preference, more precisely, a weighted preference:

$$x <^{Weight} y \text{ iff } F(f_1(x_1), f_2(x_2)) < F(f_1(y_1), f_2(y_2)), \text{ where } x = (x_1, x_2) \text{ and}$$
$$y = (y_1, y_2).$$

The intended role of composite preferences within the proposed preference-based behavior composition framework is to rank compositions. Preferences on attributes have a ripple effect. Their fulfilments are propagated from tasks to compositions. Composite preferences are a means to specify various ranking heuristics.

Example 3.1. In Fig. 2 of Example 2.1, all the tasks of agents have two attributes and their values are between parenthesis. The value of the second attribute is the price a traveler will pay for the corresponding service. The preferences for the corresponding tasks appear in the goal. The dislike preference "not $\{first\}$" indicates that the customer does not want a first class flight. He also prefers a 4-star hotel, but a 3-star hotel is acceptable. This is a favorite/alternative preference. The preferences for meals and bus are favorite preferences. The preference for the second attribute is a quantitative preference. It indicates that the customer always looks for the lowest prices.   ∎

4   Preference-Based Behavior Composition

The formal representation for behaviors need to be changed to take into account attributes and preferences. Each behavior β_i is represented by a finite-state transition system $\langle B_i, T_i, \alpha_i, \delta_i, b_{i0}, F_i, \rangle$, where all elements are defined in Sect. 2, except that there is an additional element $\alpha_i : T_i \to 2^{Att}$, which is a function assigning a subset of attributes of Att to every task. It should be noted that $\tau(\beta_i) = T_i$. The same tasks of different behaviors have the same attributes (i.e., $\alpha_i(t) = \alpha_j(t)$, if $t \in T_i \cap T_j$). Likewise, the (enacted) system behavior is $\mathcal{S} = \langle S, T, I_n, \alpha, \delta, s_0, F \rangle$, where $S = B_1 \times \cdots \times B_n$ is the set of states, with $s_0 = \langle b_{10}, \ldots, b_{n0} \rangle$ and $F = F_1 \times \cdots \times F_n$; $T = \cup_i T_i$ is the set of tasks; $\alpha(t) \subseteq \alpha_i(t)$ for $t \in T_i$; and $\delta \subseteq S \times T \times I_n \times S$ is the transition relation defined in the usual way, except that each transition is labeled by a task and an index that belongs to I_n, which indicates the behavior that may perform the task. The target behavior (goal) is $\beta_t = \langle B_t, T_t, \alpha_t, \delta_t, b_{t0}, F_t \rangle$, where $T_t \subseteq T$. For any $t \in T_t$, $\alpha_t(t) = \alpha(t)$. This means that a task of the goal has the same attributes as the ones of the corresponding task in the system.

Values must be assigned to attributes via valuations. To provide a flexible model, the way the values are assigned to attributes depends on transitions, that is, each transition is labeled by an instance of a task (a task with specific values for its attributes). In this sense, a valuation ν is a conditional valuation and $\nu(att|\langle s, t, k, s' \rangle)$ (or shortly $\nu(att)$ when the context is clear), with $\langle s, t, k, s' \rangle \in \delta$

and $att \in \alpha(t)$, denotes the value of att. The counterpart of ν for β_t is ρ, but its range is atomic preferences (*Indifference* is the default preference). For instance, $\rho(att) = Around(v)$ for a preference of type "*Around*" with argument v and $\rho(att) = Fav/Alt$ for a favorite/alternative preference with the sets Fav and Alt as arguments.

4.1 A New Version of the ND-Simulation Relation

The main notion of ND-simulation relation has been adapted, so that the match between tasks is not strict, but depends on preferences. A filter is applied on the tasks with respect to Eqs. 1 to 4.

An ND-simulation relation of β_t by $\mathcal{S}$ is a relation $R \subseteq B_t \times S$ such that $\langle s_t, s \rangle \in R$ implies:

1. if $s_t \in F_t$, then $s \in F$;
2. for all transitions $\langle s_t, t, s_t' \rangle \in \delta_t$:
   - there exists a transition $\langle s, t, k, s' \rangle \in \delta$;
   - for all transitions $\langle s, t, k, s' \rangle \in \delta$, $\langle s_t', s' \rangle \in R$ and for all $att \in \alpha_t(t)$:
     - $\nu(att) \in Fav$ if $\rho(att) = Fav$,
     - $\nu(att) \notin Dis$ if $\rho(att) = Dis$,
     - $\nu(att) \in Fav \cup Alt$ if $\rho(att) = Fav/Alt$,
     - $\nu(att) \notin Dis$ if $\rho(att) = Fav/Dis$.

This definition can be easily implemented through a fixpoint calculation procedure to obtain the largest relation R. As mentioned in Sect. 3, a final decision (acceptance or rejection of a task offered by an agent) cannot be taken due to the fact that the transitions are examined one at a time with local information. The characterization of the "best" compositions relies, among other things, on the composite preferences used to rank all candidate compositions.

4.2 Enumeration of Compositions

Based on the preceding definition of ND-simulation relation, a prototyping approach has been followed initially to generate all candidate compositions from problem instances of smaller size to evaluate the feasibility and effectiveness of the integration of a preference model into a synthesis procedure. The prototype has been implemented by using a SAT-solving environment especially developed for controller synthesis in Alloy [12].

4.3 Synthesis of Controllers

Another approach has also been taken for controller synthesis. It is based on the TLV/SMV code provided in [8]. Since the original SMV module skeletons only support functional requirements (tasks), they have been modified to include nonfunctional requirements (preferences and attributes) by exploiting set operators. When the initial state is a winning state, the controller generator can then be constructed from the maximal set of winning states (the output of TLV) and narrow controllers can be extracted from it to obtain the set of all candidate compositions.

Example 4.1. Six compositions can be identified form the controller generator depicted in Fig. 3 of Example 2.2. Four have a deterministic controller. For instance, $C_1 = \langle P_1, \{a_2, a_3\}\rangle$ with the following transitions for P_1:

$$\langle s_0, Airplaneticket(economy, 350\$), 3, s_1\rangle, \langle s_1, Hotel(4\text{-}star, 300\$), 3, s_2\rangle,$$
$$\langle s_2, Meals(vegetable, 50\$), 2, s_4\rangle, \langle s_4, Bus(shuttle, 20\$), 3, s_0\rangle.$$

Two have a nondeterministic controller. For instance, $C_6 = \langle P_6, \{a_1, a_2, a_3\}\rangle$ with the following transitions for P_6:

$$\langle s_0, Airplaneticket(economy, 350\$), 3, s_1\rangle,$$
$$\langle s_1, Hotel(3\text{-}star, 240\$), 1, s_2\rangle, \langle s_1, Hotel(3\text{-}star, 320\$), 1, s_3\rangle,$$
$$\langle s_2, Meals(vegetable, 50\$), 2, s_4\rangle, \langle s_3, Meals(vegetable, 50\$), 2, s_5\rangle,$$
$$\langle s_4, Bus(shuttle, 20\$), 3, s_0\rangle, \langle s_5, Bus(shuttle, 20\$), 3, s_0\rangle.$$

∎

Recall that, based on the current state of the system and the current task $t \in T_t$ released by the goal, the controller returns an index $k \in I_n$ such that agent a_k is ready to execute the task t, while taking into account some preferences of the goal.

5   Formulation of a Team Formation Problem

The team formation problem through preference-based behavior composition is formulated as follows:

> Given an attributed multiagent system $\mathcal{S} = \langle a_1, \ldots, a_n\rangle$ and a deterministic goal G with preferences, find a set of compositions $\{C_1, \ldots, C_m\}$, such that each composition $C_i = \langle P_i, \{a_{i_{j_1}}, \ldots, a_{i_{j_l}}\}\rangle$ realizes (through P_i) the goal G and presents the best match for the preferences, and agents involved in these compositions form the more robust team at less cost.

The original behavior composition problem is then extended to the one of finding the more robust team at less cost (i.e., the utility factors are cost and degree of robustness). It comprises distinct parts. Each of them may be declined in numerous variants. One variant is further formalized with the following multi-objective optimization problem, in which the variable x_j, y_i, and x_{ij} are Boolean variables and K is an integer variable:

$$\min[\sum_i \kappa_1(C_i)y_i + \sum_j \kappa_2(a_j)x_j + \sum_{i,j} \kappa_3(a_j, C_i)x_{ij}, -K] \tag{5}$$

subject to

$$\bigvee_i x_{ij} = x_j; \tag{6}$$

$$\sum_{a_j \in C_i} x_{ij} = |C_i| y_i; \qquad \sum_{a_j \notin C_i} x_{ij} = 0; \tag{7}$$

$$\sum_{j:t_k \in \hat{\tau}(a_j)} x_j \geq K + 1; \tag{8}$$

$$y_i, x_j, x_{ij} \in \{0, 1\};$$

$$C_i \text{ realizes } G \text{ at best.} \tag{9}$$

The two objectives of this problem concern costs (κ_1, κ_2, κ_3) and degree of robustness (K), respectively. The function κ_1 gives the global cost of a composition. The functions κ_2 and κ_3 represent the access cost to an agent and connection cost of an agent to a composition, respectively. The variables i, j, and k range from 1 to m (the number of candidate compositions), from 1 to n (the number of agents), and from 1 to $|T_t|$ (the number of tasks in the goal), respectively. There are three blocks of constraints. Constraints (6) relate the individual agents to the corresponding agents in the compositions. If agent a_j is selected (i.e., $x_j = 1$ in the solution), then a_j belongs to at least one composition, say C_i (i.e., $x_{ij} = 1$ for at least one i in the solution). Constraints (7) ensure that each composition includes only their own agents. The term $|C_i|$ denotes the number of agents in composition C_i. If composition C_i is selected (i.e., $y_i = 1$ in the solution), then its agents are necessary attached to it (i.e., for all j such that $a_j \in C_i$, $x_{ij} = 1$ in the solution). These two subblocks of constraints could also be written as follows: $\sum_j In(a_j, C_i) x_{ij} = |C_i| y_i$, where the predicate In holds whether $a_j \in C_i$. Constraints (8) correlate the degree of robustness and the number of agents that can perform the same task. The function $\hat{\tau}$ is a restriction of τ. It gives only the set tasks delegated to an agent, not all the tasks it can perform. For a given task t_k of the goal, if it is also a task of agent a_j and it is delegated to a_j then it counts for one whether a_j is selected (i.e., $x_j = 1$ in the solution). Without loss of generality, it is assumed that $\hat{\tau}(a_i) \cap \hat{\tau}(a_j) = \emptyset$, for all distinct pairs of agent a_i, a_j that belong to the same composition (care must be taken when considering a task delegated to more than one agent in the same composition). Due to the last constraint (9), the problem rests on another multiobjective optimization problem, which determines a subset of the set of candidate compositions that meet the preferences of the goal to the greatest extent possible. Its solution cannot be computed by exploiting usual mathematical programming techniques, since the maximization is over an unknown set of compositions, which must be generated while taking into account some qualitative preferences. Several heuristics and an efficient non-dominated sort algorithm [9] are used instead for approximate ranking of compositions.

5.1   Composition Ranking

As explained in Sect. 4, it is impossible to distinguish between compositions satisfying favorite preferences and those offering just alternative or non-dislike preferences due to their semantics and implementation details. A similar remark applies for the quantitative preferences. The compositions with the most desirable values cannot be identified during the generation of compositions. An additional step is required to classify compositions in a number of ranks when comparing all attribute values of their tasks with respect to the corresponding preferences of the goal. The goal here is not only to solve the optimization problem (9), but to collect and rank a large number of compositions. First, a composite preference on attributes of every task, namely Pareto, prioritized, and weighted, is applied to reflect their relative importance. Second, rating values are associated with the relevant attributes based on the goal's preferences. Finally, the rating values are aggregated into one (total value) or more (Pareto) values to determine the rank of each composition.

Example 5.1. The six compositions identified in Example 4.1 have been ranked with respect to the Pareto composite preference for attributes of each task, Boolean values (1 for the best, 0 otherwise) as rating values, and summation over them. The final rating values of C_1 to C_6 are 5, 5, 4, 4, 3, and 4, respectively. So, C_1 and C_2 have rank 1, C_3, C_4 and C_6 have rank 2, and C_5 has rank 3. ∎

Example 5.2. Let $\kappa_1(C_i) = 1$ (for all i), $\kappa_2(a_j) = 1$ (for all j), and $\kappa_3(a_j, C_i) = 1$ (for all i, j) in the optimization problem defined by Eqs. 5 to 9. Then, the total cost of compositions C_1, C_2, C_3 and C_4 is 5, and is 7 for C_5 and C_6. If the compositions with rank 1 or 2 are those considered in Eq. 9, then the Pareto front (best solutions) are C_1, C_2, C_3 and C_4. The agent team is $\{a_2, a_3\}$ and it is 0-robust. ∎

6   Experiments with a Synthetic Problem

The synthetic problem consists in n available agents that carry out tasks, ranging from groups of agents having one task to those having $p - 1$ different tasks, including the group of a single agent having p different tasks, where p is the total number of tasks in the goal. So, $n = 2^p - 1$ and the number of candidate compositions is also $2^p - 1$. Each task, in turn, has three attributes. One has a numerical value, ranging from 1 to 10 and chosen randomly. It corresponds to any sort of quantitative preference. The others have lexical terms as domains and correspond to favorite/alternative or favorite/dislike preferences. A favorite term is represented by 1 and a non-favorite or alternative term by 0. The 0 and 1 are generated randomly with the constraint that 40 % of them be 1 (favorite). The Pareto heuristic was implemented by using a non-dominated sort. Figure 4 provides the results computed by a Ruby program for $p = 7$. Results are averages calculated after 10 iterations with different random data.

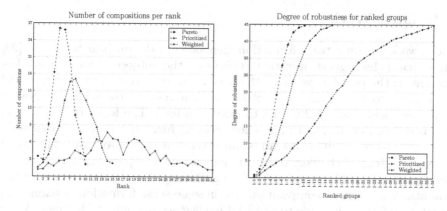

Fig. 4. Experimental results

As depicted in the left graph, the horizontal axis indicates the rank, ranging from 1 to 34, and the vertical axis shows the number of compositions. Bell-shaped curves arise for the three composite preferences (Pareto, prioritized, and weighted). The number of best and worst compositions (i.e., the most and least matchable with goal preferences, respectively) are at the extremities of the curves. They look like a normal distribution with heavier tails in the case of Pareto and prioritized preferences (e.g., like a logistic distribution), since attributes values have been generated randomly. The compositions are distributed in ten groups with the Pareto preference, and the one of rank 1 contains in average more compositions in comparison with the other groups of rank 1 for the prioritized and weighted preferences. The fluctuation among groups is less variable for the weighted preference, which tends to discriminate compositions between a larger range of ranks. The reason for that is that the prioritized preference gives importance to one attribute per task, the Pareto preference gives the same priority to all the attributes, and the weighted preference takes also into account all the attributes, but assigns different priorities (or weights) to them.

The right graph shows the degree of robustness for groups of compositions. With respect to the horizontal axis, each label of the scale has the format "1–i" and refers to all compositions with a rank between 1 and i. It can be observed that the slopes of the curves are high, except at the beginning and end. The slope is higher for the Pareto heuristic and lower for the weighted heuristic. This is consistent with the bell-shaped curves in the left graph, in particular the shape of the curves for the Pareto and prioritized heuristics is quite similar. Compared with the Pareto heuristic, more ranks and thus more groups of compositions, with a larger gap between the first and last, must be added to the team to reach the same degree of robustness. Finally, it is impossible to achieve a reasonable degree of robustness when considering only compositions of rank one.

7   Related Work

Besides work on static team formation mentioned in the introduction (e.g., [20, 21]), which include good literature reviews on the subject, a lot of work has been done in the past few years on the selection or discovery of web services and their ranking to determine which of the alternatives give the highest degree of goal achievement (e.g., [1,22], just to mention a few). The focus was mainly on formalisms (e.g., conditional preference network, fuzzy *if-then* rules, preference tree, μcalculus) to specify constraints, preferences, and trade-offs over functional requirements (e.g., behavior, data) or nonfunctional requirements (e.g., availability, privacy, reliability, security). The goal was to lay the foundation for the automatic generation of compositions (or in some sense formation of teams). In general, no reference is made to artificial-intelligence planning techniques. A few of these papers, however, exploit verification techniques.

Other related research work argue for the use of planning techniques for composition or team formation: STRIPS [6], HTN planning [24], or particular planning algorithm [27]. From a reactive planning perspective, a controller, as defined in this paper, is like a reactive plan that prescribes behavior delegations rather than domain actions [8]. There are other solutions based on control by enablement, rather than control by delegation, implemented by a state machine operating in synchronous composition with a state machine representing the system behavior [4]. Although they share common characteristics, they are notably different because there are many facets to the underlying problem and many contrasting angles to address. In most of them (e.g., [6,27]), agents are loosely coupled. Utility factors (e.g., cost) and preferences appear in an uneven way across the underlying approaches. Furthermore, none of them pay attention to runtime failures of agents, which are one of our motivations. For instance, the authors of [24] focus on gathering data operations, that is, the invocation of ν in the context of our paper. They identify conditions on when (e.g., decoupling or not from composition generation) and how (e.g., local optimization) data access can be made without compromising composition optimality. The language used to express preferences gives more freedom to the user, but it allows for the definition of only one kind of metric function (or objective function) over preferences, which can either be minimized or maximized. In some sense, a metric function is similar to a numerical preference. Services (agents) have no behavior, but tasks can be, however, chronologically ordered by adding constraints in a task network. The planning algorithm returns the globally optimal composition instead of a set of acceptable compositions from which a robust team can be identified. The reason is that only numerical composite preferences over all atomic preferences is allowed. The Pareto preference, among others, is not supported. In fact, the objectives must be combined into one single-objective scalar function.

An approach similar to the last described above also uses HTN [19], but neither information gathering nor robustness are considered. Finally, graph theory has been used as foundation to formulate and solve a basic team formation problem with the only objective to determine the minimum number of agents to satisfy a goal [26].

8   Contributions and Conclusion

Automated preference-based composition of software artifacts (e.g., agents, business processes, components, services) so far has received relatively little attention when addressed from the perspective of a team formation problem as formulated in this paper. The novel solution proposed to solve a new distinct formulation of the team formation problem (see Eqs. 5 to 9) combines existing concepts and synthesis procedures borrowed from a well-defined preference model and a sound, complete behavior composition framework. In summary, this paper makes the following contributions:

- It extends the basic robust team formation problem to include agents with behaviors, tasks with attributes, and scalar-valued functions over compositions.
- It integrates the semantics of a preference model into the notion of ND-simulation relation with implementations into two synthesis procedures.
- It considers a large number of compositions (not only one plan) without which it is impossible to cope with the Pareto preference or produce robust teams.
- It takes into account more global properties on compositions for discrimination at a higher level in order to formulate multiobjective optimization problems and solve them with usual mathematical programming techniques.
- It provides experiments with a synthetic multiagent system to show the impacts of composite preferences (or heuristics) on the distribution of compositions with respect to their rank and on the degree of robustness of a team formed from agents, which are involved in a given number of compositions.

The proposed approach is not the panacea. Further work should be done. First, recovery procedures must be defined to manage failures in a k-robust team. Some indications are given in [8], but they do not consider, for instance, the reversibility of tasks or any other assumptions on agents. Second, contrary to flat agents and tasks, compositions reveal properties at three levels: properties associated with compositions, agents, and tasks. Although a solution to this problem has been suggested herein (with no other utility factors than cost and robustness), a uniform solution must be developed for both the preference model and synthesis procedures. Third, centralized control is generally too restrictive with respect to the multiagent paradigm. Theories should be developed with synthesis algorithms to generate control policies as well as negotiation policies, which could be distributed into agents. The former is more appropriate for orchestration and the latter for choreography.

From a more general point of view, it should be interesting to further investigate how the approach proposed in this paper could be applied, for instance, to the multiple team formation problem [14]. In this problem, the goal is divided into several subgoals and a team of agents must be assigned to each of them. An agent can simultaneously participate in several teams, but its efforts must be allocated to the corresponding subgoals in some proportions.

References

1. Agarwal, S., Lamparter, S., Studer, R.: Making Web services tradable: a policy-based approach for specifying preferences on Web service properties. Web Semant.: Sci. Serv. Agents World Wide Web **7**(1), 11–20 (2009)
2. Andreasen, T., Bulskov, H., Knappe, R.: From ontology over similarity to query evaluation. In: Bernardi, R., Moortgat, M. (eds.) 2nd CoLogNET-ElsNET Symposium - Questions and Answers: Theoretical and Applied Perspectives, pp. 39–50. Elsevier, Amsterdam (2003)
3. Arp, R., Smith, B., Spear, A.D.: Building Ontologies with Basic Formal Ontology. MIT Press, Cambridge (2015)
4. Bertoli, P., Pistore, M., Traverso, P.: Automated composition of web services via planning in asynchronous domain. Artif. Intell. **174**(3–4), 316–361 (2010)
5. Binder, C.: Preference and similarity between alternatives. Rationality Markets Morals **5**, 120–132 (2014)
6. Brafman, R.I., Domshlak, C.: From one to many: planning for loosely coupled multi-agent systems. In: 18th International Conference on Automated Planning and Scheduling (ICAPS), pp. 28–35. AAAI Press, Sydney, September 2008
7. Crawford, C., Rahaman, Z., Sen, S.: Evaluating the efficiency of robust team formation algorithms. In: Osman, N., Sierra, C. (eds.) AAMAS 2016. LNCS, vol. 10002, pp. 14–29. Springer, Cham (2016). doi:10.1007/978-3-319-46882-2_2
8. De Giacomo, G., Patrizi, F., Sardiña, S.: Automatic behavior composition synthesis. Artif. Intell. **196**, 106–142 (2013)
9. Deb, K., Pratap, A., Agarwal, S., Meyarivan, T.: A fast and elitist multiobjective genetic algorithm: NSGA-II. IEEE Trans. Evol. Comput. **6**(2), 182–197 (2002)
10. Doran, J.E., Fraiklin, S., Jennings, N.R., Norman, T.J.: On cooperation in multi-agent systems. Knowl. Eng. Rev. **12**(3), 309–314 (1997)
11. Dragoni, N., Giallorenzo, S., Lafuente, A.L., Mazzara, M., Montesi, F., Mustafin, R., Safina, L.: Microservices: yesterday, today, and tomorrow (2017). arXiv:1606.04036
12. Fraikin, B., Frappier, M., St-Denis, R.: Supervisory control theory with Alloy. Sci. Comput. Program. **94**(2), 217–237 (2014)
13. García, J.M., Ruiz, D., Ruiz-Cortés, A.: An intuitive and formal description of preferences for semantic web service discovery and ranking. Technical report ISA-12-TR-07, Universidad de Sevilla, Sevilla, Spain (2012)
14. Gutiérrez, J.H., Astudillo, C.A., Ballesteros-Pérez, P., Mora-Melià, D., Candia-Véjar, A.: The multiple team formation problem using sociometry. Comput. Oper. Res. **75**, 150–162 (2016)
15. Hayano, M., Hamada, D., Sugawara, T.: Role and member selection in team formation using resource estimation for large-scale multi-agent systems. Neurocomputing **146**, 164–172 (2014)
16. Horling, B., Lesser, V.: A survey of multi-agent organizational paradigms. Knowl. Eng. Rev. **19**(4), 281–316 (2014)
17. Hua, Q.S., Wang, Y., Yu, D., Lau, F.C.: Dynamic programming based algorithms for set multicover and multiset multicover problems. Theoret. Comput. Sci. **411**(26–28), 2467–2474 (2010)
18. Kießling, W.: Foundations of preferences in database systems. In: 28th International Conference on Very Large Data Bases, pp. 311–322. VLDB Endowment, Hong Kong, August 2002

19. Lin, N., Kuter, U., Sirin, E.: Web service composition with user preferences. In: Bechhofer, S., Hauswirth, M., Hoffmann, J., Koubarakis, M. (eds.) ESWC 2008. LNCS, vol. 5021, pp. 629–643. Springer, Heidelberg (2008). doi:10.1007/978-3-540-68234-9_46

20. Marcolino, L.S., Jiang, A.X., Tambe, M.: Multi-agent team formation: diversity beats strength? In: 23rd International Conference on Artificial Intelligence (IJCAI), pp. 279–285. AAAI Press, Beijing, August 2013

21. Okimoto, T., Schwind, N., Clement, M., Ribeiro, T., Inoue, K., Marquis, P.: How to form a task-oriented robust team. In: 2015 International Conference on Autonomous Agents and Multiagent Systems (AAMAS), pp. 395–403. International Foundation for Autonomous Agents and Multiagent Systems, Istanbul, May 2015

22. Santhanam, G., Basu, S., Honavar, V.: TCP-Compose*- A TCP-net based algorithm for efficient composition of web services using qualitative preferences. In: Bouguettaya, A., Krueger, I., Margaria, T. (eds.) ICSOC 2008. LNCS, vol. 5364, pp. 453–467. Springer, Heidelberg (2008)

23. Sim, K.: Agent-based cloud computing. IEEE Trans. Serv. Comput. 5(4), 564–577 (2012)

24. Sohrabi, S., McIlraith, S.A.: Preference-based web service composition: a middle ground between execution and search. In: Patel-Schneider, P.F., Pan, Y., Hitzler, P., Mika, P., Zhang, L., Pan, J.Z., Horrocks, I., Glimm, B. (eds.) ISWC 2010. LNCS, vol. 6496, pp. 713–729. Springer, Heidelberg (2010). doi:10.1007/978-3-642-17746-0_45

25. Wang, H., Wang, H., Guo, G., Tang, Y., Zhang, J.: Measuring similarity of users with qualitative preference for service selection. Knowl. Inf. Syst. 1–34 (first online, 2016)

26. Zhang, Y., Sreedharan, S., Kambhampati, S.: A formal analysis of required cooperation in multi-agent planning. In: 26th International Conference on Automated Planning and Scheduling (ICAPS), pp. 335–343. AAAI Press, London, June 2016

27. Zhuo, H.H., Yang, Q., Kambhampati, S.: Action-model based multi-agent plan recognition. In: Pereira, F., Burges, C.J.C., Bottou, L., Weinberger, K.Q. (eds.) Advances in Neural Information Processing Systems 25 (NIPS), pp. 368–376. Curran Associates, Inc. (2012)

Collaborative Search for Multi-goal Pathfinding in Ubiquitous Environments

Oudom Kem$^{(\boxtimes)}$, Flavien Balbo, and Antoine Zimmermann

Univ Lyon, MINES Saint-Étienne, CNRS, Laboratoire Hubert Curien, UMR 5516, 42023 Saint-Étienne, France
{oudom.kem,flavien.balbo,antoine.zimmermann}@emse.fr

Abstract. Multi-goal pathfinding (MGPF) is a problem of searching for a path between an origin and a destination, which allows a set of goals to be satisfied. We are interested in MGPF in ubiquitous environments that are composed of cyber, physical and social (CPS) entities from connected objects, to sensors and to people. Our approach aims at exploiting data from various resources such as CPS entities and the Web to solve MGPF. However, accessing resources creates overheads – specifically latency affecting the efficiency of the approach. In this paper, we present a collaborative multi-agent search model that addresses the latency problem. The model handles the process of accessing resources such that agents are not blocked while data from resources are being processed and transferred. Agents search concurrently and collaboratively on different parts of the search space. The model exploits the knowledge and structure of the search space to distribute the work among agents and to create an agent network facilitating agent communications as well as separating the search from the communications. To evaluate our model, we apply it in uniform cost search, creating a collaborative uniform cost algorithm. We compare it to the original algorithm. Experiments are conducted on search spaces of various sizes and structures. In most cases, collaborative uniform cost is shown to run significantly faster and scale better in function of latency as well as graph size.

Keywords: Collaborative search · Multi-agent search · Multi-goal pathfinding · Ubiquitous environments

1 Introduction

Pathfinding is a problem that has been studied extensively due to its importance in various fields such as AI, robotics, logistics and video games. There are different variations of pathfinding problems [2,8] such as single-agent pathfinding, multi-agent pathfinding in static, dynamic and real-time environments. Numerous techniques have been proposed to address pathfinding [1]. In this paper, we focus on a particular kind of pathfinding problem, multi-goal pathfinding (MGPF) in the context of ubiquitous environments accommodating cyber, physical and social (CPS) entities such as sensors, smart objects and humans.

© Springer International Publishing AG 2017
J.O. Berndt et al. (Eds.): MATES 2017, LNAI 10413, pp. 72–88, 2017.
DOI: 10.1007/978-3-319-64798-2_5

MGPF is a problem of searching for a path between an origin and a destination, which allows a set of goals to be satisfied. Our approach to solving MGPF exploits data acquired from CPS entities in a given environment and from external resources such as the Web. It uses up-to-date and dynamic information from various resources for path computation. For path evaluation, we use generic criteria, which are not limited to distance, and quality of entities, which is determined using qualitative information from resources. To understand the underlying motivation of our approach, consider the following scenario. A traveler, Carol, arrives at an airport. Carol wants to find a path to her departure gate. Carol has a set of activities (goals) she wants to do on her way to the gate: get a trolley for her luggage, check-in, buy a takeout for lunch and find a waiting seat near a power socket to charge her laptop. Using spatial information of the airport, we can find a path to the gate. Information about the airport makes it possible to determine which locations allow Carol to satisfy each of her goals. For example, restaurant is a business which prepares and serves food and drinks to customers in exchange for money. By obtaining that piece of information from the Web, we are able to deduce that Carol can buy lunch at locations of type restaurant. Dynamic and up-to-date information from sensors and smart objects enables us to determine the optimal path for Carol. For instance, instead of going to a trolley area, which is at the opposite direction of her gate, it is possible to locate an available trolley nearby that was left by other people, thanks to data from connected trolleys. We might suggest Carol to take an escalator instead of an elevator because we know that there are too many people in the queue waiting for the elevators or that the elevators are out of service thanks to the feeds from sensors. In addition, information from social entities such as other travelers or personnel can be used to enhance Carol's travel experience. For instance, reviews by travelers (e.g. quality or availability) on restaurants enable us to choose locations that are at Carol's best interests.

Considering the aim of the approach, one might ask two challenging questions: (1) Which resources to use to solve a MGPF problem? (2) How to deal with the dynamics, mobility and heterogeneity of CPS entities? The first question is concerned with the discovery of resources that are relevant to a given MGPF problem. We address this question via the use of a data model to capture necessary knowledge enabling resource discovery. Regarding the second question, there are existing works that address these issues in the context of IoT. As an example, in [4], the authors propose a multi-agent-based socio-technical network (STN) to manage the complexity of CPS entities. In our approach, we focus on the conceptual level, and we employ one of the existing solutions such as STN to abstract away the complexity at the lower level.

In our approach, we solve MGPF by abstracting a given environment as a search space and use search algorithms to find the path. Necessary information for finding and evaluating a path during a search is acquired from various resources from CPS entities to the Web. Accessing resources creates overheads resulted from the latency of processing and transferring data from their sources. To address this issue, we propose a collaborative search model for search algorithms, which is the main contribution of this paper. The model is composed of multiple agents collaboratively and concurrently searching on different parts of a search space. It handles the process of resource accesses such that agents do not have to wait for data and are able to perform other tasks while requests to resources are being processed. It exploits the structure and knowledge of the search space to distribute the work efficiently among agents and to construct an agent network on-the-fly to facilitate agent communications and separate the search from the communications.

The rest of the paper is organized as follows. First, we review related work. Second, we present the problem addressed in this paper. Third, a detailed description of the collaborative search model is provided. Fourth, we present an application of our model in uniform cost search, and provide some experimental results. Fifth, we conclude the paper and outline future work.

2   Related Work

There are two common variants of MGPF. First, given a single start and multiple goals, MGPF is defined as a problem of searching for paths for each start-goal pair, resulting in multiple paths [12]. Second, MGPF is treated as a traveling salesman problem (TSP) in which the aim is to find a path from a start to a number of goals before reaching the destination such as in [5,13]. Our problem is close to the second definition. However, unlike the classical TSP, we have constraints on the order of goals to satisfy. The work in [21] addresses a TSP with partial order constraints. The author proposes two algorithms to solve the selection and ordering of points-of-interests (goals), which are places, for indoor navigation systems. Path computation is based on complete spatial knowledge of an environment, and distance is the sole criterion for path evaluation. In this paper, we address a problem similar to [21], but the specific property of our problem is that satisfying a goal is not limited to passing by a place, but can be any activity carried out via a CPS entity, which can be mobile and dynamic. Furthermore, we have a strict order in which goals are satisfied.

There is a rich body of literature on pathfinding. Many search algorithms have been proposed to address various aspects of the problem. The most common search algorithms are the centralized and synchronous ones such breadth-first search, depth-first search, Dijkstra's algorithm, uniform cost search and A*. A* is probably the most used heuristic algorithm due to its theoretical properties that guarantee completeness and optimality [9], provided that the heuristics are consistent. Considerable efforts have been invested to optimize A* by reducing search space [3], mitigating memory requirements [15] and adapting it to dynamic environments [11,18]. In these algorithms, each step is performed sequentially as the global state of the search is required. For example, A* selects a promising node to expand by comparing it to all the candidate nodes. With latency, sequential search will become impractical as the algorithm is blocked while waiting for requested data to determine the cost of each node.

Much work has been done [16,17,20] to address search that involves multiple agents, commonly known as cooperative pathfinding or multi-agent pathfinding.

However, such work aims at finding non-interfering paths for each agent from their current state to their respective goal state. In our case, each agent may have different starts, but they cooperate to find the same goal state. This falls under the definition of collaborative mulit-agent search as classified by the author in [6]. Parallelization techniques such as [10,19] have been used to improve search. They distribute workloads or search operators between processors using generic mechanisms independent of the problem (e.g. using hash function to assign each node to a process). Furthermore, in [14], the authors propose a multi-agent A* based on agents possessing different search operators. Workloads are distributed based on the operators (i.e. discovered nodes are sent to agents who have the operators to expand them). In our model, we separate a search space among agents based on the structure of the space, thus distributing the workload by assigning each agent a sub search space. In addition, to the best of our knowledge, there is no work that addresses the latency during search, which makes reasonable sense since accessing resources to compute node cost is specific to our approach.

3   The Problem

In this section, we present our method to abstract a ubiquitous environment into a search space. Then, we provide an overview of our approach, and describe how search algorithms are positioned in the approach.

3.1   Environment Abstraction

Spatial information is necessary but insufficient to determine the locations at which a goal can be satisfied. Up-to-date and qualitative information from CPS entities and external resources are also required to find an optimal path. Therefore, in our approach, we model a ubiquitous environment by integrating its spatial and CPS dimensions along with the notion of resources. We assume that the spatial topology of a ubiquitous environment is abstracted as a graph SG where nodes are locations in the environment. A directed edge between two nodes n and n' is defined if, in the given environment, the location represented by n' is directly accessible from that by n.

Definition 1 (*Environment*). *An environment at a given time is a tuple* $E_t = (SG, HE, CPSE, R)$ *where:*

- *SG is a search graph defined as* $SG = \langle L, C \rangle$ *where L is a finite set of nodes representing locations in E and* $C \subseteq L \times L$ *is a set of edges representing connections between locations*
- *HE represents an organizational hierarchy of E. It is a tree whose elements correspond to hierarchy entities (e.g. terminals) of E and the child relation indicates sub-hierarchy entities (e.g. zones within a terminal). Locations are grouped under hierarchy entities, so the leafs of HE are directly connected to the locations*

– *CPSE is a finite set of CPS entities located in E*
– $R = (r_n)_{n \in CPSE \cup C}$ *is a finite set of resources providing information about a CPS entity or giving information on how to move between locations. An example of a resource can be a website, a database or an API to sources of data collected from cyber-physical entities.*

Figure 1 shows an example of an abstracted environment. The top layer is the spatial dimension of an environment. The bottom layer consists of resources relevant to an environment. The middle layer integrates L with $CPSE$, and connects them to R.

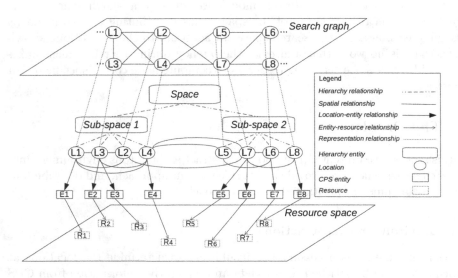

Fig. 1. An example of an environment description

Definition 2 (Multi-goal pathfinding). *By abstracting a given environment as previously described, we can formulate MGPF as a tuple MGPF = $(E_t, n_o, n_d, G, CR, f)$ where E_t is a representation of an environment at time t, $n_o \in L$ is a node representing the start location, $n_d \in L$ is a node representing the destination, G is an ordered list of goals to satisfy, CR is a set of criteria for evaluating a path and f is a cost function used to evaluate paths. Criteria are problem-specific. For instance, a criterion can be distance, price, duration or all of them combined. f determines how CR is taken into account in the decision process when choosing a path (e.g. prioritize a subset of CR or compromise all the criteria in CR). A problem is solved when an optimal path is found. A path is a list of locations through which every goal can be satisfied in the given order. A path is optimal if it has a minimum cost evaluated using f.*

3.2   The Approach

Our approach to MGPF consists of two main steps *goal-space graph generation* and *multi-layer search*. In the first step, we construct a goal-space graph to represent goals, the locations where each goal can be satisfied and the order of goals to satisfy. A goal-space graph, denoted by π, is an acyclic graph where nodes are goal-location pairs, and nodes are connected according to the order of goals defined in G. In this work, we associate a goal g to an activity a^g. We say that g can be satisfied at a location l if l contains at least one entity $cpse \in CPSE$ through which a^g can be carried out. For illustration purpose, suppose the followings are the locations where Carol's goals can be satisfied: trolley $= \{l_{21}, l_{32}\}$, check-in $= \{l_{43}, l_{64}\}$, lunch $= \{l_{15}, l_{61}, l_{11}\}$ and waiting seat $= \{l_{20}, l_{71}\}$. We can generate a goal-space graph π as shown in Fig. 2.

In the second step, we search over π to find an optimal path. π is an abstract graph built on top of SG. An edge of π is equivalent to a path that may consist of multiple nodes on SG. For instance, an edge between $(lunch, l_{15})$ and $(waitingseat, l_{20})$ may be equivalent to a sequence of nodes $(l_{15}, l_{16}, l_{28}, l_{18}, l_{20})$ on SG. Computing the cost of an edge between two nodes of π is equivalent to a pathfinding problem of two corresponding nodes on SG. Searching on SG requires accesses to resources to determine the cost of moving between nodes, which leads to the issue of latency. In this paper, we address the search on SG by providing a collaborative search model that can be used to adapt search algorithms to efficiently handle latency and to improve search efficiency.

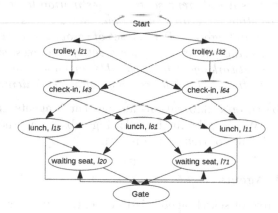

Fig. 2. An example of a goal-space graph

4   Collaborative Search Model

The aim of the collaborative search model is to manage resource accesses, thus the consequential latency, and to improve search efficiency. This model can be applied to forward-search algorithms such as breadth-first search, depth-first search, uniform cost search and A*. Generally, during each iteration, a forward-search algorithm *selects* a node from the list of candidate nodes *Frontier*, *generates* its child nodes, *prunes* some unpromising nodes, and *updates Frontier* to include the remaining children [7]. The critical point that creates latency is the *generation of child nodes*. To determine the cost for moving from an expanded node n to its child node n', we need to retrieve information from one or multiple resources. An example of the cost can be time, distance or all of them combined. Besides enabling us to determine the value of the cost, dynamic information from resources allows us to factor in cost-influencing criteria such as the fact that an elevator in the path is out of service or the path is currently blocked. This process results in latency as the algorithm has to wait for the requested information to arrive to determine the cost of child nodes and proceed the execution. The proposed model adapts each step of forward-search algorithms. More precisely, to distribute workloads, agents explore different parts of a search space concurrently by executing a search algorithm, thus *selecting* nodes from their respective part of the search space. *Child generation* is modified into an asynchronous and non-blocking process where agents are able to execute other tasks while information from resources is being retrieved. Discovered paths to a node in another part of the search space are communicated to agents responsible for that part so that they can *prune* and *update* their local search process.

Definition 3 *(Collaborative search model). A collaborative search model is a tuple* $CSM = (E_t, n_o, n_d, SA, Sa^o, RA, NA)$ *where* E_t *is an abstraction of an environment at time t as previously defined,* $n_o \in L$ *is a node representing a start location,* $n_d \in L$ *is a node representing a destination location, SA is a set of search agents executing the search algorithm,* $Sa^o \in SA$ *is the initial search agent that starts the search process, RA is a set of resource agents, each of which is responsible for retrieving information from a set of resources, and NA is a set of network agents. A network agent is responsible for managing a search process and related communications within the coverage of a set of hierarchy entities.*

The model is based on collaborations among search agents, resource agents and network agents. We describe in the following subsections the roles of these agents in realizing the aim of this search model.

4.1   The Search Agents

In our model, the role of search agents is to execute a given search algorithm. The execution cycle of a search agent consists of *expanding a node, retrieving the cost of a child node* and *processing received messages*. A search agent Sa is responsible for exploring a part of the search space. The nodes constituting the part of the search space for which Sa is responsible are dynamically and incrementally assigned by Sa's parent agent (a network agent) and are stored in *ResponsibledNodes*. The dynamic assignment and distribution of a search space is presented in depth in the following section (Sect. 4.2).

As in a forward-search algorithm, Sa has a set of candidate nodes to expand *Frontier* and a set of expanded nodes *Expanded*. In each iteration, Sa executes the search algorithm which starts by selecting a node n from $Frontier$ to expand. If n is the destination, goal verification procedure (GVP) is initiated (further explained in Sect. 4.3), and Sa continues its execution until the destination is verified or a better path to the destination is found. Otherwise, Sa generates the child nodes of n. To generate each child n', it is necessary to know the cost for moving from n to n'. We call the moving from n to n' an action $a(n, n')$. If n' belongs to Sa's part of the search space (i.e. in its $ResponsibledNodes$), Sa stores $a(n, n')$ in its $ActionList$ to be queried for its cost. Otherwise, Sa sends $a(n, n')$ to a search agent Sa' that is responsible for n' through the parent agent of Sa. Upon receiving $a(n, n')$, Sa' discards $a(n, n')$ if it already knows the path to n' with a better cost than through n; this prevents Sa' from requesting for the cost to move from n to n', which is clearly in a non-optimal path. Otherwise, Sa' adds $a(n, n')$ to its $ActionList$.

After node expansion, Sa takes an action a_q from its $ActionList$ to query for its cost. The cost of an action is determined by using information retrieved from resources associated with the action, and is computed using the cost function f given as a part of MGPF. To obtain the cost of a_q, Sa sends a request to a resource agent. A resource agent is capable of accessing a number of types of resources. Information about resource agents are provided to search agents as a part of their knowledge. Depending on the type of resource, Sa chooses a resource agent to inquire. While the cost of a_q is being retrieved, a_q is moved from $ActionList$ to $PendingActionList$ where all the actions pending for their cost are stored. Retrieving an action cost is a non-blocking process. After sending the request to a resource agent, Sa continues its execution. Once the necessary data is acquired, the resource agent sends it to Sa. This asynchronous mechanism for retrieving information enables search agents to perform other tasks while resources are being accessed, thus mitigates the latency.

After retrieving the cost of an action, Sa processes received messages. When receiving a message containing the cost of an action $a(n, n')$, Sa computes the cost of n', $f(n')$ and removes $a(n, n')$ from $PendingActionList$. Based on $f(n')$, Sa prunes unpromising nodes from $Frontier$ and updates $Expanded$. How the pruning is done depends on the actual algorithm (e.g. A*, uniform cost search). The algorithm is terminated when a verified solution is found or the entire search space has been explored. Naturally, we reach the end of a search space when all search agents have no node in their $Frontier$, no action in $ActionList$ and no pending action in $PendingActionList$.

4.2   The Network Agents

In this search model, we separate a search space based on the knowledge of the search space, in this case, the hierarchy information. A network agent is responsible for a set of hierarchy entities at a certain level of hierarchy. The role of a network agent is to manage the search process related to the hierarchy entities for which it is responsible. This management entails routing an action to a relevant search agent, distributing workloads to search agents, assigning sub-hierarchy entities to other network agents to manage, creating new search agents and network agents when necessary, and handling communications among agents. Search space separation and assignment as well as workload distribution are done on-the-fly during the search in order to focus only on the parts of the search space relevant to a given pathfinding request. This process is triggered by the routing of actions, illustrated in Algorithm 1, to their relevant search agents, and progressively, it constructs an agent network tailored to a given request.

Algorithm 1. action-routing-protocol($a\langle n, n'\rangle$)

1: *hierarchy* ← get the entire hierarchy of n'
2: **if** the executing agent Na is in charge of a hierarchy entity he in *hierarchy* **then**
3:     **if** he is the direct parent hierarchy entity (i.e. a leaf of HE) of n' **then**
4:         **if** Na has no search agent that is the agent responsible of n' **then**
5:             **if** Na has no search agents OR all search agents cannot take more responsibility **then**
6:                 create a new search agent Sa and send $a\langle n, n'\rangle$ to Sa
7:                 set Na as the parent agent of Sa and Sa as a search agent of Na
8:             **else**
9:                 select the search agent with the least responsibility and send it $a\langle n, n'\rangle$
10:             **end if**
11:         **else**
12:             send $a\langle n, n'\rangle$ to the search agent responsible
13:         **end if**
14:     **else**
15:         get he' from *hierarchy* where he' is a direct child hierarchy entity of he
16:         **if** Na has no child agents OR all child agents cannot take more responsibility **then**
17:             create a network agent Na' and make Na' responsible for he'
18:             set Na as the parent agent of Na' and Na' as a child agent of Na
19:         **else**
20:             assign he' to Na' where Na' is a child agent of Na with the least responsibility
21:         **end if**
22:         forward $a\langle n, n'\rangle$ to Na'
23:     **end if**
24: **else**
25:     **if** Na's parent agent doesn't exist yet **then**
26:         create a network agent Na^P
27:         make Na^P responsible for the hierarchy entity that is the direct parent of Na's hierarchy entity(ies)
28:         set Na^P as the parent of Na and Na as the child of Na^P
29:     **end if**
30:     forward the request $a\langle n, n'\rangle$ to the parent agent Na^P
31: **end if**

During node expansion, when a search agent Sa discovers an action $a(n, n')$ where n' is not under its responsibility, Sa sends $a(n, n')$ to its parent agent Na. However, if it is the beginning of the search, which is an exceptional case where there are no network agents yet, the initial search agent Sa^o creates the first network agent Na to route $a(n, n')$. Na becomes the agent responsible for the hierarchy entity in which n is directly located. Upon receiving $a(n, n')$, Na executes the action routing protocol (Algorithm 1) to find the search agent responsible for n'.

We separate a search space based on the hierarchy, so a search agent $Sa^{n'}$ that is responsible for n', if it exists, is under the management of a network agent that is responsible for the hierarchy entity in which n' is *directly* located. Na uses the hierarchy information of n' to guide the search (Algo:1 - L:1). The hierarchy of n' is an ascending ordered list of hierarchy entities in which n' is located. For instance, in an airport, the hierarchy of n' can be *Zone 1-Terminal 2-Airport* where n' is located directly under Zone 1. Zone 1 is a sub-hierarchy entity of Terminal 2, which is in turn a sub-hierarchy entity of Airport.

If n' is not a part of Na's search space (i.e. not located in one of Na's hierarchy entities), Na passes the control to its parent Na^p, if Na^p already exists, to do the routing (Algo:1 - L:25–30). If Na^p does not exist yet, Na creates Na^p to take charge of a hierarchy entity in which all Na's hierarchy entities are located and forward the request to Na^p. For example, suppose Na's hierarchy entities are Zone 1 and Zone 2 of Terminal 1; as Na's parent, Na^p takes charge of all the search processes in Terminal 1. Then, Na^p takes over the routing operation and executes the action routing protocol. On the other hand, if n' is located in one of Na's hierarchy entities, denoted by he^{Na}, Na takes control of the routing process (Algo:1 - L:2–23). This implies one of the two possibilities - (1) n' is *directly* under he^{Na} (i.e. he^{Na} is a leaf of HE) or (2) n' is *indirectly* under he^{Na} (i.e. n' is under a leaf, which in turns is under he^{Na}).

In the case of (1), the relevant search agent $Sa^{n'}$ should be under the management of Na. In such case, $a(n, n')$ is sent to $Sa^{n'}$ if $Sa^{n'}$ already exists (Algo:1 - L:12), and the routing operation of $a(n, n')$ is finished. If n' has not been assigned to any search agent (i.e. $Sa^{n'}$ does not exist), Na selects a search agent under its management that has the *least responsibility* to take charge of n' (Algo:1 - L:9). To determine the responsibility of a search agent, we take into account its current workload, which is the number of nodes in its *Frontier*, and number of nodes for which it is responsible *ResponsibledNodes*. The workload indicates the current tasks that a search agent has to execute, and the number nodes in *ResponsibledNodes* indicates the amount of potential tasks that it may have to do. The potential tasks include requesting the cost of actions, processing update messages and pruning. Using both criteria to measure responsibility enables us to assign more work to a search agent that is more likely to become idle (i.e. having few current tasks), and also preventing assignments to the ones that might potentially be occupied (i.e. responsible for many nodes). However, when all the search agents of Na reach the *responsibility limit*, a new search agent is created to take charge of n' (Algo:1 - L:5–7). The reason for introducing responsibility limit is to distribute workloads among the search agents exploring the same part of the search space. This is essential when the part of the search space of a network agent is large. The responsibility limit is determined according to two factors: the computational resources available and the search space. If the computational resources are limited, the responsibility limit should be high to reduce the number of search agents. This configuration, however, may affect the efficiency when working with a large graph. Otherwise, the limit should be low, resulting in more search agents exploring in parallel.

In the case of (2), $Sa^{n'}$, if it exists, is under the management of one of the direct or indirect child agents of Na. Na forwards $a(n, n')$ to its child agent Na' (Algo:1 - L:15–22). Na' is the direct child agent of Na and is the agent responsible for a hierarchy entity he' where he' is a direct sub-hierarchy entity of he^{Na} and n' is located directly or indirectly under he'. If Na' does not exist, he' is assigned to a child agent with the least responsibility (Algo:1 - L:20). The responsibility of a network agent is measured by the sum of the number of nodes under the hierarchy entity(ies) for which it is responsible. We employ such indicator because the number of nodes determine the number potential tasks such as routing and other communications a network agent has to handle. Each network agent has a responsibility limit that is the maximum number of nodes it should handle. This limit is determined by the computational resources available. Setting the limit low results in having more network agents, but this would avoid problems such as communication bottlenecks. If all child agents of Na reach the responsibility limit, he' is assigned to a new network agent and $a(n, n')$ is forwarded to the new agent, which will continue the routing.

4.3 Goal Verification Procedure, Termination and Optimality

Goal Verification Procedure. When a destination node n_d is expanded, the expanding search agent Sa^d initiates the GVP. The objective is to determine whether a found path leading to n_d is a minimum-cost path. This process is necessary because each search agent does not possess global knowledge of the search state. The verification is conducted in a distributed manner by each search agent. A path is a minimum-cost path only if all search agents reach a consensus concerning its validity. For each search agent, a path to n_d is optimal if there exists no node n where $f(n) < f(n_d)$. To verify this property, each search agent performs the following verification:

- If there is any node n in *Frontier* where $f(n) < f(n_d)$, the path is not verified.
- If there are actions in *ActionList* or *PendingActionList*, the path is not verified. The cost of those actions are still unknown, so it is impossible to determine the cost of the nodes to which those actions lead.

To start this procedure, Sa^d sends a goal verification request to its parent agent Na^d. Na^d propagates the request by forwarding the request to its other children and its parent agent. The receiving parent agent repeats the propagation process.

In this way, every search agent will receive the request from its parent agent. Each search agent keeps verifying the found path leading to n_d until the path is verified or a better path to n_d is found.

- If the found path is verified by an agent, the agent sends the response to its parent. Responses are sent back in the opposite direction of the one in which the request is propagated. Therefore, eventually, Sa^d receives all the responses directly from Na^d, who receives responses from its parent and other children.
- If a better path to n_d is found, the expanding agent initiates another GVP to replace the previous one.

Besides determining the validity of a path, GVP also enables search agents to filter nodes and actions. When the found path is under location verification of an agent, the knowledge about the found destination such as its cost is used to discard unpromising nodes from *Frontier* and actions from *ActionList*.

Termination. A search execution is terminated when a path verified by GVP is found or when the entire search space has been explored. Naturally, the end of a search space is reached when all search agents have no nodes in *Frontiers*, no actions in *ActionList* and no pending actions in *PendingActionList*.

Optimality. GVP enables us to determine whether a path has a minimum-cost. However, whether a path is optimal depends on the actual algorithm and the cost function(s) that it uses. For instance, in uniform cost search, the cost of a node is the cost from the start node to the node, which guarantees optimality. In such case, a path verified by GVP is an optimal path. However, for a greedy algorithm, a path verified by GVP is a minimum-cost path based on the algorithm's cost function, but not necessarily an optimal path.

The algorithm terminates by finding a minimum-cost path if one exists, assuming the following properties:

- The search space is finite.
- All messages arrive at their destinations.
- For every request for the cost of an action, we get a response.
- All operations take a finite amount of time.

5   Experimental Evaluation

Our experiments were conducted on a 2.4 GHz Intel Core i7 laptop with 16 GB of RAM. We used 2 types of requests: the start and destination nodes are (1) in the same hierarchy entity (same hierarchy entity request) and (2) in different hierarchy entities (inter-hierarchy entity request). The principle of our approach is that it acquires information from various resources. As a result, we introduced simulated latency in accessing resources (1, 5, and 9 ms). 1, 5 and 9 (ms) are the maximum latency of each respective case. For instance, in the 5 ms case, we generate latency values between 0 to 5 ms. We applied our collaborative search model in uniform cost search (UC), creating a collaborative uniform cost algorithm (CUC). In our experiments, we compare CUC with UC. The choice of UC for our experiments is motivated by the fact UC is independent of any domain-specific or case-based heuristics. Consequently, the impacts of the collaborative search model on UC's performance can be accurately observed.

In the first experiment, we used both algorithms to solve the two types of requests on the same environment, abstracted as graph 1. Graph 1 has a 4-level depth hierarchy (1 hierarchy entity at first level, 10 at second, 100 at third, 1000 at fourth), 10000 locations and 10000 CPS entities. Figure 3 demonstrates time efficiency in (%) gained by using CUC compared to UC to solve the two types of requests. The results show that for requests of type (1), UC is more efficient than CUC when there is no latency. This is because in type (1) requests, the start and the destination are under the same hierarchy entity containing approximately 100 nodes. In both algorithms, the solution was quickly found, but CUC takes more time because there are overheads for creating the network agent and managing communication as well as workload distribution. However, these overheads become negligible when latency is present. CUC starts to outperform UC from around 1 ms of latency. For type (2) requests, which involve multiple hierarchy entities, CUC performs better even without latency. The reason is that our model is based on concurrent agents exploring different parts of a search space (i.e. nodes under relevant hierarchy entities), which leads agents to discover the destination quicker. With latency, CUC is remarkably more efficient, reaching over 90% of time efficiency gains in the case of 9 ms latency. Regarding node expansion, in our model, each search agent has only partial knowledge of the search process, so it selects nodes to be expanded based on its limited knowledge. This may lead to expansion of costly or unpromising nodes. Despite such limitation, the results of our experiment, depicted in Fig. 4, suggest that CUC expands approximately the same number of nodes for type (1) requests and less for type (2). This is thanks to agent collaboration and the GVP. Collaborative and concurrent search leads to rapid discovery of the destination, irrespective of its optimality. Once the destination is found, the GVP is initiated, informing all search agents about the destination. While the destination is under local verification (i.e. verifying the properties described in Sect. 4.3), search agents use knowledge about the found destination to filter unpromising nodes and actions (i.e. having higher cost than the found destination).

In the second experiment, we compared CUC with UC over three different graph structures of the same size, namely graph 1, 2 and 3. Graph 2 has the same hierarchy structure and location distribution as graph 1. The only difference is that in graph 2, there is only one connection between 2 locations and 1 exit point for each hierarchy entity, while there are 3 connections and 2 exit points in graph 1. Graph 3 has a 3-level depth hierarchy (1 hierarchy entity at first level, 10 at second, 100 at third), 10000 nodes (locations) and 10000 CPS entities. Figure 5 illustrates time efficiency (in percentage) gained by using CUC compared to

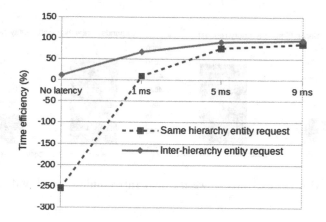

Fig. 3. Run time efficiency of collaborative uniform cost compared to uniform cost

UC on different graph structures. CUC performs best on graph 1 because there are more connections between nodes and more exits to other hierarchy entities. Our collaborative search model does not use a predefined method to separate a search space, but it dynamically and progressively distributes the search space among agents based on the structure of the space, in this case the hierarchy, during the search process. More exits to different hierarchy entities allow agents to reach more parts of the graphs faster, and thus finding the destination faster; more connections to other nodes also lead to a more efficient search since more nodes can be explored by concurrent agents. In graph 2 and 3, each node has only one neighbor node and a hierarchy entity has only one exit. With such connectivity, the algorithm takes more time to find the exits to enable agents to explore different parts of the graph. Between graph 2 and 3, CUC works better on graph 2 because locations are more distributed in graph 2. In graph 3, each 1000 locations are grouped under the same hierarchy entity, and there is only one exit from each hierarchy entity. In such case, the algorithm can only distribute the workloads, which are nodes under the same hierarchy entity, and has to expand many nodes to find an exit allowing spreading of the search to other hierarchy entities. This reason coupled with the overheads for communications and agent network management makes UC outperform CUC in graph 2 and 3 when there is no latency.

In the third experiment, we compared the two algorithms on three different graphs of the same structure and connectivity, but different sizes to examine the scalability. Graph 1, as described previously, has 10000 nodes; graph 4 has 4096 nodes, and graph 5 has 1296 nodes. Figure 6 shows the order of growth of both algorithms over the three graphs. Regardless latency, CUC outperforms UC as the graph size grows due to the concurrent graph exploration by collaborative agents. Remarkably, CUC scales much better in function of latency.

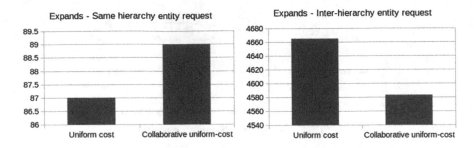

Fig. 4. Comparison of expands between collaborative uniform cost and uniform cost

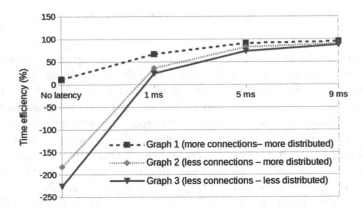

Fig. 5. Run time efficiency of collaborative uniform cost compared to uniform cost over different graph structures

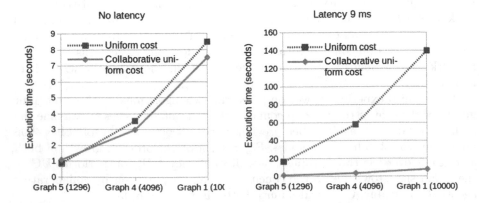

Fig. 6. Time comparison between collaborative uniform cost and uniform cost

These experimental results show the impact of graph structures, request types and latency on the efficiency of search algorithms. These factors can be used to choose a search algorithm suitable for each given MGPF problem.

6 Conclusion

This paper describes an approach to solve MGPF in ubiquitous environments by exploiting data from various resources from CPS entities to data sources on the Web. The overview of the approach was provided. We proposed a collaborative multi-agent search model that can be applied to forward-search algorithms to improve the efficiency and handle latency issue resulting from resource accesses. The model is based on agents searching collaboratively towards a shared goal. Such collaboration is enabled and facilitated by an agent network constructed by exploiting the structure and knowledge of a search space. While the collaborative search model is applicable to forward-search algorithms in general, we presented a specific example by applying it to uniform cost search. We used this example to demonstrate a concrete application of the model and to evaluate its efficiency. The results showed that the collaborative algorithm improves search efficiency in most cases, and scales better in function of latency and graph size.

In this paper, we focus on pre-trip planning. In ubiquitous environments, CPS entities are mobile and often changing their states. An activity for satisfying a goal takes a certain amount of time, during which CPS entities may be changing. Consequently, an optimal pre-planned path may lose its optimality over time. This necessitates en-route planning to keep refining the initial path according to the current state of the environment. In future work, we plan to extend our search model to support en-route planning. An agent network constructed during each search is tailored to that particular search. The network agents can be extended to support monitoring of CPS entities and resources under their coverage to detect mobility and changes. Such knowledge will then be taken in account to adapt the path on-the-fly while users are traveling.

References

1. Algfoor, Z.A., Sunar, M.S., Kolivand, H.: A comprehensive study on pathfinding techniques for robotics and video games. Int. J. Comput. Games Technol. **2015**, 7 (2015)
2. Botea, A., Bouzy, B., Buro, M., Bauckhage, C., Nau, D.: Pathfinding in games. In: Dagstuhl Follow-Ups, vol. 6. Schloss Dagstuhl-Leibniz-Zentrum fuer Informatik (2013)
3. Botea, A., Müller, M., Schaeffer, J.: Near optimal hierarchical path-finding. J. Game Dev. **1**(1), 7–28 (2004)
4. Ciortea, A., Zimmermann, A., Boissier, O., Florea, A.M.: Towards a social and ubiquitous web: a model for socio-technical networks. In: 2015 IEEE/WIC/ACM International Conference on Web Intelligence and Intelligent Agent Technology (WI-IAT), vol. 1, pp. 461–468, December 2015

5. Codognet, P.: Multi-goal path-finding for autonomous agents in virtual worlds. In: Nakatsu, R., Hoshino, J. (eds.) Entertainment Computing. ITIFIP, vol. 112, pp. 23–30. Springer, Boston (2003). doi:10.1007/978-0-387-35660-0_3

6. Denzinger, J.: Conflict handling in collaborative search. In: Tessier, C., Chaudron, L., Müller, H.-J. (eds.) Conflicting Agents: Conflict Management in Multi-Agent Systems, pp. 251–278. Springer, Boston (2002)

7. Ghallab, M., Nau, D., Traverso, P.: Automated Planning and Acting. Cambridge University Press, Cambridge (2016)

8. Graham, R., McCabe, H., Sheridan, S.: Pathfinding in computer games. ITB J. **4**(2), 6 (2015)

9. Hart, P.E., Nilsson, N.J., Raphael, B.: A formal basis for the heuristic determination of minimum cost paths. IEEE Trans. Syst. Sci. Cybern. **4**(2), 100–107 (1968)

10. Kishimoto, A., Fukunaga, A.S., Botea, A., et al.: Scalable, parallel best-first search for optimal sequential planning. In: ICAPS (2009)

11. Koenig, S., Likhachev, M., Furcy, D.: Lifelong planning A*. Artif. Intell. **155**(1–2), 93–146 (2004)

12. Lim, K.L., Yeong, L.S., Ch'ng, S.I., Seng, K.P., Ang, L.M.: Uninformed multi-goal pathfinding on grid maps. In: 2014 International Conference on Information Science, Electronics and Electrical Engineering, vol. 3, pp. 1552–1556, April 2014

13. Matai, R., Singh, S.P., Mittal, M.L.: Traveling salesman problem: an overview of applications, formulations, and solution approaches. In: Traveling Salesman Problem, Theory and Applications, pp. 1–24 (2010)

14. Nissim, R., Brafman, R.I.: Multi-agent A* for parallel and distributed systems. In: Proceedings of the 11th International Conference on Autonomous Agents and Multiagent Systems, vol. 3. pp. 1265–1266 (2012)

15. Rabin, S.: A* speed optimizations. Game Program. Gems **1**, 272–287 (2000)

16. Standley, T., Korf, R.: Complete algorithms for cooperative pathfinding problems. In: IJCAI, pp. 668–673. Citeseer (2011)

17. Standley, T.S.: Finding optimal solutions to cooperative pathfinding problems. In: AAAI, vol. 1, pp. 28–29 (2010)

18. Stentz, A.: Optimal and efficient path planning for partially-known environments. In: Proceedings of 1994 IEEE International Conference on Robotics and Automation, pp. 3310–3317. IEEE (1994)

19. Vrakas, D., Refanidis, I., Vlahavas, I.: Parallel planning via the distribution of operators. J. Exp. Theoret. Artif. Intell. **13**(3), 211–226 (2001)

20. Wang, K.H.C., Botea, A.: Fast and memory-efficient multi-agent pathfinding. In: ICAPS, pp. 380–387 (2008)

21. Werner, M.: Selection and ordering of points-of-interest in large-scale indoor navigation systems. In: 2011 IEEE 35th Annual Computer Software and Applications Conference, pp. 504–509, July 2011

Flock Stability in the Vicsek Model

Joshua M. Brown$^{(\boxtimes)}$ (iD) and Terry Bossomaier

Charles Sturt University, Panorama Avenue, Bathurst, NSW 2795, Australia
jbrown@csu.edu.au

Abstract. The Standard Vicsek Model and a popular variant—using topological neighbour interactions—are widely used models for studying flocking phenomena in the natural world. It is capable of demonstrating the ordered and disordered states of real world flocks by tuning a temperature variable η, where high η corresponds to the disordered state. Here we show that the ordered state attained at low η is not stable over indefinite time periods raising implications for simulations and settling times. Additionally, we show that the loss of coherency in the metric case is reversible, while it is permanent in topological case.

Keywords: Vicsek model · Metric interactions · Topological interactions · Flocking

1 Introduction

The motions of bird flocks are impressive in their grace and grandeur. Birds fly in complex interweaving paths that seem chaotic, yet lead to the formation of coherent flocks. Flocking behaviour is not just restricted to birds, either. Many species display similar movements, from schools of fish [12] to colonies of bacteria [9]. The behaviours that lead to this phenomenon are subject to much research [15].

One of the most widely used models for studying flocking phenomena was introduced in 1995 by Vicsek *et al.* [14]. This minimal model approximates flock members as simple point particles with position and heading, moving with constant speed in discrete time steps. At each time step, a given particle will adjust its heading to match the average direction—with some random perturbation, η—of its neighbouring particles, including itself. By adjusting the magnitude of the perturbation, one can observe the flock in ordered ($\eta = 0$) or disordered states ($\eta = 2\pi$), or any state in between, including the *phase transition* at the critical noise η_c.

The use of just an alignment rule in the Vicsek model is in contrast to the earlier model by Reynolds [11] which combines three rules to achieve flocking phenomena: *alignment*, as above, *dispersion* where flock members steer to avoid flock mates, and *cohesion* in which flock members steer towards the centre of local flock mates.

© Springer International Publishing AG 2017
J.O. Berndt et al. (Eds.): MATES 2017, LNAI 10413, pp. 89–102, 2017.
DOI: 10.1007/978-3-319-64798-2_6

Many studies have been performed using the Vicsek Model (VM), from low level analysis of criticality [2,7,14] to high level comparisons with real world flock data [1,4]. Studies investigate either some specific noise value—generally at or around criticality—or the whole noise range $[0, 2\pi]$, relying on the assumption that as $\eta \to 0$ the flocking behaviour becomes increasingly stable. This is further reinforced by work showing that when $\eta = 0$ the Vicsek model will converge to a single stable flock [8,13]. In this paper, we question this assumption and show that for the low noise regime, permanent stability—that is, over sufficiently large time scales—is not guaranteed.

In Sect. 2 we formally introduce the Vicsek model followed by a demonstration of flock instability in both the metric and topological cases in Sect. 3. We then provide a detailed analysis of the mechanics that give rise to these results in Sect. 4 and show that over large time scales, these states are unavoidable. We conclude in Sect. 5 with some discussion on managing the models to minimise instability.

2   Methods

In the Standard Vicsek Model (*SVM*) N particles move continuously in a two dimensional square space of linear size L with periodic boundary conditions. The model is updated with a time interval $\Delta t = 1$. Positions for each particle are updated according to:

$$x_i(t + \Delta t) = x_i(t) + v_i(t)\Delta t, \tag{1}$$

where the velocity $v_i(t)$ is constructed to have constant magnitude, s, and heading, $\theta_i(t)$. This method of position update—using $v_i(t)$ instead of $v_i(t + \Delta t)$—is known as Backwards Update.

Heading angles are updated according to:

$$\theta_i(t + \Delta t) = \langle\theta(t)\rangle_{i,k} + \frac{\eta}{2}\xi_i(t), \tag{2}$$

where $\langle\theta(t)\rangle_{i,k}$ denotes the average direction of k neighbours of particle i (including itself) that fit the neighbourhood criterion. In the Standard—or Metric— model the neighbourhood of particle i is all particles within radius $r = 1$. The Topological variant (TVM) instead uses the neighbourhood of the nearest k_T particles, regardless of distance. We use the definition from [14] for average angle—$\langle\theta(t)\rangle_{i,k} = \arctan[\langle\sin(\theta(t))\rangle_{i,k}/\langle\cos(\theta(t))\rangle_{i,k}]$. $\xi_i(t)$ is a realisation from the uniform interval $[-1, 1]$ and $0 \leq \eta \leq 2\pi$. Where convenient, the shorthand $\Delta\theta_i(t) = \frac{\eta}{2}\xi_i(t)$ will be used to refer to the noise term.

This work deals solely with the low noise regime, $0 < \eta \leq 0.5$, outside of the phase transition regime. Here—after a settling period—large flocks are expected to predominate. As we are considering only flocks far from criticality, we will not broach the topic of the precise nature of the phase transition in the Vicsek Model.

We denote the order, φ, of the flock with

$$\varphi(t) = \frac{1}{sN} \left| \sum_i^N v_i(t) \right|, \tag{3}$$

which defines the overall alignment of particles at time t, with $\varphi(t) = 1$ signalling all particles pointing in the same direction and $\varphi(t) = 0$ indicating complete disorder. Fluctuations of the order parameter are given by the susceptibility

$$\chi = \langle \varphi^2 \rangle - \langle \varphi \rangle^2, \tag{4}$$

where a peak in χ indicates a phase transition [16].

When analysing the topological case, we construct *swarm signalling networks* (SSN) from our simulations as described by Komareji and Bouffanais in their investigation into consensus and its resilience in topological systems [10]. The SSN shows the directed connectivity between particles—as topological interactions are not symmetric. Komareji and Bouffanais demonstrate that for a system to reach consensus the SSN must be a strongly connected super set during *most*—not necessarily all—time steps, and to achieve this, k_T should be 6 or more, in agreement with bird flocking studies [3]. We use these SSNs to analyse consensus over longer time scales.

Simulations were performed and visualised in C++, with post processing done in Matlab. Where statistics were collated, we performed 100 repetitions to calculate standard error. Free variables—ρ, N, s, k_T, r—were all varied over common values in the literature and behaved analogously to the results presented below.

3   Results

We simulated both metric and topological flocks, using a range of values for the free parameters, and found that in all cases—except degenerate cases such as $r \to L$ or $k_T \to N$—flock stability was not permanent and flocks would eventually split apart for long periods of time at low η where cohesive flocks are expected to predominate the system. In this section, we give an overview of these results, while a detailed mathematical analysis will follow in the Sect. 4.

We start with the metric case, with Fig. 1 showing the evolution of a flock from a completely ordered, singular flock into seven sub-flocks of varying sizes, demonstrating that an aligned metric flock can split apart into disjoint sub-flocks from just thermal fluctuations. At later time steps, this flock coalesces into fewer sub-flocks, before returning to a single flock at $t = 99,000$, repeating *ad infinitum*.

While the particles are still mostly ordered in Fig. 1b, with $\varphi(t) = 0.99$, this does not necessarily have to be. Sub-flocks can diverge completely to π radians from each other. However, due to the periodic boundary conditions of the system, as divergence increases so too does the chance of the sub-flocks colliding and merging into a single flock, thus—temporarily—restoring stability to the flock.

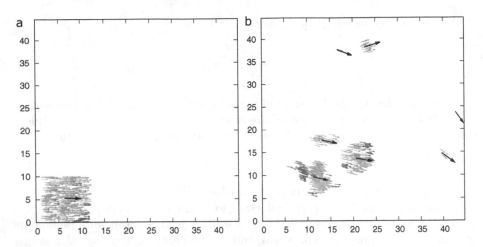

Fig. 1. Metric—Snapshots of an SVM flock at (a) $t = 10$ and (b) $t = 24,000$ with $\varphi = 1.0$ and 0.99 respectively, demonstrating instability behaviours in the metric model. Flock parameters were $N = 500, \rho = 0.25, s = 0.1, \eta = 0.1$, with all particles initialised facing right ($\theta_i(0) = 0 \ \forall \ i \in N$), in a box of local density, $\rho = 5.0$, to force a flocking event at $t = 0$. This flock behaves no differently to a flock achieved more naturally via a settling regime whereby particles are given random positions and headings and simulated for time series of at least order $t = 1 \times 10^5$. Particles are positioned at the base of each arrow, with arrow direction indicating heading. Arrow colour conveys the same information as in Fig. 6 although is unnecessary here. Extra flock information included in Fig. 6 is stripped here for clarity. Large black arrows indicate centre of sub-flock and average flock heading. (Color figure online)

The topological flock also suffers from instability, as shown in Fig. 2. Komareji and Bouffanais [10] show consensus for topological systems with $k_T = 6$ neighbours, which we recreate in Fig. 2a with $N = 1,000, \rho = 1.6$ at $t = 3,000$. Figure 2b shows the same system at a future time step, $t = 7,000$, where it has devolved to a quasi-disordered state of many flock fragments. Similar behaviours are seen for all k_T tested, $k_T \in \{3, 6, 7, 8, 9, 20, 40\}$ at $\rho \in \{0.25, 1.6\}$. The size of the fragmented flocks scales with k_T, while the time taken to devolve scales proportional to k_T, and inversely with ρ. Komareji and Bouffanais [10] also shows the case of $k_T = 3$, exhibiting similar behaviour as observed in Fig. 2b, indicating that with low enough k_T fragmentation sets in before consensus can be achieved. Simulations with other starting conditions—including those seen in Fig. 1a—all exhibited the same behaviour.

While the flocks can merge in the metric case we show later that this is not the case for the topological model. Sub-flocks continue to fragment, with a minimum bound of k_T particles per sub-flock, with no ability to merge into larger flocks for any meaningful length of time. Entering the quasi-disordered state is a one way transition for the topological flock. Figure 3 shows φ and χ of one set of simulations at low η, for a large time frame. The peak in χ and behaviour of

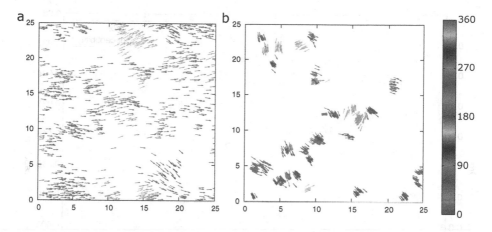

Fig. 2. Topological—Snapshots of the one flock at (a) $t = 3,000$ ($\varphi = 0.97$) and (b) $t = 7,000$ ($\varphi = 0.75$). System was initialised facing right ($\theta_i(0) = 0 \ \forall \ i \in N$), with parameters $N = 1,000, \rho = 1.6, s = 0.05, \eta = 0.1\pi, k_T = 7$ as per [10], where (a) matches Fig. 1 of [10]—noting their initial state of $\theta_i(0) = \frac{\pi}{2}$. Particle colour indicates heading angle, such that the colour of $\theta = \theta + \pi$. Note that the only headings not represented in (b) are $\frac{\pi}{2} < \theta < \pi$ indicating significant fragmentation between sub-flocks. (Color figure online)

φ indicates the system does indeed experience a quasi-phase transition from an ordered state to a not-quite-disordered one while η remains constant.

4 Discussion

In this section, we give detailed analysis of the mechanics leading to instability showing that it is inevitable in both cases.

We begin with analysis of a minimal two particle metric flock and introduce the term *drift*, $\dot{d}$, to explore how the distance between particles changes at a subsequent time step when noise is or is not applied. Specifically, $\dot{d} < 0$ indicates convergence at the future step *when noise is applied than if it is not*, while $\dot{d} > 0$ indicates the addition of noise leads to separation. The main result of Sect. 4.1 is to show that the probability of $\dot{d} < 0$ and $\dot{d} > 0$ is approximately equal in both neighbour and non-neighbour cases, while the probability of converging between time steps is 0.5 only in the neighbour case.

We extend this argument in Sect. 4.2 to show that drift plays a vital role in the instability of metric flocks and is able to explain the behaviour in Fig. 1. Notably, this instability is reversible, allowing reformation of a stable flock. This argument holds in the topological case, however does not adequately cover the phenomena in Fig. 2.

To understand the topological case we analyse a small flock and its SSN in Sect. 4.3. We show that due to a lack of dispersion rule in the Vicsek model and the asymmetric nature of topological interactions, a quasi-phase transition takes

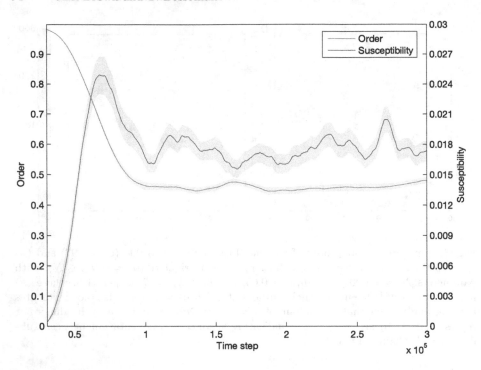

Fig. 3. Topological—Plot of order (left axis) and susceptibility (right axis)—measured over a sliding window of 3×10^4 time steps. All particles were initialised facing right $(\theta_i(0) = 0 \ \forall \ i \in N)$, using the parameters $N = 1,000$, $\rho = 0.25$, $s = 0.05$, $\eta = 0.2$, $k_T = 7$. ρ and η were reduced to increase the time taken for fragmentation to occur to better visualise χ. The peak in χ at $t = 7 \times 10^4$ indicates the flocks fragmenting into the quasi-disordered state described in text. Additionally, the non-zero χ after the peak demonstrates that the quasi-disordered state is maintained for the remainder of the simulation. Measurements repeated 100 times to calculate standard error (shaded regions).

place whereby particle flocks devolve to the fragmented clusters seen in Fig. 2b. We also show that this instability is irreversible unlike the drift instability.

4.1   Two Particle Metric Flocks

We begin with a minimal metric flock of just 2 particles, p_i and p_j, well within interaction radius—such that they remain neighbours—with centre of mass $\boldsymbol{x}_f(t)$ and velocity $\boldsymbol{v}_f(t)$ (with heading $\theta_f(t)$). For notational convenience, we will construct the flock with p_i always above p_j—i.e., $x_{i,x} \approx x_{j,x}$ and $x_{i,y} > x_{j,y}$. Note that by rotational symmetry, this is equivalent to any orientation of a 2 particle flock.

The benefit of this construction is that p_i is to the "left" of $\boldsymbol{x}_f$, that is, the z-component[1] of $(\boldsymbol{x}_i - \boldsymbol{x}_f) \times \boldsymbol{v}_f$ is positive (i.e. pointing up) and thus positive rotation of v_f points towards p_i, while p_j corresponds with negative rotations.

Since the particles are neighbours[2], $\langle\theta(t)\rangle_{i,k} = \langle\theta(t)\rangle_{j,k}$, resulting in three possibilities when updating the headings in Eq. 2:

1. $\Delta\theta_i(t) = \Delta\theta_j(t)$ - Both particles will move (at the next time step, since we are backward updating) in parallel to each other—i.e. $|\boldsymbol{x}_i(t+\Delta t) - \boldsymbol{x}_j(t+\Delta t)| = |\boldsymbol{x}_i(t+2\Delta t) - \boldsymbol{x}_j(t+2\Delta t)|$.
2. $\Delta\theta_i(t) > \Delta\theta_j(t)$ - p_i experiences a more positive (or less negative) rotation from noise than p_j, meaning either one or both of p_i, p_j is turning away from v_f. In all three possibilities, this leads to an increase in distance between $\boldsymbol{x}_i(t + 2\Delta t)$ and $\boldsymbol{x}_j(t + 2\Delta t)$ than otherwise would have been the case if $\Delta\theta_i(t) = \Delta\theta_j(t) = 0$.
3. $\Delta\theta_i(t) < \Delta\theta_j(t)$ - p_i experiences a more negative (or less positive) rotation than p_j and results in decreased distance at $t + 2\Delta t$.

Since the noise is uniformly distributed, the second two items have equal likelihood giving the relation

$$P[\Delta\theta_i(t) < \Delta\theta_j(t)] = P[\Delta\theta_i(t) > \Delta\theta_j(t)], \tag{5}$$

with $P[\Delta\theta_i(t) = \Delta\theta_j(t)]$ being negligible—both in terms of chance of occurrence as well as the consequences when it does occur.

Before continuing, we need to distinguish that the above relates to a gradient-esque term for the distance between two particles. That is, will they be closer at $t + 2\Delta t$ with $\Delta\theta_i(t), \Delta\theta_j(t)$ than they would have been with no noise. We will describe this comparative gradient property as *drift*, or $\dot{d}(\boldsymbol{x}_i, \boldsymbol{x}_j)$, with $d(\boldsymbol{x}_i, \boldsymbol{x}_j)$ referring to the actual distance. Equation 5 can be rewritten in two ways:

$$P[d_t(\boldsymbol{x}_i, \boldsymbol{x}_j) < d_{t+\Delta t}(\boldsymbol{x}_i, \boldsymbol{x}_j)] = P[d_t(\boldsymbol{x}_i, \boldsymbol{x}_j) > d_{t+\Delta t}(\boldsymbol{x}_i, \boldsymbol{x}_j)], \tag{6}$$

to denote that the distance is equally likely to increase or decrease, or

$$P[\dot{d}(\boldsymbol{x}_i, \boldsymbol{x}_j) < 0] = P[\dot{d}(\boldsymbol{x}_i, \boldsymbol{x}_j) > 0], \tag{7}$$

to denote that the probability of the drift being positive (diverging) or negative (converging) is equally likely. When the two particles are neighbours the two equalities are equal since the average angle for each particle is equal at each time step via neighbourhood averaging.

Additionally, we note the above does not quite hold for all values of $\langle\theta(t)\rangle_{i,k}$, specifically, when $\langle\theta(t)\rangle_{i,k}$ approaches parallel to the vector between the two particles—$\langle\theta(t)\rangle_{i,k} \to \pm\frac{\pi}{2}$ in this case—Eq. 7 breaks, giving a bias towards divergence, as seen in Fig. 4. This bias increases as the distance decreases between the two particles. When the distance between the two particles is sufficiently small the bias appears for all $\langle\theta(t)\rangle_{i,k}$, with $P[\dot{d}(\boldsymbol{x}_i, \boldsymbol{x}_j) < 0] \to 0$.

---

[1] We obtain a z-component by treating the simulation plane as existing in 3D, with $z = 0$ for all positions and velocities.

[2] Note that the metric case is symmetric. If p_i is a neighbour of p_j, then p_j is a neighbour of p_i. This does not necessarily hold in the topological case.

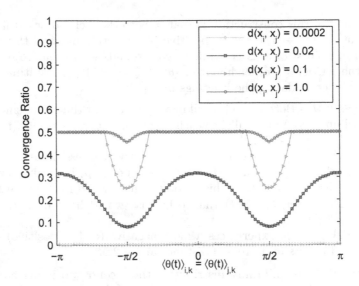

Fig. 4. Metric—Drift convergence profile for interacting two particle case described in text, where $d(\boldsymbol{x}_i, \boldsymbol{x}_j) \leq r$. The 100 linearly spaced points are the ratio of convergence events occurring over every permutation of $\Delta\theta_i(t)$ and $\Delta\theta_j(t)$ for 100 linearly spaced noise values between ± 0.25—i.e. $\eta = 0.5$. Distance convergence follows exactly.

When the particles are not neighbours however the distinction between drift and distance is pertinent. Here Eq. 7 holds for most values—with biases occurring at four singularities as above, shown in Fig. 5a—while Eq. 6 does not. Specifically, since they are no longer neighbours, the first term in Eq. 2 differs for each particle. At low η, $\theta(t)_i$ and $\theta(t)_j$ can dominate such that there is no $\Delta\theta_i(t)$ or $\Delta\theta_j(t)$ that changes the relationship between $d_{t+2}(\boldsymbol{x}_i, \boldsymbol{x}_j)$ and $d_t(\boldsymbol{x}_i, \boldsymbol{x}_j)$ and thus the particles, regardless of noise, *must* get closer or *must* separate. Figure 5b shows the dominance of $\theta(t)_i$ and $\theta(t)_j$ over the noise.

Thus when discussing drift, we can see that—aside from four singularity points—$P[\dot{d}(\boldsymbol{x}_i, \boldsymbol{x}_j) < 0] \approx P[\dot{d}(\boldsymbol{x}_i, \boldsymbol{x}_j) > 0]$ while Eq. 6 completely breaks, with one side of the equality approaching 1 for most heading combinations.

4.2   Drift in Large Metric Flocks

We can extend this to the multiple particle single flock case (multiple flocks follows on exactly by treating flocks as locally singular) by setting aside p_j and instead considering p_l, the imaginary particle representing the local neighbourhood of p_i, with $\boldsymbol{x}_l$ as the centre of mass of p_i's neighbours, and $\boldsymbol{v}_l$ representing the velocity vector of the neighbourhood. Let Ω_l represent the change of $\boldsymbol{v}_l$ arising from neighbour changes rather than from uniform noise. By the central limit theorem, Ω_l will approximately follow a Gaussian distribution with $\mu = 0$. Due to the symmetrical nature of both distributions, Eq. 7 still holds (with $\boldsymbol{x}_l$). That is, p_i is equally likely to drift away from or towards p_l. In fact, as $\langle\theta(t)\rangle_{i,k} = \boldsymbol{v}_l$ we have the neighbour case from above, meaning Eqs. 6 and 7 both hold for $\boldsymbol{x}_i$ and $\boldsymbol{x}_l$.

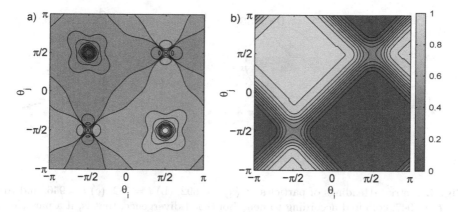

Fig. 5. Metric—(a) Drift convergence profile for non-interacting two particle case described in text at $\eta = 0.5$, with $d(\boldsymbol{x}_i, \boldsymbol{x}_j) = 2$. Measurements same as Fig. 4, extended for differing θ_i, θ_j. Singularities exist at $\pm\frac{\pi}{2}$, parallel to $\boldsymbol{x}_i - \boldsymbol{x}_j$. When signs match, both particles move together, with slight biases—converging and diverging. With opposite signs, particles face away from or towards each other, resulting in complete convergence or divergence, respectively. This can only occur once flocks have lost coherency however, thus is dismissed from discussion on losing coherency. Lower η sharpens peaks and flattens all other values. (b) Distance convergence profile, approaching equality only at $\theta_i \approx \theta_j$ and $\mathrm{sgn}(\theta_i)\pi - \theta_i \approx \theta_j$. Decreasing η increases the steepness between extremes.

This does not extend to the overall flock—i.e., $\boldsymbol{x}_i$ and $\boldsymbol{x}_f$—for similar reasons to the non-neighbour two particle case, meaning only $P[\dot{d}(\boldsymbol{x}_i, \boldsymbol{x}_f) < 0] \approx P[\dot{d}(\boldsymbol{x}_i, \boldsymbol{x}_f) > 0]$ holds true. That is, p_i is equally like to drift away from or toward p_f (the imaginary flock centre particle), however at low η, $\boldsymbol{v}_l$ constrains p_i such that equality of Eq. 6 breaks and completely favours either convergence or divergence.

In the case of a perfectly ordered flock (i.e., $\boldsymbol{v}_i = \boldsymbol{v}_l = \boldsymbol{v}_f \; \forall \; i, l$), we have symmetry in fluctuations about $\boldsymbol{v}_f$ (even though the symmetry of particle headings is broken). This will quickly change as thermal noise is introduced unless $\sum_j^{n_j} \xi_j(t) = 0$ for all local neighbourhoods. Any case of $\boldsymbol{v}_l(t + \Delta t) \neq \boldsymbol{v}_l(t)$ will constrain all connected particles, even if slightly, towards a converging or diverging trajectory—the probabilities in Eq. 6 are no longer equal. Furthermore, when particles on the boundary diverge from their neighbourhoods, they also freely diverge from the flock, while those near the centre move towards other particles and are more likely to keep $\boldsymbol{v}_{l,i} \approx \boldsymbol{v}_f$.

Even though noise is uniform, for $\boldsymbol{v}_l(t + \Delta t)$ to return to $\boldsymbol{v}_f$ an equivalent but opposite set of noise realisations is required for each connected particle. As discussed above however, particles connected to p_l will have a noise distribution centred about $\boldsymbol{v}_l$, leading to $\boldsymbol{v}_l$ staying steady. Additionally, when p_l is along the border of the overall flock, the outermost particles of p_l will have their own

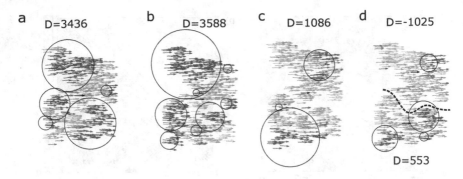

Fig. 6. Metric—Headings of particles at (a) $t = 692$, (b) $t = 782$, (c) $t = 946$, and (d) $t = t_s = 947$, coloured according to neighbourhood divergence, that is, if a particle is diverging, how many of its neighbours are also diverging. Red = 0%, green = 50% of neighbours are also diverging, purple = 100%. Black circles indicate minimum spanning circle of connected diverging sub-flocks, where each particle in the connected set has a neighbourhood divergence >80%. Number near flock represents sum of each neighbourhood divergence $D = \sum_j^{n_j} \delta(i,j)$, where $\delta(i,j) = 1$ if both particles are diverging from v_f and -1 otherwise. Black vector indicates x_f and v_f for each flock. Note the lack of divergence in (c)—the inertia has dissipated with the flock split happening in the next time step in (d). Black dashed line in (d) indicates the demarcation between the two flocks. Flock presented here is the same flock presented in Fig. 1. (Color figure online)

smaller neighbourhoods, allowing for their own v_l to diverge with more ease as they only partially reset to the inner v_l at each time step.

This inertia in the heading of each v_l is what ultimately leads to a flock split event at some future time step t_s. The inertia need not even exist at t_s and could have dissipated many time steps earlier, with the final split occurring due to minor fluctuations in the few particles linking the sub-flocks together. Figure 6 shows such a case with inertia almost completely dissipated at $t_s - 1$ and t_s.

This has implications for the symmetry breaking of the system. Typically, we have an unstable state where particles are disordered[3] and stable states of just one flock from which the system has trouble escaping giving a state space similar to Fig. 7a. However, as argued above, we have other stable states—those with more flocks—which can be reached via thermal fluctuations. This also creates additional unstable states between the stable states—different thermal fluctuations in Fig. 6c could cause a collapse back to the 1 flock stable state instead. Figure 7b shows a cross section of one possible potential function with this behaviour. Note that moving between these states is reversible, with the jump to fewer flocks being more achievable as it can also be achieved by the flocks explicitly colliding, which becomes increasingly likely the further the flock directions diverge.

---

[3] Remembering that we are dealing exclusively with the $\eta \ll \eta_c$ regime in which particles "want" to clump together.

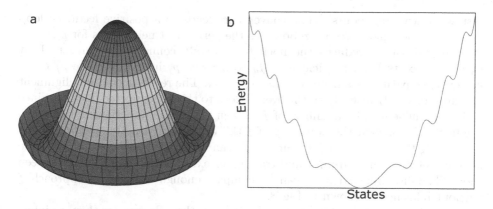

Fig. 7. Metric—(a) Goldstone's [6] *Mexican hat* potential function. The peak is analogous to the unstable disordered state of the SVM with the trough representing the single rotationally symmetric stable flock state. (b) Proposed cross section of state space for SVM. Each higher local minimum represents more flocks, with the global minimum indicating a single flock. Note that where thermal fluctuations would not return the system to the peak in (a) they could push the system up into higher buckets in (b).

4.3   Topological Flocks

We now turn our attention to the topological variant of the Vicsek model and begin by noting that the above analysis holds true here as well, with the exception that the two particle neighbour-less case is not possible. However, the subsequent distinction between the local neighbourhood and overall flock and Eqs. 6 and 7 remains valid.

As the drift analysis holds true for both cases, and explains a reversible flock instability, something else must explain the behaviour seen in Figs. 2 and 3, where the topological flock permanently enters a quasi-disordered state. The issue, in fact, stems from an interplay between the lack of dispersion rule in the Vicsek model and the asymmetric nature of topological neighbours. This allows groups of particles to contract around a local centre of mass such that they disconnect from the rest of the flock. For example, in a system with $k_T = 6$, a small flock f_d of just 6 particles can be internally connected—for each $p_i \in f_d$, all k_T neighbours $p_j \in f_d$—creating only unidirectional connections between f_d and f. In practice, these disconnected flocks are usually larger than the minimum k_T particles[4]. The lack of dispersion rule naturally leads to this outcome, as particles will move—within thermal fluctuation—in the direction of $\langle \theta(t) \rangle_{i,k}$. As with the metric case, p_i has equal likelihood of diverging or converging with p_l. Here however, at best, divergence leads to the *status quo*, local density is roughly constant

---

[4] The minimum is k_T and not $k_T + 1$ since particles are always neighbours to themselves, such that the neighbourhood is never empty in the metric case.

just with new neighbours, while convergence leads to a positive feedback loop cementing the current k_T neighbours as the permanent neighbours for p_i.

This eventually reduces the flock to a weakly connected super set. That is, a path exists from particle $p_i \notin f_d$ to particle p_j including those $p_j \in f_d$, however, no path exists from $p_i \in f_d$ to $p_j \notin f_d$. The result is that no alignment information can transfer from the overall flock to the disconnected flock f_d. Since f_d is only influenced by members of f_d, it can proceed in directions unrelated to the flock. If f_d is near the boundary of f this can quickly lead to splitting apart.

During this process, neighbours to f_d can be stripped away from f, where they either disconnect from f and trail f_d, or exist in a no-man's land between them. The disconnected flock can be compact enough that it can approach f without influence as shown in Fig. 8.

Once flocks start exhibiting these behaviours the only way for them to interact again is for the flocks to collide rather than brush near each other. However, such mergers are only temporary, as the new flock is constructed of even closer particles. Figure 9 shows two flocks merging and disbanding in under 200 time steps, resulting in two new denser flocks. Thus it is clear that once the quasi-disordered state is reached, the system will not return to an ordered state without some dispersion rule preventing contained islands of particles.

For systems with larger k_T, the above mechanism still occurs, just at a slower rate as it takes longer for the requisite islands to contract enough for fragmentation to arise.

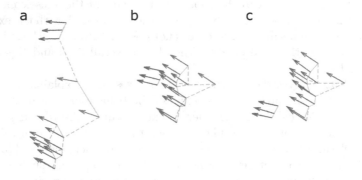

Fig. 8. Topological—Snapshots of small flock, $N = 30$ (15 shown), $\rho = 0.25, k_T = 3, s = 0.1$, demonstrating the effect of contraction. SSN super-imposed where dashed purple lines indicate asymmetric neighbours—i.e., p_i is one of p_j's k_T neighbours, but not vice versa—and full orange lines indicate symmetric neighbours. Self-connections are implicit and not drawn. Arrow colour denotes sub-flock membership as established in (a). (a) $t = 4,655$: The three red particles are connected only to themselves, while a green particle has one red neighbour. (b) $t = 4,693$: Sub-flock moves in front of the main flock. Both flocks are tight enough that no connection occurs between red and blue particles. (c) $t = 4,710$: Both flocks continue with no changes to heading. (Color figure online)

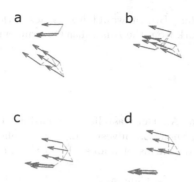

Fig. 9. Topological—Snapshots of two flocks merging then disbanding at (a) $t = 4,812$, (b) $t = 4,821$, (c) $t = 4,969$, (d) $t = 4,986$. Note in (b) the tight core of 3 particles—originating from both original flocks—occupying almost the same space—and that in (d) the two flock are made up of both red and blue particles. See Fig. 8 for colour legend. (Color figure online)

5   Conclusion

By careful inspection of how particles interact at each time step, we have demonstrated that when consensus is reached in the Vicsek Model, it is not permanent for $\eta > 0$, regardless of metric or topological interactions. The topological case is the more troublesome of the two as it clearly exhibits a state in which the original stable flock is no longer reachable, while the metric case can return to stability more easily than escaping from it in the first place.

In extensions to the SVM or TVM, such behaviour may potentially disappear, even without a rule explicitly addressing the flock instability. One such extension is the *Inertial Spin Model* (ISM) by Cavagna *et al.* [5]. The ISM introduces a spin component which influences the velocity component of particles, leading to an inertia in a particle's direction. This would invalidate Eq. 5 and would likely result in long term flock stability. Furthermore, the spin component could potentially interfere with the contraction behaviour in the topological case preventing islands from forming.

For the Vicsek model as it stands however, instability is inescapable. The key respite is that both sets of instability mechanics do require moderate time scales to occur meaning that with careful consideration of observation windows, particularly when settling time is required, data collection regimes can be structured such that flock instability is avoided. However, we note that the Vicsek model is one of the simplest flocking models available—which leads to its popularity in many numerical analyses of collective behaviour—and while it is quite informative for applied fields, it should perhaps be replaced altogether in practical applications with a more robust model rather than adjusting observation windows.

Acknowledgments. Joshua Brown would like to acknowledge the support of his Ph.D. program and this work from the Australian Government Research Training Program Scholarship.

References

1. Attanasi, A., Cavagna, A., Del Castello, L., Giardina, I., Melillo, S., Parisi, L., Pohl, O., Rossaro, B., Shen, E., Silvestri, E., et al.: Collective behaviour without collective order in wild swarms of midges. PLoS Comput. Biol. **10**(7), e1003697 (2014)
2. Baglietto, G., Albano, E.V., Candia, J.: Criticality and the onset of ordering in the standard Vicsek model. Interface Focus **2**(6), 708–714 (2012)
3. Ballerini, M., Cabibbo, N., Candelier, R., Cavagna, A., Cisbani, E., Giardina, I., Lecomte, V., Orlandi, A., Parisi, G., Procaccini, A., et al.: Interaction ruling animal collective behavior depends on topological rather than metric distance: evidence from a field study. Proc. Natl. Acad. Sci. **105**(4), 1232–1237 (2008)
4. Cavagna, A., Conti, D., Giardina, I., Grigera, T.S., Melillo, S., Viale, M.: Spatio-temporal correlations in models of collective motion ruled by different dynamical laws. Phys. Biol. **13**(6), 065001 (2016)
5. Cavagna, A., Del Castello, L., Giardina, I., Grigera, T., Jelic, A., Melillo, S., Mora, T., Parisi, L., Silvestri, E., Viale, M., et al.: Flocking and turning: a new model for self-organized collective motion. J. Stat. Phys. **158**(3), 601–627 (2015)
6. Goldstone, J.: Field theories with superconductor solutions. Il Nuovo Cimento (1955–1965) **19**, 154–164 (1961)
7. Grégoire, G., Chaté, H.: Onset of collective and cohesive motion. Phys. Rev. Lett. **92**(2), 025702 (2004)
8. Jadbabaie, A., Lin, J., Morse, A.S.: Coordination of groups of mobile autonomous agents using nearest neighbor rules. IEEE Trans. Autom. Control **48**(6), 988–1001 (2003)
9. Keller, E.F., Segel, L.A.: Traveling bands of chemotactic bacteria: a theoretical analysis. J. Theor. Biol. **30**(2), 235–248 (1971)
10. Komareji, M., Bouffanais, R.: Resilience and controllability of dynamic collective behaviors. PLoS one **8**(12), e82578 (2013)
11. Reynolds, C.W.: Flocks, herds and schools: a distributed behavioral model. In: SIGGRAPH 1987 Proceedings of the 14th Annual Conference on Computer Graphics and Interactive Techniques, vol. 21, pp. 25–34. ACM, New York (1987)
12. Shaw, E.: Schooling fishes: the school, a truly egalitarian form of organization in which all members of the group are alike in influence, offers substantial benefits to its participants. Am. Sci. **66**(2), 166–175 (1978)
13. Tahbaz-Salehi, A., Jadbabaie, A.: On recurrence of graph connectivity in Vicseks model of motion coordination for mobile autonomous agents. In: American Control Conference, pp. 699–704 (2007)
14. Vicsek, T., Czirók, A., Ben-Jacob, E., Cohen, I., Shochet, O.: Novel type of phase transition in a system of self-driven particles. Phys. Rev. Lett. **75**, 1226–1229 (1995)
15. Vicsek, T., Zafeiris, A.: Collective motion. Phys. Rep. **517**(34), 71–140 (2012)
16. Wicks, R.T., Chapman, S.C., Dendy, R.: Mutual information as a tool for identifying phase transitions in dynamical complex systems with limited data. Phys. Rev. E. **75**, 051125 (2007). https://journals.aps.org/pre/abstract/10.1103/PhysRevE.75.051125

Advancing the Performance of Complex Manufacturing Systems Through Agent-Based Production Control

Arndt Lüder[1], Jacek Zawisza[1(✉)], and Alexander Becker[2]

[1] Otto-v.-Guericke University, Universitätsplatz 2, 39106 Magdeburg, Germany
{arndt.lueder,jacek.zawisza}@ovgu.de
[2] Volkswagen AG, Berliner Ring 2, 38440 Wolfsburg, Germany
alexander.becker@volkswagen.de

Abstract. Ever increasing competition is driving the efforts to improve productivity throughout nearly all domains. In the manufacturing context, digitalization of value networks and creation of autonomous, self-optimizing systems – a vision coined '*Industrie 4.0* – is an approach that promises competitive edge over other players. One field in which this vision could lead to great productivity potentials is order scheduling and sequencing in high variety, high volume manufacturing businesses like the automobile industry. A viable technology to realize the expected gains in productivity are software agents and multi-agent systems, since they provide autonomy, flexibility, adaptiveness, and robustness to unforeseeable events. This paper proposes an agent-based control architecture that enables communication between resources and customer orders within a car body shop, so that they can negotiate the best alternative schedule and order sequence in case of disturbances. The proposed architecture allows improvement of overall production system performance in terms of output, resource utilization, delivery reliability and others. Further, the paper describes the implementation and simulation of the multi-agent system with JADE framework and discusses the simulation results, which show that significant productivity leaps can be achieved.

Keywords: Industrie 4.0 · Multi-agent systems · Production control systems · Production scheduling · Car-sequencing

1 Introduction

Customer demand simultaneously fosters product segmentation and higher product individualization [1]. Consequentially, volume of each model and product variant declines, resulting in more complex and more competitive markets [2]. In order to keep up with demand and competition, manufacturing businesses have to constantly improve their productivity, adapt quickly to changes in customer demand, and eliminate waste throughout the value chain. However, to achieve new levels of productivity, new approaches become increasingly important [3]. In this context, *Industrie 4.0*, as one of the leading research and development initiatives, has envisioned an advanced production system control architecture and engineering methodology, to achieve leaps in

© Springer International Publishing AG 2017
J.O. Berndt et al. (Eds.): MATES 2017, LNAI 10413, pp. 103–120, 2017.
DOI: 10.1007/978-3-319-64798-2_7

resource productivity and efficiency across entire value networks [4–7]. The underlying potentials are assumed to allow cost reductions of up to 40% in work in progress, up to 20% in processing, and even up to 70% in complexity reduction [2].

A field that could benefit greatly from advances in this area is the manufacturing sector, in particular, businesses with high product and production complexity, high product variety, and high volume. The automobile industry comprises a prominent representative of this kind of enterprise, where highly individual, complex products are being mass manufactured on mixed-model production lines. The same production method is also used in other segments like consumer electronics, white goods, furniture and clothing [8]. However, high product diversity requires detailed sequence planning in order to best exploit the potential of the production system [9].

This is achieved using mixed-model sequencing, which is an optimization problem from the domain of operations research and falls into the category of discrete and combinatorial optimization [10]. Research and industry have elaborated a broad range of approaches like using real options from finance domain, fuzzy goal programming, and particle swarm optimization to find satisfactory solutions in a given amount of time [11–13]. Those approaches factor in the restrictions of the underlying production system to give a near-optimal solution and have experienced considerable improvement over the last decades [14]. However, the underlying optimization problem is NP-hard, meaning that it cannot be solved in real-time [15]. Additionally, complex production systems with thousands of entities are subject to unforeseeable disruptions, that conventional, monolithic enterprise software is not designed to deal with. Multi-agent systems (MAS), on the other hand, provide the necessary properties to excel in dynamic environments [16]. This leads to the assumption, that the shortcomings of static scheduling algorithms could potentially be compensated by cooperating with dynamic multi-agent systems in order to achieve a better overall performance of production systems. Therefore, the following research questions will be discussed in this paper:

RQ1: How can decentralized control of production scheduling and sequencing with multi-agent systems improve the overall performance of complex production systems?

RQ2: How must a viable architecture for such a multi-agent system be designed and what tasks does each agent have to perform in order to realize productivity potentials?

To answer these questions, this work is structured as follows. In Sect. 2, the general mixed-model sequencing problem in the context of complex production systems is introduced and current challenges are illustrated. Following this, in Sect. 3, the approach of this work is described, requirements for the proposed MAS are derived, and the application case is presented. On this basis, the architecture of the MAS is explained and the elaborated agent communication is discussed. After this, Sect. 4 describes the basis of the performed simulations including input data and simulation approaches, and then focuses on the key performance indicators (KPI's) which are used to measure the performance of the system. The results of the simulations are discussed in Sect. 5 and the paper ends with a summary and outlook on future challenges.

In terms of scope and delimitations, the goal of this paper is to demonstrate the feasibility of applying multi-agent systems in the selected area and tapping into their potential. Therefore, focus is laid on the higher layers of the automation pyramid, mainly manufacturing execution system layer (MES). This, in turn, means that Enterprise Resource Planning (ERP) and field-level layers of the automation pyramid are not regarded. However, the work of [17, 18] shows that this is a realizable undertaking and a consequent next step. In real-world applications, deviations in cycle times of different product configurations can cause an overload of manufacturing equipment and, therefore, pose a challenge for production sequence planning [19]. However, due to the scope of this work, cycle times of each variant and within each variant type are assumed equivalent. This property can be implemented ex-post and is supported by existing sequencing algorithms as described in [8, 14], and alike. To enable future improvements, the application programming interface (API) of the designed software allows for easy exchange and adjustments of software modules and algorithms.

2 Production Scheduling and Control

2.1 Complex Products and Production Systems

Today, state of the art automobile factories produce several thousand cars per day. Each factory performs several thousand production steps to complete an order and has an equal amount of work in progress distributed on the production floor. This creates a very complex environment on production side already. On the product side, however, the situation is even more complex: due to high personalization of vehicles and thereby increasing product variety, manufacturers are confronted with billions of theoretically possible product configurations. For example, BMW offers up to 10^{17} configurations for its Series 7 and Daimler offers even up to 10^{24} for its E-Class [1, 20]. This product complexity raises production complexity even further and demands for suitable control approaches on the production side. Car wiring harnesses, for example, are each assembled individually and work only for the car it was designed for. It, therefore, is useless for any other car than this exact same one. To cope with the resulting complexity in supply chain and internal logistics, most automobile manufacturers have adopted the so-called "pearl chain logistics concept". Here, the final assembly sequence is defined several days in advance to handle complexity and required materials are picked and sequenced in the predefined order [21–23].

2.2 Approaches for Sequencing Mixed-Model Assembly Lines

In research and industry, three main types of approaches for planning the optimal order sequence on mixed-model assembly lines have emerged: mixed-model-sequencing, car-sequencing, and level scheduling.

Mixed-Model-Sequencing. As a workload-oriented approach, mixed-model-sequencing focuses on avoiding or minimizing sequence-depending work-overload at individual workstations. This approach explicitly integrates operational characteristics like cycle times, personnel restrictions, station borders, etc. It, therefore, allows for high accuracy but requires significant effort considering data collection [8].

Car-Sequencing. In contrast, car-sequencing requires significantly less effort, since it considers the above-stated operational characteristics implicitly rather than explicitly by setting sequencing rules of type $H_o:N_o$ (meaning that a maximum of H_o occurrences may be among N_o positions) [8]. The most successful implementations use heuristics like greedy algorithms, local search methods, genetic algorithms, and ant colony optimization methods [14]. Overall, this makes car-sequencing a valuable approach that is frequently used in practice, although it comes with the trade-off of lower accuracy.

Level Scheduling. The last approach to be mentioned in this paper seeks to optimize Just-in-Time (JIT) objectives, rather than workload. The overall goal is to distribute material requirements, which depend highly on the production sequence, as evenly as possible over the planning horizon. Therefore, target production rates are defined and product variants are sequenced according to those rates minimizing deviations [24].

Despite great efforts in academia describing alternative solutions, there is still a lack of empirical research evaluating the fit of sequencing approaches for real-world applications [8]. The next section tries to reduce this gap. Furthermore, manufacturers have a hard time following the specific sequence defined by the pearl chain concept, since perturbations and complex, parallel production lines tend to disrupt the planned order [25]. The resulting challenges are discussed in the following section.

2.3   Case Study: Challenges in the Automotive Sector

Both, high product and production system complexity, increase the possibility of disruptions during the manufacturing process. Even though concepts like Total Productive Maintenance (TPM) and Predictive Maintenance helped reduce previously unforeseeable failures in past decades, manufacturers constantly deal with disturbances.

Since disruptions in any of the thousands of participants of a production network are possible anytime, adaptation of the production sequence is a necessary ability. However, mixed-model scheduling is an NP-hard problem and a new near-optimal sequence cannot be calculated under real-time conditions [15]. Current algorithms require runtimes of about 30 min to calculate a new sequence, which is too slow for real-time adjustments [26]. Limiting runtime, e.g. to 10 min like in the ROADEF'05 challenge [14], enables faster reactivity, but generally leads to lower quality of the solution. As a consequence of both, dynamics of complex production systems and insufficient real-time abilities, the elaborated solution is often outdated the moment it comes into place. Therefore, it is inevitable for a robust production system to autonomously adapt to disturbances the moment they occur.

Conventional monolithic enterprise software, however, is not designed to cope with unexpected events, since it is based on a very detailed set of rules to cover very specific situations. On one hand, this allows excellent results in those predefined circumstances. On the other hand, monolithic systems tend to have poor performance when handling events that were not specifically defined in advance, because they cannot respond adequately and in a timely manner to such situations. Therefore, although many automobile factories have the possibility to virtually or physically resequence the production order at some point, they can only handle planned, predefined operations like e.g. building color blocks before entering paint shop [27]. Unplanned resequencing usually results in deviations from the originally planned sequence and causes problems down the production stream. Inconsistent data types can further increase such complications [28].

Additionally, the overall system complexity makes it extremely difficult for humans to manage the required information in real-time. However, it can be observed that humans are often the decision makers in such situations, which can lead to suboptimal results. As an example, the distribution of lead times often shows that the expected bell curve is stretched far to the right, with a significant part of orders having very long lead times [22]. However, in the experience of the authors, this effect can be found in about half of the factory output, and it can be argued, that ineffective production control is accountable for a significant part of this effect. The same can be observed in the distribution of product variants where unexpected events and disruptions often lead to unevenness of production as depicted in Fig. 1. This unevenness usually causes problems in assembly shop that can only process a certain number of variants in sequence. In a production control context, these kinds of deviations are often caused by disturbances like logistical restrictions, e.g. due to delayed material. Dispatchers counteract by releasing other orders to keep production running. These decisions, however are usually not entirely data-driven and must be taken quickly, resulting in the distributions illustrated below. Based on the experiences of the authors at different

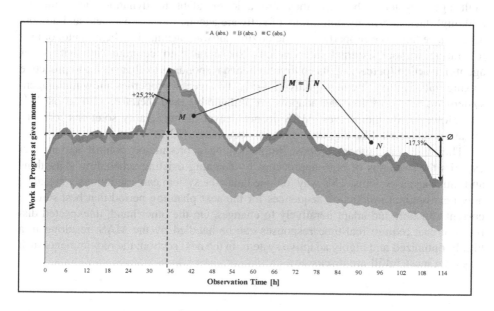

Fig. 1. Work in progress of three product variants A, B, and C

factories and manufacturers, these observations appear to be representative of the automobile sector.

To summarize, there are multiple approaches for sequencing mixed-model assembly lines and great effort is being made in both, academia and industry, to further improve the given tools. However, it can be observed that solutions like car sequencing are used in real-world applications, rather due to better interpretability for humans and lower computational effort then due to higher performance.

From this, two conclusions can be drawn: first, despite their complexity and real-time requirements, decisions in modern production systems are – to some extent – influenced by human decision-makers. And second, computation time is a critical factor for the success of a production control system in the manufacturing domain. Considering the fact that highly complex production systems with several thousand suppliers as well as hundreds of internal production resources are exposed to a substantial amount of unexpected disruptions, it seems rational to increase the amount of autonomy in that area. However, since the presented sequencing strategies already provide near-optimal solutions and significant runtime-improvements are not expected, it is difficult to achieve great productivity leaps in that area. It is far more likely to realize substantial improvements by adding more flexibility and autonomy to the production system itself, which is outlined in more detail in the following section.

3   Agent-Based Production Control System

3.1   Approach

A technology with high potential to address the challenges described above are multi-agent systems, because they are able to adapt to dynamic environments. Although there are many definitions of software agents, most researchers and authors agree on certain core properties characterizing software agents, like being autonomous (operating without external intervention), social (able to communicate with other agents), reactive (perceiving its environment and responding to changes), and proactive (taking initiative to achieve its goals) [29–31]. The agents' properties allow multi-agent systems to be highly flexible, adaptive, reconfigurable, and therefore also robust [31, 32]. However, by themselves, MAS do not deliver higher quality solutions for optimization problems, like e.g. mixed-model sequencing [33].

Therefore, the authors propose implementing a production control system that exploits the strengths of both approaches by combing existing scheduling algorithms and multi-agent systems. This way, on one hand, the system can continuously calculate new near-optimal production sequences for the next planning period that best suit the current situation and adapt iteratively to changes. On the other hand, unexpected disruptions that require real-time responses can be handled by the MAS, resulting in a highly optimized and highly adaptive system. In the next section, the requirements such a system must fulfill are discussed.

3.2 Requirements and Implementation-Framework

To address the defined challenges and equip the proposed production control system with the necessary properties a set of requirements must be met. Although multi-agent systems can provide a long list of valuable properties (see e.g. [29–31]), the following five requirements are considered especially important by the authors:

R1: Autonomy and Decentralized Control. To cope with its complex and dynamic environment, the designed system comprises of software-agents that are autonomous by definition. Each agent has its own goals and autonomously exercises plans to achieve them. Therefore, it controls its own behavior and operates without direct intervention of human supervisors [31]. It can and must, however, communicate with other agents.

R2: Flexibility and Adaptability. Unexpected disruptions must be handled effectively, meaning that agents must adapt automatically to dynamic changes in their environment. This was considered in the MAS by enabling agents to sense their environment, i.e. receiving the information they need, and to act upon it. As an example, if a resource suffers a malfunction and cannot process an order, the system must recognize this and find an alternative way to achieve its goal.

R3: Reconfigurability. Multi-agent systems offer the opportunity to provide plug & produce functionality to manufacturing businesses. In practice, this is a very valuable property, since it allows adding and removing resources depending on current demand. To ensure this functionality, the system is designed to allow registering and deregistering resources at runtime, providing all necessary information about the resource.

R4: Real-time capabilities. As shown in Sect. 2.3, it is necessary that the developed system can adequately respond to sudden changes. Since the system is working in the MES-context, response times in the range of minutes, like they are common in sequencing algorithms, are not allowed. Neither is the system responsible for direct control of field-layer equipment like PLCs, so it does not have to meet real-time requirements in the millisecond range. Therefore, the maximum response time for the system was designed to be below one second. Although most events are handled in significantly shorter time, this threshold is enough to make all required decisions.

R5: Modularity and extensibility. To facilitate modifications of the proposed system, the API was designed in a way that allows to easily replace or add modules. The system can thus be adjusted to the domain it is used in and the goals developers pursue. Examples for this are the scheduling and routing algorithms as well as simulation of resource failures. Furthermore, the API allows integrating sophisticated machine learning algorithms like reinforcement or deep learning and other kinds of artificial narrow intelligence that allow to further increase the autonomy and performance of the system.

Framework. To meet the above-stated requirements, the MAS was developed using the widespread Java Agent Development Framework (JADE) [34]. It has the advantage of being platform-independent, because it is Java-based and, in addition, provides

FIPA-compatibility and is distributed open source under the LGPL license. Furthermore, database management systems and several libraries were used to achieve the required functionality. Among them are MySQL, Apache Web Server, and phpMyAdmin for database functionality, apache commons library for mathematical functions like exponential and gamma distributions, and Dijkstra algorithm for finding the shortest path in a directed graph. The next section describes the application case on which those tools were applied.

3.3   Application Case: Car Body Weld Shop

The roots of many of the challenges described in Sect. 2.3 are linked to order release and resource allocation. Therefore, a state of the art car body weld shop was selected as an application case for this work, since it is an archetype for those challenges. It can be structured using the hierarchical structure model from [35] which divides production systems into 9 layers reaching from component to production network. The body shop covers levels 1 to 7 of those hierarchy layers. Due to the MES-focus of this work, only layers 5 to 7 are considered, i.e. work unit, production line segment, and production line. From top to bottom, on layer 7 we can find two production lines which produce different car body types, as depicted in Fig. 2. Going deeper to layer 6, these two lines consist of 13 different production line segments S11 to S80. Some of these segments, like S11 and S12, are used exclusively by either production line 1 or 2, others like S40 and S60 are shared by both production lines and build a bottleneck.

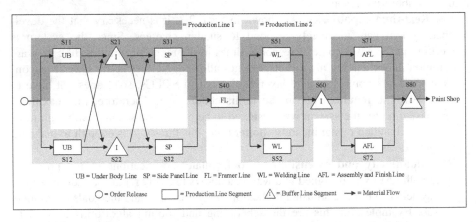

Fig. 2. Layout and technical capabilities of resources in the application case

Finally, on layer 5, each segment consists of multiple separate work units which are not depicted in the layout. They each perform separate production steps required in the production segment.

In total, the car body weld shop is able to manufacture around 70 different product variants, including different body types and market-specific models. However, all variants are based on three main body types: a two-door compact car, a four-door compact car, and a four-door compact van. To better illustrate the effects of the MAS, this paper focuses on those three main types which will be referred to as variants A, B, and C.

Production line 1 is able to produce variants A and B, while production line 2 can manufacture only variants A and C. Buffers can take all variants as shown in Table 1.

Table 1. Resource capabilities considering production of product variants A, B, and C

Variant	Production line 1				Production line 2				Shared resources				
	S11	S31	S51	S71	S12	S32	S52	S72	S21	S22	S40	S60	S80
A	✔	✔	✔	✔	✔	✔	✔	✔	✔	✔	✔	✔	✔
B	✔	✔	✔	✔					✔	✔	✔	✔	✔
C					✔	✔	✔	✔	✔	✔	✔	✔	✔

Since not all production line segments can produce all variants, it is up to the agents in the system to decide which order will be produced by which resource to achieve the best possible performance. In the next section, the architecture for these processes is explained in more detail.

3.4   Multi-agent System Architecture

The agent architecture in this work was designed using the "Designing Agent-based Control Systems"-methodology (DACS) which consists of the three steps analysis of control decisions, identification of agents, and selection of interaction protocols [36].

For the first step, the authors build upon the work of [37], where control decisions of manufacturing systems were collected, categorized, and assigned to general control tasks. As part of a student work, the specific decisions in a car body weld shop have been analyzed further and mapped to the necessary agents.

The second step, identification of agents, requires a broader look on agent-based production system architectures. Over the past two decades, a large set of architectures for manufacturing control has been developed. The work of [38] analyzes those architectures and shows that common design patterns have emerged out of them. Following those design patterns, a distributed control system architecture was designed consisting of the seven agent types shown in Table 2.

Order, Product, and Resource Agents are the most elementary agents. While Order Agents represent individual customer orders, Product Agents represent whole product variants and contain information about their constitution. Resource Agents manage the production line segments of the system and the therein contained work units. Although work units could be represented as separate Resource Agents, for the selected scenario, it suffices to represent them internally in the Resource Agents of the production line segments. Furthermore, to control and supervise those resources, a Shop Management Agent is required and the Scheduling Agent is necessary to select the next best order to be released in the dynamic environment. A not so obvious but crucial entity is the Mediator Agent, whose job it is to match supply and demand so that the best overall

Table 2. Agent types and their corresponding tasks and information in the model

Agent type	Tasks	Required information
Order Agent (OA)	• Initialize and supervise all required production steps	• Order information (e.g. order ID, variant, delivery date, priority)
Product Agent (PA)	• Manage manufacturing information for every product variant • Provide information to OAs	• Product variant • Production steps (e.g. welding spot sequence in body shop, assembly sequence in assembly shop, etc.) • Technical and sales restrictions
Resource Agent (RA)	• Process designated orders • Keep track of reservation list • Document order status • Request new orders when not occupied • Inform SMA about status (available/disturbed)	• Resource capabilities (cycle time, number of work units, variants, etc.) • Resource status (time to failure, time to repair) • Reservation list • Order status
Shop Management Agent (SMA)	• Instantiate RAs • Keep track of resource status (available/disturbed) • Provide routing information for material flow to OAs	• Shop layout and material flow graph • Resource status (available/disturbed) via message from RA
Scheduling Agent (SA)	• Manage production program • Instantiate OAs when requested by RA or SMA	• Valid production schedule (order ID, variant, sequence, delivery date) • Output and work in progress • Capabilities of requesting resource • Availability of resources in the shop and other restrictions (e.g. logistical or technical restrictions)
Mediator Agent (MA)	• Collect mediation requests from OAs and get proposals for production from RAs during reservation time frame • Match orders to resources appropriately	• Demand for production steps (number and time of requests of OAs) • Supply for production steps (number and ESOP of RAs) • Rules for prioritization of orders (e.g. delivery time, reservation time, variant, priority)
Directory Facilitator (DF)	• Register and deregister every available service in the system • Provide information to all agents	• Registered services and related information

system productivity can be achieved. However, this can only be achieved through communication and cooperation between agents, which is the third step of the DACS-methodology and the subject of the following section.

3.5   Agent Communication

Out of the control tasks listed in Sect. 3.4, the following two are described in more detail in this paper, since they have the highest impact on system performance. The first one is scheduling and releasing orders. A task especially important during disruptions. The second one is allocating orders to resources, including a reservation mechanism allowing to book resources in advance and thereby control the production sequence.

Scheduling and Order Release. The Scheduling Agent (SA) builds upon the production sequence it receives from the sequencing algorithm. This sequence includes the order-ID and related data like product variant and delivery time and is only changed if necessary. On this basis, order release works as a pull mechanism: Resource Agents (RA) of root resources (first work unit of the first production line segment) request new orders from the SA, when they finish processing the predecessor. The SA then selects the next order and instantiates an Order Agent (OA). The SA is equipped with an algorithm that aims at leveling the order release. To do this, it uses the existing production schedule, applies the real-time information it has from other agents (e.g. resource status and capabilities to produce certain variants), and prioritizes orders in a way that target ratios – defined by production system restrictions – of the respective variants are met. However, conventional production systems do not adapt to them automatically in case of disruption. Therefore, if e.g. product variant B cannot be built, it balances production by releasing the variant with the least negative effect on the target ratio one at a time. This way, the backlog of variant B leads to fewer upheavals down the production stream, i.e. paint shop and especially assembly shop, and after the resource is repaired, it can be reduced more easily.

Resource Allocation. Two things were needed to implement the required resource allocation: an interaction protocol that supports the required negotiation between agents and a reservation mechanism that allows matching orders and resources in advance to minimize waiting time. For the negotiation part, the common contract net protocol [34] was selected and extended to match the application case requirements. As the sequence diagram in Fig. 3 suggests, the Mediator Agent (MA) plays an important role in the negotiation. It coordinates the negotiation process as a broker and is triggered by a mediation request from an OA. To avoid loss of productive time during negotiations and thus compromising performance, a resource reservation mechanism was implemented.

Figure 4 shows that a reservation time window is at its core. This window starts a predefined time period before the end of the current production process (e.g. one second prior to production end), so that (a) the probability of disturbances during the current production process is low, and (b) no productive time is lost due to negotiation processes. After receiving the production request, the MA looks up available resources and makes a call for proposition (CFP). The RAs provide the estimated start of production (ESOP) and wait for a response at the end of the reservation window.

The MA then calculates the best match for all orders and resources using a specifically engineered set of rules. Those include the variants and delivery times of the requesting orders as well as their successors, the currently available resources and variants in the resources that offer the desired operation, as well as the status and available variants on the subsequent production steps. As an example, if a subsequent

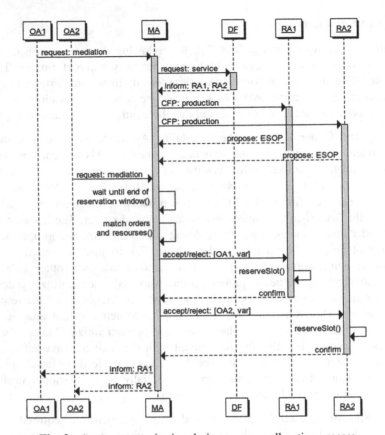

Fig. 3. Agent communication during resource allocation process

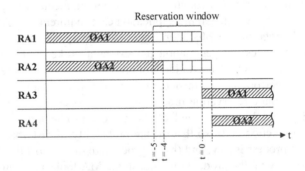

Fig. 4. Reservation mechanism with reservation window

resource offering variant 'B' is down (e.g. S51), resource S40 would not offer variant 'B', since it would block the resource for all other variants. It therefore offers 'A' and 'C' to continue production. Based on this architecture, a series of simulations was performed to examine the performance of the MAS, which is described in the following section.

4 Multi-agent Simulation

The objective of this work is to develop a solution that is tailored to the observed challenges in complex production environments. Against this background, the authors opted for using simulations with real-world data that allow emulating specific conditions instead of using abstracted benchmark-problems. The most important factors are summarized in the following.

4.1 Simulation Basis

Production Program. The starting point of the simulations is a real production program for 24 h, already sequenced by a sequencing algorithm that considers the technical restrictions of the factory. It includes a typical daily amount of about 2.000 orders of the three main body types A, B, and C. Internal delivery dates, i.e. the date when a car body must be delivered to the paint shop as an internal customer, range between 12 and 24 h from scheduled production start for regular orders. However, about 1% of the orders are fast orders with delivery dates between 10 and 12 h.

Resource Parameters. To reproduce the actual situation on the shop floor as realistically as possible, major resource parameters of the MES-layer were integrated into the model. That includes functional parameters like cycle times, variant capabilities, and capacity, as well as maintenance parameters like mean time between failure (MTBF) and mean time to repair (MTTR). Each Resource Agent is provided with the required data via a JSON-file on startup and manages its state by itself.

Resource Disturbances. To simulate resource failures, Resource Agents are provided with a function to calculate the time until the next breakdown and the time it will take to recover. The earlier is based on the MTBF-value of the resource and is approximated via an exponential distribution which is typically applied for lifetime distributions [39]. The latter, on the other hand, is based on the MTTR-value of the resource and is approximated by an Erlang distribution, since it better represents repair processes [40]. With the help of inverse transform sampling, the RA calculates those two times and takes down the resource during the disruption.

4.2 Evaluated KPI's in the Simulation Runs

To measure the performance of the system according to industry standards, the following seven categories were selected: output, resource utilization, delivery date, lead time, production program fulfillment, production sequence fulfillment, and work in progress. For each of these seven areas, specific KPI's were chosen that appropriately measure the system's performance. The list contains common KPI's used in the automobile industry as well as standard descriptive statistic methods like mean value and standard deviation, and are summarized in Table 3.

Since the simulation contains randomly selected events like MTBF and MTTR a simulation run is not replicable. To compensate outliers, the simulation was repeated multiple times for every configuration and results were averaged for each KPI. However, outliers can provide valuable information about the quality of the results and are therefore discussed in the next section.

Table 3. Selected KPI's for evaluation of production system performance

Category	KPI	Description	Unit
1. Output	• System output	• Number of good cars per time unit	jobs/hour
	• Output-mix fulfill	• Deviation from planned output-mix	(jph), %
2. Resources	• Resource-utilization	• Utilization of resources during uptime. Equal to OEE, if there are no scrap parts/orders	%
3. Delivery reliability	• Average delivery date deviation	• Mean value of delivery date deviations of all orders	Days
	• σ delivery date	• Standard deviation of delivery date	Days
4. Lead time	• Average lead time	• Mean value of lead time of all orders	Hours
	• σ Lead time	• Standard Deviation of lead time	Hours
5. Production program	• Production program fulfillment	• Degree to which the original production program is fulfilled with a tolerance window of zero	%
	• Average sequence deviation R000	• Mean value of sequence deviations at order release point (R000)	No. of cars
	• σ Production program	• Standard deviation of actual to target sequence at order release point	No. of cars
6. Production sequence	• Sequence fulfillment	• Degree to which the released order sequence mimics the planned production program with a tolerance window of zero	%
	• Average sequence deviation R800	• Mean value of sequence deviations at end of production (R800)	No. of cars
	• σ Production sequence	• Standard deviation of actual to target production sequence at end of production (R800)	No. of cars
7. Work in progress	• System filling level	• Degree to which the technical capacity of the production system is used by physical orders	%

5   Results and Critical Evaluation

To allow a direct performance comparison between a conventional production control system approach (CPCS) and the agent-based production control system (APCS), multiple simulation runs have been performed. The results of the CPCS were then set as an index, to display the direct performance delta of the APCS in a juxtaposition. The results are presented in Table 4.

As can be seen, the performance of the underlying production system is generally better when it is controlled by the agent-based control system. Good results are especially achieved in KPI's like output and resource-utilization which are interdependent. Higher resource utilization can be achieved through the systems adaptability properties, which allow it to act dynamically upon unpredicted events and therefore improve the

Table 4. Performance comparison of the two production control systems

KPI	Deterioration	Improvement
System Output [jph]		+8%
Output-Mix Fulfillment		+100%
Resource-Utilization		+8%
Avg. Delivery Date Dev. [d]		+1%
σ Delivery Date [d]		+8%
Avg. Lead Time [h]		+9%
σ Lead Time [h]		+21%
Production Program Ful.	-27%	
Avg. Seq. Dev. R000 [cars]	-36%	
σ Production Program [cars]	-32%	
Production Sequence Ful.	-22%	
Avg. Seq. Dev. R800 [cars]	-9%	
σ Production Seq. [cars]	-29%	

overall system yield. This also applies for KPI's in the area of delivery reliability. Since the system disfavors releasing orders that are subjected to current technical or logistical disturbances, the delivery reliability of the released orders increases.

On the other hand, the agent-based control system does not achieve quite as high levels of stability in the areas of production program and production sequence fulfillment. The adaptability of the system comes with the drawback of breaking a pre-defined production schedule and leads to a more mixed production sequence. This is a logical consequence of the adaptation of the system to influences of its environment and eventually leads to a more balanced workload. Although this could be seen as a challenge for manufacturers that follow the pearl chain concept, many production systems work with lead times that allow adaptation to those changes without compromising efficiency. Furthermore, on an absolute scale these KPI's decline at a single-digit rate and have therefore limited impact. So, by filling up production slots that would otherwise stay unused, production program conformity is sacrificed, but the business-wise more important KPI's considering output, resource utilization, and delivery reliability are increased. Considering the limitations of the proposed MAS, it should be noted that the system performance partly relies on predictions of the duration of disruptions which is an information many present production systems do not provide on their own. Instead, they depend on maintenance personnel or dispatchers to enter the data manually into the system, which usually comes with a delay. However, since the decisions of the MAS are being made in real-time, it can react immediately to the new information and e.g. release new orders or block them. Even in this scenario, the system would perform better than solely based on human decision making as it is common today.

6 Conclusions and Future Works

This paper has presented an approach for manufacturing business to cope with continuously rising complexity in production scheduling and sequencing in turbulent environments. The proposed approach is a hybrid between state of the art sequencing algorithms and an agent-based production control system. It allows high-quality solutions for sequencing problems while at the same time autonomously adapting to unexpected changes in the production system. The developed system architecture is based on common design patterns of agent-based production control systems and uses a Mediator Agent as a broker to allow optimal resource allocation during runtime. In simulations of an application case – a state of the art car body weld shop in the automobile industry – the system achieved significant improvements in important production system performance indicators such as output, resource utilization, and delivery time. It can therefore be assumed, that implementation of this kind of hybrid systems could help to reach substantial productivity improvements in manufacturing businesses in similarly complex environments.

Despite the achieved performance increase, there are still opportunities for further enhancements of the approach. Incremental system-specific improvements could be achieved by advancing e.g. message exchange efficiency, code heaviness, and action timing of agents. More potential, however, lies in the implementation of artificial intelligence like reinforcement learning to improve decision making. Finally, a consequent next step is the gradual implementation of the APCS into a state of the art factory to exploit the described potentials and demonstrate applicability in practice.

References

1. ElMaraghy, H., Schuh, G., ElMaraghy, W., Piller, F., Schönsleben, P., Tseng, M., Bernard, A.: Product variety management. CIRP Ann. Manuf. Technol. **62**(2), 629–652 (2013)
2. Bauernhansl, T.: Die vierte industrielle revolution – der weg in ein wertschaffendes produktionsparadigma. In: Vogel-Heuser, B., Bauernhansl, T., Hompel, M. (eds.) Handbuch Industrie 4.0 Bd.4. SRT, pp. 1–31. Springer, Heidelberg (2017). doi:10.1007/978-3-662-53254-6_1
3. Monger, M., Nicherson, J., Woerner, S.l.: Digital Transformation: The Race to Become Future-Ready. https://emarketing.alixpartners.com/rs/emsimages/2017/pubs/DIG/AP_The_race_to_become_future_ready_Apr_2017.pdf. Accessed 25 Apr 2017
4. Kagermann, H., Wahlster, W., Helbig, J. (eds.): Recommendations for implementing the strategic initiative INDUSTRIE 4.0 – securing the future of German manufacturing industry, Final report of the Industrie 4.0 Working Group, April 2013. http://www.acatech.de/fileadmin/user_upload/Baumstruktur_nach_Website/Acatech/root/de/Material_fuer_Sonderseiten/Industrie_4.0/Final_report__Industrie_4.0_accessible.pdf. Accessed 01 Feb 2016

5. Arbeitsgruppen der Plattform Industrie 4.0: Umsetzungsstrategie Industrie 4.0 - Ergebnis-bericht der Plattform Industrie 4.0, April 2015. https://www.bmwi.de/BMWi/Redaktion/PDF/I/industrie-40-verbaendeplattform-bericht,property=pdf,bereich=bmwi2012,sprache=de,rwb=true.pdf. Accessed 01 Feb 2016
6. Bauernhansl, T., ten Hompel, M., Vogel-Heuser, B. (eds.): Industrie 4.0 in Produktion, Automatisierung und Logistik. Springer, Wiesbaden (2014). doi:10.1007/978-3-658-04682-8
7. Manzei, C., Schleupner, L., Heinze, R.: Industrie 4.0 im internationalen Kontext. VDE Verlag, Offenbach (2016)
8. Sarker, B.R., Pan, H.: Designing a mixed-model, open-station assembly line using mixed-integer programming. J. Oper. Res. Soc. **52**, 545–558 (2001)
9. Boysen, N., Fliedner, M., Scholl, A.: Sequencing mixed-model assembly lines. Survey, classification, and model critique. Eur. J. Oper. Res. **192**, 349–373 (2009)
10. Waldmann, K.-H., Stocker, U.M. (eds.): Operations Research Proceedings. Springer, Heidelberg (2006). doi:10.1007/978-3-540-69995-8
11. Rahimi-Vahed, A., Rabbani, M., Tavakkoli-Moghaddam, R., Jolai, F., Manavizadeh, N.: Mixed-model assembly line sequencing using real options. In: Waldmann, K.-H., Stocker, U.M. (eds.) Operations Research Proceedings, pp. 161–167. Springer, Heidelberg (2006). doi:10.1007/978-3-540-69995-8_27
12. Rabbani, M., Rahimi-Vahed, A., Javadi, B., Tavakkoli-Moghaddam, R.: A new approach for mixed-model assembly line sequencing. In: Waldmann, K.-H., Stocker, U.M. (eds.) Operations Research Proceedings, pp. 169–174. Springer, Heidelberg (2006). doi:10.1007/978-3-540-69995-8_28
13. Mirghorbani, S.M., Rabbani, M., Tavakkoli-Moghaddam, R., Rahimi-Vahed, A.R.: A multi-objective particle swarm for a mixed-model assembly line sequencing. In: Waldmann, K.-H., Stocker, U.M. (eds.) Operations Research Proceedings, pp. 181–186. Springer, Heidelberg (2006). doi:10.1007/978-3-540-69995-8_30
14. Solnon, C., Cung, V.-D., Nguyen, A., Artigues, C.: The car sequencing problem. Overview of state-of-the-art methods and industrial case-study of the ROADEF'2005 challenge problem. Eur. J. Oper. Res. **191**, 912–927 (2008)
15. Brucker, P., Knust, S.: Complex Scheduling. GOR-Publications, 2nd edn. Springer, Heidelberg (2012). doi:10.1007/978-3-642-23929-8
16. Verstraete, P., Valckenaers, P., Van Brussel, H., Saint Germain, B., Hadeli, K., Van Belle, J.: Towards robust and efficient planning execution. Eng. Appl. Artif. Intell. **21**, 304–314 (2008)
17. Wannagat, A., Schütz, D., Vogel-Heuser, B.: Einsatz von Softwareagenten am Beispiel einer kontinuierlichen, hydraulischen Heizpresse. In: Göhner, P. (ed.) Agentensysteme in der Automatisierungstechnik. Xpert.press, pp. 169–185. Springer, Berlin (2013). doi:10.1007/978-3-642-31768-2_10
18. Göhner, P. (ed.): Agentensysteme in der Automatisierungstechnik. Xpert.press, pp. 169–185. Springer, Berlin (2013)
19. Schwede, C., Klingebiel, K., Pauli, T., Wagenitz, A.: Simulationsgestützte Optimierung für die distributions-orientierte Auftragsreihenfolgeplanung in der Automobilindustrie. In: März, L., Krug, W., Rose, O., Weigert, G. (eds.) Simulation und Optimierung in Produktion und Logistik, pp. 151–170. Springer, Heidelberg (2011). doi:10.1007/978-3-642-14536-0_13
20. Pil, F.K., Holweg, M.: Linking product variety to order-fulfilment strategies. Interfaces **34**, 394–403 (2004)
21. Meissner, S.: Logistische Stabilität in der automobilen Variantenfließfertigung. Dissertation, Technische Universität München, Garching b. München (2009)
22. Herlyn, W.J.: PPS im Automobilbau. Produktionsprogrammplanung und -steuerung von Fahrzeugen und Aggregaten, Hanser (Fahrzeugtechnik), Munich (2012)

23. Scheffels, G.: The pearl chain logistics concept. JOT **5**(2), 18–21 (2012)
24. Boysen, N., Fliedner, M., Scholl, A.: Level-Scheduling bei Variantenfließfertigung. Klassifikation, Literaturüberblick und Modellkritik. Journal für Betriebswirtschaft **57**, 37–66 (2007)
25. Boysen, N., Zenker, M.: A decomposition approach for the car resequencing problem with selectivity banks. Comput. Oper. Res. **40**, 98–108 (2013)
26. Downing, N., Feydy, T., Stuckey, P.J.: Explaining flow-based propagation. In: Beldiceanu, N., Jussien, N., Pinson, É. (eds.) CPAIOR 2012. LNCS, vol. 7298, pp. 146–162. Springer, Heidelberg (2012). doi:10.1007/978-3-642-29828-8_10
27. Boysen, N., Scholl, A., Wopperer, N.: Resequencing of mixed-model assembly lines. Survey and research agenda. Eur. J. Oper. Res. **216**, 594–604 (2012)
28. Lüder, A., Schmidt, N., Hell, K., Röpke, H., Zawisza, J.: Description means for information artifacts throughout the life cycle of CPPS. In: Biffl, S., Lüder, A., Gerhard, D. (eds.) Multi-Disciplinary Engineering for Cyber-Physical Production Systems, pp. 169–183. Springer, Cham (2017). doi:10.1007/978-3-319-56345-9_7
29. Wooldridge, M., Jennings, N.R.: Intelligent Agents. LNCS, vol. 890. Springer, Heidelberg (1995)
30. Botti, V., Giret, A.: ANEMONA: A Multi-agent Methodology for Holonic Manufacturing Systems, 1st edn. Springer, London (2008). doi:10.1007/978-1-84800-310-1
31. Unland, R.: Software agent systems. In: Leitão, P., Karnouskos, S. (eds.) Industrial Agents: Emerging Applications of Software Agents in Industry, pp. 3–22. Elsevier, Amsterdam, Oxford, Waltham (2015)
32. Roidl, M.: Kooperation und Autonomie in selbststeuernden Systemen. In: Günthner, W., ten Hompel, M. (eds.) Internet der Dinge in der Intralogistik, pp. 65–78. Springer, Heidelberg (2010). doi:10.1007/978-3-642-04896-8_9
33. Mönch, L.: Agentenbasierte Produktionssteuerung komplexer Produktionssysteme, Deutscher Universitäts-Verlag GWV Fachverlage GmbH (Wirtschaftsinformatik), Wiesbaden (2006)
34. Bellifemine, F., Caire, G., Greenwood, D.: Developing Multi-agent Systems with JADE. Wiley Series in Agent Technology (Reprinted). Wiley, Chichester (2008)
35. Röpke, H., Lüder, A., Hell, K., Zawisza, J., Schmidt, N.: Identification of "Industrie 4.0" component hierarchy layers. In: 21st IEEE Conference on Emerging Technologies and Factory Automation (ETFA), 6–9 September 2016, pp. 1–8, Berlin. IEEE, Piscataway (2016)
36. Bussmann, S., Jennings, N.R., Wooldridge, M.: Multiagent Systems for Manufacturing Control. A Design Methodology. Springer, Heidelberg (2004). doi:10.1007/978-3-662-08872-2
37. Zawisza, J., Hell, K., Röpke, H., Lüder, A., Schmidt, N.: Generische Strukturierung von Produktionssystemen der Fertigungsindustrie. In: 17. Branchentreff der Mess- und Automatisierungstechnik - Automation 2016 - Secure & Reliable in the Digital World, VDI-Berichte 2284, 16 p., VDI-Verlag GmbH, Düsseldorf (2016)
38. Lüder, A., Calá, A., Zawisza, J., Rosendahl, R.: Design pattern for agent based production system control – a survey. Submitted to 13th IEEE Conference on Automation Science and Engineering August 20–23, Xi'an, China (2017)
39. Kütting, H., Sauer, M.J.: Elementare Stochastik. Mathematische Grundlagen und didaktische Konzepte. Springer, Berlin (2014)
40. Birolini, A.: Reliability Engineering. Theory and Practice, 7th edn. Springer, Heidelberg (2014). doi:10.1007/978-3-642-39535-2

shopST: Flexible Job-Shop Scheduling with Agent-Based Simulated Trading

Frank Yukio Nedwed[1], Ingo Zinnikus[2], Maxat Nukhayev[2],
Matthias Klusch[2(✉)], and Luca Mazzola[2]

[1] Saarland University, Saarbruecken, Germany
s9frnedw@stud.uni-saarland.de
[2] German Research Center for Artificial Intelligence (DFKI), Saarbruecken, Germany
{ingo.zinnikus,maxat.nukhayev,matthias.klusch,luca.mazzola}@dfki.de

Abstract. Paradigms in modern production are shifting and pose new demands for optimization techniques. The emergence of new, versatile, reconfigurable and networked machines enables flexible manufacturing scenarios which require, in particular, planning and scheduling methods for cyber-physical production systems to be flexible, reasonably fast, and anytime. This paper presents an approach to flexible job-shop manufacturing scheduling with agent-based simulated trading, called shopST. Aspects of real manufacturing scheduling problems form the basis for a physical decomposition of the planning system into agents. The initial schedule created by the agents in shopST through reactive negotiation is successively improved through the exchange of resource binding constraints with an additional market agent. shopST is evaluated in comparison to selected other different solution approaches to flexible job-shop scheduling.

Keywords: Agents · Simulated trading · Flexible job-shop scheduling

1 Introduction

Modern production facilities are increasingly relying on networked machines for their benefits caused by increased flexibility and the ability for self organization. In order to further enhance economic factors, scheduling methods are needed, that take advantage of these features and can cope with the rising amount of complexity. Flexible job-shop scheduling (FJSS) is an extension of the classical job-shop scheduling problem, which is NP-hard and among the hardest combinatorial optimization problems [1]. There are several different types of solution methods available, though most of them disregard some constraints in order to simplify the problem or only regard a single cost function, e.g. makespan. The combination of several criteria or additional constraints generalizes the problem and further enhances its complexity. There is a wide range of approaches for using multi-agent systems in manufacturing in general and for job-shop scheduling in particular [2,11,12,16,17,19,20,25]. In this paper, we present a novel

© Springer International Publishing AG 2017
J.O. Berndt et al. (Eds.): MATES 2017, LNAI 10413, pp. 121–137, 2017.
DOI: 10.1007/978-3-319-64798-2_8

approach, shopST, that applies agent-based distributed simulated trading [3] to solve dynamic FJSS problems. In particular, shopST complements locally optimizing reactive agent scheduling with long-term planning via simulated trading. The results of a comparative experimental evaluation revealed that shopST is competitive in highly flexible manufacturing environments with multi-purpose machines.

The remainder of the paper is structured as follows. Section 2 shortly introduces the problem of flexible job-shop scheduling, and gives an overview of the solution and its implementation. Section 3 presents the comparative performance evaluation results, while related work is briefly discussed in Sect. 4. Section 5 concludes the paper with a short summary.

2   The shopST Solution for FJSS

This section introduces the problem of flexible job-shop scheduling and the first agent-based approach that makes use of simulated trading for this purpose.[1]

2.1   Flexible Job-Shop Scheduling

The problem of flexible job-shop scheduling (FJSS), in general, is to find an optimal, valid job-shop schedule S that minimizes a cost function c (e.g. makespan) for a given configuration of jobs, operations on multi-purpose machines, and is subject to certain constraints of processing. FJSS is an extension of the classical job-shop scheduling problem. Classical job-shop scheduling solutions determine a schedule for a set of jobs on a set of machines with the objective to minimize a certain criterion subject to the constraint that each job has a specified processing order through all machines, which are fixed and known in advance. A more flexible job-shop scheduling allows, for example, one operation to be performed on one machine out of a whole set of alternative machines. In the following, the type of FJSS problems our solution approach can cope with is described in more detail.

A set $J = \{j_1, \ldots, j_n\}$ of $n \in jobs$, which corresponds to factory workpieces, needs to be processed with a set $M = \{m_1, \ldots, m_p\}$ of p machines, while every job j_i has a number of $k_i \leq p$ operations $O_i = \{o_1, \ldots, o_{k_i}\}$, which have to be performed in order for the job to be completed. Performing a job j_i on a machine m_j is denoted as an operation o_{ij}, which requires the exclusive, uninterrupted use of m_j over a time period p_{ij}, called *processing time*. It is assumed that the processing time can be deterministically deduced from the system in advance. A schedule S is a bijective assignment $(S(o_i) \rightarrow (m, f_i))$ of every operation o_i to a processing machine $m \in M_i^{op}$ and a *completion date* f_i, with completion dates f_{ij} for every operation and job j. The schedule is *valid*, if all time intervals, which are assigned to a machine are free of overlaps and precedences are met

---

[1] The source code for this project is publicly available at https://sourceforge.net/projects/shopst/.

among the other additional constraints to the system. Each possible schedule S can be evaluated by assigning a cost c to every possible state of S via a *cost function* $c(S)$. To find an *optimal*, valid schedule then requires either to compute a valid S with minimal costs c, or to take an existing schedule and continually decrease its cost.

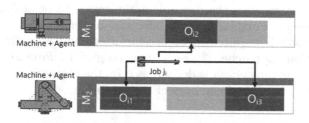

Fig. 1. Abstract example of a job-shop schedule for two machines M_1 and M_2

The following types of processing constraints are part of an extended flexible job-shop scheduling problem specification. First, any operation o_k can be performed by a number of machines M_k^{op} and it is possible that the processing time p_{ij} *varies* depending on j_i and m_j. We assume the constraint $|M_k^{op}| > 1$, which implies flexible job-shop scheduling with *multi-purpose* machines. We speak of $|M_k^{op}|$ as the factory flexibility for the remainder of this paper. Second, the schedule may also have to follow a given order of precedences for the operations to be performed. These *operation precedences* are encoded in a directed, acyclic precedence graph $G_i^{prec} = (V_i, E_i)$, where the number of vertices equals a subset of the operation set $V_i \subseteq O_i$. A directed edge $(o \rightarrow o') \in E_i$ for $o, o' \in O_i$ is part of the graph, if and only if operation o' has to be performed before operation o. In contrast to classical job-shop scheduling, the non-linear precedence constraints of the flexible version allow an arbitrary order between some processing steps of the job (e.g. drilling holes with different machines) and other precedences that are fixed (e.g. paint job only after all drilling is completed). Inflexible job-shop scheduling problems have completely linear precedence graphs. Third, possible tool changes on a multi-purpose machines may require a certain amount of time for it to prepare in between the processing of two operations. Such a *sequence-dependent setup time* s_{ikj} is the time period in which the machine cannot process any job, and which is dependent on the two operations o_{ij} and o_{kj} that shall be performed in succession. In practice, these times obey the triangle inequality $s_{ikj} + s_{kuj} \geq s_{iuj}$. Besides, jobs j_i that enter the system at a *release time* r_i cannot have their operations processed before that time, and can have a *due date* $d_i > r_i$ before which their completion is preferable, if stated in the cost function. Deadlines are mostly relevant for tardiness related cost functions like maximum lateness. We assume that already started operations o_{ij} cannot be interrupted (no preemption).

Finally, we focus on a *dynamic* version of FJSS with sequence dependent setup times and multi-purpose machines: $J\text{-}MPM|prec, r_i, d_i, sdst|c$ in the established $\alpha|\beta|\gamma$ notation for scheduling problems, whereas c denotes an arbitrary cost function [10]. The α field contains the overall class of the problem and the beta field describes additional constraints in the setup. In particular, the sets J, M and M^{op} of FJSS problems may dynamically change during optimization of the schedule, since new jobs may enter the system, and changes to the operation sequences, machine breakdowns and other unexpected events may occur at any time. That requires the dynamic optimization to be sufficiently robust against such changes. Furthermore, the information exchange between networked machines and tools is required to be decentralized, that is, unlike most state-of-the-art solution approaches [7], we assume no global information blackboard for this purpose, as the system is decomposed by the physical constraints of the machines and not the functional ones of the algorithm.

2.2 shopST System: Overview

The proposed FJSS optimization system, shopST, consists of two phases: In the first phase, agents create a valid schedule by scheduling the resource binding constraints (operations) through standard contract net protocol based interaction in a reactive manner. In the second phase, the valid schedule is improved by the long-term schedule optimization via agent-based simulated trading. These phases are executed in succession whenever an unanticipated event disrupts the validity of the planning. The first phase creates a valid solution, which is improved in the second phase.

The use of an arbitrary short term agent-based planning system in the first phase enables local optimization of the machine schedules and a heterogeneous agent system. We used a standard contract net protocol for the local short term planning in this paper, but others can be used. The factory environment can be highly dynamic because of machine breakdowns, or other events, such that the plans have to be adapted immediately in order to commence production, which requires an anytime solution. Long-term planning with simulated trading, as first introduced by Bachem et al. [3], is a method to find approximated solutions through several rounds of hypothetical trading between trading agents and a common market agent, followed by a consolidation round. In the following, we focus on the application of simulated trading and required modifications to fit the planning domain. An overview of the agent interaction is given in Fig. 2.

Agent Mapping. The trading agents are the instances in the system, which want to optimize their cost function. Thus, every machine in the system provides one trading agent. An additional non-physical market agent is existent in the network. The communication in the network is enabled via common agent technologies as described in Sect. 2.3.

Each agent is equipped with a cost function $c(m)$, $m \in M$, that on the one hand, resembles a good evaluation of the local performance of the machine. On the other hand, the summed local costs over all agents $\sum_{m \in M} c(m)$ should be a good indicator of the overall factory performance. We experimented with

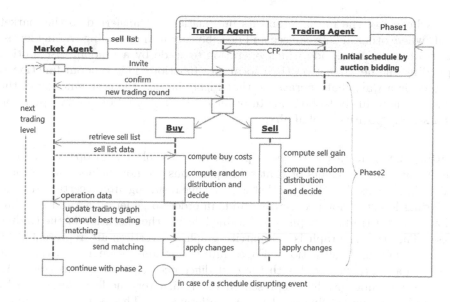

Fig. 2. Algorithm sequence and agent system structure

different possibilities for such cost functions with varying complexity. Simple cost functions like the total operation completion date (TOpC) $c(m) = \sum f_i$ for all f_i that have a pair (m, f_i) in the schedule S or the total operation lateness (TOpL) seem to work well and are computationally inexpensive. shopST also offers total operation tardiness (TOpT) and slack time (TOpSL) as cost functions.

Initialization. At the beginning of the simulated trading protocol, all participating agents are invited by the market agent to perform successive trading steps. In each such step, called a trading level, every agent chooses either to sell a resource binding constraint to the common market agent, or to buy such a constraint from it. Resource binding constraints of the trading machine agents in the planning domain are their processed operation plans. Whether to buy or sell is determined evenly randomized. The decision, whether a certain operation is traded or not, is not solely made in a greedy manner by local criteria, because in this case, agents would always sell the costliest operation at the moment and never buy because their resources are bound by this action. Because of this behavior, the trading is randomized and the used random distribution still depends on the anticipated buying cost or selling gain respectively, as follows. Because buying an operation from the market does almost always result in a deterioration of the local cost function, buying probabilities are derived from the difference of the cost difference the selling agent achieved, and the current buying cost. A trading agent can only buy an operation from the market if it can process this operation on the machine it is representing and successfully integrate it into its current schedule. If an operation is sold, it is deleted from the local schedule of the machine and its information is transferred to the market agent, where other agents can see and possibly buy it in upcoming trading levels. The trading agents decide which operation to trade by a random distribution depending on the impact on their local cost function. This random function is designed in a way, that operations, that highly impact the cost function of the agent are more likely to be sold. In order to avoid stagnation, every operation has a strictly positive probability.

Trading Graph. In the previous phase, it is possible for an operation to be bought by multiple agents or that sold operations are not included in the plan again. This means that the hypothetical schedule resulting after a certain amount of trading levels is not necessarily valid. In order to generate a valid schedule of lower cost, a trading graph is maintained during the execution of the trading phase. The trading graph is a bipartite graph, its vertices are represented by the single buy and sell actions. Edges link the actions belonging to the same operation and are weighted with the cost difference achieved by this trade. An exemplary trading graph is represented in Fig. 3. Every node is annotated by the number of the trading level it was performed in. This results in a unique identification using trading agent and trading level, as every agent trades exactly one operation per level.

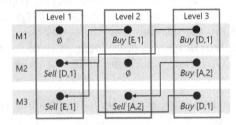

Fig. 3. Trading graph example for machine agents M1 to M3. Jobs are referred to by letters, their operations are numbered.

Trading Match. In order to get to a valid schedule again, a so called trading match has to be found. This matching is a subset of the trading graph and has to satisfy the following conditions:

- A sold operation may only be bought by exactly one agent, this property is equivalent to a matching graph.
- If a vertex of round i is part of the matching, then every vertex of the same trading agent with level smaller than i has to be part of the graph, too.
- The overall weight of the graph has to be negative, which means that if the trading actions belonging to the graph are all executed, the overall cost of the system is decreasing.

In Fig. 4, two trading matchings with three trading levels are displayed, which may result from the trading graph in Fig. 3.

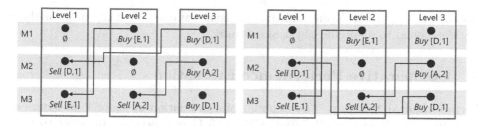

Fig. 4. Matching graphs of the trading graph in Fig. 3

Consolidation and Anytime Feature. If a trading match is found, the according trading actions are communicated to the corresponding agents. Because of the structure of the trading matching, the resulting schedule is valid and the overall costs decrease; this concludes the trading round. As each round generates another valid schedule and costs do not deteriorate after a round, the system can take new properties of the factory into account after each round. Algorithms that behave in such a way belong to the class of anytime algorithms, as they can be interrupted arbitrarily and still deliver a valid result, which is at least as good as the initial state.

Incorporated Aspects of Simulated Annealing. A main property of simulated annealing is the acceptance of system states with higher costs [18]. In order to avoid early stagnation of the shopST algorithm, we adopted aspects of simulated annealing. Several simulated trading rounds are clustered into a super round. In a single super round, the quality of the schedule may also decrease by accepting trading matchings with positive weight up to a certain limit imposed by the temperature. The temperature decreases from round to round, similarly to the original simulated annealing meta-heuristic. In order to not affect the reactivity of the system, the sizes of these super rounds have to be adapted to the frequency of disturbances of the system. For the remainder of this paper, we will refer to the number of trading rounds in a single super round as round size.

2.3   Implementation

The shopST system has been implemented in Java. For the reactive agent planning, we used standard contract net protocol based interaction between the agents. The agent framework was built according to FIPA standards [5] and uses ACL messages to communicate between agents. For the transference of information and to keep the system generic, an ontology was used, which was specifically designed for this task. The transferred information is especially relevant for the trading agents to compute whether they can handle a workpiece operation and if they do, at which cost. The search for an optimal matching graph during the consolidation phase is computationally costly and mainly contributes to the overall runtime of the algorithm. However, its costs can be transferred into the network by the market agent and thus, make use of convenient resources as they are not bound to a specific physical instance.

3   Comparative Performance Evaluation

Experimental Setting. The experimental evaluation of shopST was run on a laptop with Intel Core i5-5300U CPU@2.3 GHz processor. In order to test shopST performances, we pragmatically determine some optimal values for its main parameters first. The main metrics used for the comparison are the quality of the produced solutions and the effects the factory flexibility has on solutions. As the criterion of solution quality, the total length of the computed schedule, i.e. the makespan, has been taken. Regarding the testing of flexibility, we adopted its definition from [14], i.e. the average number of machines that can execute a given operation, and the best makespan reached as a measure for different settings of this parameter. The solution quality of shopST was compared with that of the most recent and successful FJSSP solving algorithms: HTSA [21], Zhang GA [33], AIA [4], X2010 [31], MOGA [28], P-DABC [23], X2009 [30], MOPSO [13], and HSFLA [22]. Whenever available, experimental results from the original papers were reused. The Zhang GA had to be re-implemented due to the unavailability of the original code, in order to run it on the same infrastructure and to support more detailed comparisons with shopST. Every run was repeated five times on the same instance, in order to obtain meaningful and comparable results. For the makespan analysis, the best result was adopted, in accordance with the general approach reported by the compared algorithms; for flexibility analysis, the results were averaged to overcome the non-deterministic nature of the shopST algorithm.

Three popular collections of problem instances have been used for testing, namely:

1. Kacem et al. [15]: 4 problems with total flexibility and different number of operations per job; every operation can be processed on any one of the machines. The number of machines ranges from 5 to 10, number of operations from 12 to 56.
2. Brandimarte [6]: 10 problems, which were randomly generated using a uniform distribution between two given units. The number of jobs ranges from 10 to 20, number of machines from 4 to 15, number of operations per job from 3 to 103 and number of machines per operation from 2 to 6.
3. Hurink et al. [14]: 129 test problems divided by flexibility levels into sdata, edata, rdata and vdata subsets. The number of jobs ranges from 6 to 30 and the number of machines ranges from 5 to 15.

Based on the number of operations, machines and flexibility, the problem instances from Brandimarte [6] and Hurink et al. [14] datasets were grouped as specified in Table 1. The problems were arranged by the number of machines and operations into three groups (small, average, and large). Each group was

Table 1. Selected problems grouped by size and flexibility from [6,14]

Size	Flexibility level	Problem	Operations	Machines	Flexibility
Small	Low	Mk01	55	6	3
		la05(vdata)	50	5	2.5
		la06(rdata)	75	5	2
	High	Mk02	58	6	6
Average	Low	Mk04	90	8	3
		la11(rdata)	100	5	2
		la25(rdata)	150	10	2
	High	Mk07	100	5	5
		la18(vdata)	100	10	5
		Mk03	150	8	5
Large	Low	la26(rdata)	200	10	2
		la36(rdata)	225	15	2
		la31(rdata)	300	10	2
	High	la36(vdata)	225	15	7.5
		la26(vdata)	200	10	5
		Mk09	240	10	5

split further by its flexibility level into two subgroups with low and high flexibility. The *small* size group, *high flexibility* sub-group presents only a single instance, as only one small highly flexible problem is included in the aforementioned datasets. The test problems were chosen to cover to a certain extent the full data space for every defined subgroup. It is worth to be noted that based on the very limited extension of the Kacem dataset (4 problems) and its full flexibility, the set contains only outliers with respect to the classification dimension and consequently no representative of it was selected, as for Table 1.

The solving of each problem listed in Table 1 has been tested with different values of round size, ranging from 1 to 5000. Based on the experimental results shown in Table 2, one can see that there is a direct correlation between the problem size and the round size: larger problems require larger round sizes. A comparison of flexibility levels shows that more flexible problems require more rounds to converge, which can be explained by the higher number of trade options for the agents. The result of an example run of such complex, highly flexible problems from la26(vdata) is shown in Fig. 5 in which, for readability reasons, the range of round size is divided into representative discrete values (10/100/500/1000/2500/5000).

Based on experiments, the other parameters of shopST have been chosen as five trading levels, 100 super rounds and TOpC as cost function. The initial solution for shopST has been generated by randomly assigning operations to suitable machine agents.

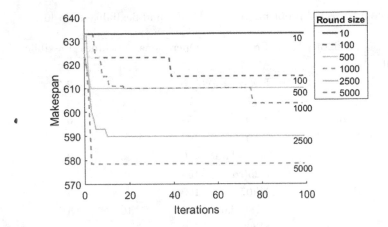

Fig. 5. Makespan convergence of la26(vdata) problem with different round sizes

Table 2. Optimal round size by size and flexibility

Size	Flexibility level	Optimal round size
Small	Low	100
	High	100–500
Average	Low	1000–2500
	High	2000–5000
Large	Low	2500–5000
	High	5000

Solution Quality. The solution qualities produced by all tested algorithms including shopST for different datasets are shown in Tables 3 and 4. As a result, shopST produces a solution quality that is comparable to that of the selected representative state-of-art solution algorithms although it has not found the best solutions most of the time. The last rows of these tables show the relative deviation with respect to shopST. The relative deviation for each problem instance is defined as

$$dev = [(MK_{comp} - MK_{shopST})/MK_{shopST}] * 100\%$$

where MK_{shopST} is the makespan obtained by shopST and MK_{comp} is the average makespan of all the other algorithms shopST is compared to. As a result, shopST underperformed by an average of 13.5% (ranging from 0% to about 25%). Zhang GA [33] found 8 out of 10 best solutions and for this reason was chosen for a more detailed comparison with shopST. Please keep in mind that the notion of iteration differs for shopST and Zhang GA [33]: While in Zhang GA one iteration is one evolution of the population and takes around 60 ms in shopST one iteration corresponds to one super round of simulated trading, which can run from several seconds to several minutes depending on the round size.

Table 3. Makespan results for Kacem et al. [15] data, best solutions in bold

Algorithms	Instance 1	Instance 2	Instance 3
shopST	12	**7**	13
Zhang [33]	**11**	**7**	**11**
HTSA [21]	**11**	**7**	**11**
AIA [4]	-	**7**	**11**
Xing [31]	12	**7**	**11**
MOGA [28]	**11**	**7**	**11**
P-DABC [23]	**11**	**7**	**11**
MOPSO [13]	**11**	**7**	**11**
dev(%)	−6.9	0.0	−15.4

Table 4. Makespan results for Brandimarte [6] data, best solutions in bold

Algorithms	MK01	MK02	MK03	MK04	MK05	MK06	MK07	MK08	MK09	MK10
shopST	47	34	229	84	196	80	164	558	342	267
Zhang [33]	**40**	**26**	**204**	**60**	173	**58**	144	**523**	**307**	**198**
Xing [30]	42	28	**204**	68	177	75	150	**523**	311	227
MOGA [28]	**40**	**26**	**204**	66	173	62	**139**	**523**	311	214
HTSA [21]	**40**	**26**	**204**	61	**172**	65	140	**523**	310	214
HSFLA [22]	**40**	**26**	**204**	62	173	64	141	**523**	311	215
AIA [4]	**40**	**26**	**204**	**60**	173	63	140	**523**	312	214
MOPSO [13]	**40**	**26**	**204**	61	173	62	**139**	**523**	310	214
dev(%)	−14.3	−22.7	−10.9	−25.5	−11.5	−19.8	−13.5	−6.3	−9.3	−20.0

Execution Time. In order to compare the runtimes of shopST and Zhang GA, both algorithms have been executed with optimal parameters on the la40(vdata) problem instance. The experiment was run 10 times for each algorithm, and the best results were selected. The results, as shown in Fig. 6 for shopST and in Fig. 7 for Zhang GA, reveal that the execution time of shopST is three orders of magnitude larger than that of Zhang GA and appears to be connected with the high round size requirement for reaching an optimal solution by shopST.

Flexibility. For the second evaluation metric, the effects of problem flexibility on solution quality were addressed in the following experiment: shopST and Zhang GA were executed on problems with different degrees of flexibility. In order to simulate different levels of flexibility, an original non-flexible problem la40(sdata) from Hurink dataset was modified by the application of a new parameter P, representing the probability that a particular machine can execute a particular operation. This is to simulate flexible manufacturing environments with multi-purpose machines. The results shown in Fig. 8 reveal that shopST

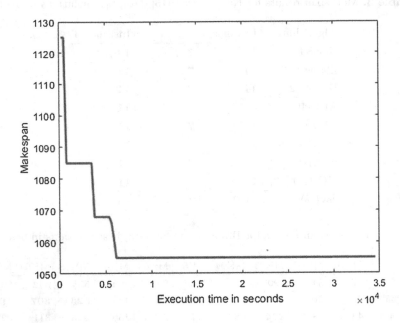

Fig. 6. Execution time of shopST

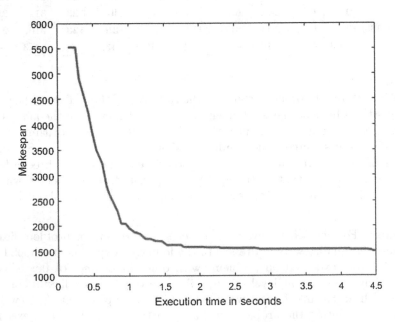

Fig. 7. Execution time of Zhang et al. [33]

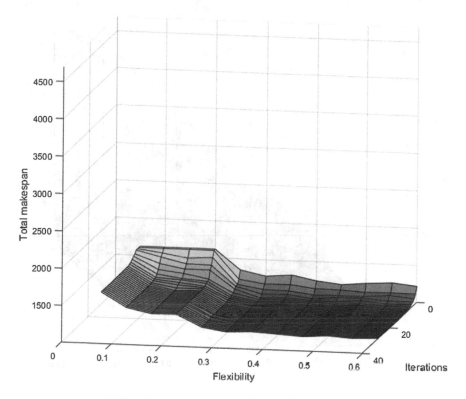

Fig. 8. Results of flexibility test on shopST

significantly improves its solution quality for more flexible problems, and outperforms Zhang GA in this regard. In particular, Zhang GA shows a decrease in its performance with increasingly flexible problems, as depicted in Fig. 9. Allowing more machines to execute particular operations results in an increase in the problem search space, that increases the probability for Zhang GA to be stuck in a local minimum, hindering its capability of converging to a globally optimal value. ShopST, on the other hand, works solely on flexible problems, because exchanges between agents are only enabled if multiple machines can exchange operations. As a consequence, a more flexible problem enables a larger number of exchange points and therefore the performance of shopST greatly improves with a greater flexibility of the multi-purpose machines.

One main strength of shopST is that it excels in solving highly flexible JJS problems with agent-based simulated trading. Besides, it natively adapts online to dynamic events that affect the problem that is currently being solved without the need of a full restart. These advantages, however, come at the cost of a comparatively higher execution time. Overall, shopST can be considered as a valuable solution for job-shop scheduling in highly flexible and dynamic cyber-physical production systems and environments, if there are no hard time constraints for solution availability.

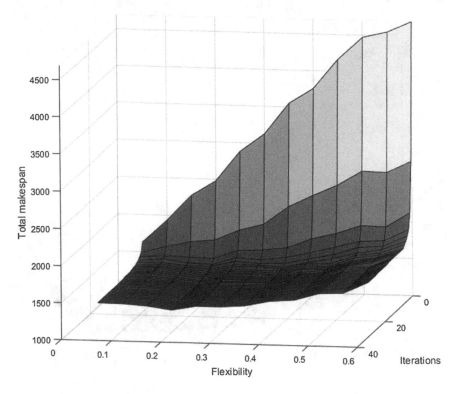

Fig. 9. Results of flexibility test on Zhang GA [33]

4   Related Work

For the comparative performance evaluation of shopST, we selected different types of state-of-the-art FJSS problem solving approaches including multi-agent system based ones. The solutions qualities of shopST are close to those of these approaches, which utilize genetic algorithm, artificial immune, knowledge-based ant colony optimization, Pareto-based discrete artificial bee colony, modified discrete particle swarm optimization, shuffled frog-leaping, hybrid tabu search. Of course, there are many other agent-based approaches for dynamic and distributed job-shop scheduling in manufacturing [2,11,12,17,19,20,29,32]. For example, [29] presents an actor-based approach to job-shop scheduling using Lagrangian relaxation which may adapt its schedule after dynamic events quickly but no values are given for comparison. BnB-ADOPT [32] is a memory-bounded asynchronous distributed constraint optimization problem solver that uses the agent framework of ADOPT. It performs exceptionally well in regard to runtime and solution quality but, in contrast to shopST, the dynamic constrained optimization problem description has to be explicitly encoded for every agent in prior. However, to the best of our knowledge, shopST is the first agent-based approach with simulated trading used to solve the class of FJSS problems defined above.

From the results of the comparative experimental testing of flexibility it became evident that shopST has its general strength in highly flexible manufacturing environments with multi-purpose machines.

Scheduling approaches can be characterized as constructing a schedule vs. optimizing a given schedule. In the first case an (ideally) exact solution for a given problem is generated (cf. [24] for a thorough overview of classical approaches). Optimization approaches improve an already existing schedule with respect to a cost function and are in general based on heuristics or meta-heuristic procedures and generate solutions iteratively, at the expense of non-optimal schedules [27]. A related field is online scheduling [26], where information about the problem domain is restricted (e.g. incoming jobs are only known when they arrive and processing times only after a job is completed). shopST addresses the problem of the optimization and repair of schedules in flexible and dynamic manufacturing environments with multi-purpose machines. Closely related approaches are based on (meta-)heuristics, since standard algorithms assume complete knowledge about the problem domain which usually implies a restart of the algorithm after a change of the problem domain. In recent years, a number of job-shop scheduling approaches based on meta-heuristics have been proposed for this purpose. [6,14] used tabu search for solving the FJSS problem, while [8] combine approaches using tabu search with simulated annealing. Several approaches for the JSS and FJSS based on evolutionary algorithms have also been developed (for a survey see e.g. [9]). Genetic algorithms such as those developed by Zhang et al. [33] or Xing et al. [30], for example, are an efficient way for schedule optimization. However, they have two major drawbacks: The first is that their information structure is functional and does not take advantage of an underlying agent encapsulation. The other is that they lose performance and solution quality in more flexible factory layouts, a use case which gets more and more common.

5   Conclusions

We presented a novel approach, shopST, that applies agent-based simulated trading to solve dynamic FJSS problems. shopST complements locally optimizing reactive agent scheduling with long-term optimization of the valid schedule via simulated trading. The results of a comparative experimental evaluation revealed that shopST is particularly competitive in highly flexible manufacturing environments with multi-purpose machines. Future work includes further investigation of robustness against disruptive events and performance trade-offs compared to other negotiation-based approaches when applicable to the same problem.

Acknowledgements. The work described in this paper was partially funded by the German Federal Ministry of Education and Research (BMBF) in the project INVERSIV and the European Commission in the project CREMA.

References

1. Adams, J., Balas, E., Zawack, D.: The shifting bottleneck procedure for job shop scheduling. Manag. Sci. **34**(3), 391–401 (1988)
2. Aydin, M.E., Oeztemel, E.: Dynamic job-shop scheduling using reinforcement learning agents. Robot. Auton. Syst. **33**(2), 169–178 (2000)
3. Bachem, A., Hochstättler, W., Malich, M.: The simulated trading heuristic for solving vehicle routing problems. Discret. Appl. Math. **65**(1–3), 47–72 (1996)
4. Bagheri, A., et al.: An artificial immune algorithm for the flexible job-shop scheduling problem. Future Gener. Comput. Syst. **26**(4), 533–541 (2010)
5. Bellifemine, F., Poggi, A., Rimassa, G.: JADE-A FIPA-compliant agent framework. In: Proceedings of PAAM, vol. 99, London (1999)
6. Brandimarte, P.: Routing and scheduling in a flexible job shop by tabu search. Ann. Oper. Res. **41**(3), 157–183 (1993)
7. Cohen, P.R., Cheyer, A., Wang, M., Baeg, S.C.: An open agent architecture. In: AAAI Spring Symposium, vol. 1 (1994)
8. Fattahi, P., Mehrabad, M.S., Jolai, F.: Mathematical modeling and heuristic approaches to flexible job shop scheduling problems. Intell. Manuf. **18**(3), 331–342 (2007)
9. Gen, M., Lin, L.: Multiobjective evolutionary algorithm for manufacturing scheduling problems: state-of-the-art survey. Intell. Manuf. **25**(5), 849–866 (2014)
10. Graham, R.L., et al.: Optimization and approximation in deterministic sequencing and scheduling: a survey. Ann. discret. Math. **5**, 287–326 (1979)
11. Nouri, H.E., Driss, O.B., Ghédira, K.: A classification schema for the job shop scheduling problem with transportation resources: state-of-the-art review. In: Silhavy, R., Senkerik, R., Oplatkova, Z.K., Silhavy, P., Prokopova, Z. (eds.) Artificial Intelligence Perspectives in Intelligent Systems. AISC, vol. 464, pp. 1–11. Springer, Cham (2016). doi:10.1007/978-3-319-33625-1_1
12. Hsu, C.Y., Kao, B.R., Lai, K.R.: Agent-based fuzzy constraint-directed negotiation mechanism for distributed job shop scheduling. Eng. Appl. Artif. Intell. **53**, 140–154 (2016)
13. Huang, S., et al.: Multi-objective flexible job-shop scheduling problem using modified discrete particle swarm optimization. SpringerPlus **5**(1), 1432 (2016)
14. Hurink, J., Jurisch, B., Thole, M.: Tabu search for the job-shop scheduling problem with multi-purpose machines. Oper. Res. Spektrum **15**(4), 205–215 (1994)
15. Kacem, I., Hammadi, S., Borne, P.: Pareto-optimality approach for flexible job-shop scheduling problems: hybridization of evolutionary algorithms and fuzzy logic. Math. Comput. Simul. **60**(3), 245–276 (2002)
16. Kapahnke, P., Liedtke, P., Nesbigall, S., Warwas, S., Klusch, M.: ISReal: an open platform for semantic-based 3D simulations in the 3D internet. In: Patel-Schneider, P.F., Pan, Y., Hitzler, P., Mika, P., Zhang, L., Pan, J.Z., Horrocks, I., Glimm, B. (eds.) ISWC 2010. LNCS, vol. 6497, pp. 161–176. Springer, Heidelberg (2010). doi:10.1007/978-3-642-17749-1_11
17. Karageorgos, A., Mehandjiev, N., Weichhart, G., Hämmerle, A.: Agent-based optimisation of logistics and production planning. Eng. Appl. Artif. Intell. **16**(4), 335–348 (2003)
18. Kirkpatrick, S., et al.: Optimization by simulated annealing. Science **220**(4598), 671–680 (1983)
19. Leitao, P.: Agent-based distributed manufacturing control: a state-of-the-art survey. Eng. Appl. Artif. Intell. **22**, 979–991 (2009)

20. Leitao, P., et al.: Smart agents in industrial cyber-physical systems. Proc. IEEE **104**(5), 1086–1101 (2016)
21. Li, J., Pan, Q., Liang, Y.C.: An effective hybrid tabu search algorithm for multi-objective flexible job-shop scheduling problems. Comput. Ind. Eng. **59**(4), 647–662 (2010)
22. Li, J., Pan, Q., Xie, S.: An effective shuffled frog-leaping algorithm for multi-objective flexible job shop scheduling problems. Appl. Math. Comput. **218**(18), 9353–9371 (2012)
23. Li, J.Q., Pan, Q., Gao, K.Z.: Pareto-based discrete artificial bee colony algorithm for multi-objective flexible job shop scheduling problems. Adv. Manuf. Technol. **55**(9), 1159–1169 (2011)
24. Pinedo, M.: Scheduling. Theory, Algorithms, and Systems. Springer, Cham (2016)
25. Pooja, D., Joshi, S.: Auction-based distributed scheduling in a dynamic job shop environment. Prod. Res. **40**(5), 1173–1191 (2002)
26. Pruhs, K., Sgall, J., Torng, E.: Online scheduling. In: Handbook of Scheduling Algorithms, Models, and Performance Analysis. Chapman and Hall/CRC (2004)
27. Rossi, A., Dini, G.: Flexible job-shop scheduling with routing flexibility and separable setup times using ant colony optimisation method. Robot. Comput.-Integr. Manuf. **23**(5), 503–516 (2007)
28. Wang, X., et al.: A multi-objective genetic algorithm based on immune and entropy principle for flexible job-shop scheduling problem. Adv. Manuf. Technol. **51**(5), 757–767 (2010)
29. Weichhart, G., Hämmerle, A.: Multi-actor architecture for schedule optimisation based on lagrangian relaxation. In: Klusch, M., Unland, R., Shehory, O., Pokahr, A., Ahrndt, S. (eds.) MATES 2016. LNCS, vol. 9872, pp. 190–197. Springer, Cham (2016). doi:10.1007/978-3-319-45889-2_14
30. Xing, L.N., Chen, Y.W., Yang, K.W.: An efficient search method for multi-objective flexible job shop scheduling problems. J. Intell. Manuf. **20**(3), 283–293 (2009)
31. Xing, L.N., et al.: A knowledge-based ant colony optimization for flexible job shop scheduling problems. Appl. Soft Comput. **10**(3), 888–896 (2010)
32. Yeoh, W., Felner, A., Koenig, S.: BnB-ADOPT: an asynchronous branch-and-bound DCOP algorithm. In: Proceedings of the 7th International Joint Conference on Autonomous Agents and Multiagent Systems, vol. 2. IFMAS (2008)
33. Zhang, G., Gao, L., Shi, Y.: An effective genetic algorithm for the flexible job-shop scheduling problem. Expert Syst. Appl. **38**(4), 3563–3573 (2011)

Lagrangian Relaxation Realised in the NgMPPS Multi Actor Architecture

Georg Weichhart[1,2](✉) and Alexander Hämmerle[1]

[1] Distributed Information Systems, Profactor GmbH, Steyr, Austria
[2] Department of Communications Engineering - Business Informatics,
Johannes Kepler University, Linz, Austria
{Georg.Weichhart,Alexander.Haemmerle}@Profactor.at

Abstract. In the research project NgMPPS – DPC (*Next-Generation Multi-Purpose Production Systems - Distributed Production Control*) a distributed, actor-based system has been realised, that uses Lagrangian Relaxation for optimising *Flexible Job Shop Scheduling with Transport Times* (FJSSTT) problems. The design of the architecture builds on the actor model. This design allows to combine operations research with distributed computing and is driven by the mathematical formulation of the Lagrange Relaxation approach. Runtime experiments with the initial implementation of the architecture have been done. The performance of the multi actor-based implementation is compared to other approaches finding solutions to the $\mathcal{NP}$-hard FJSSTT problem.

Keywords: Lagrangian relaxation · Actor system · Schedule optimisation

1 Introduction

Future Enterprise Systems will be S^3 Enterprises (Sensing, Smart and Sustainable Enterprise) [42]. These systems form complex adaptive socio-technical systems, where machines, workers are networked and through the sensing capabilities are able to identify changing environmental conditions. The (assumed) built-in smartness supports swift adaptation to changing (customer) demands. The interconnection of the systems parts make the S^3 Enterprise System a Complex Adaptive System. However, business performance is not only measured in terms of adaptability or resilience but also using traditional performance criteria of production time and manufacturing costs. This networked system is in the need of an approach that supports maintaining high quality processes and optimal production schedules while still be able to adapt to disturbances.

In the *Next-Generation Multi-Purpose Production Systems - Distributed Production Control* (NgMPPS - DPC) project algorithms are developed for distributed optimisation of manufacturing schedules in production networks. A focal point is dynamic rescheduling, where disruptions such as machine failures or transport delays impede the execution of planned schedules, and adapted schedules have to be calculated in real time.

© Springer International Publishing AG 2017
J.O. Berndt et al. (Eds.): MATES 2017, LNAI 10413, pp. 138–155, 2017.
DOI: 10.1007/978-3-319-64798-2_9

The presented distributed schedule optimisation approach builds on a formal mechanism called Lagrangian Relaxation which may be interpreted as a market price mechanism for optimisation. That mechanism is implemented using a distributed architecture. The NgMPPS - DPC actor-based architecture design was introduced earlier [41]. In this paper we go into details with respect to the underlying mathematical formulation, the detailed design and report on the implementation of the system and its runtime behaviour and computational results. The scheduling performance of the system is compared to other approaches using published, open problems sets and solution data. The above mentioned re-scheduling mechanism is currently under development and will be presented in the future.

This discussion is organised in the following way. Section 2 introduces the algorithmic approach en détail. It is followed by a presentation of the software design, including the rationales for using an actor based architecture. With respect to runtime behaviour we compare the quality of results and performance with other systems and report on solutions found to the *Flexible Job Shop Scheduling with Transport Times* (FJSSTT) problem.

2   Lagrange Relaxation

In this section, first the problem and then the mathematical formulation of the solution are presented. As mentioned above, focus here is on the currently implemented formulation of the static problem. This formulation (and its implementation) is the basis for later work that will enhance it for dynamic re-scheduling.

2.1   Schedule Optimisation

The overall optimisation scenario targeted by this architecture is one of distributed manufacturing facilities engaged in the production of goods. Each order for a good, called job (a), needs different machines, where (b) each of the operations necessary to realise a job may be done on one or more machines. Between facilities (and hence between machines) transport times exist (c), and finally the distribution of all job-operations to machine should be optimal with respect to being on time.

The optimisation problem is to be solved, respecting the following constraints.

- Processing time constraints: Every operation requires a deterministic, machine-dependent process time.
- Precedence constraints of job operations: Simple, chain-like precedence relations between operations belonging to the same job are modelled.
- Machine capacity constraints: At every time slot only one operation may be processed on a single machine.
- Operations have to be processed non-pre-emptively: Once an operation is started it may not be interrupted.

The above scenario is called Flexible Job Shop Scheduling with travel times between machines (FJSSTT). This optimisation problem is a computational problem which is a complex combinatorial problem, more specifically a non-deterministic polynomial-time hard ($\mathcal{NP}$-hard) problem. This implies, that even for a small number of jobs and machines the determination of the optimal schedule becomes practically infeasible [20, 24].

2.2   Formal Model

In the following a mathematical formulation for the FJSSTT problem with min-imisation of total weighted tardiness, as objective function, is described. An integer program for the FJSSTT problem is developed, and Lagrangian relaxation is applied by relaxing machine capacity constraints. The resulting Lagrangian problem is decomposed into independent job-level sub-problems.

Problem Formulation. This formulation is based on an integer programming formulation by Wang et al. [37]. I jobs with individual due dates are scheduled on M available machines, where jobs are immediately available. The set of jobs $\mathcal{I}$ is $\{0, 1, ..., I-1\}$ and each job i consists of a set of J_i non-preemptive operations ($\mathcal{J}_i = \{0, 1, ..., J_i - 1\}$), where operation j of job i is denoted as (i, j).

We regard simple, chain-like precedence constraints amongst operations belonging to the same job. The set of machines $\mathcal{M}$ is $\{0, 1, ..., M-1\}$. The set of alternative machines for operation (i, j) is denoted as $\mathcal{H}_{ij}$, with machine-specific processing times.

The scheduling horizon consists of K discrete time slots, the set of time slots $\mathcal{K}$ is $\{0, 1, ..., K-1\}$. The beginning time of an operation is defined as the beginning of the corresponding time slot, and the completion time as the end of the time slot.

The following parameters are defined for a specific problem instance. Decision variables span the solution space for the scheduling problem.

Parameters

$D_i, i \in \mathcal{I}$: Job due dates.
$P_{ijm}, i \in \mathcal{I}, j \in \mathcal{J}_i, m \in \mathcal{H}_{ij}$: Processing time of operation (i, j) on machine m.
$R_{mn}, m \in \mathcal{M}, n \in \mathcal{M}$: Travel time from machine m to machine n.
$W_i, i \in \mathcal{I}$: Job tardiness weight.

Variables

$\delta_{ijmk}, i \in \mathcal{I}, j \in \mathcal{J}_i, m \in \mathcal{M}, k \in \mathcal{K}$: The binary variable δ_{ijmk} is 1, if operation (i, j) is processed on machine m at time slot k, and 0 otherwise.
$b_{ij}, i \in \mathcal{I}, j \in \mathcal{J}_i$: Beginning time of operation (i, j).
$c_{ij}, i \in \mathcal{I}, j \in \mathcal{J}_i$: Completion time of operation (i, j).
$m_{ij} \in \mathcal{H}_{ij}, i \in \mathcal{I}, j \in \mathcal{J}_i$: The machine assigned to operation (i, j).

The decision variables δ_{ijmk}, b_{ij} and c_{ij} are not independent, the following relation holds:

$$\delta_{ijmk} = \begin{cases} 1 & \text{if } b_{ij} \leq k \leq c_{ij} \\ 0 & \text{otherwise.} \end{cases} \tag{1}$$

The optimisation objective is the minimisation of the weighted sum of job tardiness, the optimisation problem is then

$$\mathcal{Z} = \min_{b_{ij}, m_{ij}} \sum_{i \in \mathcal{I}} W_i T_i, \tag{2}$$

with

$$T_i = max(0, C_i - D_i), \tag{3}$$

where C_i is the completion time for job i, i.e. $C_i = c_{i, J_i - 1}$.

Constraints. Equation (2) has to be solved subject to a number of constraints. The machine capacity constraints are expressed as

$$\sum_{i \in \mathcal{I}} \sum_{j \in \mathcal{J}_i} \delta_{ijmk} \leq 1, \forall m \in \mathcal{M}, \forall k \in \mathcal{K}. \tag{4}$$

Equation (4) states that at each time slot a machine cannot process more than one operation. Processing time constraints define the relation between beginning time and completion time of operations:

$$c_{ij} = b_{ij} + P_{ijm} - 1, \forall i \in \mathcal{I}, \forall j \in \mathcal{J}_i, \forall m \in \mathcal{H}_{ij}. \tag{5}$$

The precedence constraints between job operations are

$$b_{ij} \geq c_{i,j-1} + 1 + R_{m_{i,j-1} m_{ij}}, \forall i \in \mathcal{T}, \forall j \in \mathcal{J}_i. \tag{6}$$

The term "1" in (5) and (6) occurs due to the definition of operation beginning time and completion time, respectively. The precedence constraints consider travel times R_{mn} between machines. For operations $(i, j - 1)$ and (i, j) Eq. (6) states that the beginning time of (i, j) cannot be earlier than the arrival time at machine m_{ij}. We assume immediate availability of transport resources to move workpieces corresponding to jobs between machines. In a production network, the travel time between machines located in different job shops covers transport between the shops as well as shop-internal logistics activities.

The occurrence of the term $R_{m_{i,j-1} m_{ij}}$ in (6) renders the constraint non-linear. This non-linearity can easily be resolved, in fact the mathematical model can be formulated as a linear integer program, which is outside the scope of this paper.

Lagrangian Relaxation. With respect to the problem solving approach, *Lagrangian relaxation* (LR) is used. In this approach hard problems are divided into multiple, much easier to solve, problems, by inclusion of constraints in the objective function. The objective function of the original problem is formulated with the relaxed constraints multiplied with a Lagrange multiplier.

These multipliers are often interpreted as shadow prices of the corresponding constraints. The values indicate how much it costs to violate a constraint. In addition to this, using this interpretation allows to think about a distributed architecture that implements the mathematical formulation.

The relaxed problem is *easier* to solve than the original problem. An optimal solution to the *relaxed* problem provides a lower bound (for minimisation problems) on the optimal objective value of the original problem. However, the simplification comes with a price: in addition to the original set of decision variables we have to determine the values for the Lagrange multipliers. The multiplier values are determined by solving the Lagrangian dual problem, with Lagrange multipliers being the dual variables. Due to the relaxation of constraints, solutions to the dual problem are generally infeasible with respect to the original problem. Hence only a lower bound is found and a feasibility repair mechanism has to be applied.

In flexible job shop scheduling, there are two possible constraint relaxation approaches: job-operation precedence constraint relaxation and machine capacity constraint relaxation. The relaxation of precedence constraints and decomposition into independent machine-level subproblems is hampered by the structure of the precedence constraints (6), as the term $R_{m_{i,j-1}m_{ij}}$ couples the precedence constraints across machines. The relaxation of machine capacity constraints (4) in $\mathcal{Z}$ results in the following relaxed problem.

$$\mathcal{Z}_D(\lambda) = \min_{b_{ij},m_{ij}} \sum_{i \in \mathcal{I}} W_i T_i + \sum_{m \in \mathcal{M}} \sum_{k \in \mathcal{K}} \lambda_{mk} \left[\sum_{i \in \mathcal{I}} \sum_{j \in \mathcal{J}_i} \delta_{ijmk} - 1 \right], \qquad (7)$$

where λ is the vector of Lagrange multipliers.

$\lambda_{mk}, m \in \mathcal{M}, k \in \mathcal{K}$: Lagrange multiplier for time slot k on machine m.

A solution to (7) has to be found, constraint by (5) and (6). For a given pair of indices m, k the term in brackets is positive if the capacity constraint for time slot k on machine m is violated. $\mathcal{Z}_D(\lambda)$ can be reformulated as

$$\mathcal{Z}_D(\lambda) = \min_{b_{ij},m_{ij}} \sum_{i \in \mathcal{I}} W_i T_i + \sum_{i,j} \sum_{k=b_{ij}}^{c_{ij}} \lambda_{m_{ij}k} - \sum_{m,k} \lambda_{mk}. \qquad (8)$$

The structure of $\mathcal{Z}_D(\lambda)$ allows the decomposition into independent job-level subproblems

$$\mathcal{S}_i = \min_{b_{ij},m_{ij}} W_i T_i + \sum_{j \in \mathcal{J}_i} \sum_{k=b_{ij}}^{c_{ij}} \lambda_{m_{ij}k}. \qquad (9)$$

$\mathcal{S}_i$ is a one job scheduling problem and can be characterised as follows, cf. [8]. A job requires the completion of a set of operations, and each operation can be performed on one of several alternative machines. The job operations must satisfy a set of chain-like, non-linear precedence constraints (6), considering travel times between machines. Furthermore processing time constraints (5) have to be satisfied. Each machine has a marginal cost for utilisation at each time slot within the scheduling horizon under consideration. The scheduling problem is to determine the machine and the completion time of each operation of the job to minimise the sum of job tardiness and the total cost of using the machines to complete the job, where the cost of using machine m at time k is given as λ_{mk}.

The one job scheduling problem with standard precedence constraints is not $\mathcal{NP}$-hard, and it can be efficiently solved with dynamic programming, cf. [6,8,21,37].

With the introduction of subproblems $\mathcal{S}_i$, the relaxed problem can be reformulated,

$$\mathcal{Z}_D(\lambda) = \sum_{i \in \mathcal{I}} \mathcal{S}_i - \sum_{m,k} \lambda_{mk}. \tag{10}$$

The Lagrangian dual problem, optimising the Lagrange multiplier values, is

$$\mathcal{Z}_D = \max_{\lambda} \mathcal{Z}_D(\lambda). \tag{11}$$

In [12] it is shown that $\mathcal{Z}_D(\lambda)$ is concave and piece-wise linear, thus hill-climbing methods like subgradient search can be applied to solve the dual problem.

This formal model, requires an architecture that supports the advantage of solving subproblems concurrently.

3 Actor-Based Design

In this section we discuss possible architectural approaches that have been considered for implementation. The chosen design paradigm needs to be capable to allow a straight forward mapping from the formal Lagrange Relaxation to the system's computational units.

For the NgMPPS design the Multi-Agent Systems, Holonic and Multi Actor System approach have been analysed for their suitability to implement the formal model.

All three general approaches are discussed in the following for their suitability to implement the formal model.

3.1 Decentralised Systems

Multi-agent-systems (MAS) have been applied in a number of application areas within the domain of manufacturing with respect to adaptability and optimisation under disturbances.

MAS can be used for planning and control of complex adaptive systems such as factories [38]. MAS technologies allow to realize Complex Adaptive Systems (CASs) [18].

Multi Agent Systems are systems composed out of autonomous (sub-)systems called agents [43]. *Agents* are capable of sensing their environment. Agents have a name, address, provide a function or service, are autonomous, smart, learn and are able to interact, communicate with other agents and their environment enlarge [17].

In a *multi agent system* there are infrastructure services provided through the environment. Multi agent system services support agents in their doing, being. One well known service is the Directory Facilitator [11] which has a well-known address, and which may be queried about agents providing a certain service. Hence, the identity and address of an agent may be discovered at runtime. This particular functionality increases the adaptability of the overall system. It is possible to replace agents with agents having the same capabilities.

A similar approach to MAS are multi-actor systems, where actors are more lightweight and are attributed less intelligence, when compared to agents. In contrast to agents, do actors posses a lower level of intelligence, less knowledge processing capabilities. Actors are seen to be more reactive where agents are seen to be pro-active [19].

The term *Actor* as a model for decentralised problem-solving was first coined by Hewitt [15] and a detailed architecture was developed by Agha [1]. An actor system is composed of independent actors that coordinate through message passing. Actors have a message-inbox and a set of behaviours where the active behaviour determines the reaction to a message. An actor is autonomous and may send messages to other known actors (identity and address of the receiver is to be known), create new actors and determine its own subsequent behaviour [19]. A typical actor system is hierarchically organised with parent - child relationships.

Within the intelligent manufacturing systems domain, also the holonic approach is of importance [29]. A *holonic system* is composed out of systems called holons. The word holon is composed from the Greek word *hólos*, meaning the entire whole, and the suffix *on*, indicating that it is a part or a particle. The concept holon signifies that this system is a closed whole and a part of something bigger at the same time [22]. In a holonic system, a holon is an autonomous self-governing sub-system, integrating other (sub-)holons. The other way around, a group of holons form a (super-)holon. This nested structure of holons composed out of holons forms a so called holarchy. However, control is not imposed from the top to the bottom but the "lower" holons are the source of resources and power for the higher (super-)holons.

The holonic view places emphasis on the dynamics, and holons may be created dynamically according to the requirements. For example business networks can be seen as a temporarily existing holon where enterprises are holons within the network-holon. Each enterprise itself consist of departmental holons, and so on.

The communication-based interaction of the above briefly discussed autonomously acting systems (agents, actors, holons) facilitates adaptability. Each unit is independent and through the message passing, communication interface coupled with other units. However, neither the dynamic behaviour of the individual units nor the message exchange protocol is pre-determined. Adaptability is observed on both levels, the overall systems level and the agent level. This leads to complexity and emergent behaviour and to an overall complex adaptive system [18]. Loose coupling through messages allows emergent behaviour on the overall systems level, where here behaviour cannot be predicted as it is not directly understood by observing the individual units' behaviour. These properties are of importance when adaptation of the overall system is needed.

Also a mix of the above paradigms is possible. Due to their flexibility and adaptivity, multi agent systems have been organised using holonic principles. The terms holonic agent and holonic agent system refer to agent systems organised according to the holonic paradigm [24].

The important aspect of the architectural design is that the active units have to fit the Lagrange Relaxation model. Overall the system's algorithm has a particular structure where subproblems are solved concurrently, but after each round of subproblem solving the partial solutions need to be combined.

The structural nature of the problem solving algorithm is hierarchical, but the encapsulation in holons is not straight forward, as the same machines are assigned to multiple jobs. That lead to the conclusion that a multi actor system is conceptually the closest to the algorithmic formulation.

3.2 Detail Design

We have chosen akka [27] as actor system for the implementation of the above architecture. That has influence with respect to the structural organisation of the actor system:

> "Akka implements a specific form called "parental supervision". Actors can only be created by other actors—where the top-level actor is provided by the library—and each created actor is supervised by its parent. This restriction makes the formation of actor supervision hierarchies implicit and encourages sound design decisions. It should be noted that this also guarantees that actors cannot be orphaned or attached to supervisors from the outside, which might otherwise catch them unawares. In addition, this yields a natural and clean shutdown procedure for (sub-trees of) actor applications." [27][1]

Figure 1 shows the actors, their parent-child relationships and Fig. 2 the messages used for coordination.

There is a single root actor (Fig. 1) started by the user. It starts the resource manager actor who is responsible for starting resource actors, representing machines and transporters. The resource actors are configured with process times

---

[1] http://doc.akka.io/docs/akka/current/general/supervision.html

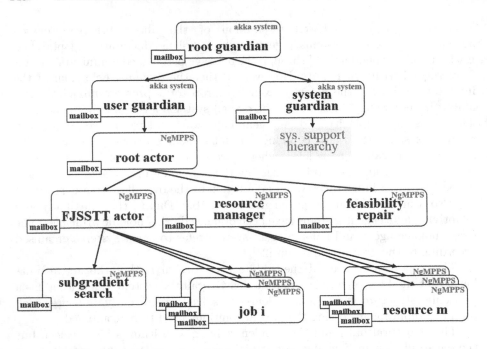

Fig. 1. NGMPPS actor architecture

for particular job operations and travel times between machines. The root agent also starts the feasibility repair actor, being responsible for repairing the infeasible schedules resulting from solving the dual problem $\mathcal{Z}_D$. For each FJSSTT problem to be solved, a corresponding FJSSTT actor is started. This hierarchy allows to distribute know-how about different aspects to different branches of the structure.

From an abstract behavioural point of view, an overview is given in Fig. 2. This diagram shows how the individual actors interact to solve the overall problem. This interaction diagram hence shows how the above described mathematical formulation is distributed among a of actors. The used subgradient search method is an adaptation of the gradient method [4,12]. Due to the usage of subgradients, the method is applicable to nondifferentiable functions, like the Lagrangian dual function $\mathcal{Z}_D(\lambda)$ in Eq. (7). For the current version, we have implemented two flavours of this subgradient search in the architecture: a standard subgradient search method requiring $\mathcal{Z}_D(\lambda)$ to be fully optimised, and additionally a surrogate subgradient method which allows that $\mathcal{Z}_D(\lambda)$ is only solved approximately.

Initial interactions of the actors shown in Fig. 2 concern the creation of the above described actor hierarchy (Fig. 1). In order to solve the dual problem $\mathcal{Z}_D$, a subgradient search actor is created. For each job in a FJSSTT problem a job actor is created. It is configured to use a particular subgradient search actor, and it is also introduced to resource actors knowledgeable of process and travel times. The main task of an actor representing job i is to solve a subproblem $\mathcal{S}_i$. We have implemented two problem solving methods for $\mathcal{S}_i$: (1) a dynamic programming algorithm for exact solutions, based on [37], and (2) a variable neighbourhood search for approximate solutions, allowing to solve larger problem instances than with dynamic programming. We refer to [14] for an introduction to variable neighbourhood search.

The subgradient search procedure is iterative: the vector of Lagrange multipliers λ is calculated based on the subgradients in the current iteration, and λ is communicated to the job actors. The subgradient γ_{mk}^l can be interpreted as the violation of the capacity constraint for machine m at time slot k in iteration l, more formally

$$\gamma_{mk}^l = \sum_{i \in \mathcal{I}} \sum_{j \in \mathcal{J}_i} \delta_{ijmk}^* - 1. \tag{12}$$

The term δ_{ijmk}^* denotes the optimal value for δ_{ijmk} in iteration l.

The job actors use the updated Lagrange multipliers to solve their subproblems, and send their solutions to the subgradient search actor. With the job solutions the subgradient search actor compiles the complete, generally infeasible schedule for the FJSSTT problem and calculates new subgradients.

The FJSSTT actor receives the infeasible schedule from the subgradient search actor and asks the feasibility repair actor to generate a feasible schedule. For feasibility repair we have implemented a list scheduling heuristic based on [16]. Machine actors are informed about the feasible schedule, and a machine actor is informed about the jobs that are scheduled on the machine.

4   Runtime Behaviour

As mentioned above, for the implementation the akka actor library[2] had been used. The general implementation had been done in java. Initially a parallel threading approach did exist. That was re-implemented to the actor-based architecture. Having the source code of both systems allowed to also benchmark runtime performance.

The overall performance may be measured with respect to the found solution quality and with respect to runtime-performance (i.e. how fast a solution is found). The problem instances of a particular class identified as "WT" (without TT; transport times) are based on [5] and are available online [28]. The WT set with transport time (TT) are novel generated problem sets based on the ones with similar name. Details on the generation process are reported in [13].

Not going into details, the problem instances consist of the following number of elements. WT1 consists of 10 Jobs, 5 Machines, and 5 Operations. WT2 consists of 20 Jobs, 5 Machines, 5 Operations. Transport times in this case are between 0,09 and 1,1 of the minimum make span of the Jobs in the respective sets. Transport times are assigned randomly (cf [13]).

---

[2] ©Lightbend Inc. http://akka.io.

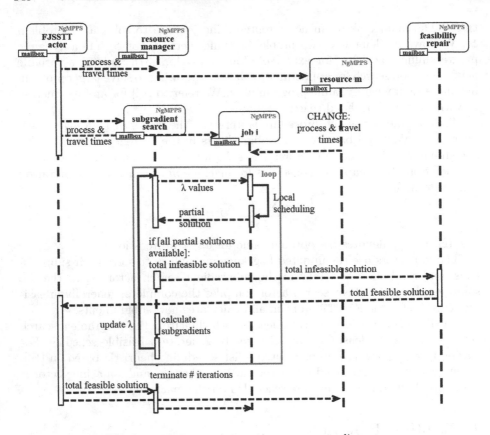

Fig. 2. NgMPPS actor interaction - sequence diagram

UB (upper bound) is the best feasible solution produced. The global optimum schedule will be equal or better than the UB. With respect to TWT (Total Weighted Tardiness) better means lower values. In addition to calculating the UB, the taken approach finds the LB (lower bounds). UB and LB is a corridor, within which the global optimum really is. If UB equals LB it is proven, that the optimum is found.

4.1 Solution Quality

The best known optimal values (UB*) for the WT1, WT2 instances in Table 1 are based on a shifting bottleneck implementation [32]. The concrete reference problems have been made available as open data set (see [28]). With respect to the found solution quality, the UB and LB produced by the NgMPPS-DPC system for the WTx instances are above and below the UB*.

The best known values for WTxTT problem instances reported in Table 1 have been generated by a simple list scheduling algorithm. This is due to the novelty of the problem instances and the need to establish an initial baseline for our system. That simple algorithm produced results (UB*) with low quality. Therefore the improvement is very high with respect to the best known upper bound in WT with travel times (WT1TT, WT2TT).

Table 1. Benchmarking NgMPPS-DPC with the best known Upper Bound (UB*).

Test instance Id	UB*	Max LB	Min UB
WT1	57	43,9	61,0
WT1TT	138	58,0	86,0
WT2	252	127,8	274,0
WT2TT	911	213,3	412,0

Table 1 shows that the solution quality produced by the NgMPPS-DPC system for WT1, WT2, is on par with the solutions documented in the literature as best known solutions [28,32]. For the instances with transport times (WT1TT,WT2TT, we provide now initial values of Upper Bounds. The problem description and the transport matrix used to calculate the values are made available on the web[3] and will (hopefully) serve as benchmarks for colleagues.

4.2   Runtime Performance

Since the tackled problem is of $\mathcal{NP}$-hard nature, not only the solution quality found is of interest, but also the runtime performance. That is an indicator, if the used approach is scalable on a single machine, and later on a network of machines. If the overhead of the actor library on a single machine has a negative impact on runtime performance that would limit the number of times the subgradient search may be executed in a particular time.

Table 2 shows the difference of the java parallel threads and akka actor system implementation on a single machine.

Since the system was implemented by the same team, we where able to test it on the same hardware for comparable results. This comparison was done to estimate the impact of using an actor library on the runtime performance. The results did surprise us.

Most of the time the solution quality found by the akka system is better or on par with the parallel implementation. However, the runtime performance of the actor system is always better than with the parallel system, i.e. less time is needed to find a solution.

In this comparison the instances with transport times are much more relevant than in the solution quality comparison shown above in Table 1.

We have expected the akka implementation to perform worse than the threading implementation. With respect to akka performing better to java threads

---

[3] https://www.profactor.at/en/research/industrial-assistive-systems/distributed-info rmation-systems/.

because of coding skills, this can be ruled out to a great extend, due the fact that the same team has implemented both systems.

We attribute this performance to the effective handling of threads in akka.

Table 2. Parallel vs. Actor Performance for total weighted tardiness problems; LB...Lower Bound; UB...Upper Bound; Par...Parallel Impl.; Act...Actor Impl.; WTx[TT]...without [with Transport Times]; *emph* marks the better value

Test instance	Max LB		Min UB		Time [s]	
	Par	Act	Par	Act	Par	Act
WT1	43,9	43,9	*57,0*	61,0	51,3	*48,7*
WT1TT	*58,1*	58,0	86,0	86,0	27,8	*27,3*
WT2	127,8	127,8	284,0	*274,0*	50,7	*48,8*
WT2TT	213,1	*213,3*	421,0	*412,0*	49,5	*47,8*

5   State of the Art

In this section we first focus on methods for decentralised scheduling, with an emphasis on distributed artificial intelligence (DAI) methods. At the end of this section we discuss briefly job shop scheduling.

From a historic DAI point of view are initial developments for advanced production planing and scheduling based on the holonic idea, followed more recently by Multi Agent Systems approaches. Several MAS prototypes for networked planning and their implementation in production environment were documented in the scientific literature [26,30,31]. A detailed overview of industrial MAS implementation is given in [25,26] A well-known example of an MAS for adaptive production control is the myJoghurt Demonstrator at Technical University Munich[4] [36].

Agent technology has been applied to manufacturing enterprise integration, supply chain management, manufacturing scheduling and control, material handling and logistics service provision [7,20,25]. Multi Agent Systems negotiation is used as a means to reduce the number of alternative solutions and to distribute the problem solving.

In several approaches, the holonic paradigm was applied to address the openness and dynamism of enterprises and enterprise networks [33,35,39].

Adaptive and distributed approaches for (re)scheduling of production schedules are discussed in the following with focus on Multi Agent Systems, Holonic Systems, and Actor based systems.

An important holonic architecture for distributed manufacturing execution is the Product Resource Order Staff Architecture (PROSA) cooperative control reference architecture [30,35].

---

[4] http://i40d.ais.mw.tum.de/.

The *PROSA* architecture allows a separation of concerns and continuous replanning in the manufacturing domain. This architecture has been built to allow solving large and complex problems by allowing solutions to emerge combining sub-solutions [34]. The PROSA architecture has been used as a basis for ant-based algorithms for production plans that are constructed over time [33]. The ant and agent types existing in the system are product ants (knowing what operations are needed in which sequence for a product), resource agents (know the current state and capability of a particular resource), order ants (in charge for scheduling a particular operation on a particular machine for a order of a particular product). Staff agents support the other agents/ants in their activities. Product ants run in the virtual production system upstream and leave a pheromone trail of possible routes for order ants. These run downstream and use these routes. Order ants determine possible schedules for customer orders. One of these schedules may be chosen at the end of the planning process. PROSA supports emergent and robust solutions. For example if a new machine is introduced, it will be discovered by the ants and new pheromone trails will start to appear which signify to the order agents new routes. When a machine breaks down order agents are not able to follow a given path as the broken machine interrupts the route. Since now the pheromone trail can not be refreshed anymore, the pheromones vanish and product, order ants search for new routes leaving new pheromone trails where the best trail is used when orders are produced.

PROSA has been extended towards ensuring adaptive behaviour of agent-based manufacturing control systems by introducing adaptive staff agents [44]. Staff agents communicate across different production facilitates and modify parameters used by the other agents or ants in order to guide their decision process and search for an optimal solution.

ADACOR² is a distributed scheduling architecture also based on a holonic modelling approach [3,24]. The overall problem is divided into subproblems and subproblems are solved taking the level of granularity into account. In ADACOR² each scheduler is composed from a swarm of schedulers. *ADACOR²* is capable of self-organising the macro structure based on behaviour changes of holons. The other way around, the behaviour of holons is influenced by the global structure.

Multi Agent Systems technology is capable of realising reactive schedule execution systems. Approaches exist that support schedule execution, advanced planing and optimisation for manufacturing networks and supply chains. In the IntLogProd project [20] a distributed infrastructure has been implemented that makes of FIPA contract net protocols [11] for scheduling production machines and transport for simple products in a production network. Optimisation is done on multiple levels. On the Network level partial solutions are combined focusing on cost considerations. The partial solutions in turn are optimised using local strategies. Each job shop (manufacturing facility) may be optimised according to its own goals [40].

A hierarchical approach for a centralised control of distributed manufacturing systems which share (some) resources is realised by the *DSCEP* framework [2].

This system supports indirect cooperation between customer agents (C) and producer agents (P). Where each customer agent represents one order and each producer agent represents one resource (machine or human). Synchronisation between c and p agents is facilitated by the environment agent e. The overall system is controlled by a supervisor agent S. Through the introduction of virtual c and virtual p agents a distributed system may be designed.

The work of [23] deals with a classical job shop scheduling problem, with total weighted tardiness as the objective function. Applying Lagrangian Relaxation, machine capacity constraints are relaxed, and the resulting Lagrangian function is decomposed into independent one job scheduling problems. Auction protocols are used to solve the dual problem, determining optimal values for the Lagrange multipliers. In [9,10] the authors tackle a dynamic scheduling problem, where machine failures and new jobs are regarded as disruptions during schedule execution. The approach is similar to [23], with one fundamental difference: while in [23] one auctioneer is coordinating the jobs, in [9,10] each machine acts as an auctioneer. As soon as a machine becomes inactive, an auction is initiated, with all jobs requiring the machine as bidders.

6   Conclusions and Next Steps

We have presented the mathematical foundation, the actor based design, and performance results of the NgMPPS-DPC project. For evaluating the solutions produced by the implementation, we use open data problem instances [28]. The results with respect to solution quality are promising and are on par with state of the art solution approaches of the same problem. Additionally the runtime performance of the actor implementation is better than expected. We compared our system on a single machine to a java threading approach, and found good solutions in shorter time.

Currently the system is extended to be able to handle machine failures and dynamic rescheduling events. After having optimised a schedule, it is executed. During execution, disrupting events like machine failures occur. These events lead to deviations in process/travel times. As a consequence, the planned schedule can not be further executed. *Dynamic rescheduling* catches the disruptions and calculates an adapted feasible schedule: a resource actor detects a disruption and informs the job actors which are affected by the disruption. For job i, the deviating process/travel times and the reduced set of operations to be scheduled are reflected in a subproblem S'_i, with Lagrange multipliers from the final iteration of the preceding subgradient search. Affected job actors solve subproblems S'_i and send the solutions to the subgradient search actor, which starts a new subgradient search. Depending on the severity of the disruption, and the changes in job-level schedules, it is likely that in the course of the new search procedure other jobs than the initially affected are forced to re-calculate their schedules. This effect propagation of a disruption may be deliberately limited, e.g. by explicitly "freezing" the schedules of high-priority jobs.

As mentioned above, the system's performance will be evaluated in a network environment with multiple limited computational devices executing part of the overall algorithm. Runtime performance impact of different configuration parameters will be evaluated. The problem description (jobs, operations, machines) and the according transport time matrices are published on the web[5]. When new results become available these will also be documented there.

Acknowledgement. The research leading to these results is funded by the Austrian Ministry for Transport, Innovation and Technology www.bmvit.gv.at through the project NgMPPS-DPC: Next-Generation Multi-Purpose Production Systems – Decentralised production control based on distributed optimisation.

References

1. Agha, G.A.: Actors: a model of concurrent computation in distributed systems. Ph.D. thesis, Artificial Intelligence Laboratory of the Massachusetts Institute of Technology (1985). http://oai.dtic.mil/oai/oai?verb=getRecord& metadataPrefix=html&identifier=ADA157917
2. Archimede, B., Letouzey, A., Memon, M.A., Xu, J.: Towards a distributed multi-agent framework for shared resources scheduling. J. Intell. Manuf. **25**(5), 1077–1087 (2013). http://dx.doi.org/10.1007/s10845-013-0748-8
3. Barbosa, J., Leitão, P., Adam, E., Trentesaux, D.: Self-organized holonic multi-agent manufacturing system: the behavioural perspective. In: 2013 IEEE International Conference on Systems, Man, and Cybernetics (SMC), pp. 3829–3834, October 2013
4. Bragin, M.A., Luh, P.B., Yan, J.H., Yu, N., Stern, G.A.: Convergence of the surrogate lagrangian relaxation method. J. Optim. Theory Appl. **164**(1), 173–201 (2014)
5. Brandimarte, P.: Routing and scheduling in a flexible job shop by tabu search. Ann. Oper. Res. **41**(3), 157–183 (1993)
6. Buil, R., Piera, M.A., Luh, P.B.: Improvement of lagrangian relaxation convergence for production scheduling. IEEE Trans. Autom. Sci. Eng. **9**(1), 137–147 (2012)
7. Camarinha-Matos, L., Afsarmanesh, H.: Elements of a base VE infrastructure. Comput. Ind. **51**(51), 139–163 (2003)
8. Chen, H., Chu, C., Proth, J.M.: An improvement of the Lagrangean relaxation approach for job shop scheduling: a dynamic programming method. IEEE Trans. Robot. Autom. **14**(5), 786–795 (1998)
9. Dewan, P., Joshi, S.: Implementation of an auction-based distributed scheduling model for a dynmaic job shop environment. Int. J. Comput. Integr. Manuf. **14**(5), 446–456 (2001)
10. Dewan, P., Joshi, S.: Auction-based distributed scheduling in a dynamic job shop environment. Int. J. Prod. Res. **40**(5), 1173–1191 (2002)
11. FIPA - Foundation for Intelligent Physical Agents: Standard FIPA Specifications (2005). http://fipa.org/repository/standardspecs.html, http://www.fipa.org
12. Fisher, M.L.: The Lagrangian relaxation method for solving integer programming problems. Manage. Sci. **50**(12 Suppl.), 1861–1871 (2004)

---

[5] https://www.profactor.at/en/research/industrial-assistive-systems/distributed-information-systems/.

13. Hämmerle, A., Weichhart, G.: Variable neighbourhood search solving sub-problems of a Lagrangian flexible scheduling problem. In: Proceedings of the 6th International Conference on Operations Research and Enterprise Systems, ICORES, vol. 1, pp. 234–241 (2017)
14. Hansen, P., Mladenovic, N.: Variable neighborhood search. In: Handbook of Metaheuristics, pp. 145–184. Kluwer Academic Publishers (2003)
15. Hewitt, C.: Viewing control structures as patterns of passing messages. Artif. Intell. **8**(3), 323–364 (1977). http://www.sciencedirect.com/science/article/pii/0004370277900339
16. Hoitomt, D.J., Luh, P.B., Pattipati, K.R.: A practical approach to job-shop scheduling problems. IEEE Trans. Robot. Autom. **9**(1), 1–13 (1993)
17. Holland, J.H.: Hidden Order: How Adaptation Builds Complexity. Basic Books, New York (1996)
18. Holland, J.H.: Emergence: From Chaos to Order. Basic Books, New York (1998)
19. Kafura, D., Briot, J.P.: Actors & agents. IEEE Concurr. **6**(2), 24–29 (1998)
20. Karageorgos, A., Mehandjiev, N., Weichhart, G., Hämmerle, A.: Agent-based optimisation of logistics and production planning. Eng. Appl. Artif. Intell. **16**(4), 335–348 (2003)
21. Kaskavelis, C.A., Caramanis, M.C.: Efficient Lagrangian relaxation algorithms for industry size job-shop scheduling problems. IIE Trans. **30**(11), 1085–1097 (1998)
22. Koestler, A.: The Ghost in the Machine. Arkana Books, London (1989)
23. Kutanoglu, E., Wu, S.D.: On combinatorial auction and Lagrangean relaxation for distributed resource scheduling. IIE Trans. **31**, 813–826 (1999)
24. Leitão, P., Barbosa, J.: Adaptive scheduling based on self-organized Holonic swarm of schedulers. In: 2014 IEEE 23rd International Symposium on Industrial Electronics (ISIE), pp. 1706–1711, June 2014
25. Leitão, P., Mařík, V., Vrba, P.: Past, present, and future of industrial agent applications. IEEE Trans. Industr. Inf. **9**(4), 2360–2372 (2013)
26. Leitão, P., Karnouskos, S., Ribeiro, L., Lee, J., Strasser, T., Colombo, A.W.: Smart agents in industrial cyber - physical systems. Proc. IEEE **104**(5), 1086–1101 (2016)
27. Lightbend Inc.: Akka Documentation (2017). http://doc.akka.io/docs/akka/current/
28. Mönch, L.: Problem Instances for Flexible Job Shops with Due Dates (2015). http://p.2schedgen.fernuni-hagen.de/index.php?id=174
29. Monostori, L.: Cyber-physical production systems: roots, expectations and R&D challenges. Procedia CIRP **17**, 9–13 (2014)
30. Monostori, L., Valckenaers, P., Dolgui, A., Panetto, H., Brdys, M., Csáji, B.C.: Cooperative control in production and logistics. Ann. Rev. Control **39**, 12–29 (2015)
31. Neubauer, M., Stary, C. (eds.): S-BPM in the Production Industry. Springer International Publishing, Heidelberg (2017)
32. Sobeyko, O., Mönch, L.: Heuristic approaches for scheduling jobs in large-scale flexible job shops. Comput. Oper. Res. **68**, 97–109 (2016). http://dx.doi.org/10.1016/j.cor.2015.11.004
33. Valckenaers, P., van Brussel, H., Hadeli, Bochmann, O., Saint Germain, B., Zamfirescu, C.: On the design of emergent systems: an investigation of integration and interoperability issues. Eng. Appl. Artif. Intell. **16**(4), 377–393 (2003). http://www.sciencedirect.com/science/article/pii/S0952197603000800

34. Valckenaers, P., Kollingbaum, M., van Brussel, H., Bochmann, O., Zamfirescu, C.B.: The design of multi-agent coordination and control systems using stigmergy. In: Proceedings of the third International Workshop on Emergent Synthesis (IWES01) (2001)
35. Van Brussel, H., Wyns, J., Valckenaers, P., Bongaerts, L., Peeters, P.: Reference architecture for holonic manufacturing systems: PROSA. Comput. Ind. **37**(3), 255–274 (1998). http://www.sciencedirect.com/science/article/pii/S016636159800102X
36. Vogel-Heuser, B., Fay, A., Schaefer, I., Tichy, M.: Evolution of software in automated production systems: challenges and research directions. J. Syst. Softw. **110**, 54–84 (2015)
37. Wang, J., Luh, P.B., Zhao, X., Wang, J.: An optimization-based algorithm for job shop scheduling. Sadhana **22**(2), 241–256 (1997)
38. Weichhart, G.: Agent technologies for production systems. In: Proceedings of SAISIA Workshop (2006)
39. Weichhart, G., Fessl, K.: Organisational network models and the implications for decision support systems. In: Piztek, P. (ed.) Proceedings of 16th IFAC World Congress. IFAC, Praha (2005)
40. Weichhart, G., Affenzeller, M., Reitbauer, A., Wagner, S.: Modelling of an agent-based schedule optimisation system. In: Taisch, M., Filos, E., Garello, P., Lewis, K., Montorio, M. (eds.) IMS International Forum, pp. 1080–1087. Cernobbio, Italy (2004)
41. Weichhart, G., Hämmerle, A.: Multi-actor architecture for schedule optimisation based on Lagrangian relaxation. In: Klusch, M., Unland, R., Shehory, O., Pokahr, A., Ahrndt, S. (eds.) MATES 2016. LNCS, vol. 9872, pp. 190–197. Springer, Cham (2016). doi:10.1007/978-3-319-45889-2_14
42. Weichhart, G., Molina, A., Chen, D., Whitman, L., Vernadat, F.: Challenges and current developments for sensing, smart and sustainable enterprise systems. Comput. Ind. **79**, 34–46 (2016). http://www.sciencedirect.com/science/article/pii/S0166361515300208
43. Wooldridge, M.J., Jennings, N.R.: Intelligent agents: theory and practice. Knowl. Eng. Rev. **10**(2), 115–152 (1995)
44. Zimmermann, J., Mönch, L.: Design and implementation of adaptive agents for complex manufacturing systems. In: Mařík, V., Vyatkin, V., Colombo, A.W. (eds.) HoloMAS 2007. LNCS, vol. 4659, pp. 269–280. Springer, Heidelberg (2007). doi:10.1007/978-3-540-74481-8_26

Extending OWL with Custom Relations for Knowledge-Driven Intelligent Agents

Lixin Tao[✉]

Computer Science Department, Pace University, New York, NY 10038, USA
ltao@pace.edu

Abstract. Ontology is one of the popular models for knowledge representation, and Web Ontology Language (OWL) is the current industry standard for supporting ontology in semantic web and knowledge encoding for various application domains including healthcare and cyber-security.

But ontology basically only supports one relation "is-a" between the classes. Even though OWL introduced object properties to emulate other relations, it lacks effective support for fundamental relations like part-of, which is very popular in engineering knowledge, and the temporal relation, which underpins all algorithms for most computer science knowledge.

This paper introduces our minimal syntax extension to OWL to allow domain experts to declare and apply custom relations with various mathematical properties, and our extension to Stanford University's Protégé project so that it can be used to encode intuitively knowledge with custom relations, and our Pace-Jena project that can use the extended OWL documents to empower knowledge-driven decision making in software agents. Important use cases illustrate how this approach supported effective drug side-effect detection, efficient software diagnostic message pattern specification and detection, and an intelligent online tutoring system that supports effective cyberlearning with knowledge navigation, specialization and generalization as well as assessment-based learning.

Keywords: Knowledge representation · OWL · Intelligent agents · Ontology · Protégé

1 Introduction

Knowledge representation is the foundation of any intelligent system/agent. Popular knowledge representation models include the rule-based approach, the logic approach, the algorithmic approach, the code-based approach, and ontologies. Knowledge can be at various levels from observed statements and true statements about entities, and abstract or distilled knowledge about classes of entities. As examples for the former, Resource Definition Language (RDF) is for making statements about entities, normally in the subject-verb-object triple format, and deep learning algorithms aim at identifying patterns from ill-understood observed statements and represent the resulting knowledge in weight parameters of the neural networks. As an example of the latter, Web Ontology Language (OWL) [5, 19] is the current industry standard for representing well-understood relations among the abstractions or classes of entities to encode

© Springer International Publishing AG 2017
J.O. Berndt et al. (Eds.): MATES 2017, LNAI 10413, pp. 156–166, 2017.
DOI: 10.1007/978-3-319-64798-2_10

domain knowledge as ontologies, and the semantic web search frameworks use such ontologies to describes the relationship or linkage among the web data for improving web search efficiency.

While the current industry standard uses OWL to represent knowledge in ontologies, we believe that ontology is not enough or natural to represent most domain knowledge that needs to support relations beyond is-a or inheritance. For example, most engineering knowledge heavily uses variations of relation part-of, and most computer science knowledge is in form of algorithms for which time dependency is the key relation among the activities. Emulating custom relations with object properties in OWL is cumbersome at the best and not suitable for domain experts to encode and validate knowledge.

This paper introduces our research to extend ontology into Pace University Knowledge Graph that is basically ontology with custom relations. We have extended OWL with minimal syntax extension to support custom relations as the "first-class" relations. We have extended Stanford University project Protégé, an open-source IDE for visually developing OWL based knowledge representation, to support the declaration of custom relations with various mathematical properties and the creation of Knowledge Graphs by subject domain experts who have limited IT background.

This paper also presents three important applications of the Knowledge Graphs in effective drug side-effect detection, efficient software diagnostic message pattern specification and detection, and an intelligent online tutoring system that supports effective cyberlearning with knowledge navigation, specialization and generalization as well as assessment-based learning.

2 Related Work

The foundation of any intelligent system is how to represent knowledge in a form that a computer can understand and use. While the AI research has adopted various knowledge representation schemes including logic-based, rule-based and code-based, the current industry dominant approach is to use RDF to specify statements or relations between resources/entities, and OWL to define knowledge types or concepts (abstraction of resources/entities) and relations among the concepts. Ontology is the mathematical model behind OWL, connected by the "is-a" or inheritance relation [6–8].

For example, vehicle, car and truck are example concepts, and car and truck are special cases of, or "is-a", vehicle. The red car with plate AMB501 is an instance of a car. Since car is a vehicle and any vehicle has wheels, this red car is also a vehicle and it must have wheels.

But most knowledge involves custom relations between the concepts, or relations that are not "is-a". For example, most engineering knowledge heavy uses various forms of relation part-of, and the main computer science knowledge bodies are in form of algorithms or processes for which time dependency is a foundation relation among the activities.

The current industry standard OWL doesn't support such custom relations. We have to use object properties to emulate such custom relations. Since each object property must have unique domain-range combination, a knowledge representation must use different part-of relation definitions for different domain-range pairs, leading to cumbersome and inaccurate knowledge representation.

Since 2014 Pace University researchers have extended OWL with minimal syntax extension so domain experts can freely introduce custom relations with various mathematical properties in knowledge representation [2, 7]. The resulting ontology extended with custom relations is called Knowledge Graphs. Stanford University open-source OWL GUI editor Protégé has also been extended to support the intuitive creation of the Knowledge Graphs. This research uses Knowledge Graph representation of course concepts and relations to encode course knowledge structure.

3 Extending Owl to Support Knowledge Graphs

3.1 Knowledge Representation

While OWL is the current industry standard for knowledge representation, it doesn't support custom relations like part-of which is very important in engineering knowledge modeling. Knowledge modelers have to declare multiple part-of object properties to model the same part-of relation between different pairs of domain-ranges, leading to unnecessary complication and inaccuracy.

We have extended OWL syntax to support custom relations, thus extending the ontology behind OWL into the much more expressive Knowledge Graph. The following is an example declaration of custom relations "partOf" and "implement".

```
<rel:NewRelation rdf:about="http://pace.edu/
    semweb.owl#partOf"/>
<rel:NewRelation rdf:about="http://pace.edu/
    semweb.owl#implement"/>
```

The following example declares that ServletContainer is part of the Tomcat Web server.

```
<owl:Class rdf:about="http://pace.edu/
    semweb.owl#ServletContainer">
 <rel:partOf rdf:resource="http://pace.edu/
    semweb.owl#Tomcat"/>
</owl:Class>
```

and the following example declares that Cookie is used to implement SessionID.

```
<owl:Class rdf:about="http://pace.edu/
    semweb.owl#Cookie">
 <rel:implement rdf:resource="http://pace.edu/
    semweb.owl#SessionID"/>
</owl:Class>
```

3.2   Knowledge Encoding with Protégé

We have extended Stanford University open-source OWL editor Protégé to support the
visual declaration of custom relations, and encode knowledge into Knowledge Graphs.
Figure 1 is an example Protégé screen for knowledge representation for the sample
Web tutorial use case described in the next section.

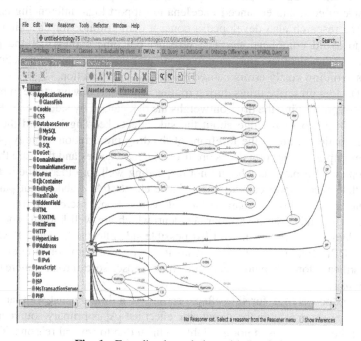

Fig. 1. Encoding knowledge with Protégé

3.3   Knowledge Parsing and Reasoning with Pace

PaceJena is our OWL/Knowledge Graph parser and validator [9–11]. It reads in an
OWL or Knowledge Graph document, validates its contents against the syntax standard, conduct necessary logic reasoning to find out implied knowledge, and expose the
knowledge to other applications through public APIs. For example, when the tutoring
system needs to find out example concepts of concept "web server", it would invoke
PaceJena's public method `derivedClasses("web server")`, which will return
an enumeration of the derived concepts including "Apache" and "Tomcat".

4   Drug Side Effect Inferencing Using Knwoledge Graphs

Drug adverse reaction data contains important constraints about side effects and conflict
avoidance of component and compound drugs [12–17]. We observe that many of these
constraints are transitive in nature due to the relationship between drug and drug

classes. Current drug side effects representations in XML does not have a proper knowledge representation mechanism to clearly specify all kinds of dependencies among the drug components and drugs. Even the recently introduced OWL based approach for medical drug side effects data representation still suffers from several shortcomings inherent to the OWL restrictions like using "is-a" relationship and usage of object property emulations.

We used Knowledge Graphs to represent the complex relationships among the drugs for side effects, and enhanced PaceJena to support logic inferencing among the relations. The research also developed a concept demonstrator for checking out pre-scriptions to avoid complications. The research outcome shows that the proposed model allows the doctors and caregivers to derive dynamic information about side-effects avoiding costly errors caused by human interpretation.

While Doctors prescribe drugs during routine visits, they always strive to make sure the benefits of prescribing the drug outweighs the risk caused by side effects. Here they always seek in-depth knowledge about the side effects keeping in mind the ultimate safety of the patient's life at the forefront of the drug prescription strategy [4].

As an example, Saxagliptin drugs are used to treat diabetes and they are the newest treatment options for patients who are not responding well for other diabetic treatment options. While Saxagliptin causes a set of side effects ($|A|$ - abdominal pain, motor dysfunction, hyperhidrosis, malaise, nasal congestion, increased blood sugar, arrhythmia, rash, and cerebro vascular accident) which are well known, doctors often find that it does not represent the full list possible side effects. Actually, Saxagliptin's parent class DPP4Inhibitors (gliptin) causes its own set of common side effects ($|B|$ - nausea, diarrhea, stomach pain, headache, runny nose, sore throat, pancreatitis, and severe join pain).

When the doctors look for side effects caused by a drug against what are reported by patents, they often rely on the direct side effect list $|A|$ as primary source as the full spectrum of the side effects is not available to them due to several reasons. This could cause them to overlook side effects like pancreatitis which is in $|B|$. Studies show that while emulations with object properties are used to capture these additional relations they often cause other problems like high cost of maintenance on data modelers.

Linking the component and compound drugs using the proposed knowledge graph based approach allows the domain experts to capture the full spectrum side effects of the drug ($|A| + |B|$) by including all possible side effects while reducing syntax burden to knowledge modelers compared with any other workarounds like object properties. Such a dynamic data representation model will also provide a full spectrum side effects to the doctors and patient helping them immensely to benefit to either adapt newer treatment models without fear or just to choose a suitable treatment model beneficial to the patient. Even when the knowledge about the drug side effects is available, the current knowledge representation makes it harder to help the doctor in clinical diagnostics.

Figure 2 shows a sample piece of Knowledge Graph related to Saxagliptin through two custom relations "part of" and "cause".

A web application is developed for the doctors to find direct/indirect side effects for patient prescriptions based on a subclass of drugs. PaceJena's real-time inference

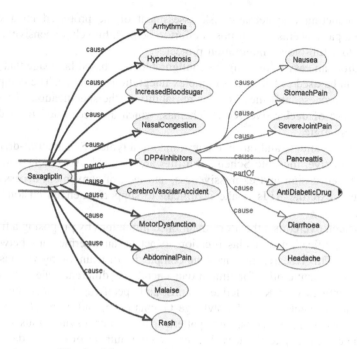

Fig. 2. Adverse reactions caused by Saxagliptin

capacity takes full advantage of the Knowledge Graphs about the drug side effect causality and significantly improved the prescription quality control.

5 Reducing Complexity of Diagnostic Message Specification and Recognition

Different companies in the same line of business can have similar computer systems with built-in diagnostic routines, and the ability to regularly send error-driven or event-driven environmental diagnostic messages in XML back to the system manufacturer. The system manufacturer typically uses these to determine faults in the system. The outcome of this troubleshooting can also assist end-users and clients in solving problems, and provide the production team valuable information that can be used to improve future versions of the product [3].

Consider that company A acquires company B, and seeks to integrate the IT infrastructure of the acquired company that processes incoming diagnostic XML files from field-resident systems into its existing inbound file processing infrastructure for efficient identification and explications of actionable system faults. Because different teams were involved in the production of the different field-resident products, with no XML formatting standard, the inbound files contain similar information, but in different formats. This is a classic case of the XML Semantic Rule Complexity and Heterogeneity Problem. Controlling the complexity of specifying exception-handling patterns to validate and process the various formats and dialects is a herculean task.

After conducting a systematic risk assessment of the proposed integration, the acquiring company deems the proposed effort to be prohibitively expensive, and seeks alternatives to a full-blown integration project.

Schematron, an easy to use, highly configurable, rule-based language that validates XML files can be used to tackle this complex integration challenge. The complexity of the validation process, and the need for reusability in the specification of validations requires the use of declarative XML schemas, which are decoupled from the application business logic.

However, to validate and enforce constraints in a typical Schematron-driven XML integration initiative, multiple Schematron files are required. Also, Schematron's limited XSLT-based design and expressiveness, and lack of convenient access for invocation through external APIs, make it difficult to support extended custom semantic constraints.

This research overcomes the afore-mentioned limitations by proposing a framework for pattern identification and classification to act as an intermediary between both infrastructures. This research manages the complexity of maintaining various versions of Schematron semantic rules for similar data encoded in different dialects by modeling the business entities with Knowledge Graphs, and specifying business semantic constraints on the concepts of the Knowledge Graphs once, and automatically generate concrete business semantic constraints/patterns based on data syntax thus significantly reducing the complexity to work with ever-growing number of diverse data formats.

Figure 3 shows our system architecture for data integration and knowledge-driven error classification.

The process starts when a file arrives. The system inspects the received file to try to identify the dialect. If the dialect is recognized, it proceeds on to the abstract level to extract the abstract rule, perform the abstract to concrete rule conversion, populates the place-holder variables with actual values, and proceeds on to validate the received diagnostic message file. If the validation is successful and it is able to identify an actionable error, that has the potential to cause a critical problem, it emits an alert, invokes PaceJena, to extract the semantics and relations relevant to that error and

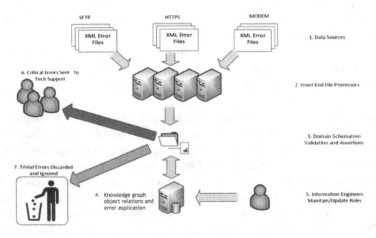

Fig. 3. System architecture for data integration and knowledge-driven error classification

escalate to technical support staff, to prevent catastrophic damage to business-critical systems. If the error is spurious and deemed trivial, then it just discards the file and goes back to the beginning to check for additional files, and if additional files exist, it goes through the entire process again for the new files. Figure 4 shows the three levels of knowledge representation that support this solution.

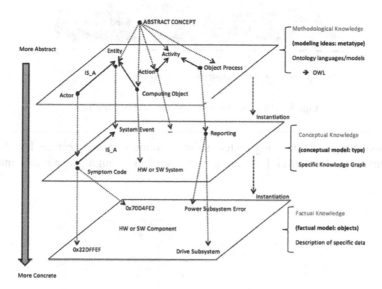

Fig. 4. The three levels of knowledge representation

6 Knowledge-Driven Tutoring System for Effective Cyberlearning

Cyberlearning is characterized by endless volume and type of learning resources freely and readily available to the students through the Web; the lack of personized guidance by experienced instructors as to learning resource selection and learning order recommendation including concept specialization and generalization; and the lack of an assessment-based learning process [1].

This research developed a complete intelligent Web-based tutoring system layered framework for easy adoption by the instructors for the delivering of courses in any subject. To adopt this framework, the instructor will first use Pace-extended Protégé GUI to model intuitively the course knowledge concepts and relations with the Pace Knowledge Graph model, and specify the mathematical properties of the custom relations. Instructor experience in form of recommended learning paths for students at different levels is also coded in the Knowledge Graph. Pace-extended Protégé will convert Knowledge Graph into a Pace-extended OWL file. PaceJena, a Pace-extended OWL parser, will read in the Pace-extended OWL file, support logic reasoning, and expose public API to empower the tutoring system runtime educational components. The tutoring web application is implemented with Java Servlets/JSP and web services [18] (Fig. 5).

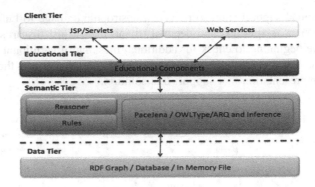

Fig. 5. PaceJena tutoring system architecture tiers

The following is the tutoring system solution framework architecture. It is designed for customization by non-IT instructors in any subject through graphic user interfaces (Fig. 6).

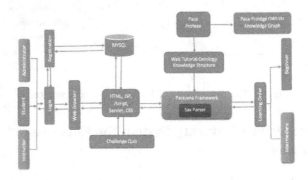

Fig. 6. Tutoring system architecture

For an instructor to adopt this Web based tutoring system for a specific subject, he/she needs to complete the following steps:

1. Describe the main concepts of the course, and describe various relations among the concepts. Declare custom relations if necessary.
2. Select suitable open-source learning objects/resources for each concept that can be presented in the Web. Each concept could have multiple alternative learning objects using different media or approaches for different student preferences.
3. Design assessment questions for each learning object. Learning object's integrated assessment questions could be used.
4. Specify recommended learning order for students with different background.

To use such a tutoring system, a student needs first to register with it, take a quiz, and create a student profile. The profile will be updated after each study session. The student can follow the recommended learning order, or request the tutoring system to show application examples of a generic concept, or show the foundation concepts of an application concept. After a student completes a course module, the student needs to pass an online quiz. If the student passes the quiz, he/she can move on to the next topic/module suitable for his/her level. Otherwise the student will be presented alternative learning modules to study the current topic from a different angle.

The main contributions of this work includes:

- Pace Knowledge Graph is used to better model the knowledge structure of a course as well as recommended learning paths so the tutoring system could support free knowledge navigation and the common learning patterns including specialization and generalization.
- A tutoring system framework is developed so instructors without IT background can customize the framework into a full-fledged online tutoring system on any subject with any learning objects, quizzes and recommended learning orders.

7 Conclusion

This paper introduced Pace University Knowledge Graph, an extension to OWL, for more effective knowledge representation. It also introduced three important applications of the Knowledge Graph as examples of knowledge-driven intelligent systems. Related current research includes integrated syntax/semantic data validation and pattern specification on data concept models instead of XML representations.

References

1. Sette, M., Tao, L., Gai, K., Jiang, N.: A semantic approach to intelligent and personal tutoring system. In: The 2nd IEEE International Conference of Scalable and Smart Cloud (IEEE SSC 2016), Beijing, 25–27 June 2016
2. Asamoah, C., Tao, L., Gai, K., Jiang, N.: Powering filtration process of cyber security ecosystem using knowledge graph. In: The 2nd IEEE International Conference of Scalable and Smart Cloud (IEEE SSC 2016), Beijing, 25–27 June 2016
3. Alipui, G., Tao, L., Gai, K., Jiang, N.: Reducing complexity of diagnostic message pattern specification and recognition on in-bound data using semantic techniques. In: The 2nd IEEE International Conference of Scalable and Smart Cloud (IEEE SSC 2016), Beijing, 25–27 June 2016
4. Jayaraman, S., Tao, L., Gai, K., Jiang, N.: Drug side effects data representation and full spectrum inferencing using knowledge graphs in intelligent telehealth. In: The 2nd IEEE International Conference of Scalable and Smart Cloud (IEEE SSC 2016), Beijing, 25–27 June 2016
5. Destefano, R.J., Tao, L., Gai, K.: Improving data governance in large organizations through ontology and linked data. In: The 2nd IEEE International Conference of Scalable and Smart Cloud (IEEE SSC 2016), Beijing, 25–27 June 2016
6. Altowayan, A., Tao, L.: Simplified approach for representing part-whole relations in owl-dl ontologies. In: IEEE 17th International Conference on High Performance Computing and Communications (HPCC), pp. 1399–1405, New York, NY (2015)

7. Patel, K., Dube, I., Tao, L., Jiang, N.: Extending OWL to support custom relations. In: IEEE 2nd International Conference on Cyber Security and Cloud Computing, pp. 494–499, New York (2015)
8. Yu, L.: Introduction to Semantic Web and Semantic Web Services. Chapman & Hall/CRC, Boca Raton (2007)
9. Tao, L., Golikov, S., Gai, K., Qiu, M.: A reusable software component for integrated syntax and semantic validation for services computing. In: 9th International IEEE Symposium on Service-Oriented System Engineering, pp. 127–132, San Francisco Bay, USA (2015)
10. Tao, L., Golikov, S., Gai, K., Qiu, M.: A reusable software component for integrated syntax and semantic validation for services computing. In: IEEE SOSE, pp. 127–132, San Francisco, Mar 2015
11. Tao, L., Golikov, S.: Integrated syntax and semantic validation for services computing. In: 10th International Conference on Services Computing, CA, 27 June–2 July 2013
12. Henriques, G., Lamanna, L., Kotowski, D., Hlomani, H., Stacey, D., Baker, P., Harper, S.: An ontology-driven approach to mobile data collection applications for the healthcare industry. Netw. Model. Anal. Health Inform. Bioinf. **2**(4), 213–223 (2013)
13. Lambers, H., Zeeuw, D., Wie, L., Leslie, B., List, J.: Dapagliflozin a glucose-regulating drug with diuretic properties in subjects with type 2 diabetes. Diab. Obes. Metab. **15**(9), 853–862 (2013)
14. Pattanawongsa, A., Chau, N., Rowland, A., Miners, J.: Inhibition of human UDP-glucuronosyltransferase enzymes by canagliflozin and dapagliflozin: implications for drug-drug interactions. Drug Metab. Dispos. **43**(10), 1468–1476 (2015)
15. Doulaverakis, C., Nikolaidis, G., Kleontas, A., Kompatsiaris, I.: GalenOWL: Ontology based drug recommendations discovery. J. Biomed. Semant. **3**, 14 (2012)
16. Hanna, J., Joseph, E., Brochhausen, M., Hogan, W.: Building drug ontology based on RxNorm and other sources. J. Biomed. Semant. (2013)
17. Doulaver, C., Nikolaidais, G., Kleontas, A., Kompatsiaris, I.: GalenOWL: ontology-based drug recommendation discovery. J Biomed. Semant. **3**(1), 14 (2012)
18. Oracle: The Java EE Tutorial (2014). https://docs.oracle.com/javaee/7/JEETT.pdf
19. W3C: OWL Web Ontology Language Overview. https://www.w3.org/TR/owl-features/

Plan Acquisition in a BDI Agent Framework Through Intentional Learning

Wulfrano Arturo Luna Ramirez$^{(\boxtimes)}$ and Maria Fasli

School of Computer Science and Electronic Engineering, University of Essex,
Colchester CO4 3SQ, UK
{waluna,mfasli}@essex.ac.uk

Abstract. Inspired by the theory of practical reasoning, Belief-Desire-Intention (BDI) agents are perhaps the most well-known type and architecture of cognitive agents. Such agents can reason about their environment and perform complex plans to bring about their objectives and goals. Within the context of ever-changing environments though, one desirable feature for agents is that of learning, implemented in BDI agents as Intentional Learning, a framework focused on the monitoring of the mental states to include learning as part of the agent goals. In this paper, we consider and develop intentional learning within the Jason BDI framework for agents focused on a plan acquisition strategy addressing the cases of learning plans composed of one action, sequences or a repetition of actions that allow an agent to improve its behaviour at run-time. This is done at the pure BDI agent level, the repertoire of plans is directly updated without using external planning tools.

We take as a testbed the simple vacuum cleaning environment and how new plans are acquired for accomplishing tasks of different level of complexity: escape from tunnel-like paths and wall-following. Furthermore, we integrate in a novel way the use of NetLogo as an environment to locate Jason agents, maintaining a clear delineation between decision making and action in the environment with the decision-making firmly anchored within the BDI agent's reasoning cycle.

Keywords: Intentional learning · BDI-agents · Cognitive agents · Planning in agents · Jason · NetLogo

1 Introduction

From their roots in Distributed Artificial Intelligence (DAI), research in agents and multi-agent systems has seen immense growth. An agent can be considered as an entity which acts for the sake of a given purpose, interacting with the environment by means of perceptions and actions. A range of agent models and architectures have been developed, with one essential distinction being made between reactive and cognitive/intentional agents while achieving their objectives: the capability of maintain a mental representation of the environment. Cognitive agents transcend the reactive approach being capable of exhibit a

© Springer International Publishing AG 2017
J.O. Berndt et al. (Eds.): MATES 2017, LNAI 10413, pp. 167–186, 2017.
DOI: 10.1007/978-3-319-64798-2_11

richer behaviour and more capabilities [11]. Perhaps the most well-known architecture for cognitive agents is the Belief-Desire-Intention (BDI) architecture [18] which is inspired by the theory of practical reasoning [6].

One notable and desirable feature for agents is that of being able to learn and adapt to their environment.

Learning can help to cope with unexpected situations in design time as those present in a changing environment. An agent can improve its performance even for tasks that are part of its repertoire, but are further refined based on past experience. Many algorithms and approaches have been developed to enable agents to learn and adapt to changes, such as reinforcement learning, neural networks and genetic algorithms among others. A number of works have been directed towards reactive agents, while some proposals have been directed towards cognitive ones [16,28].

Despite that the original BDI notion of agency lack of the learning capability, some works have demonstrated the potential to include learning into it (mainly reinforcement, and intentional learning – inductive or abductive) [7,8,17,26].

We are interested in intentional learning, a process based on the use of meta-level plans to monitor the agent intentions identifying when learning is needed. Hence, we consider and develop a plan acquire strategy within the Jason BDI framework. We address the cases of learning plans composed of one action, sequences or a repetition of actions that allow for improvements in the agent behaviour.

The contribution of this work is three-fold. Firstly, we progress the state of the art in agent programming by demonstrating the potential to include intentional learning for plan acquisition at the agent level in a pure logic-based BDI framework. To this end we use the basic scenario of a vacuum cleaning agent environment. Secondly, we integrate in a novel way the use of NetLogo as an environment to locate Jason agents, maintaining a clear delineation between action in the environment and decision-making that is firmly anchored within the BDI agent's reasoning cycle. Finally, our work represents the first step towards the extension of the IL mechanism to the multi-agent systems (MAS) case.

This paper is organised as follows. In Sect. 2, we provide a brief overview of intentional learning. The implementation of intentional learning in Jason is exposed in Sect. 3. Section 4 show the basis for plan acquisition in a pure BDI framework. Section 5 shows the experimentation and the results obtained in the vacuum cleaning scenario. This is followed by a brief revision of the related work and the discussion in Sect. 6. Finally, the paper ends with the conclusions and plans for our future work.

2   Intentional Learning

One approach that has been proposed to address the need for learning within the BDI framework is the *Intentional Learning* (IL) framework, where learning is a behaviour driven by the mental attitudes characterising BDI agents, namely, beliefs, goals and intentions [24–26]. IL involves learning in three main areas [25]:

1. Goals [3,17]. Focused on monitoring the beliefs and adjusting them as needed in order to select the applicable plan to the current state of affairs.
2. Plans [24–26]. Learning is goal-directed, described in pre-specified plans in a reactive-like manner. New skills are gained by adding new plans to the agent's repertoire.
3. Plan's contexts and applicability [1,7,8,23]. Focused on the adjustment of the triggering conditions of plans given certain contexts. The plans remain the same, but the agent learns that they can be applied in different contexts (situations).

Our work is focused on learning at the activities level, i.e. plan level, as it is the only one that includes the possibility of new behaviour generation.

With regard to the implementation of IL within a BDI framework, the authors in [26], raise a number of key issues that need to be taken into consideration: (a) Capturing the intention structure at run time; (b) Updating the plan library (at run time); (c) Controlling the execution of an intention (by another intention); (d) Monitoring actions to check their feasibility before including them into a plan body.

The last point represents the most important requirement to decide when and what to learn. According to [26], this can be done through the implementation of meta-level plans that allow controlling deliberation, the execution of commitments and explicitly driving the learning process through cycles of abduction on hypothesis testing.

As described in [26], IL is not a set of algorithms, but a framework: it provides the general framework to accomplish learning (like plans updating/generation) within intentional systems, namely, BDI agents. IL has been tried by adding ideas and techniques from other ML techniques, like Reinforcement Learning (RL), Inductive Logic Programming, and Manipulative Abduction (MA). MA is a deliberation method based on templates of plans that represent the behavioural response to finding patterns or regularities in the environment, i.e. the templates build new plans from the repertoire of actions [26].

One central issue in IL, is the selection of the actions to include in the updating of the plan library, particularly when creating new plans. In [24,26] a method inspired by RL and MA is proposed based on three main templates of learning to perform IL when updating a plan: adding one action, repetitions and sequences of actions. So, observing their applicability and past usage the learning procedure can select the actions to be included in the new plan. Templates acts as a shortcut in the search of suitable actions that helps the RL-like procedure to find feasible actions for a new plan [24].

Finally, IL directed at learning the plans' context of applicability and driving of goals has been considered from the agent-level point of view within the scope of a set of agents in works such as [2,8,10,15–17,29]. In this regard and in contrast to these other proposals, the work described here forms the basis to include IL (at the level of plan acquisition) in BDI MAS, i.e. through undertaking the essential first step which is to include IL in a pure BDI environment at the level of the individual agent.

3   BDI Agency in Jason

Jason is a fully fledged multi-agent programming environment based on AgentS-peak, an extension of logic programming to implement the BDI agent-based architecture [5,18], and as such offers a concrete framework for implementing BDI agents and MAS directly making use of mentalistic attitudes. Since its incep-tion, it has been extended and it offers many features that makes it amenable to developing a wide range of systems and applications. In Jason, the knowledge of the agent is encoded through beliefs expressed as first-order logic predicates [4]. A detailed description of the language can be found in [5,18]. Moreover, Java classes are used to extend the agent capabilities (known as *internal actions*), interfacing packages to link the BDI engine with other systems, including even the potential of linking and reusing legacy code. Additionally, it is the potential to develop complex environments in a different platform and interfacing it with Jason by extending the environment class.

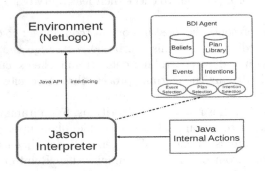

Fig. 1. The components of the Jason BDI environment. [internal actions allow to imple-ment IL].

As illustrated in Fig. 1, a BDI agent in Jason comprises: *Beliefs* (the agent's knowledge and perceptions), *Events* (the stimuli external or internal that the agent perceives), a *PlanLibrary* (the repertoire of courses of action that an agent is capable of performing in response to events; these courses of action are expressed as *plans*), and *Intentions* (the commitment to action the agent undertakes as a response to some event). The agent's reasoning cycle involves three functions to perceive, deliberate and act:

- *event selection*: a single event is chosen of those available through perceiving changes in the environment or in the list of intentions due to beliefs being updated;
- *option selection or applicable plan selection*: take a course of action suitable for the chosen event creating and intention; and
- *intention selection*: choose the next intention of a particular plan to be executed.

All the courses of action an agent has at its disposal are encoded in the plans stored in the *PlanLibrary*.

The main components of a plan are: `triggering_event`, `context`, and `body`. The `triggering_event` defines the name of a plan and determines when it can be initiated, hence, during the execution loop of the agent when an event (internal or external) matches this name, this plan is eligible for execution. There may be multiple plans that can have the same event as a trigger. The `context`, formed by a conjunction of first-order literals, defines the applicability of the plan given some condition or state of affairs in the environment translated into the agent perceptions or beliefs. Therefore, the `context` specifies under what conditions a plan applies and could be executed and this may vary from plan to plan. As a result, an agent can have multiple plans with the same triggering event differentiated by their `context`. Finally, the `body` of a plan is composed either of `subgoals`, which are calls to other plans (defined in the *PlanLibrary*), or internal actions (defined in Java code).

3.1   Agent and Environment Representation

Jason provides the facilities to develop external complex environments where agents can take action, and interface the execution of the agents within such environments, i.e. keeping the deliberation process on the Jason side (following a pure logic-based definition). Then, it is possible to interface Jason and NetLogo (a rapid and flexible prototyping tool[1]) due to both are Java-based free pieces of software with API facilities that grant their interoperability.

In order to develop and demonstrate our work, we configure a simple vacuum cleaning environment as a model in NetLogo: a 11×11 grid-like environment populated by walls an a single cleaning agent operating in it. The objective was to reproduce the same simple environment as used in [26] but adjusted within the pure BDI agent framework currently Jason makes available. Hence, the model is the scenario where the actions will be performed and from where the agent will gather its perceptions. The vacuum cleaning agent is represented as a NetLogo *turtle* and as a Jason agent. The functionality of the vacuum agent, is defined in Jason in terms of actions and plans plans included in the *PlanLibrary*. A translation step from Jason code to NetLogo and vice versa is performed whenever sensing and acting is needed.

The situated BDI agent has a limited perception of the environment: an array of cells in front of it restricted to a sight of one cell of depth represented as five predicates: $[o1(C), o2(C), o3(C), o4(C), o5(C)]$, where $C = \{0, 25\}$ values denote: cleared space, boundaries or walls, respectively. Also, the agent is constrained to moving according to the 4-connected way: only the cells in front and both sides are allowed to move in. The movement through the environment is based on the following primitives: (i) `moveForward`: advance one position ahead when no obstacle is present; (ii) `turnRight`: change its perspective turning 90° to the right; and (iii) `turnLeft`: turning 90° to the left.

---

[1] http://ccl.northwestern.edu/netlogo/.

The unique function of these actions is to return a command to be sent to the environment (the actual NetLogo model) to make the *turtle* execute the corresponding movement (go further one patch/cell, turn left or right).

Once the system starts, the environment sends the start perception to the Jason agent, it configures the command to create the *turtle* in the environment, and begins to run wandering throughout the environment using its plans to move.

4   Intentional Learning in Jason

The earlier implementation of IL regarding the generation of plans (i.e. in the activities level) was performed both in pure NetLogo and in a hybrid NetLogo-BDI architecture [26]. In contrast, the developments presented here are aimed at including the complete learning process in a full BDI agent framework, Jason, and where tested by learning a different behaviour: the left-handed wall-following.

The main issues around the implementation of IL are: capturing the intention structure and changing the plan library at run time; controlling the execution of intentions (by means of another intention); monitoring an action to check its failure; and controlling the deliberation process at the meta-level.

To manage these points Jason provides methods to retrieve the agent's intentions stack, and meta programing facilities as meta-plans and meta-events to manage intention (suspend, resume, fail) and to change the repertoire of plans (add, delete or modify).

The purpose of IL in the BDI architecture is to generate new plans to be added into the *PlanLibrary* of the learning agent in order to increase its range of actions. To do so, three learning templates are defined to produce new plans, namely, including one action, repetition and sequence of actions. The criteria of plan updating and acquisition follows a RL-like strategy based in the utilities reported by the plans when running. Furthermore, the action selection mechanism implemented in Jason by its Java *plan selection* function can be extended to adjust the way the plans are selected to be executed in case they are applicable and share the name. This is the case of the movement plans of the vacuum cleaning agent including the new learned plans. As a result, this function is modified to choose the most beneficial plans according to their computed utilities.

Plan Acquisition. In the current implementation there are two types of plans: *movement* plans and *primitives* (moveForward, turnRight, turnLeft). The former are triggered by the main loop of action of the agent whenever a movement is required in the environment. Once any of these plans is fired, i.e. it is applicable due to the environment and the current mental state of the agent, the plan fires a *primitive*.

IL is demonstrated by reaching a couple of behaviours virtually from scratch as they are not defined by the movement plans: (a) manage tunnel-like structures; and (b) reach a left-handed wall-following behaviour.

In the first case, the given movement plans can drive to a failure when a tunnel-like structure is found in the environment as any of them are applicable in such a case. The inapplicability of movement plans is monitored by a *fail* plan (coded in Jason as other plans). Once the failure occurs, the fail plan fires the learning procedure by calling an internal action implemented in Java by extending the default internal action Java classes.

On the second case, the intended wall-following behaviour is not included in the movement plans. Plans are annotated with utilities to indicate its adequacy in pursuing the task. Whenever a movement plan is fired the meta-level plans evaluate its utility and determine if the learning should be triggered. In this way, each time a plan is fired, the utility is computed based on the primitive's rewards. Rewards are discrete values $\{1, -1\}$ provided in design time depending on its contribution to the intended wall-following behaviour: 1 if the agent touches a wall with the left-hand, -1 otherwise. Under this framework a different behaviour could be targeted, in such a case the primitives would be different in order to fulfil the objective of the task and consequently, the set of rewards should be changed accordingly to contribution of each primitive to the intended behaviour.

Then, the learning is triggered as a consequence of either a failure or when the movements of the agent lose their utility. In both cases, the result of the learning function is is a new plan added to the agent's *PlanLibrary*.

There are three templates to guide the learning of new plans: one action, repetition, and sequences.

The first template generates a plan with only **one action** in its body. The actions considered as candidates to be added in the new plan belong to the set of actions included in the other plans' bodies. The selection criteria are the applicability of the candidate actions to the current context, for instance the context that gave rise to the failure, and the reward of the action for the current state of affairs of the environment.

The second template concerns the generation of more complex plans, i.e. plans with **repetitions of actions**, that can potentially give rise to more useful behaviours due to the interaction with the environment and the new set of actions included in them. The number of action is given by a parameter N setup at design time.

The last template for implementing IL produces a new plan including an alternate **sequence of actions**. Differently from [26] where plans and actions are stored in a list to avoid repetitions, in our system the selection of the actions is based on the applicability according to the current context and the utility of actions in the history of executions, i.e. sampling the trace of executed plan/action so far. In this case the length of the sequence is also defined by the parameter N.

The development of the last template requires additional changes in comparison with the previous ones, namely, collecting a sequence of fired actions while the agent is interacting with the environment before a failure occurs in order to track sequences of valid actions according to their demonstrated past applicability and utility. Thus, there is a need to track the times an action is triggered, and the pre and post conditions when it does so, i.e. the transitions between states and the actions to perform those changes. This is accomplished by setting tracking beliefs of the actions undertaken by the agent and computing its utility. The belief tAB/13 is used to collect the transitions of the context when a primitive plan is fired, i.e. the array of cells of the agent's line of sight [o1(C) ...o5(C)]; the belief lastMove/13 collects the past execution of a plan for moving (the last previous movement action).

The template of learning to generate alternate sequences of actions is showed in Algorithm 1. Once the set of relevant plans (those who match the failed trigger TFL) are stored in RelPlans by the function RelevantPlan (line 1), the actions of the body of each plan in RelPlans are collected by the function GetActions (line 2) taking into account the context when the failure occurs (cntx). Then, they are ranked via the function GetMaxRankedAction based on their utility showed so far (line 3). Context pcntx is initialised with the value of cntx (line 4) in order to query the belief tAB/13 looking for an applicable action cAct. From the tracked beliefs, the learning performs a sequence by matching the contexts of the past fired actions (while loop in line 5) stored in the list Actions (line 7). In addition, the context must be a logical consequence of the agent's beliefs at the current moment, i.e. the current perceptions of the environment (line 6). Contexts and applicable actions are updated accordingly to the belief's content (lines 8 and 9). The process continues until chaining at most N actions.

Algorithm 1. The template for adding a plan with sequences of actions

---

Data: TFL: the failed trigger; $cntx$: failed plan context
Result: A new plan to be added into the agent's $PlanLibrary$
begin

    /* Get actions from other plans matching the context   */
1    $RelPlans = \text{RelevantPlans}(TFL)$
2    $cActions = \text{GetActions}(RelPlans, cntx)$
3    $cAct = \text{GetMaxRankedAction}(cActions)$
    /* Select actions from $tAB/13$ */
4    $pcntx = cntx$
5   **while** *(cAct in tAB/13 with pcntx) and ($|Actions| < N$)* **do**
6   **if** *agentBelieves(pcntx)* **then**
7   *Actions*.add(*cAct*)
8            $cAct = $ action in tAB with $pcntx$
9            $pcntx = $ post-context in $tAB/13$ with $cAct$
10   Building the new plan $[TFL : cntx : Actions]$ annotated with $learn(1)$

In any of the aforementioned cases, the utility of a new plan is taken from the utility of the last executed plan augmented in 0.1, to give it higher precedence and this plan can be chosen in the first place when the applicability could compete with other plans already stored in the $PlanLibrary$.

Exploration and Exploitation. A characteristic issue in learning is the exploitation and exploration dilemma, and in our case this regards the option of keep using the learned plans versus continuing to add new ones. To this end, the agent has the following elements to help it decide: (a) An exploration parameter e; and (b) Re-learning stages.

The first case introduces variations in the eligibility of actions by transferring the RL e-*greedy* strategy [27] from the action selection to the learning process. In other words, instead of applying that strategy every time the agent acts here it is restricted only to the learning case, keeping the action selection mechanism based on the plan utilities. As a result, low ranked actions (which suggest lower order of preference) are able to be part of a new plan. e is set to 0.01 as in [27].

Re-learning stages are related with the fulfillment of the task. They are implemented in meta-plans as a learning asking arising when a number of executions exceeded an adequacy threshold, i.e. when the number of executions with negative utilities reaches the threshold experimentally set to 10 due the number of possible steps in the environment (at most 9 steps without reaching a wall). On this basis, re-learning stages address the agent to two possible outcomes: (a) plan revision, applicable when a learned plan seems to has lost its adequacy for pursuing the task (as described below); or (b) the addition of a new plan, applicable when the plan belongs to the original given set of plans.

Utility Updating. The learning templates generate a new plan in the *Plan-Library* with a utility based on the last executed plan. As explained above, the plan's applicability is defined by the context, i.e. the array of cells in front of the agent's line of sight: [o1..o5], and its utility. In other words, the more beneficial the plan, the more likely it is it will be used and consequently its utility will increase respectively. This establishes a criterion of plan selection that determines the behaviour of the agent while running and confers the capability of keep learning as required by the environment changes when pursuing its intended task.

In order to keep the utilities updated, two tracking beliefs are used: qr/8 and q/7. The former stores the rewards of a primitive action belonging to a certain plan; the latter stores the utility q_c of a plan once it has been triggered, i.e. this utility takes into account just the current state of the agent when fires that plan. Then the utility is computed by means of a RL-inspired formulae [27]:

$$q_c = \sum_i^n q_i \tag{1}$$

Where q_i are each of the values stored in q/7 matching the plan's name and the current context. In the case of plans with only one action, q_i is the past value, otherwise it is the summation of all the primitives belonging to the plan fired similar contexts.

On the other hand, the values of the q_r values are computed according to the Q-Learning utility updating:

$$q_r = q_r + \delta * (R + \gamma * q_i - q_r) \qquad (2)$$

Where δ is the learning rate set to 0.1; γ is the discount factor set to 0.95; and q_i as defined in (1) is the plan utility. This keep the balance between past and current utilities, allowing the updating to take into account the new observations from the environment.

Plan Revision. The learning templates generate three kind of plans based on partial information, i.e. the perceptions of the agent up to a given moment. In some cases, the sub-goals of a plan could not complete their execution. Consequently, a revision of the plan is needed. Moreover, plan revision is a form of tuning mechanism for learning to improve the agent's behaviour once the learned plans' results are not good enough to fulfil an intended task or to reach certain behaviour. There are two cases where plan revision is needed:

- In the basic case, to cope with the inapplicability of sub goals; and
- When a plan seems no longer helpful to fulfil a task given its negative utility and it has been executed surpassing the fixed threshold. Then, plan revision aims to increase the utilities of a plan again.

In both cases, the target plan is reviewed and some of the actions are substituted by new ones. In the first case, an action is eligible to be deleted from a plan whenever it fails. On the other hand, the actions in the plan are rearranged based on its utility and their context of applicability, given priority to the most beneficial sequences. The candidate actions are taken based on the beliefs tAB/13 and qr/13 and their matching context of application.

5   Experiments and Results

The vacuum cleaning agent starts its behaviour by wandering around the environment, taking decisions about moving based on its plans.

Two cases were used to test the learning: (a) Failure handling: a failure occurs as the given agent plans are not capable to manage tunnel-like structures in the environment; and (b) Reach a left-handed wall-following behaviour. In both cases the agent lacked from the given plans to fulfil the task.

Different configurations to test the learning under diverse conditions have been used. The learning templates were run 5 times in each scenario. Each run lasts for 3500 movement actions for learning and 1750 for testing. What is reported here is the mean of those runs.

5.1   Failure Handling

While the agent traverses the environment, at a certain point it reaches a tunnel-like structure which cannot be managed by its given movement plans. Figure 2 illustrates when the agent starts the learning process. In (A) the agent reaches a tunnel-like structure, as the plans in its *PlanLibrary* cannot cope with this situation the fail arises. Subsequently, the learning process is started using the templates described earlier; while in (B) after the learning process is finished, a new plan is added to the *PlanLibrary*. After learning, the agent has a plan with a context applicability able to cope with tunnel-like structures. Then, the agent's code is saved on the hard disc and the agent now has increased its set of abilities.

A) The learning process firing   B) The learned plan

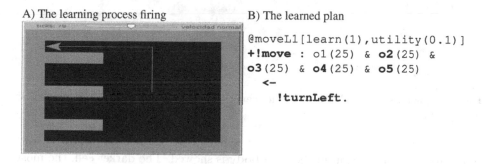

```
@moveL1[learn(1),utility(0.1)]
+!move : o1(25) & o2(25) &
o3(25) & o4(25) & o5(25)
   <-
   !turnLeft.
```

Fig. 2. When no applicable plan exists, the learning generates a new one to be directly added to the *PlanLibrary*.

Learning of plans with one action and repetitions in their body suffices to solve the task in all the cases, while the sequences of actions are more sensible to the history of environment observations: when early applied can result in loops of turns left and right, keeping the agent into the tunnel-like structure. In such a case, plan revision is applied.

5.2   Wall-Following

In addition to managing the tunnel-like structures, this test is focused on learning a left-handed wall-following type of behaviour not included in the given plans. The behaviour is reached after hundreds of interactions (sensing-acting) with the environment as a result of the generation of new plans and the tuning of the utility as the agent traverses the environment. It is important to note that the agent has restricted scope of sight making it impossible to sense when it has left or reached a wall through a corner increasing the difficulty degree of this task. The wall-following behaviour is depicted in Fig. 3 using three different scenarios, the yellow lines mark when the agent touches a wall on the left side. In Fig. 4 the cumulated times of a cell has been visited in each of the scenarios using the

Fig. 3. The agent achieving the left-hand wall-following behaviour in different scenarios.

B) Scenario 1   B) Scenario 2   C) Scenario 3

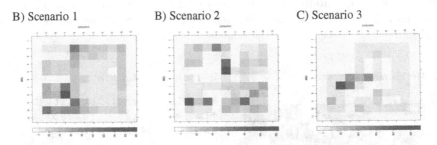

Fig. 4. Cumulated visited of cells in the scenarios using the template to add one action in the plan.

template with one action in the plan body is showed. The darker cell, the most visited one. As can be seen, the boundaries of the environment are the most visited illustrating the wall-following behaviour.

Table 1 includes a summary of the plans on 5 runs showing the number of useful actions, i.e. the times when the agent touches a wall with the left side, reviews and the liveness of the plans (their execution frequency) which gives a hint about how a plan is being used during the run due its applicability and its adequacy for the task.

Table 1. Summary of the wall-following behaviour tests on diverse scenarios tested up to 3500 movements after 1750 testing actions. Letters stand for Scenario (S), Template (ILT), Learned Plans (LrPl), Revisions (PRev), Plan Liveness (PLiv), Useful Actions (UsAc), where (O) denotes one action and (S) refers to sequences of actions.

S	ILT	LrPl	PRev	PLiv	UsAc
1	O	21	827	406	548
	S	19	445	85	135
2	O	27	867	370	501
	S	24	814	535	431
3	O	26	806	408	538
	S	19	816	119	139

As can be seen, the learning template with one action in their body populates the agent with more number of plans than the other strategy and the template with more than one action require more plan reviews than learned plans. This can be noticed when comparing the differences between the scenarios: the template with one action included 6 more plans in the second scenario than in the first one and 40 more revisions were required; while the template with sequences of actions included 5 more plans but implied 369 more revisions in the same scenarios.

Comparing the second and third scenarios, the template with one action decreased in 1 plan the number of learnt plans requiring 61 less revisions, while the other template decreased in 5 the number of learnt plans but increased in 2 the revisions.

Finally, comparing the third and first scenarios, the one action template increased 5 the learnt plans and decreased in 21 the revisions, while the other template keeps the same number of learnt plans but implies 371 more revisions.

This is explained by two causes: firstly, each scenario configures a different experience for the agent, which is reflected in the learning of the agent (particularly in the plan revision), and secondly, because the narrow scope of applicability of plans with more than one action in the body, i.e. the plan context is determined by the context where either an error arose or a revision was performed, and the applicability or benefit of the actions can be affected as the state of affairs in learning could be different of those exhibit when the plan is fired, consequently, template with longer plans receive less feedback from the environment and need to be constantly reviewed.

Finally, Fig. 5 (A) shows the plan utilities of an agent running using the learning templates. As explained before, in addition to the plan applicability the action-selection function considers the plan utility to establish a precedence in the execution of plan. Accordingly, the plans with the better rewards and utility will be selected most frequently. On the other hand, despite of their applicability, some plans could decrease their utility reaching cases where their reported benefit to the task is lower or even negative. It also could be the case that some plans be seldom applied due the features of the scenario and the movements of the agent after this plan is added to the *PlanLibrary*. The plot shows a snapshot of the plan utilities while the agent is running and how the plans are varying their utilities where in early stages they have similar values and they became different during the run. In (B) a plot of the plans generated by the three templates are showed while running up to 3500 actions. As can be seen, the strategy that includes more plans is the one action template, this is explained also because the longer plans include more actions and the plans take more time to be evaluated delaying the addition of new plans. It has an impact in the training as more cycles are required for the repetition and sequences.

The agent starts exploring the environment and the learning fires as the utilities of the plans decreased. The behaviour is reached as a result of the addition of new plans and plan revisions.

A) Plan utilities

B) Number of plans learned

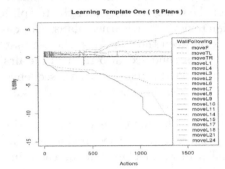
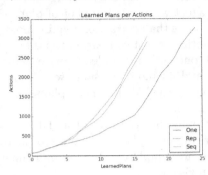

Fig. 5. (A) Plan utilities when the agent is running and with the one action learning template (B) plot of the plans generated by the three learning strategies in same scenario.

6   Related Work and Discussion

Plan acquisition in cognitive agents has been of interest in the agent and MAS community and several works to include planning and learning in BDI agents have been proposed. In [26], the Intentional Learning framework is implemented in two ways: (a) developing a BDI layer upon NetLogo, and (b) on a hybrid NetLogo-BDI architecture (using JAM as the BDI engine) [30]. Furthermore, in [19, 20] a very basic BDI implementation in pure NetLogo programing language is reported, mainly focused on teaching the MAS BDI foundations. This approach includes communication capabilities and a straightforward way to implement intentions (as a list of commands). However, being a basic implementation, it lacks a proper definition of plans and other facilities offered by other BDI oriented platforms [19], and it was not conceptualised to include learning. Other works have focused o IL just in the level of plan applicability using other learning strategies, mainly based on logical tree induction algorithms (either using external tools or including them as Jason libraries) [7,9,22,31], or learning goals [17] even implemented a pure RL approach in Jason [3].

On the other hand, in [13], an integrated version of Jason and a STRIPS-like planner is proposed, allowing the agent to add new plans as a result of the planner. To couple the two systems a bidirectional translation stage from AgentSpeak to the plan's representation in the planner is required to update the *PlanLibrary* of the agent. More recently, in [12], a successful probabilistic method of learning using the tracked interactions with the environment has been proposed. Despite using first-order logic to represent the agent knowledge, this work is further away from BDI agents. Consequently, it does not use AgentSpeak to encode the plans but the Relational Dynamic Influence Diagram Language (RDDL) [21].

In contrast with the aforementioned work on IL, which main focus is on learning the context of plan applicability and goals adjustment without considering to acquire new plans (i.e. no new skills are learned by the agent), the aim of our work has been to include IL in cognitive agents on the plan acquisition level within the same framework without using external systems. We have shown how this is feasible in Jason, a pure BDI agent oriented framework, through a set of templates for learning different types of plans which we have demonstrated through the implementation of the single-agent vacuum cleaning scenario. Furthermore, IL was implemented making use of the NetLogo as the environment where the agent is located.

A noteworthy feature of our work is that plans are directly represented in Jason's code (AgentSpeak). As a result, the use of external tools (like planners) is avoided, consequently, there is no need of translation processes between different plan representations. Moreover, the agent built new behaviours based only on its primitive actions and the interactions with the environment.

As it is shown in Fig. 2, the addition of new plans enables the agent to follow walls while it is capable of coping with tunnel-like structures, which is not equipped to deal with by default. The results of this work contribute to the state of the art in both IL and in BDI Multi-Agent Systems by exhibiting the feasibility of including learning driven by intentions and manipulative abduction in a pure BDI agent environment in a very simple scenario with a narrow repertoire of actions, namely, move forward, turn left and turn right.

The learning templates addressed as part of this work are: (1) learning plans with one action; (2) plans involving repetition of the same action; and (3) sequences of actions.

For the first type, in the most simple case, the learning process is just required to find a matching action with the current perceptions (an array of five cells in its line of sight) of the environment to produce a new plan. This is reached by observing the utility an action has when previously fired in a given state. On this basis, the agent can select the most useful action that matches the state of affairs at the time that the learning has started. Once the learned plan is added, the agent can use it in the following steps of reasoning and manage to escape from tunnel-like structures.

Concerning the second template, this generates a repetition of one action N times. In essence, such a plan represents a loop of execution of the same action.

The result of the last template, focused on generating sequences of actions, is a new plan which includes different actions in an alternate sequence.

The behaviour of learning new skills has been reached in both a simple problem of managing tunnel-like structures and a more complex behaviour which has been achieved essentially from scratch, namely, wall-following.

The first learning template seems to be sufficient for solving the task, by including several plans it captures a wider range of applicability of them. Plans with more than one action in their body requires more steps of plan revision due that their applicability (its pre condition) is closer related to the state of affairs when they were added to the set of plans, becoming more demanding of the revision stage to keep its utilities.

The template with one action also requires less learning steps than the repetitions and sequences and it could be considered more valuable for the intended behaviour accordingly with its higher reported number of useful actions. On the other hand, repetitions and sequences allow the agent to explore and perform a kind of map from the environment, and can easily derive to patterns of behaviours (like oscillatory and square trajectories in the domain presented here) potentially helpful in building higher level tasks not explored here.

The advantages of the work presented here can be summarized as: (a) The procedural knowledge of the agent is reused either for failure handling or to improve the agent behaviour. By plan acquisition the agent is capable of performing tasks not specified in design time. (b) The use of RL techniques for action selection confers the agent the capability of learning through interacting with the environment, on this way, the agent can approximate the model of the world by encoding this knowledge in the set of plans and the capability of refine this procedural knowledge from new interactions. Despite the work presented here relies in basic RL techniques for the selection criteria, other ranking methods can be used as long as they allow to establish a way of determining when an action is beneficial for an intended task. (c) The learning mechanism is fully integrated in the BDI framework without the use of external planning tools, progressing in enhancing agents with plan acquisition (IL in the level of activities). (d) The Manipulative Abduction component of the approach (the set of learning templates) is able to be changed, i.e. changing the templates to organize the actions in a structurally different way or even to incorporate domain knowledge when pursuing a different task.

On the other hand, some limitations of the present work can be pointed out: (a) As the applicability of plans generated by the learning templates with more than one action is affected by the narrow space of feedback that the agent gets when the learning occurs, these learnt plans demand further refinements steps. On this regard, the current implementation is focused on demonstrating the plan acquisition possibilities but nothing prevent the use of IL in the other levels, namely learning in the level of goals and plan applicability [7,22]. Furthermore, a simple version of plan revision based on the reported utility and the applicability of actions when the learning process is triggered was implemented, although a more robust analysis of the interactions with the environment could be incorporated, for instance, by adopting a more flexible action selection that consider other contexts apart from the current one. (b) In order to scale the approach to a more difficult environment or task, both the relevant set of plans and a set of applicable rewards to the aimed task must be provided as they are specific for an intended behaviour. In the simple problem presented here, the pre and pos conditions of the actions where captured by sampling the state perceived by the agent before and after executing a movement action. Consequently, jointly with the use of ad hoc learning templates an important aspect for scaling to reach behaviours with higher level of complexity is the configuration of the primitives and their precedence that should be expressed accordingly to the intended task. To do so, in [12,14] some relevant techniques that could be considered are mentioned. (c) Additionally, the re-learning stages are driven by a measure of the adequacy of the plans when pursuing a task, in the left-handed wall-following behaviour the negative utility indicates when a new learning process is needed. When changing the task this criteria should be adjusted as required to fit the new conditions.

Finally, it is worth noting that working with a logic-based programming language poses additional challenges to IL and planning in general. An example of a challenge is the case of conditional actions: despite the fact that conditional actions can be integrated in learning, the logic programming paradigm splits the condition in different structures according to the options (i.e. plans), which implies in terms of plan generation the need to build different plans instead of just one. This is an open question which is currently under consideration and will be addressed as part of our future work.

7   Conclusions and Future Work

Learning in cognitive systems has been addressed from different perspectives, including using traditional Machine Learning algorithms that are called by the agents in certain circumstances, or other proposals that are more aligned with the paradigm of cognitive agents. This latter line of work includes Intentional Learning, which has been developed in different directions: learning referring to goals, plan selection and plan acquisition.

In this paper, we have presented a first implementation of IL taking the plan acquisition direction, i.e. learning of plans driven by intention monitoring and guided by Manipulative Abduction. The scenario that we have experimented and demonstrated our work is the well-known vacuum cleaning agent located in a grid-like environment with the purpose of traversing the 11×11 cells that comprise the environment following the walls on the left-hand side.

We have developed and implemented three cases of learning within a declarative BDI system, the Jason BDI framework. To the best of our knowledge, this work represents the first such inclusion of IL in a fully fledged BDI declarative environment. Although we have demonstrated the concepts and templates in a simple environment, we would argue that the inclusion of IL in a BDI agent provides the means to develop agents that are able to learn at run-time and modify their behaviour and cope with situations that have not been taken into account in terms of their provided plan library. Altogether, plan generation and plan revision allow the agent to keep in an ever-learning mode, a desirable feature in dynamic domains.

This is an essential first step in developing Intentional Learning within a multi-agent environment consisting of BDI agents that can learn on their own, but also by working together.

The work presented here shows the primitives for including IL in Jason, addressing the cases of three learning templates as the guiding mechanism. Additionally, it is successfully exploits the inter-operation of Jason and Net-Logo, taking the advantage of the latter as a rendering tool for environments and agents, while the reasoning is kept on the side of the BDI engine. While it is not restricted to the current domain, it inspires to try more complex applications using both powerful MAS frameworks.

Our endeavour is ongoing and there are a number of avenues that are currently under exploration and will be considered as part of future work:

- The current experimental setting is limited and we aim to test the learning processes developed in more challenging environments and in different domains where a different set of learning templates could be explored.
- Additionally to continue exploring the plan revision (concerned with the content of the plans) and the acquisition of several plans (in order to cover a wider scope of cases), IL at the level of context of applicability is a promising extension of this work. Moreover, the parameter N in sequences and repetitions of plans should be determined automatically.
- Finally, our ultimate goal is to progress the state of the art by including IL within a multi-agent system set up and in particular, we would like to study the influence of a group of agents in the learning process. One of the main aspects in MAS organization is the exchange of messages between agents and the agreement that can be obtained in order to tackle a common goal or task. Within such a context, there are different views/levels of information that need to be considered: partial/individual information; partial collective information; and environmental information.

Acknowledgment. We would like to thank to the project no. 48510384 of SEP-DSA/UAM-169, for the support provided to this work.

References

1. Airiau, S., Padgham, L., Sardiña, S., Sen, S.: Enhancing the adaptation of BDI agents using learning techniques. IJATS **1**(2), 1–18 (2009)
2. Alonso, E., D'inverno, M., Kudenko, D., Luck, M., Noble, J.: Learning in multi-agent systems. J. Knowl. Eng. Rev. **16**, 277–284 (2001)
3. Badica, A., Badica, C., Ivanovic, M., Mitrovic, D.: An approach of temporal difference learning using agent-oriented programming. In: 2015 20th International Conference on Control Systems and Computer Science, pp. 735–742, May 2015
4. Bordini, R.H., Hübner, J.F.: Jason: Java-based AgentSpeak interpreter used with saci for multi-agent distribution over the net (2005)
5. Bordini, R.H., Hübner, J.F.: BDI agent programming in agentspeak using *Jason*. In: Toni, F., Torroni, P. (eds.) CLIMA 2005. LNCS (LNAI), vol. 3900, pp. 143–164. Springer, Heidelberg (2006). doi:10.1007/11750734_9
6. Bratman, M.E.: Intention, Plans, and Practical Reason. Harvard University Press, Cambridge (1987)
7. Guerra-Hernández, A., Fallah-Seghrouchni, A., Soldano, H.: Learning in BDI multi-agent systems. In: Dix, J., Leite, J. (eds.) CLIMA 2004. LNCS (LNAI), vol. 3259, pp. 218–233. Springer, Heidelberg (2004). doi:10.1007/978-3-540-30200-1_12
8. Guerra-Hernandez, A., Ortiz-Hernandez, G.: Toward BDI sapient agents: learning intentionally. In: Mayorga, R., Perlovsky, L. (eds.) Toward Artificial Sapience, pp. 77–91. Springer, London (2008). doi:10.1007/978-1-84628-999-6_5

9. Guerra-Hernandez, A., Ortiz-Hernandez, G., Luna-Ramirez, W.A.: Jason smiles: incremental BDI MAS learning. In: Sixth Mexican International Conference on Artificial Intelligence - Special Session 2007, MICAI 2007, pp. 61–70, November 2007
10. Hao, J., Leung, H.F., Ming, Z.: Multiagent reinforcement social learning toward coordination in cooperative multiagent systems. ACM Trans. Auton. Adapt. Syst. 9(4), 20:1–20:20 (2014)
11. Jennings, N.R., Wooldridge, M.: Agent-oriented software engineering. Artif. Intell. 117, 277–296 (2000)
12. Martínez, D., Alenyà, G., Torras, C., Ribeiro, T., Inoue, K.: Learning relational dynamics of stochastic domains for planning. In: Proceedings of the Twenty-Sixth International Conference on Automated Planning and Scheduling, ICAPS 2016, London, UK, pp. 235–243, 12–17 June 2016
13. Meneguzzi, F., Luck, M.: Declarative planning in procedural agent architectures. Expert Syst. Appl. 40(16), 6508–6520 (2013)
14. Meneguzzi, F., De Silva, L.: Planning in BDI agents: a survey of the integration of planning algorithms and agent reasoning. Knowl. Eng. Rev. 30(1), 1–44 (2013)
15. Ortiz-Hernandez, G.: Aprendizaje incremental en sistemas multi-agente BDI. Master's thesis, Departamento de Inteligencia Artificial, Fac. de Fisica e Inteligencia Artificial, Universidad Veracruzana, Mexico, September 2007
16. Van Dyke Parunak, H., Brueckner, S.A.: Engineering swarming systems. In: Bergenti, F., Gleizes, M.P., Zambonelli, F. (eds.) Methodologies and Software Engineering for Agent Systems, vol. 11, pp. 341–376. Springer, Heidelberg (2004). doi:10.1007/1-4020-8058-1_21
17. Phung, T., Winikoff, M., Padgham, L.: Learning within the BDI framework: an empirical analysis. In: Khosla, R., Howlett, R.J., Jain, L.C. (eds.) KES 2005. LNCS (LNAI), vol. 3683, pp. 282–288. Springer, Heidelberg (2005). doi:10.1007/11553939_41
18. Rao, A.S., Georgeff, M.P.: BDI agents: from theory to practice. In: Proceedings of The First International Conference on Multi-Agent Systems (ICMAS-95), pp. 312–319. AAAI (1995)
19. Sakellariou, I., Kefalas, P., Stamatopoulou, I.: Enhancing netlogo to simulate BDI communicating agents. In: Darzentas, J., Vouros, G.A., Vosinakis, S., Arnellos, A. (eds.) SETN 2008. LNCS (LNAI), vol. 5138, pp. 263–275. Springer, Heidelberg (2008). doi:10.1007/978-3-540-87881-0_24
20. Sakellariou, I., Kefalas, P., Stamatopoulou, I.: Teaching intelligent agents using netlogo. In: Proceedings of the ACM-IFIP Informatics Education Europe III Conference, IEEIII Venice, Italy (2008)
21. Sanner, S.: Relational dynamic influence diagram language (RDDL): language description. Unpublished ms, Australian National University (2010)
22. Singh, D., Sardina, S., Padgham, L., James, G.: Integrating learning into a BDI agent for environments with changing dynamics. In: Proceedings of the Twenty-Second International Joint Conference on Artificial Intelligence, IJCAI 2011, Vol. 3, pp. 2525–2530. AAAI Press (2011)
23. Singh, V., Singh, G., Pande, S.: Emergence, self-organization and collective intelligence - modeling the dynamics of complex collectives in social and organizational settings. In: 2013 UKSim 15th International Conference on Computer Modelling and Simulation (UKSim), pp. 182–189, April 2013
24. Subagdja, B., Rahwan, I., Sonenberg, L.: Learning as abductive deliberations. In: Yang, Q., Webb, G. (eds.) PRICAI 2006. LNCS (LNAI), vol. 4099, pp. 11–20. Springer, Heidelberg (2006). doi:10.1007/978-3-540-36668-3_4

25. Subagdja, B., Sonenberg, L.: Learning plans with patterns of actions in bounded-rational agents. In: Khosla, R., Howlett, R.J., Jain, L.C. (eds.) KES 2005. LNCS (LNAI), vol. 3683, pp. 30–36. Springer, Heidelberg (2005). doi:10.1007/11553939_5
26. Subagdja, B., Sonenberg, L., Rahwan, I.: Intentional learning agent architecture. Auton. Agents Multi-Agent Syst. **18**(3), 417–470 (2009)
27. Sutton, R.S., Barto, A.G.: Introduction to Reinforcement Learning, 1st edn. MIT Press, Cambridge (1998)
28. Tan, A.H., Xiao, D.: Self-organizing cognitive agents and reinforcement learning in multi-agent environment. In: IEEE/WIC/ACM International Conference on Intelligent Agent Technology, pp. 351–357, September 2005
29. Tuyls, K., Weiss, G.: Multiagent learning: basics, challenges, and prospects. AI Mag. **33**(3), 41–52 (2012)
30. Wilensky, U.: Netlogo. Center for Connected Learning and Computer-Based Modeling. Northwestern University, Evanston (1999)
31. Guerra-Hernández, A., González-Alarcón, C.A., El Fallah Seghrouchni, A.: Jason induction of logical decision trees: a learning library and its application to commitment. In: Sidorov, G., Hernández Aguirre, A., Reyes García, C.A. (eds.) MICAI 2010. LNCS, vol. 6437, pp. 374–385. Springer, Heidelberg (2010). doi:10.1007/978-3-642-16761-4_33

Understanding the Behaviour of Learning-Based BDI Agents in the Braess' Paradox

João Faccin[1(✉)], Ingrid Nunes[1,2], and Ana Bazzan[1]

[1] Universidade Federal do Rio Grande do Sul, Porto Alegre, Brazil
{jgfaccin,ingridnunes,bazzan}@inf.ufrgs.br
[2] TU Dortmund, Dortmund, Germany

Abstract. The Braess' paradox is a well-known problem associated with route choice and traffic distribution. Agent-based simulations that investigate this paradox typically model driver's behaviour using reactive agent architectures, which simplify and abstract an inherently complex behaviour. The BDI architecture is an alternative widely used in multi-agent systems, which has not been evaluated as a suitable solution to deal with this problem. We thus in this paper detail an empirical evaluation of the BDI architecture, enhanced with a learning-based plan selection, to address the Braess' paradox. We describe the results of two simulations configured to reproduce the paradox behaviour. Results indicate that agents are able to soften the effects of the Braess' paradox using only local information, as opposed to existing alternatives, including when the environment is dynamic.

Keywords: Braess' paradox · Agent-based Modelling and Simulation · Traffic simulation · BDI architecture

1 Introduction

Traffic-related problems have been extensively investigated in the last decades. They are fundamental problems in the society, because solving them not only improves transportation but also address environmental issues. These traffic-related problems are particularly observed in large city centres and metropolitan areas, which tend to concentrate most of the vehicle fleet of a region, and range from constantly emerging traffic jams to increased air pollution.

In order to provide solutions for these problems, *software simulations* arise as a valuable resource, as they allow the replication of real-world scenarios in a controlled environment without the constraints imposed by the need for a physical infrastructure of roads and vehicles. *Agent-based Modelling and Simulation* (ABMS) [8,11] is a paradigm particularly suited for the development of these simulations. It differentiates from the most conventional simulation paradigms by being a *bottom-up approach* in which individuals of a scenario are modelled as *agents*. It is thus possible to model heterogeneous scenarios comprising agents

© Springer International Publishing AG 2017
J.O. Berndt et al. (Eds.): MATES 2017, LNAI 10413, pp. 187–204, 2017.
DOI: 10.1007/978-3-319-64798-2_12

with behaviours that may vary in complexity and sophistication. The interactions among these agents, or between them and their environment, originate the (sometimes unexpected) phenomena one wants to observe and analyse.

The Braess' paradox [3] is one of these phenomena. It states that in a scenario with different routes from a given origin to a given destination in which drivers choose their routes selfishly, the addition of a new route with reduced commuting time may increase the drivers' travel time. In such a scenario, the driver's preference for a route is specified by the road utility, which is based on the time required to commute in that route. Such time is defined by a function regarding the number of vehicles using the route in a given moment. Although initially presented as a traffic-related problem, instances of the Braess' paradox can be found in several different domains, such as in chemistry and energy-related scenarios [9,15], for example.

Several approaches were proposed in the context of ABMS to provide solutions capable of softening or even solving this paradox [2,6]. Traditionally, simulations of scenarios that reproduce this problem are modelled using reactive agent architectures. However, this design choice can sometimes abstract and simplify the complexity inherent to the human behaviour, which may compromise the validity of such simulations regarding real-world situations. Moreover, most of the existing approaches able to achieve promising results in this scenario require information or resources that are not typically available in realistic situations, such as the awareness of global travel time of agents. Despite the exploration of multiple solutions to address this paradox, there are various approaches that could still be explored to possibly mitigate limitations of existing work. An example is *cognitive agents*, which have been widely investigated in the context of multi-agent systems.

In this paper, we thus explore the use of cognitive agents to address the Braess' paradox. More specifically, we exploit an extension [4] of the well-known BDI (Belief-Desire-Intention) architecture [14] for modelling drivers in our scenario. This architecture structures an agent in terms of beliefs, desires (or goals) and intentions. These mental attitudes represent, respectively, the information an agent has about the world, the states of the world it wants to bring about, and the goals an agent is committed to achieve and for which it has suitable plans. When integrated into a reasoning cycle, these mental attitudes endow agents with a flexibility that does not exist in purely reactive agents. Additionally, the extended architecture used in this work makes agents able of learning the relationship between their context and the outcomes of their plans. Therefore, an agent can predict plan outcomes based on its current context, and to select for execution the plan expected to perform better according to agent preferences. To assess the benefits provided by using these learning-based BDI agents in a scenario that replicates the Braess' paradox, we compare their behaviour against agents with two different plan selection strategies.

The remainder of this paper is organised as follows. In Sect. 2, we present an overview of ABMS and how existing approaches exploit it to address the Braess' paradox, also introducing the extended BDI architecture used in this work. In

Sect. 3, we describe the modelled problem and the setup of our simulations in two different scenarios. The results of such simulations are presented and discussed in Sect. 4. Finally, we conclude this paper in Sect. 5.

2   Background and Related Work

Modelling and simulation are two fundamental activities in research in several application areas [12]. When combined, these activities allow researchers to study phenomena that cannot be easily reproduced in the real world due to their scale or even technical limitations, e.g. the disappearing of an entire civilisation. These modelling and simulation activities comprise the development of a model, i.e. a system representation, and its execution, respectively. There are different approaches that provide guidelines on representing and executing models. Next, we briefly overview that used in this work, followed by further background needed to understand our work and a discussion regarding related work.

2.1   Agent-Based Modelling and Simulation

The Agent-based Modelling and Simulation (ABMS) paradigm is particularly suited for modelling complex systems with emergent behaviour. Models based on this paradigm rely on the specification of three main components: (i) the set of agents; (ii) the environment; and (iii) the interactions among agents and between agents and the environment. The first characterises the set of individuals that actively participate in a scenario. The behaviour of such individuals can be separately specified so that a scenario with agents behaving heterogeneously can be easily modelled. The second component concerns all other simulation elements, such as resources and elements without active behaviour [8]. Finally, how the interactions among model elements are specified determines the dynamics of a system. These interactions may originate the phenomena one aims to observe, analyse or predict, and such generative nature characterises one of the main features of the ABMS paradigm. The execution of a model, i.e. its simulation, requires additional information, such as parameters indicating the number of agents to be inserted in a system and how they must be initialised.

Building and simulating agent-based models become particularly useful for the development of traffic simulations. In real world scenarios, the dynamics of an entire traffic-system emerge from individual drivers' behaviour, which may vary from driver to driver, and may involve complex reasoning processes. Therefore, modellers can leverage the existence of a diversity of agent architectures to model drivers with different characteristics. Moreover, agent-based simulations can have their dynamics analysed from at least two viewpoints: one considering individual agents, the other regarding the entire system [8]. It not only allows modellers to validate what is being simulated but also provides a way of analysing how subtle changes in drivers' behaviour may impact the overall system. In fact, several traffic-related problems have been replicated and studied by means of the use of ABMS. Next, we present one of such problems, named the Braess' paradox, which we address in this paper.

2.2   The Braess' Paradox

The Braess' paradox [3] consists of a counter-intuitive idea whose characteristics have been widely investigated [1,13]. It states that, contrary to popular belief, adding an extra route with reduced commuting time to a traffic network may increase drivers' travel time. Such phenomenon was firstly noticed by Dietrich Braess in 1968 when analysing the scenario depicted in Fig. 1.

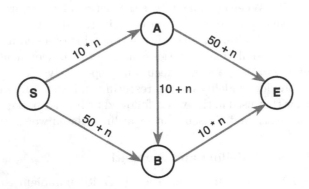

Fig. 1. The five-link network originally proposed by Braess et al. [3].

In this scenario, drivers must commute from a starting point S to an ending point E. For this purpose, there are initially two possible routes: routes SAE and SBE, passing by points A and B, respectively. Travelling by each route link has a particular cost, which is defined according to a linear function directly dependent on the number of vehicles on each link. Figure 1 depicts cost functions in the original scenario, where n is the number of vehicles currently travelling on a link. Considering six vehicles in the network and this initial four-link setup, it is possible to notice that the user equilibrium (UE), i.e. the vehicle distribution in which each route has the same cost and thus drivers have no incentive to change their routes, is achieved when vehicles are equally distributed between routes SAE and SBE—three vehicles for each route, taking 83 time units to commute from S to E. Such vehicle distribution also corresponds to the system optimum (SO) distribution regarding travel costs, i.e. the situation in which travel time considering all drivers is minimised (in this case, 498 time units).

Although the SO remains the same, the addition of an extra link with *reduced cost* that connects points A and B—thus leading to a new route $SABE$ between the start and ending points—modifies the UE. In this five-link setup, the system reaches an equilibrium when the traffic is evenly distributed among the three existing routes. In this scenario, the commuting time of each driver is 92 time units, which is 9 time units higher than the scenario without the SABE route. This increase in the final commuting time characterises the paradox. Table 1 presents the costs of each route as well as travel costs considering all drivers associated with different vehicle distributions in the original scenario proposed by Braess et al. [3].

Table 1. Cost of routes and total cost for different vehicle distributions ($N = 6$).

Number of drivers			Cost of route			Sum of costs of all drivers
SAE	SBE	SABE	SAE	SBE	SABE	
3	3	0	83	83	70	498
2	2	2	92	92	92	552
6	0	0	116	50	70	696
0	6	0	50	116	70	696
0	0	6	110	110	136	816

The ABMS paradigm was adopted by several approaches whose aim is to deal with the Braess' paradox, ranging from the use of learning strategies to the manipulation of the information provided to drivers. Klügl and Bazzan [7], for example, proposed an approach for binary route choice based on reinforcement learning, which can be adapted to scenarios that reproduce the paradox. In their approach, agents decide which route to select based on the average of previous rewards obtained selecting those routes. The reward provided by a route is inversely proportional to the travel time of an agent using it. Different agent behaviours specified based on a user experiment—namely impulsive, proportional and radical—were evaluated by Forno and Merlone [5]. These behaviours vary according to the rate at which agents change their choices. Decisions are based on the last travel time provided by each route. If a certain route presented a shorter travel time than the last route selected by an impulsive agent, this agent can change to that route in the next iteration. Proportional agents, in turn, have their changing rate proportional to the difference in travel time between routes. Finally, radical agents tend to stick to their last choice. In their simulations, homogeneous populations of these agents were unable to avoid the effects of the paradox.

Simulations with better outcomes were presented by Bazzan and Klügl [2]. These simulations show how manipulating the information provided to agents impacts traffic distribution. In their approach, a traffic control centre is responsible for giving to drivers information about the current traffic situation, which may or may not be accurate in order to avoid the effects of the Braess' paradox. Despite these positive results, this proposal depends on centralising, processing, and distributing information regarding the entire network, which may be infeasible in realistic scenarios. Results obtained by Hasan et al. [6] were also promising. They proposed a solution that relies on the existence of a social network traffic application, which uses traffic-related information provided by agents to compute route utilities. Thus, agents can use the application to make route choices. Although being able to solve the paradox, we must highlight that this approach requires substantial engagement from agents, which may be considered an issue in a real world scenario.

Although there are approaches able to solve (or at least mitigate the effects of) the Braess' paradox, there are issues that still need to be addressed. Some of these approaches assume that agents have access to information regarding the social impact of their choices and consider such information in a more altruistic way when selecting their routes. However, these assumptions may be unrealistic. First, because knowing the exact number of vehicles commuting in a route a priori, particularly in large-scale scenarios, is impractical even with the current availability of traffic density data. Second, altruism is not a typical characteristic of drivers, which tend to act selfishly in every situation thus caring only for their own performance (considering that there is no penalty for such behaviour). Another issue is related to the fact that drivers are frequently modelled as reactive agents, even with the existence of approaches proposing the use of cognitive agent architectures as a suitable alternative to model their behaviour [10]. Next, we overview one of these architectures, which provide agents with learning and adaptive capabilities, and can potentially address the Braess' paradox.

2.3   BDI Agents with Learning

The BDI architecture [14] is perhaps one of the most widely used agent architectures. It structures agents in terms of mental attitudes of beliefs, desires (also known as goals) and intentions, which are integrated to several abstract functions into a reasoning cycle. In this reasoning cycle, an agent updates its beliefs based on the perception of external and internal events and updates its goals accordingly. From the set of existing goals, it selects those it will commit to achieve and transforms them into intentions. Finally, suitable plans able to achieve the given intentions are selected and executed, and the cycle restarts. One of the abstract functions comprising this reasoning cycle is the plan selection function, which is responsible for the selection of suitable plans for execution. In typical implementations of the BDI architecture, this function selects plans according to a First In, First Out (FIFO) policy. However, it does not correspond to the way humans reason when choosing how to act.

In a previous work [4], we extended the BDI architecture to provide agents with a sophisticated plan selection strategy. Agents based on our approach are able to learn how particular *influence factors* impact *outcomes* of plan executions. This knowledge is then used by agents to predict how plans are expected to perform according to the current agent context. The plan selected for execution is that with an expected performance that best satisfies agent *preferences* over given *softgoals*. This learning-based plan selection strategy comprises two different stages. In the first, the agent selects plans randomly, collecting data related to influence factors and plan outcomes. When there is enough collected data, such an agent builds a prediction model for each of its plans. In the second stage, it starts to select plans according to the predictions provided by existing prediction models. Data is still being collected during this stage, and prediction models are updated following a pre-specified update rate.

3 Simulation Modelling

We investigate the use of this introduced learning-based plan selection strategy to deal with the Braess' paradox through two different simulations. The scenario in which these simulations are placed comprises a five-link network similar to that originally presented by Braess et al. [3]. The only difference relies on the cost functions of each link, which are specified according to a system of equations and inequalities proposed by Bazzan and Klügl [2] that, when solved, is able to determine cost functions that reproduce the paradox for any given number of vehicles. Figure 2 depicts the network and its cost functions, where n is the number of vehicles currently travelling a link. It is possible to notice that, in this scenario, commuting through links SB, AB or AE results in fixed travel costs. These links may represent highways with several lanes in which travel time is not affected by the number of vehicles commuting through them. Costs from links SA and BE, in turn, are directly dependent on this number, and travel times tend to increase as more vehicles use these routes. These links are the bottlenecks of our network and may represent, e.g., bridges with limited capacity.

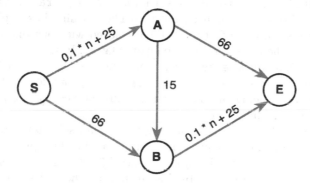

Fig. 2. The five-link network used in this work.

3.1 Standard Simulation

In the first simulation, we populate our network with *390 agents* representing drivers and their vehicles. This number of agents gives the conditions so that the Braess' paradox can occur in the proposed scenario. Considering the four-link network (without the existence of the AB link), the UE and the SO vehicle distributions correspond to agents being balanced between the two existing routes (SAE and SBE), i.e. 195 agents in each route with a travel cost of 110.5 time units per agent. The addition of the fifth link (route SABE) changes the UE to an even distribution among the three possible routes, i.e. 130 agents in each route with a travel cost of 117 time units per agent. The SO distribution, in turn, remains the same. Table 2 presents these distributions and their corresponding travel costs.

Table 2. Cost of routes and total cost for different distributions of drivers (N = 390).

Number of drivers			Cost of route			Cost over all drivers
SAE	SBE	SABE	SAE	SBE	SABE	
195	195	0	110.5	110.5	104	43095
130	130	130	117	117	117	45630
390	0	0	130	91	104	50700
0	390	0	91	130	104	50700
0	0	390	130	130	143	55770

Every driver in this simulation is modelled according to the extended BDI architecture already presented. Therefore, each agent has a goal move(S,E), which must be reached in order to move between points S and E. To achieve this goal, there are three available plans, namely SAEPlan, SBEPlan and SABEPlan, each of them representing one of the existing routes. When acting towards the achievement of move(S,E), agents must aim for the satisfaction of the softgoal Minimise Travel Time. To assess this, they monitor the travel time obtained as the outcome from their plan executions. The learning-based plan selection technique requires influence factors to be associated with outcomes, thus allowing agents to learn how the former impacts the latter. In this simulation, agents consider the number of agents in the entire network as such a factor. However, it is important to notice that such number of agents does not vary during this simulation, thus being provided just to fulfil the need of the plan selection technique for an influence factor.

As described in Sect. 2.3, the learning-based plan selection strategy can be split into two stages. One, for collecting information, in which plans are randomly selected. The other, for exploiting the knowledge obtained by selecting plans according to predicted outcomes. In this simulation, the first stage is performed in the first *50* executions of each plan. Thus, a *linear regression model* is used to build the corresponding prediction models, which are updated every *250* plan executions. To avoid local minima while in the second stage of the plan selection process, agents are able to explore plans that may not have the best-predicted outcomes in the current context. During this exploration activity, all suitable plans have the same probability of being selected. Such exploration is specified to occur in *5%* of the executions of the plan selection. Table 3 summarises the attributes of the learning-based plan selection strategy in this simulation.

3.2 Context-Dependent Simulation

The second simulation aims to investigate the behaviour of agents in a *context-dependent* scenario. While the standard simulation described above has a fixed number of agents in every episode, in this second simulation this number varies, with each episode representing a day of the week with different traffic loads, ranging from 150 to 510 agents (see Table 4). This traffic load variation allows

Table 3. Additional attributes of the plan selection strategy.

Attribute	Value
Initial data collection	50 plan executions
Prediction model update rate	250 plan executions
Exploration rate	5% of plan selections
Learning model	*linear regression*

Table 4. Traffic load in different days of the week.

Day of the week	Number of drivers
Monday	150
Tuesday	390
Wednesday	261
Thursday	390
Friday	510

us to observe how agents behave in four particular situations, which are described as follows.

Episodes that represent Mondays have *150* agents commuting in our network. Although the cost functions remain the same, the reduced number of agents significantly impacts the UE and SO of the scenario. With such configuration, the Braess' paradox does not occur, given that choosing route SABE gives to agents the shortest travel time compared to avoiding that route. However, although the UE corresponds to all agents commuting through SABE, the SO distribution regarding social cost can only be achieved with some agents travelling through SAE and SBE and accepting a travel time greater than that obtained by others. Table 5 presents costs for different distributions of a fleet with 150 agents.

In episodes representing Tuesdays and Thursdays, the number of agents is the same as in the standard simulation, i.e. *390* agents. Characteristics of such scenario configuration, which reproduces the Braess' paradox, were already pre-

Table 5. Cost of routes and total cost for different distributions of drivers (N = 150).

Number of drivers			Cost of route			Cost over all drivers
SAE	SBE	SABE	SAE	SBE	SABE	
75	75	0	98.5	98.5	80	14775
50	50	50	101	101	85	14350
150	0	0	106	91	80	15900
20	20	110	104	104	91	14170
0	0	150	106	106	95	14250

sented in Sect. 3.1. The paradox also occurs on Wednesdays, whose number of agents commuting from S to E is *261*. The difference is that, in this scenario, the UE leads to a distribution in which almost every agent uses route SABE, with a single agent travelling through each of the remaining routes. The SO distribution, in turn, requires an even distribution between routes SAE and SBE. Table 6 presents these and other possible distributions as well as their corresponding travel costs.

Table 6. Cost of routes and total cost for different distributions of drivers (N = 261).

Number of drivers			Cost of route			Cost over all drivers
SAE	SBE	SABE	SAE	SBE	SABE	
130.5	130.5	0	104.05	104.05	91.1	27157.05
87	87	87	108.4	108.4	99.8	27544.2
261	0	0	117.1	91	91.1	30563.1
0	261	0	91	117.1	91.1	30563.1
1	1	259	117	117	117	30537

Finally, in episodes representing Fridays, *510* agents travel between the start and ending points. Although the paradox is still occurring in such configuration, the increased number of agents impacts the UE in a way that it becomes close to the SO. Therefore, a reasonable sub-optimal solution may arise naturally. In UE, there are 500 agents equally distributed between routes SAE and SBE, and 10 agents travelling through SABE. In the SO distribution, route SABE is completely avoided. Table 7 presents some agent distributions and corresponding travel costs.

Table 7. Cost for routes and total cost for different distributions of drivers (N = 510).

Number of drivers			Cost of route			Cost over all drivers
SAE	SBE	SABE	SAE	SBE	SABE	
255	255	0	116.5	116.5	116	59415
250	250	10	117	117	117	59670
170	170	170	125	125	133	65110
510	0	0	142	91	116	72420
0	0	510	142	142	167	85170

Agents in this context-dependent simulation are similar to those described in Sect. 3.1, maintaining the same goal, softgoal, plans and outcome previously specified, as well as the same additional attributes of the plan selection strategy (see Table 3). The only difference consists of influence factors. The number of agents on the network is replaced by the day of the week, which is a factor that impacts plan outcomes in our scenario, being also an information easily provided in realistic scenarios.

4   Simulation Results

Both simulations described in Sect. 3 were executed for 50,000 episodes, each of them representing one travel from S to E. For the first 5,000 episodes, only routes SAE and SBE were available for use; therefore, agents are only able to perform the two corresponding plans, i.e. SAEPlan and SBEPlan. In episode 5,001, the link AB is added to the network, making route SABE available, and every agent is able to perform the plan SABEPlan. It is important to notice that, when an agent does not have a built prediction model for a particular plan, such plan receives the same expected utility than the current best predicted plan. It motivates agents to select such plan more often and build its prediction model as soon as possible, but the best plan can still be selected. Next, we present results obtained with our two simulations.

4.1   Standard Simulation

In our simulations, the distribution of vehicles in our network does not initially follow any particular trend, as agents select their routes randomly. After existing plans have their prediction models built, vehicle distribution approximates to the SO (see Table 2), being almost balanced between routes. As expected, there is a variance related to the exploration activity performed by some agents in each episode. With the addition of the link AB to the network, several agents start commuting through it (because this plan has the same probability of being chosen as the plan with the best expected utility), and at some point they have a prediction model built for the SABEPlan. However, due to this extensive use, agents associate the route SABE with the longest travel times and start avoiding it, returning to a distribution similar to that presented before the existence of that route. Such phenomenon can be observed in Fig. 3, which depicts the distribution of agents among the three routes along our simulation.

It is interesting to highlight what happens near episode 15,000. Although agents avoid to use SABE almost completely, this route is still being used by a few different agents in every episode, which is caused by the exploration activity performed by some of them. In such situation, SABE provides a shorter travel time than the other routes. Suppose that 10 agents are commuting through SABE while the other 380 are evenly distributed between SAE and SBE. In such an episode, those 10 agents will have a travel cost of 101 time units, which is lower than the 109 time units spent by agents using the other routes. As this situation repeats along the simulation and prediction models start to get updated, route SABE becomes very attractive to an increasing number of agents, as can be seen in Fig. 3. However, agents can recognise when such increase exceeds a threshold

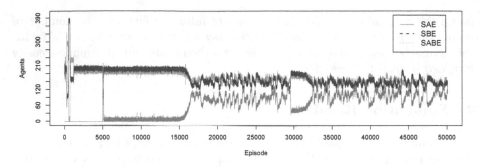

Fig. 3. Standard simulation: agent distribution between routes SAE, SBE and SABE.

in which SABE is no longer better than SAE or SBE, and they then abandon this route. It leads to SABE providing a shorter travel time again, which attracts more agents, resulting in a cyclic behaviour. This cycle tends to happen in shorter intervals along the simulation, and can be observed in Fig. 3 near episodes 29,000 and 34,000, for instance. Therefore, agents end in a distribution that constantly oscillates between the SO and the UE.

To evaluate the performance of our learning-based plan selection strategy in this scenario, we measured the travel cost over all agents and compared it with results from simulations using two different approaches for route selection. In the first, which is referred to as *greedy*, agents have the information about the cost functions of each route but not about the number of agents in the network. Thus, agents always select the route providing the shortest travel cost regarding a single vehicle. Such reasoning is similar to that presented by drivers that have different available routes, know their corresponding lengths, and select that with the shortest length disregarding possible traffic jams. The second approach, in turn, provides agents with a plan selection strategy based on *reinforcement learning*. In this case, the rewards (or costs) considered by an agent are the average times obtained through previous travels in each route. It is important to note that agents in these simulations are capable of exploring routes, as in our approach. Figure 4 presents the comparison of these two approaches with ours. A careful reader may notice that there are episodes in which the obtained global travel cost is plotted below the SO line. It happens because in such episodes, few agents may not process in time and commute after the others. Although such behaviour impacts the immediate global travel time, it does not affects the results of the overall simulation.

The greedy approach presents the worst performance regarding the global travel costs. Given their characteristics, every agent tends to select SABE, overloading that route and having a high travel cost. Our approach, in turn, has the best result considering the first ten thousands episodes after the addition of route SABE, almost reaching the SO. After this initial period, its performance is comparable to that presented by the reinforcement learning approach. Such result is due to the similar plan selection strategy performed by both approaches. In our

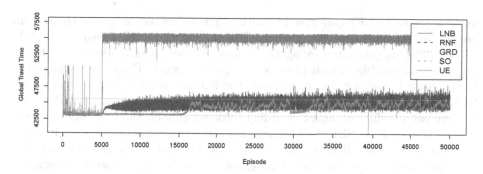

Fig. 4. Standard simulation: global travel costs of our plan selection strategy (LNB) compared with reinforcement learning (RNF) and greedy (GRD) approaches as well as to the system optimum (SO) and user equilibrium (UE).

simulation, agents have a single influence factor whose value is fixed. Therefore, outputs from prediction models correspond to the average outcome of previous plan executions, which is exactly the same reward considered by agents on the reinforcement learning approach. Despite this similarity, the global cost remains, on average, bellow the one obtained in UE (44250.6 vs. 45630 time units, respectively), indicating that agents provided with our learning-based plan selection strategy are able to mitigate the effects of the Braess' paradox. These results are even more interesting when we consider that (i) they were achieved without explicit communication among agents, (ii) agents do not know the social impact of their actions, and (iii) agents are not aware of the cost functions of each route.

4.2   Context-Dependent Simulation

Our aim with the context-dependent simulation is to evaluate how agents adapt to changes in their environment. On Mondays (150 agents on the route), agents using our learning-based plan selection strategy are able to achieve a distribution that performed better than the UE. This can be seen in Fig. 5, which shows the global travel costs of our plan selection strategy (LNB) compared with reinforce-

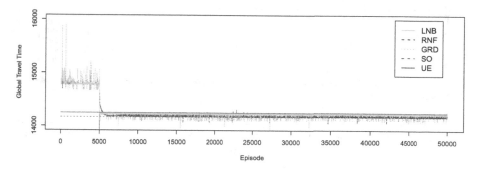

Fig. 5. Context-dependent simulation: Mondays.

ment learning (RNF) and greedy (GRD) approaches as well as to the system optimum (SO) and user equilibrium (UE) on Mondays. This result is slightly worse than that presented by agents choosing routes using reinforcement learning, and comparable to that obtained by greedy agents. There are reasons that justify such behaviour. First, to reach the SO distribution, some agents must have a longer travel time by travelling through routes SAE and SBE. However, as they act selfishly, no agent is willing to do so. In fact, the majority of agents that choose SAE or SBE on Mondays are due to the exploration activity. Second, the UE and SO distributions are very close regarding the global travel time obtained in each of them. Therefore, given their selfishness, it seems reasonable for agents to accept a very attractive reward that will have a small impact on the final global travel time. Finally, agents commuting on Mondays are also the only agents commuting in every day of the week. It is possible that such information overlap impacts the outcome prediction and consequently the plan selection.

Mixing information from different days of the week is also evidenced by the results of Tuesdays and Thursdays, which have the same number of agents (390) but surprisingly distinct results. On Tuesdays, agents using our plan selection strategy have their global travel time initially oscillating between the UE and SO values. However, their performance decreases during the simulation, becoming worse than the UE distribution for most of the time (Fig. 6). This can be explained by the fact that some agents commuting on Tuesdays do not commute in other days of the week. Therefore, their prediction models tend to be built later than those from agents who commute throughout the week. In this particular case, what occurs is that agents who had their prediction models built first tend to select SABE more often than those who did not (remember that these agents commute on Mondays, in which SABE can be considered the best choice). Added to the exploration activity, it results in a much higher number of agents selecting SABE during the initial episodes. Such behaviour triggers the cyclic phenomenon described in Sect. 4.1. The difference is that, in long term, the number of agents attached to route SABE impacts the update of prediction models of other agents, making them associate routes SAE and SBE with higher travel times, and also migrate to SABE. The apex of such migration can be

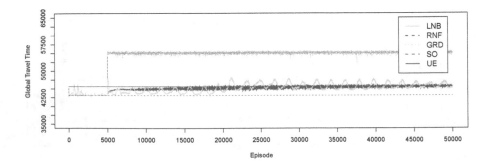

Fig. 6. Context-dependent simulation: Tuesdays.

noticed near the episode 21,000. However, it is possible to observe that, during
the last ten thousand episodes, the amplitude of the global travel time starts to
reduce, slowly moving towards the UE.

On Thursdays, in turn, results are exceptionally good—agents are able to
achieve an almost optimal distribution for a long period of time. In fact, the
global travel time obtained by these agents is only greater than that from UE
near the episode 5,000, in which the link AB is recently added to the network
and thus very attractive to drivers. On average, global travel times were also
better than those obtained from greedy and reinforcement learning plan selection
strategies, as can be seen in Fig. 7. The difference between the results from
Tuesday and Thursday can be explained by the surrounding days of the day of
the week that we are analysing. As a regression model is built, and we represent
the days of the week as natural numbers, the behaviour in the surrounding days
affects the prediction regarding a particular day of the week.

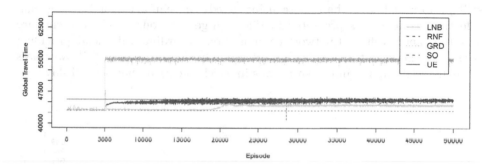

Fig. 7. Context-dependent simulation: Thursdays.

Good results were also obtained in episodes representing Wednesdays. As
described in Sect. 3.2, these episodes also replicate the Braess' paradox. In this
context, agents have a behaviour similar to that presented on Thursdays, initially reaching an almost optimal distribution and then having a slightly decrease
in their performance as agents start the cyclic behaviour described in Sect. 4.1.
Actually, the implicit coordination to avoid the use of route SABE is facilitated
in this scenario. Differently from Tuesdays and Thursdays, the UE and SO distributions are completely different from each other. Therefore, even with some
agents regularly exploring SABE, the entire agent population does not become
attracted by that route. Such behaviour is depicted in Fig. 8.

On Fridays, in turn, the UE and the SO distributions are very similar, as can
be seen in Table 7. In general, agents present the same behaviour as in other days
that reproduce the paradox, initially reaching an almost optimal distribution and
gradually decreasing their performance. As we pointed out in Sect. 3.2, in this
particular scenario the UE corresponds to 10 agents selecting SABE while the
other 500 are equally distributed between routes SAE and SBE. Due to the
considerably high exploration rate (5%), there are often more than 10 agents

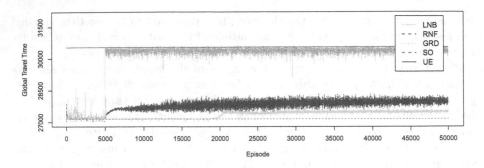

Fig. 8. Context-dependent simulation: Wednesdays.

selecting that route. As a consequence, agents slightly move away from both UE and SO distributions. Despite this particularity, agents using our approach had still performed better than those using greedy or reinforcement learning plan selection strategies, as presented in Fig. 9. In general, our cognitive agents are able to adapt to different network configurations regarding traffic load, providing social outcomes that are typically achieved only through the explicit awareness of such social impact and in situations in which agents do not act selfishly.

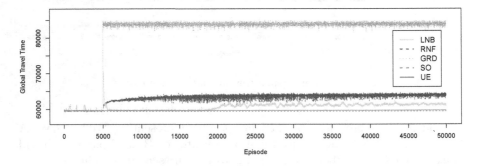

Fig. 9. Context-dependent simulation: Fridays.

Observing these simulations also allows us to point out some interesting details. In some cases, the non existence of the Braess' paradox in a given scenario may influence the performance of sophisticated route selection techniques when compared to the simpler ones. It occurs because, in this scenario, the best route choice is commonly equivalent to the naive choice performed by these simpler selection techniques. Sophisticated approaches, in turn, tend to look for complex solutions that may be incorrect. Moreover, as the number of agents in a network is modified, the UE and SO distributions also change. Therefore, comparing travel times obtained from such distributions with those obtained from any other distribution may be subjective. In a given scenario, for instance, reaching a distribution close to the user equilibrium can be a reasonable result if it is also close to the optimum solution.

5 Conclusion

The Agent-based Modelling and Simulation (ABMS) paradigm has been a powerful solution for investigating scenarios that cannot be easily replicated in the real world. Such paradigm is particularly suited for modelling and simulating traffic-related problems, such as the Braess' paradox. Although being able to soften or even solve the paradox, existing agent-based solutions addressing this problem typically model drivers as reactive agents, also requiring information that may be infeasible to obtain in real world situations or relaxing some assumptions concerning the paradox itself, e.g. drivers acting as altruistic agents.

In this work, we proposed the use of cognitive agent architectures as a suitable alternative to model driver behaviour and a potential solution to the Braess' paradox. We exploited an extended BDI architecture that provides agents with the ability of learning the relation between the context and the outcomes of their choices. Results indicate that the use of cognitive agents is able to effectively soften the effects of the Braess' paradox. Our approach differentiates from those existing given that there is no need for providing to agents additional information, e.g. the awareness of the social impact of their choices, and no additional engagement required from agents. A study on the impact of having several influence factors as well as different setups for the attributes of the learning-based plan selection technique, e.g. prediction model update rate and exploration rate, are subjects of future work.

References

1. Arnott, R., Small, K.: The economics of traffic congestion. Am. Sci. **82**(5), 446–455 (1994)
2. Bazzan, A.L., Klügl, F.: Case studies on the braess paradox: simulating route recommendation and learning in abstract and microscopic models. Transp. Res. Part C: Emerg. Technolog. **13**(4), 299–319 (2005)
3. Braess, D., Nagurney, A., Wakolbinger, T.: On a paradox of traffic planning. Transp. Sci. **39**(4), 446–450 (2005)
4. Faccin, J., Nunes, I.: BDI-agent plan selection based on prediction of plan outcomes. In: WI-IAT 2015, vol. 2, pp. 166–173, December 2015
5. Forno, A.D., Merlone, U.: Replicating human interaction in braess paradox. In: WSC 2013, pp. 1754–1765 (2013)
6. Hasan, M.R., Bazzan, A.L.C., Friedman, E., Raja, A.: A multiagent solution to overcome selfish routing in transportation networks. In: ITSC 2016, pp. 1850–1855 (2016)
7. Klügl, F., Bazzan, A.L.: Route decision behaviour in a commuting scenario: simple heuristics adaptation and effect of traffic forecast. J. Artif. Soc. Soc. Simul. **7**(1) (2004). http://jasss.soc.surrey.ac.uk/7/1/1.html
8. Klügl, F., Bazzan, A.L.: Agent-based modeling and simulation. AI Mag. **33**(3), 29 (2012)

9. Lepore, D.M., Barratt, C., Schwartz, P.M.: Computational models of chemical systems inspired by braess' paradox. J. Math. Chem. **49**(2), 356–370 (2011)
10. Lützenberger, M., Ahrndt, S., Masuch, N., Heßler, A., Hirsch, B., Albayrak, S.: The BDI driver in a service city. In: AAMAS 2011, pp. 1257–1258 (2011)
11. Macal, C.M.: Everything you need to know about agent-based modelling and simulation. J. Simul. **10**(2), 144–156 (2016)
12. Macal, C., North, M.: Introductory tutorial: agent-based modeling and simulation. In: WSC 2014, pp. 6–20. IEEE Press (2014)
13. Pas, E.I., Principio, S.L.: Braess' paradox: some new insights. Transp. Res. Part B: Methodol. **31**(3), 265–276 (1997)
14. Rao, A.S., Georgeff, M.P.: BDI agents: from theory to practice. In: ICMAS 1995, 312–319 (1995)
15. Sousa, A.A., Chaves, A., Farias, G.A., Peeters, F.M.: Braess paradox at the mesoscopic scale. Phys. Rev. B **88**, 245417 (2013)

Eavesdropping Opponent Agent Communication Using Deep Learning

Thomas Gabel[✉], Alaa Tharwat, and Eicke Godehardt

Faculty of Computer Science and Engineering,
Frankfurt University of Applied Sciences, 60318 Frankfurt am Main, Germany
{tgabel,aothman,godehardt}@fb2.fra-uas.de

Abstract. We present a method for learning to interpret and understand foreign agent communication. Our approach is based on casting the contents of intercepted opponent agent communication to a bit-level representation and on training and employing deep convolutional neural networks for decoding the meaning of received messages. We empirically evaluate our method on real-world data acquired from the multi-agent domain of robotic soccer simulation, demonstrating the effectiveness and robustness of the learned decoding models.

1 Introduction

Communication plays a central role in many multi-agent systems. The ability to communicate with one another can, among others, enable agents to coordinate their behavior or to overcome problems arising from partial state observability by, e.g., sharing local observations with one another. While these usages of communication adhere to cooperative multi-agents systems, it may be of importance in an adversarial setting as well. More particularly, in an adversarial multi-agent system it is very tempting to intercept the messages opponent agents exchange and understanding them can bring about significant benefits for the eavesdropping agent.

In this paper, we focus on settings in which the communication within a team of adversarial agents can be heard easily, but where the "language" used by those opponent agents is unknown. Thus, the challenge for the listening agent is to learn a model of the opponent agents' communication which effectively allows for interpreting the contents of messages received and to possibly act upon that information. The basic idea of our approach is to leverage state of the art deep learning techniques for recognizing the meaning of intercepted communication. To achieve this we formalize the problem as a supervised learning problem and develop a deep, bit-level convolutional neural network model that is trained on real, non-encrypted, and non-compressed communication data. The application area we are targeting is the domain of robotic soccer simulation where communication across agents, like in real soccer, plays a crucial role. Besides this multi-agent application, we are convinced that the basic ideas of our approach

© Springer International Publishing AG 2017
J.O. Berndt et al. (Eds.): MATES 2017, LNAI 10413, pp. 205–222, 2017.
DOI: 10.1007/978-3-319-64798-2_13

might be utilized also for other message-based tasks such as reverse engineering or decoding data transfer in bus systems (like controller area networks).

We start this paper with some technical and algorithmic foundations and a summary of relevant related work. In Sect. 3 we present in detail our problem modeling and learning approach, followed by an empirical evaluation of our learned deep models (Sect. 4), applying them in the context of the competitive multi-agent world of robotic soccer simulation. Finally, Sect. 5 concludes. Since this paper makes use of quite some mathematical notation, the Appendix provides an overview of the most important symbols we use and a brief explanation of their meaning.

2   Foundations

We start off by providing some basics of our multi-agent application domain, simulated robotic soccer, before we continue to elaborate on foundations required for our deep communication learning approach. Also, this section is meant to provide references to related work.

2.1   Robotic Soccer Simulation

RoboCup [22] is an established international research initiative that aims at fostering research in AI, intelligent robotics, and multi-agent systems. Annually, there are championship tournaments in several leagues. Among these, the most tactically advanced and richest in terms of behavioral complexity is the 2D Soccer Simulation League, where two teams of simulated soccer-playing agents compete against one another using the Soccer Server [15]. This software implements a real-time soccer simulation system which puts into practice all aspects that are of relevance to multi-agent systems research.

The Soccer Server allows autonomous software agents to play soccer in a client/server-based style: The server simulates the playing field, communication, the environment and its dynamics, while the clients are permitted to send their actions once per simulation cycle to the server (each cycle lasts 100 ms). Then, the server takes all agents' actions into account, computes the subsequent world state and provides all agents with (partial) information about their environment.

Robotic Soccer represents an excellent testbed for machine learning and, particularly, for multi-agent tasks. Several research groups have dealt with the task of learning parts of a soccer-playing agent's behavior autonomously (e.g. [5,12,16]) and even more have defined [9,20] and investigated [2,11,19] various multi-agent related (sub-)tasks in robotic soccer. However, to the best of the authors' knowledge, the work we are presenting here is the first one that aims at learning and understanding the contents of opponent communication.

2.2   Communication in Simulated Soccer

As outlined, decision making must be performed in real-time or, more precisely, in discrete time steps: Every 100 ms the agents can execute a low-level action (like to *dash*, to *kick* the ball, *turn* their body or neck, or to *point* with their arm into some direction) and the world-state will change based on the individual actions of all players. Beyond these actions which influence the physical behavior of the agent, each agent is additionally allowed to communicate. In many existing multi-agent systems with communicating agents, the agents are allowed to use a reliable, high-bandwidth, and low-cost communication [23]. By contrast, in simulated soccer communication is unreliable, is restricted to low bandwidth, and uses a single shared communication channel for all 22 agents, thus mimicking the way spoken messages are transmitted and heard by humans in real soccer.

2.2.1 Technical Details

Direct agent-to-agent communication is strictly forbidden (more exactly, it would be considered a fraud attempt during competitions). Instead, each agent is allowed to broadcast a string of up to 10 characters in each time step. The broadcast is received by the Soccer Server and will be conveyed to selected players in the next simulation cycle, implying that any form of communication in soccer simulation is inherently delayed. Moreover, the communication channel is shared which imposes the restriction that each player can hear only one message from a teammate plus one from an opponent in each simulation step. The selection of the teammate and/or opponent to listen to can also be influenced by each agent by focusing its listening attention to exactly one specific player (otherwise random messages will be received). As a consequence, communication in soccer simulation is inherently unreliable since no agent can ever be sure whether some teammate has heard its say message or not. If all agents speak all the time, on average two of every eleven messages will be heard.

2.2.2 Communication Examples

Given these restrictions, at RoboCup competitions some teams make more intensive use of communication while others do less. Considering the amount of information sent to the Soccer Server during an average game, the share of communication data relative to the overall amount of information that needs to be transmitted in order to control all simulated parts of the agent's body is as high as

- 54% and 36% for former champion teams WrightEagle and Brainstormers/FRA-UNIted, implying that each agent sends a message in each time step,
- 17% and 13% for last year's finalists Gliders and Helios, meaning hat each agent sends a say message in one of every six time steps on average.

Having a look at an excerpt of the text log file (created by the Soccer Server, storing all actions and commands issued by all players) of the 2016 final match, we can easily detect communicated say messages among other data transmitted by the agents (Fig. 1). For example, we see that in time step 7 Helios' agent #4 dashed with 60% power, while #6 kicked the ball. We also observe, that four out of the six agents listed made use of communication by sending a 10-char *say* message, though we have a hard time understanding its meaning.

```
7,0 Recv Gliders2016_6: (dash 100)(turn_neck 41)(say "-EsQdKhGQI")
7,0 Recv HELIOS2016_4: (dash 60)(turn_neck -47)
7,0 Recv HELIOS2016_6: (kick 89.676 3.5062)(turn_neck 84)(attentionto off)(say "paw07w4-v ")
7,0 Recv Gliders2016_9: (dash 100)(turn_neck -5)(say "fbkHkNRaZP")
7,0 Recv Gliders2016_1: (dash 100)(turn_neck 0)(attentionto our 6)
7,0 Recv HELIOS2016_9: (dash 100)(turn_neck -55)(say "RZvS?uDYKw")
```

Fig. 1. Excerpt of the text log file of RoboCup 2016's final match.

2.3   Feed-Forward and Convolutional Neural Networks

Artificial neural networks are known for their excellent performance in different areas of machine learning. They are frequently applied for classification, regression, prognosis, as well as in reinforcement learning tasks. Specifically, multi-layer perceptron neural nets were shown to be universal function approximators [8].

In recent years, deep learning methods have witnessed significant improvements and brought about a number of breakthroughs in classic AI tasks that at times outperform human-level performance [14], including traditional multi-agent scenarios with imperfect information [4]. Additionally, deep (convolutional) neural networks as critic or actor in a reinforcement learning setting were, in combination with more classic tree search algorithms, able to beat human champions in challenging games like Go [18].

2.3.1   Multi-layer Perceptron Neural Networks

A multi-layer perceptron is a neural network whose units (neurons) are connected in an acyclic graph. When calculating the activation of a neuron, we first calculate the net input to this neuron which is a weighted sum derived from all predecessor neurons' activations and the corresponding connection weights. In a second step, the net input to this neuron is passed through a differentiable monotonous activation function (e.g. the $tanh$, the logistic sigmoid function, or the rectified linear activation unit $ReLu$ [7]), thus yielding the neuron's output.

In a multi-layer perceptron neural network all of its neurons are arranged in layers that are disjoint from one another in that there are no connections among units within the same layer. Data is propagated through the network (forward propagation) by providing inputs to the network's first layer (input layer) and, subsequently, calculating the activations of all neurons in all successive layers (hidden layers) till the final, so-called output layer. For a given training set

$$\mathbb{P} = \{(x^p, t^p) | p \in \{1, \ldots, |\mathbb{P}|\}\} \tag{1}$$

of training patterns (x^p, t^p) with input vectors $x^p = (x_1^p, \ldots, x_m^p) \in \mathbb{R}^m$ and target values $t^p = (t_1^p, \ldots, t_n^p) \in \mathbb{R}^n$, a multi-layer neural net can be trained using one of the many variants of the back-propagation algorithm which essentially performs a gradient descent-based adaptation of the net's connection weights such that the summed squared error between the net's outputs under input of pattern x^p and the corresponding target values t^p is minimized. For more basics on neural networks the reader is referred to [6,17].

2.3.2 Convolutional Neural Networks

Convolutional neural networks (CNNs, [13]) are a specialized type of neural networks for processing data with a grid-like topological layout, like image data where pixels form a 2D grid. CNNs differ from standard feed-forward neural nets in that they use convolution as a special linear operation in some of their layers. That operation is not limited to two-dimensional data, but can be applied to one-dimensional problems as well, e.g. for time series data.

Discrete convolution over an input $I \in \mathbb{R}^{m \times n}$ using a convolution kernel $K \in \mathbb{R}^{k \times k}$ with kernel size k produces a matrix $S \in \mathbb{R}^{m \times n}$ whose entries $S[i, j]$ are defined as

$$S[i,j] = (K * I)[i,j] = \sum_{p=1}^{m} \sum_{q=1}^{n} I[i - p, j - q] \cdot K[p, q]$$

This definition is a well-known operator in computer vision and it trivially extends to one-dimensional data, if $m = 1$. In machine learning, the input is usually an array of data (training examples) and the kernel's entries are the parameters that are adapted by the learning algorithm similar to what has been described in Sect. 2.3.1. The linear output of convolution is then run through a non-linear activation function such as *tanh* or *ReLu*. The output of the non-linear activation is often followed by maximum or average pooling layers that are meant to downsample the overall input, representing the output calculated so far by some summary of it. Besides, it should be stressed that each convolutional layer does not just employ a single, but a larger number of convolutional kernels, also called filters, each of which represents its own representation for the next layer of the network. Lastly, deep feed-forward neural networks do usually employ a number of stacked convolutional layers as described before, followed by one or more fully connected layer(s) to form the net's final output(s). A comprehensive and more detailed introduction and overview of CNNs can be found in [6].

3 Problem Modeling

As we saw in the previous section, intercepting opponent communication can be done easily in robotic soccer simulation. The agent can simply put its listening attention to a desired opponent and will receive its next say message in the subsequent simulation cycle given that the wire-tapped opponent has said something. In this section, we describe our approach to interpreting and understanding the contents of the received opponent message.

3.1 General Approach

Our goal is to pose the communication understanding task as a supervised learning problem. Generally, the to-be-predicted contents of a 10 char opponent say message could contain anything, from an agent's internal stamina state to high-level results of reasoning about our team's playing strategy. However, it is natural to assume that in a competitive application domain like robotic soccer any agent is likely to frequently communicate such information that is most beneficial to its teammates with respect to the real-time properties and the partial observability of the simulation. Among such highly beneficial pieces of information are

1. the ball location and its velocity,
2. locations of teammates and opponent players,
3. pass announcements or requests,
4. locker room agreements and corresponding team strategy information (e.g. formation, role assignments, player markings etc. [21]).

In the remainder of this paper, we are going to specifically address points 1. and 3. In order to tackle these tasks with supervised learning we require a training data set $\mathbb{P}$ (cf. Eq. 1) containing a substantial amount of training patterns (x^p, t^p).

Inputs x^p are communicated messages $\mathcal{C} = (c_s, \ldots, c_0)$ with maximal message size S and $s < S$ as well as with literals c_i from an alphabet A which in our case is the printable subset of ASCII-128 characters (cf. Fig. 1). Since the length of each message is restricted to a length of S, the discrete set of possible communication messages is

$$\mathcal{A} = \cup_{i=0}^{S} A^i.$$

In our targeted application domain it holds $|\mathcal{A}| \approx 5.4 \cdot 10^{19}$ since $S = 10$ and A represents the set of 94 printable 7-bit ASCII characters (without quote sign).

Input Vector: A naive approach to learning a model for recognizing the contents of opponent say messages would be to feed a numeric representation of each letter c_i into the first layer of the network. This approach could be expected to bring about acceptable results already, if we could guarantee that the payload is never spread across multiples letters. Given the limited communication bandwidth in the type of multi-agent system we are considering, however, such an assumption is unrealistic as it would, for example, be wasteful to use one full letter (7 bit) for transmitting the unique number of some other agent for whose encoding 4 bit are sufficient.

By contrast, we suggest to define and utilize a bit-level representation for any received say message $\mathcal{C} = (c_s, \ldots, c_0)$ for the following reasons:

- Such a more fine-grained representation allows for capturing payload data that is spread across multiple characters c_i. Moreover, it allows for covering chunks of information that start at arbitrary bit positions within $\mathcal{C}$.
- Assuming that the communicating agents do not apply some kind sophisticated encryption/decryption techniques, the bit representation is likely to contain patterns that hint to the type of information contained (e.g. an identifier indicating it is a pass announcement) as well as bit patterns that contain the details or parameters (e.g. the starting point or velocity of a pass).
- The bit-level representation enables the usage of convolutional neural networks to detect features (i.e patterns) within the bit sequence that makes it possible to classify a message's type, its contents or for doing regression on the encoded parameters it contains.

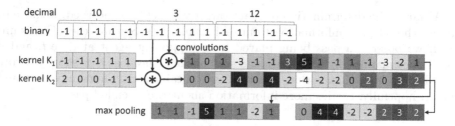

Fig. 2. One-dimensional Bit-level convolution

Given a new say message $C \in \mathcal{A}$ we use a function

$$b : \mathcal{A} \to \{0, 1\}^B \tag{2}$$

which maps C to a bit sequence $b(C)$ of length $B = S\lfloor \log_2 |\mathcal{A}| \rfloor$ where A is the underlying alphabet (in our application it holds $B = 10\lfloor \log_2 94 \rfloor = 70$. In Sect. 3.3.2, we will discuss possible concrete implementations of b.

Figure 2 visualizes our approach for an exemplary bit vector of length 15 containing some "identifiers", including one represented by the decimal number 3 encoded as a 5-bit binary number. The figure also shows two 1D convolutional kernels that might be understood as the result of learning. Apparently, K_1 is able to "detect" a possible location of the searched for identifier "3" in the bit sequence, whereas K_2 is obviously meant to recognize other bit features.

Target Values: In what follows, we distinguish between two different types of learning problems that we want to tackle.

(a) Classification Problems: Here, we aim at the recognition of the type of information that is contained in a say message C. Since each message can contain multiple chunks of information (and these in an arbitrary order, too), this amounts to a multi-label binary classification problem where $t^p \in \{true, false\}^l$ with l denoting the number of information chunks considered. If we, for example, aim at recognizing communicated ball information (one class), pass announcements (one class) as well as player information (one class for each player on the field) simultaneously, we arrive at $l = 24$. In the experiments reported below, we focus on ball and pass classification with $l = 1$ in each setting.

(b) Regression Problems: Assuming that our trained model in (a) states that a certain piece $\mathcal{P}$ of information is contained in C (e.g. data about the ball's location), the next logical step is to also extract the details or parameters of $\mathcal{P}$. In the example of a ball location such details are its x and y position on the field, in the case of a pass announcement it might be the unique number of the receiving agent or the pass velocity. As a consequence, in this setting the challenge for the trained model is to extract numerical data from C which corresponds to a classical regression problem. Thus, $t^p \in \mathbb{R}^l$ with l taking a value that depends n the kind of information $\mathcal{P}$ contains.

As far as the determination of exact target values t^p is concerned, we have to extract the relevant information from real simulated soccer matches. For example, if we observe a pass being played by an opponent agent at time t, and if this is accompanied by a say message sent by that player at t or shortly before t, we have a high chance that this message contains a pass announcement and that it, hopefully, carries more information about the intended pass.

3.2   Model Architecture

We use a deep neural network architecture that is identical for all settings and learning tasks we are considering. As pointed out, input to the network is a bit-level representation $x^p = b(\mathcal{C})$ of an opponent agent's received say message $\mathcal{C}$ containing B bits. The positive and negative level of each bit a mapped to -1 and 1, respectively, which prevents us from simply ignoring all zero bits in the context of the convolutional operation (cf. Sect. 2.3.2).

The input is fed into a first convolutional layer of 128 one-dimensional convolutional filters of size 13, followed each by rectified linear activation units, whose output is then handed on to a maximum pooling layer with a stride of two. The second convolutional layer uses exactly the same layout as the first one with the exception of reduced kernel sizes of seven, and is also followed by *ReLu* activations and max pooling. The output of this layer is fed into a standard fully connected layer with 512 hidden units whose outputs are linearly combined to form the single (or multiple) output(s) of the net. The number of neurons in the output layer depends on the specific learning task as described in Sect. 3.1. To enforce regularization during learning we apply drop-out in the fully connected layer [3] with a drop-out rate of 0.5.

3.3   Communication En-/Decoding

In order to define a suitable bit-level representation function $b : \mathcal{A} \to \{0,1\}^B$ (cf. Eq. 2) that maps an opponent say message $\mathcal{C} \in \mathcal{A}$ to a bit vector, we need to reflect about common ways for encoding some payload data efficiently in a message of limited size S over a given alphabet A. This means, for a moment (Sect. 3.3.1), we adopt the perspective of an opponent agent opp_1 and compare different approaches for defining a function $enc^{opp} : \mathcal{D} \to \mathcal{A}$ that encodes a given tuple $V = (v_1, \ldots v_d) \in \mathcal{D}$ of payload data, i.e. of numeric values v_i, to a maximally S-letter message $\mathcal{C}$ over alphabet A that can be decoded easily by one of its teammates opp_2 that receives $\mathcal{C}$.

3.3.1   Encoding Payload Data as Say Message

As a general note, we make the fundamental assumption that *all* agents do *not* apply any form of error detection or recovery since, on the one hand, the communication channel (simulated by the Soccer Server) does not introduce transmission errors and, on the other hand, agents are expected to maximize the amount of information transmitted (making check bits superfluous). Furthermore, we proceed on the assumption that no agent performs any kind of sophisticated data encryption which would render our entire approach useless.

(a) One Letter per Value: The most intuitive approach is to discretize the domain $D_i = [d_i^{min}, d_i^{max}]$ of v_i to $|A|$ values and map v_i to its nearest representative according to

$$enc_i^{opp} : D_i \rightarrow A \text{ with } v_i \mapsto A\left[\left\lfloor |A| \frac{v_i - d_i^{min}}{d_i^{max} - d_i^{min}}\right\rfloor\right]$$

where $A[j]$ provides access to the jth element of the alphabet. While easy to implement, this approach is suboptimal as it allocates one letter to each v_i and disregards the requirements on the resolution. For example, using one character for encoding a unique player number $v_i \in \{1, \dots, 11\}$ is wasteful, whereas for conveying an x position on the field[1] this approach would yield a rather coarse discretization of steps with size $\frac{105}{|A|}$ which is 1.11 m for printable 7-bit ASCII characters. It is unlikely that any of the existing robotic soccer teams is adopting such a basic encoding approach.

(b) Information-Oriented Bit Allocation: A clearly more efficient approach is to specify the required number of bits β_i for each piece of information v_i and to then create a block code (without error correction) from it. Hence,

$$enc_i^{opp} : D_i \rightarrow \{0,1\}^{\beta_i} \text{ with } v_i \mapsto bin\left(\left\lfloor 2^{\beta_i} \frac{v_i - d_i^{min}}{d_i^{max} - d_i^{min}}\right\rfloor\right)$$

where bin takes a natural number, converts it to a binary number, and represents it as a bit string of fixed length β_i. From this, a trivial block code can be created by simple string concatenation bs of the bit strings returned from each enc_i^{opp}, i.e. $bs^{opp}(V) = \oplus_i enc_i^{opp}$.

Given, for instance, the data $V = (v_1, v_2, v_3)$ where v_1 stands for one out of a set of 32 identifiers and $\binom{v_2}{v_3}$ represents the ball's location. Then, five bit are sufficient for encoding v_1 whereas one might spend 1024 possible discrete values (i.e. ten bit) for encoding the ball's x location on the pitch and 512 discrete values (nine bit) for its y location. This yields a sufficiently accurate resolution of $\frac{105}{1024} = 10.3$ cm and $\frac{68}{512} = 13.3$ cm in x and y direction, respectively. Concatenating the three binary numbers yields a 24-bit string as shown in Fig. 3 for a payload extended by two more data fields.

(c) Fixed-Length Encoding: A straightforward approach for turning the block-code bit string $bs^{opp}(V)$ into a message $C = (c_{S-1}, \dots, d_0)$ is to split it into pieces of identical size σ, interpret each such piece as a natural number n, and to map it to a character c_i using some bijective index function $idx_A : A \rightarrow \{0, \dots, |A| - 1\}$ (the "code") such that $n = idx_A(c_i)$.

---

[1] Pitch size in 2D simulated soccer is 105×68 m.

Given the size $|A|$ of the alphabet, it is natural to set $\sigma = \lfloor \log_2 |A| \rfloor$ and to use only a 2^σ-element subset of A. Knowing that $|A| = 94$ in our application, an agent using this approach encodes each $\sigma = 6$ bit from $bs^{opp}(V)$ by one character from A (see Fig. 3, left-hand side).

(d) Base- $|A|$ *Encoding:* The fixed-length encoding in (c) is still wasteful in the sense that it does not fully exploit the available alphabet. The bit string $bs^{opp}(V)$ formed in (b), however, corresponds to a (possibly large) base-2 number N_2. Therefore, it is standing to reason to convert that number into a base-$|A|$ number and to simply employ that as the encoded message to be sent. Thus,

$$enc^{opp} : D \to C \text{ with } V \mapsto base_{|A|}(bs^{opp}(V))$$

where $base_{|A|} : \{0,1\}^{\sum_i \beta_i} \to C$. A binary number N_2 can be written in base $|A|$ as $N_2 = N_{|A|} = \sum_{i=0}^{S-1} idx_A(c_i)|A|^i$. So, the function $base_{|A|}$ yields a string $base_{|A|}(N_2) = (c_{S-1}, \ldots, c_0)$ over alphabet A with S denoting the maximal size of a message. Here, again, $idx_A : A \to \{0, \ldots, |A|-1\}$ refers to the index assigned to each letter from A (thus, depicting the agent's code).

3.3.2   Bit-Level Representation of Say Messages

We now return to our agent's point of view and, hence, to the question on how to interpret intercepted communication.

Naive Bit-Level Representation: Given an opponent's say message $C = (c_s, \ldots, c_0)$, we can naively represent it as a bit vector using the individual characters' 7-bit ASCII code representation. Thus,

$$b_{asc} : A \to \{0,1\}^B \text{ with } (c_s, \ldots, c_0) \mapsto \oplus_{i=0}^s asc(c_i)$$

where $asc(c_i)$ returns the index of c_i in the ASCII-128 table as a bit string of length 7. This way, we might easily retain the structure contained in a say message encoded using the fixed-length regime from above.

Base-$|A|$ Bit-Level Representation: Instead of the naive approach, throughout the rest of this paper, we are going to use the following more sophisticated one in which we take account of the base-$|A|$ encoding possibly applied by the communicating agent. Here, we define

$$b_{|A|} : A \to \{0,1\}^B \text{ with } (c_s, \ldots, c_0) \mapsto bin\left(\sum_{i=0}^{S-1} idx_A(c_i)|A|^i\right)$$

where bin returns a bit string as defined in Sect. 3.3.1 (b) and idx_A provides the index of a letter in the code as introduced above.

For this approach to be applicable, we need to know the full contents of the alphabet A used by the opponent agent. While we can infer the exact value of $|A|$ after having intercepted a sufficient number of messages, we have no chance

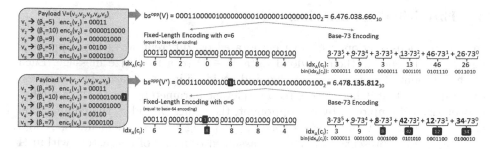

Fig. 3. Influence of a single bit swapped under fixed-length and base-73 encoding: although only the least significant bit in only one of the five values v_i has changed from V to V', the resulting encoded message looks totally different under base-73 while the Hamming distance is only one under fixed-length encoding.

of getting to know how the opponent agent's code idx_A is defined. In order to get along with this we assume some arbitrarily chosen function idx_A (e.g. with character indices sorted identically to the asc function from above) and rely on the learned deep representation of our approach to do the actual decoding work.

3.3.3 Encoding Remarks and Example

It is important to emphasize that the fixed-length encoding in Sect. 3.3.1 (c) is a special case of the base-$|A|$ encoding in (d) for $|A| = 2^\sigma$. Accordingly, our bit-level representation $b_{|A|}$ in Sect. 3.3.2 is capable of handling both of them.

We have, however, presented them separately in order to highlight that:

- For a message size of $S = 10$ over an alphabet A with $|A| = 94$ we find that in (c) a payload of 60 bits can be transmitted per message. By contrast, in (d) the payload is effectively as high as $\log_2(94^{10} - 1) = 65.5$ bit.
- In general, a base-κ encoding can be employed by the opponent agents with any value $\kappa \leq |A|$.
- If, however, κ is *not* a power of two, then this has severe implications for our bit pattern recognition approach based on convolutional neural networks.

To understand the last of these three points, consider the example shown in Fig. 3. Here, we have a tuple of payload data V that is altered by just the least significant bit of v_2 forming V'. Under an opponent-side fixed-length encoding (i.e. with κ a power of two) the encoded message changes by only one bit, too, whereas for values of κ that are not a power of two (in the figure: $\kappa = 73$) the encoded message $\mathcal{C}$ is mutated heavily. As a consequence, payload data with very similar contents is mapped to strongly differing say messages which makes it difficult, if not impossible, for a convolutional neural network to learn patterns within the data that do generalize across communicated messages. For these reasons, it is essential to our approach to apply the base-$|A|$ bit-level representation $b_{|A|}$, if the opponent agent has encoded its payload data using a base-$|A|$ encoding function enc^{opp} as outlined above.

4   Empirical Evaluation

In the previous section, we have elaborated on different ways how opponent agents might encode their payload data $V \in \mathcal{D}$ to a fixed-size message. Each of the encoding functions is bijective and could be inverted easily by our eavesdropping agent, if it had access to the relevant parameters, i.e. to the alphabet subset size $|A|$ employed by the opponent, the values β_i and σ, the composition of the elements within V as well as the mapping between elements of A and their numeric representation (i.e. the assumed ordering of characters within A belonging to idx_A). Since, however, we do not have access to the internals of the opponent agent, it is a challenging task to learn a deep representation of them which allows us to decode opponent agent messages.

4.1   Experiment Overview

As a proof of concept, we start with the task of eavesdropping and correctly understanding the contents of out own team's (FRA-UNIted) communication. This is indeed a particularly straightforward task since we know the basic principles of our communication and how they are implemented. After that, we will put our focus on the communication of a selection of current top teams.

While we consider communicated ball information as part of our proof of concept, the main focus of this evaluation is on eavesdropping information about passes. In any case this includes both, classifying whether some message contains a certain piece of information as well as, if it does, extracting the numeric details of that information.

Our model has been implemented in Python using TensorFlow 1.0 [1] and was trained on a single Intel i7 machine with two GeForce GTX1080 GPUs using the Adam optimizer [10] with learning rate 10^{-4} minimizing the l_2 loss using stochastic gradient descent with a batch size of 64. A single epoch of stochastic gradient descent requires approximately 1.5 ms on this hardware which is a speed-up by a factor of ten compared to training on a CPU, only.

When applying a learned model on a standard PC with an i7 CPU (as it is likely to be the case during competitions, for example), processing of a single say message (forward pass through the deep convolutional neural network) takes circa 0.5 ms on average using TensorFlow's Python API. Given the time frame of 100 ms per time step imposed by the Soccer Server, the computational requirements of our approach in terms of evaluating a learned model do, therefore, not represent an obstacle for a practical application under real-time requirements.

4.2   Proof of Concept: Ball Information

The communication system of our soccer-playing agents currently supports 8 different payload types including ball and ball holder information, pass announcements and requests, information on individual players as well as free-form messages. Our implementation employs the information-oriented bit allocation approach (cf. part (b) of Sect. 3.3.1) and can, thus, embed multiple payload

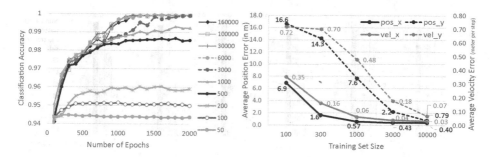

Fig. 4. Uncovering ball information: classification accuracy achieved when trying to predict whether some message contains ball data for different training set sizes subject to neural network training epochs (left) and correctness of predicting ball position and velocity information from the messages' contents subject to increasing training set sizes (right).

types in a single message. The agents employ a fixed-length encoding with $\sigma = 6$ (Sect. 3.3.1 (c)) using a 64-element subset of 7-bit ASCII characters as code.

In this section, we focus on communicated ball information which is a data chunk of 36 bits that can be placed at an arbitrary position within a say message (e.g. preceded by a pass request or followed by information about some other player). It contains a 5-bit payload type identifier, the encoded ball position and its velocity (each made up of an x and a y component) plus two 3-bit values indicating the age of the position and velocity values.

Our data set $\mathbb{P}$ consists of 200k say messages recorded from a single player in the course of more than thirty matches. 40k samples are left as an independent test set. We investigate the effectiveness of learning for different training set sizes sampled randomly from the remaining examples. Note that only a small subset (5.8%) of these messages contains a ball information, i.e. $\mathbb{P}$ contains about 16 times as many negative examples as positive ones.

Figure 4 (left) shows that 500 samples are sufficient for obtaining an average quality classifier, whereas about 3000 samples (i.e. the data from approximately one half-time of a match) yield a classification of the type of the say message with nearly zero error. As the right part of that figure shows, in order to also accurately decode the contents of the ball information, most prominently its position and velocity on the field, again the data collected within one half-time is sufficient. For assessing the usefulness of the accuracy of the decoded data it is worth noting that the domain of pos_x is $[-52.5, 52.5]$ (in meters), of pos_y is $[-34, 34]$ (in meters), and of $vel_{x/y}$ is $[-3, 3]$ (in meters per time step).

4.3   Pass Classification

Next, we aimed at classifying whether messages contain pass announcements. This time, however, we focused not just on our own team, for which we can

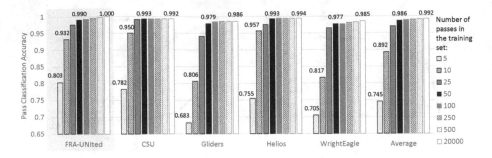

Fig. 5. Pass classification: accuracy of detecting the membership of pass announcing information in a say message subject to different opponent agents and to different amounts of observed passes with accompanying messages.

create accurate class labels easily, but on a selection of current top-level teams[2]. We made these teams play a series of matches, recording both, their passes played as well as their entire communication. From this data we built a set $\mathbb{P}^+$ of 20k positive training examples by associating any actual pass played with the say message sent concurrently or shortly before the pass by the passing player.

Accordingly, the built training data set may contain wrong labels if, for example, some player played a pass, but did not announce it and, instead, broadcast some other information concurrently. Without knowing the internals of other agents, it is difficult to quantify that level of noise, though we expect it to be low since playing and announcing passes is a fundamental soccer skill that is likely to be mastered nearly perfectly by any of the opponent agents considered. Henceforth, all accuracy values reported refer to the classification performance on independent training examples that originate from the same data distribution including the same potential level of noisy labels.

In this series of experiments, we are also interested in assessing how many passes need to be observed until a reliable classifier can be trained. Therefore, in each run we selected a specific number p of samples from $\mathbb{P}^+$ and joined it with p negative examples (for which we used randomly selected say messages received during non-pass situations), thus forming $\mathbb{P}$. Again, 40k samples are left out as an independent test data set on which all results reported are evaluated.

Figure 5 summarizes the results obtained after applying stochastic gradient descent optimization after 5k epochs. Note that a random classifier, e.g. an untrained net, would yield a classification accuracy of 0.5 due to our data set compilation. Also, note that during an average match approximately 50 passes (sometimes more) are played by a team. Thus, for any of the teams considered we are able, for instance, to learn a pass announcement detector with an accuracy of above ≈93% using the intercepted communication data from a single half-time. The average accuracy using pass and communication data from a single game (black series) is as high as ≈98% despite the fact that labels are possibly noisy.

---

[2] Binaries of all contemporary teams are available at `chaosscripting.net`.

4.4   Pass Regression: White and Black Box Experiments

The final stage of our experiments aims at decoding the payload data, i.e. the exact numeric details, of messages that were previously classified as containing pass information. Such details can contain the starting position $p = \binom{p_x}{p_y}$ of the pass, its velocity $v = \binom{v_x}{v_y}$ or, eventually, the unique number of the intended pass-receiving player.

To this end, we emphasize that the Soccer Server adds small random Gaussian noise to all actions performed by the agents (e.g. to kicks that are intended to play a pass) as well as, in each time step, to all movement vectors of objects on the field (e.g. the velocity vector of the ball). As a consequence, each pass actually played will most likely deviate slightly (in terms of its direction and its speed) from the intended pass whose properties were communicated by the pass-playing agent. Therefore, our training data set $\mathbb{P}$ contains inherently noisy target values, since we build the data set from actually observed passes.

White Box Agents: Since it is straightforward to generate pass announcements for agents of our team (as we do have access to their source code), we started by building a dataset of $200k$ such pass-announcing messages that we could label perfectly. We trained our decoder on 80% of the data, leaving $40k$ pass messages as an independent test set. After 10^6 epochs of neural network training, i.e. after about half an hour wall clock time, the error on the test set had dropped on average to $\binom{0.34}{0.50}$ for the pass start position and $\binom{0.03}{0.04}$ for the velocity (units: meters and meters per time step, respectively). Interestingly, even for much smaller data sets (e.g. $|\mathbb{P}| = 5k$, cf. Table 1) a decoding accuracy can be achieved that would be sufficient for taking appropriate counter measures during a game. Figure 6 visualizes the quality of the decoded information for FRA-UNIted as well as for the (black box) agents from team Helios.

Black Box Agents: To create the necessary data sets for other opponent agents (black box agents to whose source code we have no access), we made each agent team considered play a series of 1000 simulated matches of soccer (each one lasting 10 min wall clock time) during which we recorded their communication. Again, our deep decoding model was trained using the same parameterization, employing up to $20k$ examples in the training set and an independent test set covering $40k$ passes.

As can be read from Table 1, outstanding results could be obtained for all opponents considered with the exception of WrightEagle (no learning progress w.r.t. p and v at all). Here, we found, however, that a pass announcement by an agent from that team contains different pieces of data, namely the number of the targeted pass-receiving teammate as well as the absolute value of the pass velocity. Then, when modifying the labels of $\mathbb{P}$ accordingly, for a (extended) training set of $50k$ passes we are able to achieve an error of the pass velocity of 0.04 ± 0.05 meters per time step and an error in classifying the pass receiver (one out of 11 classification) of 21.6%.

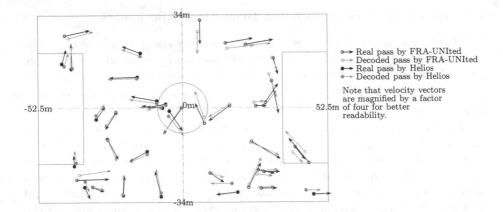

Fig. 6. For two of the teams considered, 20 randomly chosen (not cherry-picked) passes are visualized, opposing the real passes played and the information extracted from pass announcing say messages that were sent by pass-playing agents and decoded using our learned models.

Table 1. Average errors (in meters and meters per time step, respectively) and their standard deviations for the decoded pass data (pass start position p, pass velocity v, unique number r of pass receiver) intercepted from different opponent agent teams.

$|\mathbb{P}|$	FRA-UNIted				CSU_Yunlu			
	p_x	p_y	v_x	v_y	p_x	p_y	v_x	v_y
500	1.18 ± 1.70	13.1 ± 16.7	$.13 \pm .22$	1.37 ± 1.65	2.78 ± 5.16	4.20 ± 5.77	$.28 \pm .44$	$.14 \pm .28$
5000	0.54 ± 0.85	4.15 ± 6.48	$.06 \pm .07$	0.37 ± 0.56	0.86 ± 2.28	1.47 ± 3.34	$.14 \pm .25$	$.10 \pm .20$
20000	0.48 ± 0.55	1.43 ± 2.21	$.04 \pm .04$	0.09 ± 0.15	0.44 ± 1.62	1.04 ± 2.86	$.13 \pm .21$	$.10 \pm .18$

Gliders				Helios				WrightEagle	
p_x	p_y	v_x	v_y	p_x	p_y	v_x	v_y	$|v|$	r
3.01 ± 5.97	4.50 ± 6.48	$.30 \pm .46$	$.16 \pm .37$	2.31 ± 4.16	3.61 ± 4.91	$.28 \pm .36$	$.13 \pm .26$	$.41 \pm .52$	$.672$
1.50 ± 4.18	1.86 ± 4.39	$.14 \pm .31$	$.12 \pm .32$	0.69 ± 2.21	1.22 ± 2.24	$.10 \pm .19$	$.09 \pm .20$	$.29 \pm .40$	$.332$
0.79 ± 2.85	1.23 ± 3.71	$.11 \pm .21$	$.10 \pm .23$	0.45 ± 1.34	0.74 ± 1.85	$.09 \pm .16$	$.09 \pm .18$	$.19 \pm .28$	$.251$

5 Conclusion

In this paper, we have presented an approach that aims at understanding foreign agent communication using deep learning. Our learner intercepts fixed-size messages from opponent agents, casts their contents to a bit-level representation, and uses deep convolutional neural networks to interpret the contents of the message. Our work has been embedded into the multi-agent domain of robotic soccer simulation. In our experiments, we have shown that our approach is capable of correctly classifying the type of the payload data contained in a message as well as inferring numeric values therein. While we have shown that our approach works well for recognizing ball and pass information, in future work we aim at recognizing further categories of data communicated by opponent agents. Our very next step, however, is to do the engineering work for integrating the approach presented into our competition team in such a manner that it adheres to all real-time constraints of the soccer simulation domain and such that it can be utilized during competitions.

Appendix

Notation and mathematical symbols used and their meaning in order of their appearance.

$\mathbb{P}$	training data	d_i^{max}	upper bound of D_i
x^p	input of pth training pattern	β_i	number of bits used to encode v_i
t^p	target value of pth training pattern	bin	mapping from natural number
$\mathcal{C}$	communicated message		to binary
c_i	ith character in message	bs	mapping from payload tuple to
S	maximal message size		bit string
A	alphabet	idx_A	mapping from character to its
$A[j]$	character at index j in alphabet		index in the alphabet
$\mathcal{A}$	set of all formable messages	σ	number of bits mapped to one
b	mapping from message to bit string		character (fixed-length encoding)
B	length of bit string	$base_{|A|}$	mapping from binary number to
V	tuple of payload data		a base-$|A|$ number
v_i	ith numeric value in payload data	asc	mapping from character to its
$\mathcal{D}$	domain of payload data		index in the ASCII table
enc^{opp}	encoding of payload data to message	b_{asc}	mapping from message to bit
$\oplus$	concatenation of bit strings		string using ASCII indices
D_i	domain of ith value in payload data	$b_{|A|}$	mapping from message to bit
d_i^{min}	lower bound of D_i		string using indices in alphabet

References

1. Abadi, M., Agarwal, A., Barham, P., Brevdo, E., Chen, Z., Citro, C., Corrado, G., Davis, A., Dean, J., Devin, M., Ghemawat, S., Goodfellow, I., Harp, A., Irving, G., Isard, M., Jia, Y., Jozefowicz, R., Kaiser, L., Kudlur, M., Levenberg, J., Mané, D., Monga, R., Moore, S., Murray, D., Olah, C., Schuster, M., Shlens, J., Steiner, B., Sutskever, I., Talwar, K., Tucker, P., Vanhoucke, V., Vasudevan, V., Viégas, F., Vinyals, O., Warden, P., Wattenberg, M., Wicke, M., Yu, Y., Zheng, X.: TensorFlow: Large-Scale Machine Learning on Heterogeneous Systems (2015). http://tensorflow.org/
2. Almeida, F., Abreu, P., Lau, N., Reis, L.: An automatic approach to extract goal plans from soccer simulated matches. Soft Comput. **17**(5), 835–848 (2013)
3. Ba, J., Frey, B.: Adaptive dropout for training deep neural networks. In: Advances in Neural Information Processing Systems (NIPS), pp. 3084–3092 (2013)
4. Brown, N., Sandholm, T.: Safe and nested endgame solving for imperfect-information games. In: Proceedings of the AAAI workshop on Computer Poker and Imperfect Information Games (2017)
5. Gabel, T., Riedmiller, M.: Learning a partial behavior for a competitive robotic soccer agent. KI Z. **20**(2), 18–23 (2006)
6. Goodfellow, I., Bengio, Y., Courville, A.: Deep Learning. MIT Press, Cambridge (2017)

7. Hahnloser, R., Sarpeshkar, R., Mahowald, M., Douglas, R., Seung, H.: Digital selection and analogue amplification coexist in a cortex-inspired silicon circuit. Nature **405**(6789), 947–951 (2000)
8. Hornick, K., Stinchcombe, M., White, H.: Multilayer feedforward networks are universal approximators. Neural Netw. **2**, 359–366 (1989)
9. Kalyanakrishnan, S., Liu, Y., Stone, P.: Half field offense in robocup soccer: a multiagent reinforcement learning case study. In: Lakemeyer, G., Sklar, E., Sorrenti, D.G., Takahashi, T. (eds.) RoboCup 2006. LNCS (LNAI), vol. 4434, pp. 72–85. Springer, Heidelberg (2007). doi:10.1007/978-3-540-74024-7_7
10. Kingma, D., Ba, J.: Adam: a method for stochastic optimization. In: Proceedings of the 3rd International Conference on Learning Representations (2015)
11. Kok, J., Spaan, M., Vlassis, N.: Non-communicative multi-robot coordination in dynamic environments. Robot. Auton. Syst. **50**(2–3), 99–114 (2005)
12. Kuhlmann, G., Stone, P.: Progress in learning 3 vs. 2 keepaway. In: Polani, D., Browning, B., Bonarini, A., Yoshida, K. (eds.) RoboCup 2003. LNCS (LNAI), vol. 3020, pp. 694–702. Springer, Heidelberg (2004). doi:10.1007/978-3-540-25940-4_68
13. LeCun, Y.: Generalization and network. Design strategies. Technical report CRG-TR-89-4, University of Toronto (1989)
14. Mnih, V., Kavukcuoglu, K., Silver, D., Rusu, A., Veness, J., Bellemare, M., Graves, A., Riedmiller, M., Fidjeland, A., Ostrovski, G., Petersen, S., Beattie, C., Sadik, A., Antonoglou, I., King, H., Kumaran, D., Wierstra, D., Legg, S., Hassabis, D.: Human-level control through deep reinforcement learning. Nature **518**(7540), 529–533 (2015)
15. Noda, I., Matsubara, H., Hiraki, K., Frank, I.: Soccer server: a tool for research on multi-agent systems. Appl. Artif. Intell. **12**(2–3), 233–250 (1998)
16. Riedmiller, M., Gabel, T., Hafner, R., Lange, S.: Reinforcement learning for robot soccer. Auton. Robots **27**(1), 55–74 (2009)
17. Rumelhart, D., Hinton, G.: Learning representations by back-propagating errors. Nature **323**, 533–536 (1986)
18. Silver, D., Huang, A., Maddison, C., Guez, A., Sifre, L., Driessche, G., Schrittwieser, J., Antonoglou, I., Panneershelvam, V., Lanctot, M., Dieleman, S., Grewe, D., Nham, J., Kalchbrenner, N., Sutskever, I., Lillicrap, T., Leach, M., Kavukcuoglu, K., Graepel, T., Hassabis, D.: Mastering the game of go with deep neural networks and tree search. Nature **529**(7587), 484–489 (2016)
19. Stolzenburg, F., Murray, J., Sturm, K.: Multiagent matching algorithms with and without coach. J. Decis. Syst. **15**(2–3), 215–240 (2006)
20. Stone, P., Kuhlmann, G., Taylor, M.E., Liu, Y.: Keepaway soccer: from machine learning testbed to benchmark. In: Bredenfeld, A., Jacoff, A., Noda, I., Takahashi, Y. (eds.) RoboCup 2005. LNCS (LNAI), vol. 4020, pp. 93–105. Springer, Heidelberg (2006). doi:10.1007/11780519_9
21. Stone, P., Veloso, M.: Task decomposition, dynamic role assignment, and low-bandwidth communication for real-time strategic teamwork. Artif. Intell. **110**(2), 241–273 (1999)
22. Veloso, M., Balch, T., Stone, P.: RoboCup 2001: the fifth robotic soccer world championships. AI Mag. **1**(23), 55–68 (2002)
23. Woolridge, M.: Reasoning about Rational Agents. MIT Press, Cambridge (2003)

Multi-agent Autonomous Decision Making in Smart Micro-Grids' Energy Management: A Decentralized Approach

Sajad Ghorbani[1(✉)], R. Rahmani[3], and Rainer Unland[1,2]

[1] Institute of Computer Science and Business Information Systems,
University of Duisburg-Essen, Essen, Germany
{sajad.ghorbani,rainer.unland}@icb.uni-due.de
[2] Department of Information Systems, Poznan University of Economics,
Poznan, Poland
[3] Faculty of Science, Engineering and Technology,
Swinburne University of Technology, Hawthorn, VIC 3122, Australia
rrahmani@swin.edu.au

Abstract. Current energy grids are moving toward utilization of renewable and non-polluting energy sources. Micro-grids, as an emerging means for a localized management, supervision, and control of energy production and consumption are changing the traditional centralized grid topology, making it more distributed and autonomous. However, the fluctuating nature of renewable energy systems make the energy demand control very complex. Hence, one of the challenges in Micro-grid energy control and management is to handle any deviation from the prior forecasted power generation/consumption by optimizing the usage of storage and backup generation units in a way that preserves the users' convenience level. The majority of the proposed optimization approaches only use the centralized load shedding schemes, neglecting the effect of inconvenience it may cause to the users. In this paper, we propose a Multi-agent based decentralized algorithm for a residential grid-connected Microgrid. The focus of our work is on how to handle possible power imbalance situations with the help of an Autonomous Decentralized Multi-agent approach consisting of user agents, storage agent, and grid agent considering the users' consumption preferences as an important factor in the decision making. We investigate the application of our proposed algorithm over a PV-based Microgrid scenario.

Keywords: Multi-agent systems · Microgrid · Autonomous decision making · Decentralized · Energy management

1 Introduction

The number of Micro-grid projects is increasing all over the world [1, 2]. Mannheim-Wallstadt Micro-grid in Germany, Bronsbergen Micro-grid in Netherlands, and Kithnos islands Micro-grid in Greece are just a few examples of the Micro-grid installations in Europe [2, 3]. There has been a lot of research going on in the field of microgrid control and management specially in renewable energy based microgrids

© Springer International Publishing AG 2017
J.O. Berndt et al. (Eds.): MATES 2017, LNAI 10413, pp. 223–237, 2017.
DOI: 10.1007/978-3-319-64798-2_14

[4, 5]. One of the main control issues of microgrids with high dependency to renewable sources of energy is dealing with the intermittency of these sources which makes the energy demand control very complex. Hence, there should be a mechanism to handle any deviation from the prior forecasted power generation/consumption by optimizing the usage of storage, backup generation, and/or the power purchase from the main grid. There have been some studies addressing the power imbalance issue in the power electronic level using blind load curtailments to decrease the cost of imbalance handling. However, considering the socio-economic factors such as consumers' satisfaction alongside the cost of energy may lead to intensive cooperation of users in so-called demand-side management programs. Most of the existing research uses a centralized approach in which utility functions are considered to represent user's priorities for certain appliances at the time of unforeseen event. The drawbacks of this strategy is twofold, first, the centralized approach incurs a massive computational burden on the system whereas all the calculations must be performed by one calculation unit. Secondly, modelling the utility functions for power appliances is user sensitive and depends on the time of use as well; therefore, there is no consensus for power appliances' utility functions among the researchers in this field.

This paper proposes a decentralized autonomous multi-agent based algorithm for handling unforeseen events in a smart microgrid consisting of a photovoltaic system as the main power generation unit. In this methodology, the users' inconvenience due to load curtailment has been taken into account as a monetary cost integrated into the power purchase cost from the main grid. Instead of using utility functions for modelling the appliances, we use some ratings denoting the importance of usage for each user, which will be sent to the microgrid control agent (MCA) and the MCA chooses the best proposals using the proposed cost function model. The agents are able to communicate within the iterations towards reaching the minimal cost for handling the situation. Meanwhile we ensure that if load curtailment is applied there will be no satisfaction drop in the community due to it, as the inconvenience is calculated in the costs and can be paid to the respective users as incentives. The results obtained show the feasibility of the proposed algorithm in a case based scenario developed for the evaluation.

2 Related Work

In fact, there is no standard way to model the utility functions of various appliances belonging to different users. Some studies [6–8] have taken into account the power consumption level of appliances as a measurement to demonstrate their utility. A simple comparison between the power consumption of lighting and TV consumption (roughly about 100 times the amount) may show the lack of these algorithms to model users' consumption preferences. Researchers also tried to model the utility functions of the appliances based on their type [9, 10]. For instance, taking into account the ambient temperature is a way to model air-conditioners and fans, regardless of their power rating. However, even if all the utility functions of different appliances could be described, it still should be individual users' preferences that determines the priority of consumption.

The focus of this research is how to handle possible power imbalance situations with the help of an Autonomous Decentralized Multi-agent approach, preserving the users' level of satisfaction. The aim is to choose an optimized combination of storage, grid power purchase, and load curtailment (Fig. 1), taking into account the inconvenience caused by each combination to the consumers. Utilization of Multi-agent based architectures in the Microgrid power management is of a paramount interest [11, 12] in recent years. The concept of unified energy agent is proposed in [13, 14] in order to fill the gap between the power engineering part of the energy grid and its higher control levels such as the optimization and market functionalities. In this scheme, any component of the energy grid can be represented by an agent and all the energy conversion happening in the grid environment can be modeled using this Multi-agent based demonstration of the energy grid [15–17].

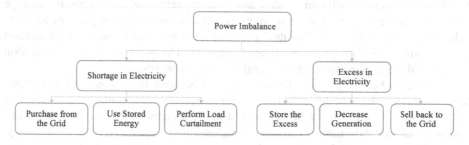

Fig. 1. Possible solutions for handling power imbalance situations

In the proposed algorithm, user agents are responsible to reflect the respective users' preferences while hiding this information from the micro-grid control agent. It is worth mentioning that authors in [18] proposed a decentralized algorithm which considers the users' level of inconvenience when load curtailment. They use a combination of back-up diesel generation, PV generation, and load curtailment in order to address the *power mismatch* issue in an isolated Microgrid. Unlike their work, in this paper, we considered grid connection as an option of power trading and removed the backup generation, as usage of diesel generation is not very common is German energy grid. In the next section, the proposed autonomous decentralized multi-agent based algorithm, which is designed to handle the power generation and consumption imbalance, is explained. As a use-case, the application of the proposed decentralized control technique is described in a given micro-grid scenario.

3 Problem Description

Finding an optimal schedule for electricity generation, consumption, and storage is addressed as a solution for an optimization problem aiming to minimize the cost function, mainly consist of the electricity cost. In contrast to the existing energy management techniques, in this study we consider the users' satisfaction drop alongside with the energy cost as a part of cost function. The optimal solution x^* can be generally described as:

$$x^* = arg_m f(x) \tag{1}$$

$$s.t. \begin{cases} g(x) \leq 0 \\ h(x) = 0 \end{cases}$$

where $f(x)$ is the cost function for the unforeseen event, and x consists of desecrate or continuous variables. The constraints of the problem are represented using $g(x)$ and $h(x)$ and the optimization must be performed subject to these constraints consisting of information for load and generation units as well as the storage system. The maximum and minimum power generation are defied as the constraints of generation units. Maximum charging/discharging rates and total capacity are constraints for storage units. Whilst the minimum and maximum power consumption of appliances are considered as constraints for load units. In case of any undesired event, the optimization process will be performed on the related time-slot. The solution of the optimization process will be applied to the Micro-grid system afterwards.

From the scheduling point of view loads can be generally categorized as controllable, which can be scheduled and non-controllable. The non-controllable appliances (e.g. electric cooking) cannot be considered in the scheduling. The appliances which consumptions are deferrable (such as washing machine) or power-level controlled (e.g. air conditioner) can be taken into consideration. For a deferrable load the starting point can be deferred over a specified period. The power-level controlled loads may alter their power around the nominal power rating.

In the proposed methodology, PV system is considered as the main generation unit of the Microgrid and also a 24 h power consumption of the load units are forecasted and available. In this study, we only focus to handle power imbalance situations that may occur due to any deviation from the forecasted PV power generation.

3.1 Power Imbalance Definition

We use the following terms in our definitions. *Forecast Load*, the consumption timetable which shows the exact usage time for users' appliance; *Forecast PV*, the predicted power generation of PV systems for the next 24 h; *Actual Load*, the real-time consumption monitored by users' smart meters; *Actual PV*, the real-time PV generation.

We refer to *imbalance* as any deviation of the *Actual Load* from the *Forecast Load* or the *Actual PV* from the *Forecast PV*.

The aim of the proposed algorithm is to minimize the total daily cost of imbalance handling by minimizing the cost of each time-slot, considering the user inconvenience as cost.

4 Proposed Mathematical Model

4.1 Mathematical Imbalance Model

In this section, we describe our proposed mathematical model of imbalance. We also model the cost function of handling imbalance situation. The objective of the proposed algorithm is to handle the imbalance by choosing an optimized combination of storage, load curtailment, and purchasing power from the grid (Fig. 1), taking the inconvenience caused by each combination to the consumers into account. An example of the combined solution is importing power from the main grid along with the load curtailment. The amount of deviated energy form the forecast PV generation in timeslot t is assumed to be as follows:

$$\Delta E_g = E_{g,f} - E_{g,a} \tag{2}$$

where E, is the energy amount (kWh) with subscript g indicating PV generation while a and f denote *actual* and *forecast*, respectively. There is another parameter in the model showing the amount of stored energy (E_{strg}) that is preferred to be used at the time of energy shortage. The amount of *energy shortage* (E_{shrt}) is required to be covered by the grid. In case of excess in the electricity E_{shrt} is negative.

If the amount of energy shortage can be supplied from the stored energy or compensated by conserving energy from load curtailment, we will not need to buy it from the grid anymore. However, it will cause a drop in the respective users' satisfaction which should also be considered in the cost. Equation (3) shows the specific amount of energy (E_{cnsr}) that can be conserved by load curtailment:

$$E_{cnsr} = \sum_{u=1}^{\mathcal{N}} \sum_{i=1}^{\mathcal{M}} E_u(i) \tag{3}$$

where $\mathcal{N}$ denotes the number of users affected by the load curtailment, $\mathcal{M}$ is total number of appliances to be removed or re-scheduled, and $E_u(i)$ is the energy usage of ith appliance of uth user. It is assumed that each household is equipped with a user agent which can communicate with the MCA on behalf of the user by representing his/her priorities in terms of cost. The priorities can be directly given to the agent or being calculated by the agent itself through monitoring the time of use, power consumption, etc. It is worth mentioning that the calculation of the user priorities is out of scope of this research and we assume different costs representing the priorities of different users in the simulations. Therefore, the new cost of importing power from the grid for covering imbalance would be $f_g(E_{shrt} - E_{cnsr})$.

Model of Inconvenience. In case of load curtailment, there will be a change in satisfaction of the users who are affected. This change is proportional to the importance of the appliances for a specific user whose appliances are removed or rescheduled. As mentioned before, the preference of individual users may vary, hence, every user experience a different amount of satisfaction drop (I_u) which is formulated in Eq. (4) for the uth user.

$$I_u = \sum_{i=1}^{\mathcal{M}} I_{u,i} \tag{4}$$

Overall change in the community's satisfaction level is:

$$I = \sum_{u=1}^{\mathcal{N}} \sum_{i=1}^{\mathcal{M}} I_{u,i} \tag{5}$$

where $\mathcal{N}$ is the number of users whose satisfaction are affected by the imbalance.

Cost Function of Power Imbalance. Equation (6) denotes the overall cost of imbalance based on the calculation above:

$$C_{Imb} = f_{Imb}(E_{shrt}, E_{cnsr}, I) = f_g(E_{shrt} - E_{strg} - E_{cnsr}) + I \tag{6}$$

where $f_g(E)$, is returning the cost of importing electricity from the grid (€). The goal of imbalance handling process is to minimize the cost function f_{Imb}. The amount of energy shortage (E_{shrt}) and community satisfaction drop (I) are used in the iterations to minimize the cost function.

5 Proposed Autonomous Decentralized Multi-agent Control and Management System

In our proposed Autonomous Decentralized Multi-agent Control and Management System (ADMCM), the main objective is to minimize the imbalance cost (C_{Imb}), in each time-slot. The system consists of four main unit types namely, *Micro-grid Control Agent, User agent, Storage agent,* and *Grid agent.*

In case of any power imbalance occurrence, the ADMCM communicate with the User agents (UAs) to receive the monetary value of using each appliance from the specific user's perspective. If the curtailment is included in the optimal solution, Micro-grid Control Agent (MCA) unit will curtail the load and pay the respective price, based on the value determined by each user. User can always update the monetary value of each appliance. Hence, the curtailment of the appliances is directly based on the importance of them to the respective user at each time-slot.

The overall communication of the four unit types is described as follows:

- *Micro-grid Control Agent (MCA)* monitors the actual PV generation and actual load, and calculates the amount of power imbalance at each time-slot (t). It also dynamically communicates with user agents which reflect the users' consumption priorities and perform the optimization.
- *User agent (UA)* is responsible to reflect the respective user's consumption priorities to the MCA. It is physically connected to the appliances and can switch them on and off upon request from MCA. Local optimization is performed by UA on the level of user's appliances.

- *Storage agent (SA)* is physically connected to storage units and capable of charging and discharging them. This agent communicates with MCA and receive the request to control the storage units.
- *Grid agent (GA)* connect to the main grid in order to import or export the amount of energy requested by MCA. The connection is to buy the power when the combination of PV generation and storage cannot solely serve the loads. Moreover, in case of over generation, the excess energy can be sold back to the grid (Fig. 2).

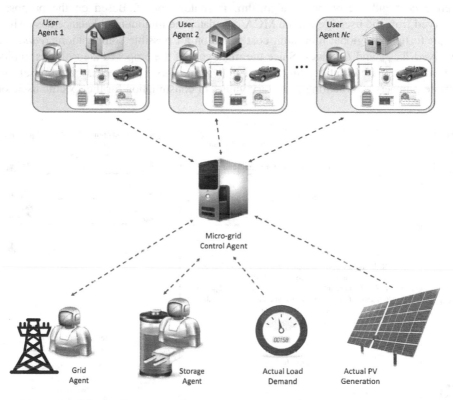

Fig. 2. The proposed autonomous decentralized algorithm

5.1 Decentralized Algorithm Description

The main goal of the proposed algorithm is to minimize the imbalance cost (C_{Imb}) in each time slot. At the beginning of the algorithm, the energy shortage (E_{shrt}) is checked. The positive and negative value of E_{shrt} means the shortage and excess energy respectively. δE_{strg} denotes the energy stored in each time slot t, and $E_{strg}(t)$ shows the accumulated stored energy in the battery until the time slot t. Importing power from the grid is only done when the battery is run out of energy.

In case of energy shortage ($E_{shrt} > 0$) the imbalance cost (C_{Imb}) and share of every user in the cost are calculated. In contrast to centralized approaches user agents (UAs) participate in the decision making in the decentralized algorithm. UA has to reflect the priorities of the respective user in the form of utility values defined for each appliance. It also should locally minimize the user cost and return the energy conservation ($E_{cnsr,u}$) and inconvenience cost (I_u) to the micro-grid control agent (MCA) as a proposal. If any UA tries to misrepresent the inconvenience cost in the proposal sent to the MCA, the chance of it being accepted will be very low. The reason is that the MCA calculates the cost respective to all combinations of all proposals received from the UAs and the minimum cost is the objective from which the optimal solution is chosen. Hence, there is no incentive for the UAs to misrepresent their real inconvenience cost and the proposed algorithm is strategy proof. Based on the proposals received from the user agents, the MCA calculates the minimum imbalance cost. MCA ought to find the global minimum cost based on all possible combinations (***comb***) of received $E_{cnsr,u}$ and I_u values. Since the main goal of the proposed algorithm is to hide the information about utility function of individual users' appliances, the proposals are simple numbers representing monetary values of consumption for the specific users on

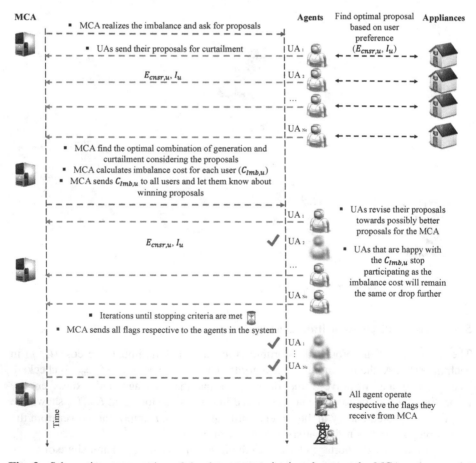

Fig. 3. Schematic representation of the data communications between the MCA and agents in the proposed decentralized imbalance handling algorithm

a certain time-slot. Iterations of communication happen between MCA and UAs to ensure global minimum costs. After performing the optimization and computing C_{Imb} and user costs ($C_{Imb,u}$), MCA lets the users know about the share of cost and also the acceptance or rejection of their proposals. The iterations advance until the C_{Imb} is not greater than a given tolerance value (ε). The same process is happening to the optimizations at users' level, a tolerance value is determined by each user (ε_u) at which the algorithm stops the iterations.

The control signals are going to be sent by MCA to the storage agent (SA) and grid agent (GA) when required (Fig. 3).

6 Case Study

In this section, we present the application of the proposed decentralized control technique in a Microgrid scenario. As mentioned earlier, in our model the consumption preferences of the users may be different from each other. Therefore, the monetary value of using the same appliances are not identical for different users. To show the impact of users' satisfaction in the final decision making we create a community behavior including user types with various consumption preferences. Then, we create a load forecast profile based on users load constraints defined, and a generation profile based on the forecast PV electricity production. In the end, we create power imbalance scenarios to show the application of our autonomous decentralized algorithm to handle those power imbalance situations. The simulated Microgrid consists of 10 residential units, photovoltaic generation system, battery storage, and grid connection possibility.

6.1 Model of User Behavior in Negotiation

In order to demonstrate the impacts of user preferences and behaviors on the negotiation process and the hourly imbalance cost, three different user types are assumed as shown in Table 1. Different user types present different monetary constraints and different preferences for inconvenience and electricity cost to be paid. Type A refers to the users for whom less imbalance cost incurred is relatively more important than the inconvenience. Type B denotes the user who care about their inconvenience rather than cost incurred. And Type C represent the user with normal preferences, i.e., their constraint and preferences are around rational values based on the electricity retail price from the grid. In the considered community, we assume to have 3 users for Type A and B while 4 users are from Type C.

Table 1. User types with their preferences in the negotiation.

User type	Maximum $C_{Imb,u}$ [€]	$\frac{I_u}{E_{cnsr,u}}$ [€/kWh]
Type A	0.05	0.5
Type B	0.5	4
Type C	0.12	1.5

In the assumed power imbalance scenarios that will be described later, every user will send a proposal consisting of the inconvenience cost and the respective energy to be conserved by the user. In order to focus on the impacts of user behavior on the cost, the basic consumption profile is assumed to be the same for all users.

6.2 Model of PV-Based Micro-Grid

The assumed Micro-grid consists of 10 households with anonymous appliances situated in a residential area. An array of Photovoltaic (PV) panels with the overall size of 9 kW is set to produce the needed energy, and with a possibility of grid connectivity, serve the whole consumption. The given Micro-grid is equipped with a battery storing system of 3 kW which is used to store the excess solar generation and discharge it later in the evening (Fig. 4). Figure 4 shows the generation, storage and consumption profiles for 24 h while the Microgrid is in its balanced condition, i.e., the PV generation and load consumption are as forecasted. In this situation, the total energy generated by PV is 57.548 kWh, the total load consumption is 56.259 kWh and the net energy purchased from the grid is 2.667 kWh. It is worth mentioning that the grid connection is very useful to handle the morning peak and sell back the excess of PV generation which cannot be stored. It is widely accepted that the size of battery storage system cannot be chosen more than a rational portion of renewable energy generation. In this study the size of battery storage system has been considered as 30% of rated PV generation. Also, the battery degradation due to charge and discharge cycles are ignored in this study. In the designed balanced Microgrid system, the net energy

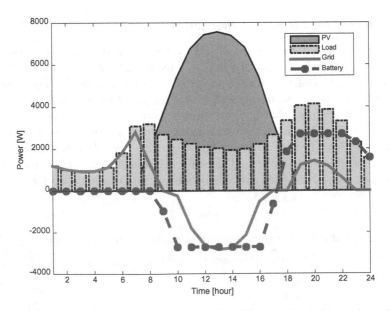

Fig. 4. Assumed balanced Microgrid with load profile, PV generation, grid supply, and storage energy.

purchased from the grid covers only 4% of the total load consumption, and the other 96% is provided by the PV generation. The energy retail price for purchasing from the grid is assumed to be flat at 0.3 € while the sellback price is fixed at 0.2 €. As an example of showing cost calculations, the total cost incurred when the Microgrid is in balanced situation is 2.09 € with the hourly profile shown in Fig. 5. For the simulation set-up, we used MATLAB R2016b release. The simulations have been performed on a PC with *Intel (Core i7)* processor with *24 GB RAM*.

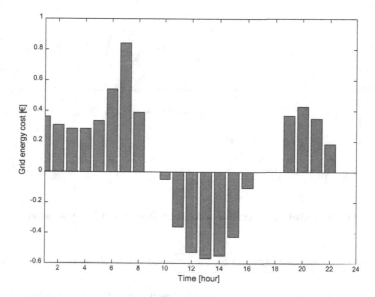

Fig. 5. Hourly grid cost when the Microgrid is in balanced mode.

6.3   Power Imbalance Scenarios

The balance between the actual production and consumption is being monitored by the control agent. In case of any imbalance between production and consumption, the cost of handling the imbalance is calculated through the proposed decentralized algorithm described in previous section.

In order to analyze the proposed algorithm, four imbalance scenarios are taken into consideration. For the sake of simplicity, imbalance scenarios with 20, 40, 60 and 80% of shortage in the PV generation, as shown in Fig. 6 are considered. More realistic shortage model in PV generation which for instance, considers the cloud coverage model are investigated in [19, 20]. The obtained cost for each imbalance scenario is reported and compared with the cost of purchasing the shortage energy from the grid, as shown in Table 2.

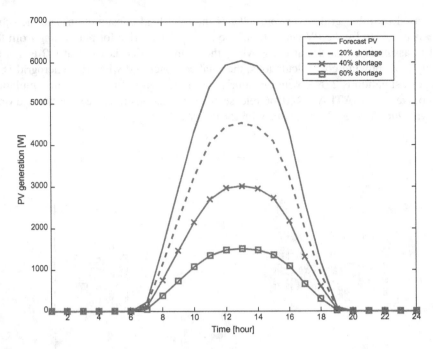

Fig. 6. Imbalance scenarios – different shortages in PV generation.

Table 2. The optimized cost obtained by the proposed decentralized algorithm for imbalance scenarios.

PV generation shortage	C_{Imb} proposed algorithm (€)	C_{Imb} grid purchase (€)
20% shortage	1.26	1.73
40% shortage	3.61	4.43
60% shortage	5.57	7.88
80% shortage	8.38	11.33

6.4   Comparison of the Proposed Decentralized Algorithm with Centralized Approaches

The key differences and benefits of the proposed autonomous decentralized solution in comparison with the centralized control and management systems to handle power imbalance are as follows:

For a centralized entity, it is needed to access all users' information and have ability to process it in a reasonable time, in order to reach a global optimum solution. Implementing such a system which is capable of calculating the optimal imbalance handling cost and performing the respective load curtailment at a reasonable cost and time may be hard to achieve. In the proposed approach, each user agent autonomously performs local optimizations and only needs to send the results as a proposal to the microgrid agent. This will considerably reduce the overall decision time by permitting concurrent calculations. It also permits omitting the need for retrieving details about users' consumption behaviors.

Due to the lack of a standard approaches for modelling the utility functions of various appliances of different users there is no realistic appliance utility function model that properly considers all users' consumption preferences. In contrast, the utility functions of users' appliances are either unknown or non-existent to the micro-grid control agent in the decentralized case. It is the user agents' liability to keep track of the related consumers' preferences and prioritize the appropriate load schemes.

The need for a sophisticated data communication structure is another issue of a centralized approach. This and the need for extra programming in order to add any agent to the system will make the reliability and scalability issues more severe. The proposed decentralized approach, instead, works based on constricted necessary data exchange. Moreover, the decentralized approach is able to easily adopt and embed a new programmable agent in the system, such as a DER unit, user agent, etc.

7   Conclusion and Future Work

In this paper, we addressed one of the challenges in Micro-grid energy control and management, which is to handle unforeseen events in a smart microgrid consisting of a photovoltaic system as the main power generation unit, A Multi-agent decentralized imbalance handling architecture was presented optimizing the overall imbalance cost, considering different users' power consumption priorities. Any deviation from the prior forecasted power generation/consumption is compensated by optimizing the usage of storage unit in a way that preserves the users' convenience level. In this methodology, the users' inconvenience due to load curtailment has been taken into account as a monetary cost integrated into the power purchase cost from the main grid. Instead of using utility functions for modelling the appliances, we use some ratings denoting the importance of usage for each user, which will be sent to the microgrid control agent (MCA) and the MCA chooses the best proposals using the proposed cost function model. The agents are able to communicate within the iterations towards reaching the minimal cost for handling the situation. Meanwhile we ensure that if load curtailment is applied there will be no satisfaction drop in the community due to it, as the inconvenience is calculated in the costs and can be paid to the respective users as incentives. The results obtained show the feasibility of the proposed algorithm in a case based scenario developed for the evaluation.

We investigated the application of our proposed autonomous decentralized algorithm in a PV-based Microgrid assuming various power imbalance scenarios. In order to show the effect of users' consumption preferences in the decision making, we created Microgrid users' community with various users' consumption behavior and took into account respective monetary values for the imbalance cost minimization. We compared the effect of using our proposed decentralized imbalance handling with the case of not having demand flexibility, over the simulation. The results show a considerable reduction in the final imbalance handling cost compared with only compensating the imbalance by importing power from the grid. Moreover, our proposed model made participation of the users possible by taking into account the effect of their consumption preferences in optimization process. However, the strategy of choosing the best proposals at the moment is exhaustive search which is not efficient if the number of proposals is high and so as the number of their combinations. In this case, a very high computational cost will be incurred if the optimal operation is required. One way to tackle this problem is to propose an effective methodology for choosing the best proposals at each iteration using a heuristic search algorithm which reduces the computations significantly. In our future work, we will improve our imbalance handling model trying to address this issue. Moreover, the impact of having more realistic electricity price model and imbalance scenarios, storage optimization approaches, and also using other storage and back-up generation technologies such as fuel cell on the proposed model will be explored.

References

1. Barnes, M., Kondoh, J., Asano, H., Oyarzabal, J., Ventakaramanan, G., Lasseter, R., Hatziargyriou, N., Green, T.: Real-world MicroGrids-an overview. In: 2007 IEEE International Conference on System of Systems Engineering, pp. 1–8 (2007)
2. Hatziargyriou, N., Asano, H., Iravani, R., Marnay, C.: Microgrids. IEEE Power Energy Mag. 5, 78–94 (2007)
3. Planas, E., Andreu, J., Gárate, J.I., de Alegría, I.M., Ibarra, E.: AC and DC technology in microgrids: a review. Renew. Sustain. Energy Rev. 43, 726–749 (2015)
4. Bayindir, R., Hossain, E., Kabalci, E., Perez, R.: A comprehensive study on MicroGrid technology. Int. J. Renew. Energy Res. (IJRER) 4, 1094–1107 (2014)
5. Olivares, D.E., Mehrizi-Sani, A., Etemadi, A.H., Cañizares, C.A., Iravani, R., Kazerani, M., Hajimiragha, A.H., Gomis-Bellmunt, O., Saeedifard, M., Palma-Behnke, R., Jiménez-Estévez, G.A., Hatziargyriou, N.D.: Trends in Microgrid control. IEEE Trans. Smart Grid 5, 1905–1919 (2014)
6. Samadi, P., Mohsenian-Rad, A.H., Schober, R., Wong, V.W.S., Jatskevich, J.: Optimal real-time pricing algorithm based on utility maximization for smart grid. In: 2010 First IEEE International Conference on Smart Grid Communications, pp. 415–420 (2010)
7. Remani, T., Jasmin, E.A., Imthias Ahamed, T.P.: Load scheduling with maximum demand using binary particle swarm optimization. In: 2015 International Conference on Technological Advancements in Power and Energy (TAP Energy), pp. 294–298 (2015)
8. Yang, P., Tang, G., Nehorai, A.: A game-theoretic approach for optimal time-of-use electricity pricing. IEEE Trans. Power Syst. 28, 884–892 (2013)
9. Li, N., Chen, L., Low, S.H.: Optimal demand response based on utility maximization in power networks. In: 2011 IEEE Power and Energy Society General Meeting, pp. 1–8 (2011)
10. Mohajeryami, S., Schwarz, P., Baboli, P.T.: Including the behavioral aspects of customers in demand response model: real time pricing versus peak time rebate. In: 2015 North American Power Symposium (NAPS), pp. 1–6 (2015)
11. Nunna, H.K., Doolla, S.: Multiagent-based distributed-energy-resource management for intelligent MicroGrids. IEEE Trans. Ind. Electron. 60, 1678–1687 (2013)
12. Rohbogner, G., Hahnel, U.J., Benoit, P., Fey, S.: Multi-agent systems' asset for smart grid applications. Comput. Sci. Inf. Syst. 10, 1799–1822 (2013)
13. Derksen, C., Linnenberg, T., Unland, R., Fay, A.: Structure and classification of unified energy agents as a base for the systematic development of future energy grids. Eng. Appl. Artif. Intell. 41, 310–324 (2015)

14. Derksen, C., Unland, R.: Energy agents - foundation for open future energy grids. In: Position Papers of the 2015 Federated Conference on Computer Science and Information Systems, vol. 6, pp. 259–264 (2015)
15. Derksen, C., Unland, R.: The EOM: an adaptive energy option, state and assessment model for open hybrid energy systems. In: Proceedings of the 2016 Federated Conference on Computer Science and Information Systems, FedCSIS 2016, Gdansk, Poland, 11–14 September 2016, pp. 1507–1515 (2016)
16. Ghorbani, S., Unland, R.: A Holonic multi-agent control system for networks of micro-grids. In: Klusch, M., Unland, R., Shehory, O., Pokahr, A., Ahrndt, S. (eds.) MATES 2016. LNCS, vol. 9872, pp. 231–238. Springer, Cham (2016). doi:10.1007/978-3-319-45889-2_17
17. Loose, N., Nurdin, Y., Ghorbani, S., Derksen, C., Unland, R.: Evaluation of aggregated systems in smart grids: an example use-case for the energy option model. In: Bajo, J., Escalona, M.J., Giroux, S., Hoffa-Dąbrowska, P., Julián, V., Novais, P., Sánchez-Pi, N., Unland, R., Azambuja-Silveira, R. (eds.) PAAMS 2016. CCIS, vol. 616, pp. 369–380. Springer, Cham (2016). doi:10.1007/978-3-319-39387-2_31
18. Rahmani, R., Moser, I., Seyedmahmoudian, M.: Multi-agent based operational cost and inconvenience optimization of PV-based microgrid. Sol. Energy 150, 177–191 (2017)
19. Seyedmahmoudian, M., Horan, B., Soon, T.K., Rahmani, R., Oo, A.M.T., Mekhilef, S., Stojcevski, A.: State of the art artificial intelligence-based MPPT techniques for mitigating partial shading effects on PV systems – a review. Renew. Sustain. Energy Rev. 64, 435–455 (2016)
20. Seyedmahmoudian, M., Mekhilef, S., Rahmani, R., Yusof, R., Renani, E.T.: Analytical modeling of partially shaded photovoltaic systems. Energies 6, 128–144 (2013)

Learning Policies for Resolving Demand-Capacity Imbalances During Pre-tactical Air Traffic Management

Theocharis Kravaris[1,2], George A. Vouros[1,2(✉)], Christos Spatharis[1,3],
Konstantinos Blekas[1,3], Georgios Chalkiadakis[1,4],
and Jose Manuel Cordero Garcia[1,5]

[1] University of Piraeus Research Centrer, Piraeus, Greece
[2] Department of Digital Systems, University of Piraeus, Piraeus, Greece
georgev@unipi.gr
[3] Department of Computer Science & Engineering, University of Ioannina,
Ioannina, Greece
[4] School of Electrical and Computer Engineering, Technical University of Crete,
Chania, Greece
[5] CRIDA - Reference Center for Research, Development and Innovation in ATM,
Madrid, Spain

Abstract. In this work we propose and investigate the use of *collaborative reinforcement learning* methods for resolving demand-capacity imbalances during pre-tactical Air Traffic Management. By so doing, we also initiate the study of data-driven techniques for predicting multiple correlated aircraft trajectories; and, as such, respond to a need identified in contemporary research and practice in air-traffic management. Our simulations, designed based on real-world data, confirm the effectiveness of our methods in resolving the demand-capacity problem, even in extremely hard scenarios.

1 Introduction

The current Air Traffic Management (ATM) system worldwide is based on an time-based operations paradigm that leads to demand-capacity balancing (DCB) issues. These further impose limitations to the ATM system that are resolved via airspace management or flow management solutions, including regulations that generate delays (and costs) for the entire system. These demand-capacity imbalances are difficult to be predicted in pre-tactical phase (prior to operation) as the existing ATM information is not accurate enough during this phase.

With the aim of overcoming these ATM system drawbacks, different initiatives, notably SESAR in Europe[1] and Next Gen in the US[2], have promoted the transformation of the current ATM paradigm towards a new, *trajectory-based*

---

[1] SESAR 2020, http://www.sesarju.eu/.
[2] NextGen, https://www.faa.gov/nextgen/.

© Springer International Publishing AG 2017
J.O. Berndt et al. (Eds.): MATES 2017, LNAI 10413, pp. 238–255, 2017.
DOI: 10.1007/978-3-319-64798-2_15

operations (TBO) paradigm. In the future ATM system, the trajectory becomes the cornerstone upon which all the ATM capabilities will rely on. The trajectory life cycle describes the different stages from the trajectory planning, negotiation and agreement, to the trajectory execution, amendment and modification. This life cycle also provides new opportunities in terms of both information quality and availability among ATM stakeholders, as it requires collaborative planning processes, before operations. The envisioned advanced decision support tools required for enabling future ATM capabilities will exploit trajectory information to provide optimised services to all ATM stakeholders—Airspace users, Air Navigation Service Providers, Network Manager, and so on.

The proposed transformation requires high-fidelity aircraft trajectory prediction capabilities, supporting the trajectory life cycle at all stages efficiently. This is also evidenced by the fact that improvements in trajectory prediction are fully aligned with FlightPath 2050[3] goals, in particular with those related to societal and market needs (with focus on improved, weather-independent arrival punctuality), protecting environment and energy supply, and ensuring safety and security. Single trajectory prediction refers to the process of predicting an individual trajectory considering it in isolation from the overall ATM system. Accounting for network effects and their implications on the execution of planned trajectories of individual flights requires considering interactions among these trajectories; moreover, it requires considering other operational conditions that influence the actual trajectory of any flight.

State-of-the-art techniques for predicting flights' trajectories, enable predictions based on specific physical models of aircrafts' movement, or on the exploitation of historical trajectory data that are obtained from surveillance systems (e.g., radar or ADS-B tracks) or directly from the aircraft (e.g., Quick Access Records). Two important drawbacks of such prediction methods are that *(a)* they are limited to single trajectory predictions, and *(b)* their prediction horizon is a short time one. Indeed, the trajectories are predicted one-by-one based on the information related to the individual flights, ignoring the expected traffic at the prediction time lapse. Consequently, the network effect resulting from the *interactions of multiple trajectories* is not considered at all, which may lead to huge prediction inaccuracies. This is due to the complex nature of the ATM system, which impacts the trajectory predictions in many different ways. Capturing aspects of that complexity, and being able to devise prediction methods that take the relevant information into account, would greatly improve the current trajectory prediction approaches.

Against this background, our main objective in this paper is to demonstrate how machine learning methods can help in refining single trajectory predictions (learned from surveillance data linked to weather data and other contextual information), considering cases where demand of airspace use exceeds capacity, resulting to *hotspots*. This is referred as the *Demand and Capacity Balance (DCB)* problem. In our work we study and determine the way trajectories are

---

[3] "Flightpath 2050" European Commission. Available Online: http://ec.europa.eu/transport/modes/air/doc/flightpath2050.pdf.

affected due to the influence of the surrounding traffic (i.e., considering interactions among individual predicted trajectories), taking into account an important aspect of ATM system complexity.

Our overall, long-term goal is to deliver an understanding on the suitability of applying data-driven techniques for predicting single and multiple correlated aircraft trajectories. However, our focus in this article is on the DCB problem in Air Traffic Management, whose solution takes place during the so-called "flights' planning phase", during which the eventual conflicts resolutions adopted by air-traffic controllers in the actual flights are not taken into consideration. As such, our immediate objective is to predict delays that are applied to the flight plans, due to the demand and capacity imbalances occurring in hotspots.

To this end, this paper makes the following contributions:

- It formulates the DCB problem as an MDP.
- It proposes the use of specific *collaborative reinforcement learning* techniques for tackling this problem.
- It presents evaluation results in simulated, varying traffic conditions based on real-world data, showing the potential of our methods. All our methods managed to successfully resolve the DCB problem i.e., to produce schedules without any conflict seven in the hardest of our scenarios.

In the remainder of this paper we first state the operational context of our research in detail, motivate our work and state the problem to be solved (Sect. 2). Then in Sect. 3 we formulated the DCB problem in an MDP framework, and present collaborative reinforcement learning methods of choice. In Sect. 4 we present evaluation results for all our three methods. Section 5 presents relevant work; and finally, Sect. 6 concludes the paper.

2   The Air Traffic Management Operational Context and Motivation for Research

The operational scenarios for trajectory predictions considered in our research agenda assume that the process of predicting traffic happens at the planning phase (i.e., days before operation), as opposed to the tactical phase (i.e. in real-time during operation). The scenarios are considered to be developed in a specific geographical area (without affecting the generality of the solutions proposed), and interests of different stakeholders, such as Air Navigation Service Providers and airspace users, are taken into account: Air Navigation Service Providers require resolving the demand-capacity imbalances efficiently, while airspace users (e.g. airlines) aim to operate safely and efficiently without large delays.

Considering the ATM network effects and multiple trajectories prediction, our objective is to demonstrate how machine learning methods can help in refining single trajectory predictions considering cases where demand of airspace use exceeds capacity. Doing so, we aim to study and determine the way trajectories are affected due to the influence of the surrounding traffic. During the planning phase, conflict resolutions adopted by Air Traffic Controllers are not considered at all, so the resulting trajectories are not conflict-free.

2.1 The Demand-Capacity Balance Problem in ATM

The DCB problem (or process) considers two important types of objects in the ATM system: *aircraft trajectories* and *airspace sectors*.

Aircraft trajectories are series of spatio-temporal points of the generic form $(long_i, lat_i, alt_i, t_i)$, denoting the longitude, latitude and altitude, respectively, of the aircraft at a specific time point t_i. At the same time, *flight plans* are *intended trajectories*, which consist of events of flights crossing air blocks and sectors, and flying over specific waypoints. Each event specifies the element that is crossed (air block or sector), the entry and exit locations (coordinates + flight levels), and the entry and exit times, or the time that the flight will fly over a specific time. Other information such as estimated take-off time are specified, and, in case of delay, the calculated take-off time.

Sectors are air volumes segregating the airspace, each defined as a group of airlocks. These are specified by a geometry (the perimeter of their projection on earth) and their lowest and highest altitudes. As an example, Fig. 1 depicts projections of airblocks above Europe. Airspace sectorization may be done in different ways, depending on sector configuration. Such a configuration determines the number of active (open) sectors. Only one sector configuration can be active at a time. Airspace sectorization changes frequently during the day, given different operational conditions and needs. This happens transparently for flights.

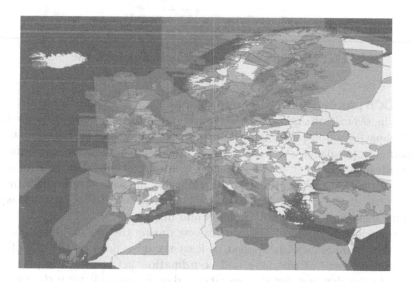

Fig. 1. Airlocks in 2D: sectors are groups of adjacent airblocks.

The *capacity of sectors* is of utmost importance: this quantity determines the maximum number of flights flying within a sector during a specific time interval.

The *demand* for each sector is the quantity that specifies the number of flights that co-occur (or predicted to occur) during a specific interval within a sector. Demand must not exceed sector capacity for any time interval. There are different types of measures to monitor the demand evolution, with the most common ones being *Entry Rate* and *Occupancy Count*. In this work we consider Occupancy Count.

The Occupancy of a given sector is defined as the number of flights inside the sector during a selected period, referred as *Occupancy Counting Period*. In turn, this Occupancy Counting Period is defined as a picture of the sector occupancy taken every time step value along an interval of fixed duration: The Step value defines the time difference between two consecutive Occupancy Counting Periods. The Duration value defines the time difference between start and end times of each Occupancy Counting Period. For instance, considering the example in Fig. 2 for a specific sector, the occupancy counts corresponding to the set of flights at different moments P with duration of 1 min and step of 1 min are: (a) At P: 1, 2, 3; (b) at P+1: 1, 3, 4, 5; (c) at P+2: 3, 4, 6; and (d) at P+3: 4, 6, 7, 8.

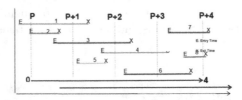

Fig. 2. Occupancy step = 1 min., Duration = 1 min.

The DCB process is divided in three phases: Strategic, Planning and Tactical Phase. The overall objective is to optimise traffic flows according to air traffic control capacity while enabling airlines to operate safe and efficient flights.

Planning operations start as early as possible - sometimes more than one year in advance. Given that the objective is to protect air traffic control service of overload [5], this service is always looking for optimum traffic flow through a correct use of the capacity, guaranteed: safety, better use of capacity, equity, information sharing among stakeholders and fluency.

We consider the demand-capacity process during the *pre-tactical* phase. Pre-tactical flow management is applied at least six days prior to the day of operations, and consists of planning and coordination activities. This phase aims to compute the demand for the operations day, compare it with the predicted airspace capacities on that day, and make any necessary adjustments to the flight plans. Since our goal is trajectory prediction in a TBO environment, we consider individual predicted trajectories instead of flight plans, in order to determine the delay that should be imposed on them due to traffic. At this phase, trajectories are sent to the Network Manager who takes into account sector capacities to detect problematic areas. The main objective of this phase is to optimise efficiency and balance demand and capacity through an effective organisation of resources. In fact, DCB work today involves a collaborative decision making process among stakeholders, resulting to a corresponding Air Traffic Flow Control Management Daily Plan.

Tactical flow management takes place on the day of operations and involves considering, in real time, those events that affect the Air Traffic Flow Control Management Daily Plan and make the necessary modifications to it. This phase aims at refining the measures taken during the pre-tactical phases towards solving the demand -capacity imbalances that may appear. Tactical flow management is not within the scope of our work.

Figure 3 shows a snapshot of the Air Traffic Flow Control Management human-machine interface that is currently being used by the Network Manager, for supporting collaborative decision-making between all stakeholders: This snapshot shows the occupancy count of a specific sector in consecutive periods.

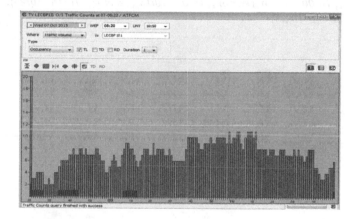

Fig. 3. Occupancy indicator. The y axis represents the occupancy count, and the x axis time. Columns show occupancy counts, yellow line shows sustainable capacity and orange line shows the peak capacity (Color figure online)

Concluding the above, our objective is to demonstrate how machine learning methods can help in trajectory forecasting when planned demand exceeds sectors capacity, taking into account interactions among trajectories, and thus traffic. In this case, regulations of type C (i.e. delays) are applied to the trajectories.

2.2 Problem Specification

Let there be N trajectories in T that must be executed over the airspace in a total time period of duration H (e.g. hours). The airspace consists of a set of sectors, denoted by *Sectors*. Time can be divided in intervals of duration Δt, equal to that of the Occupancy Counting Period.

As already defined above, each trajectory is a sequence of timed positions in airspace. This sequence can be exploited to compute the series of sectors that each flight crosses, together with the entry and exit time for each of these sectors. For the first (last) sector of the flight, i.e. where the departure (resp. arrival) airport resides, the entry (resp. exit) time is the departure (resp. arrival) time. However, there may exist flights that cross the airspace but do not depart and/or arrive in any of the sectors of our airspace: In that case we only consider the entry and exit time of sectors within the airspace of our interest.

Thus, a trajectory T in $\mathcal{T}$ is a time series of elements of the form:

$$T=\{(sector_1, entry_{t_1}, exit_{t_1})....(sector_m, entry_{t_m}, exit_{t_m})\},$$

where $sector_l \in Sectors, l = 1, ...m$.

For instance, considering the trajectories T_1 and T_2 in Fig. 4, these are specified as follows:

$T_1 = \{(sector_5, 10:00, 10:20), (sector_2, 10:20, 10:45)\}$
$T_2 = \{(sector_1, 10:00, 10:05), (sector_2, 10:05, 10:15), (sector_7, 10:15, 10:25),$
$\quad (sector_{12}, 10:25, 10:35)\}$

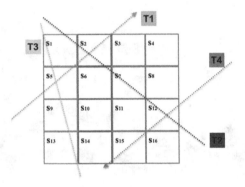

Fig. 4. Example of trajectories crossing sectors

This information per trajectory suffices to measure the demand $D_{s_i,p}$ for each of the sectors $sector_i \in S$ in the airspace in any Occupancy Counting Period p of duration Δt.

Specifically, $D_{s_i,p} = |T_{s_i,p}|$, i.e. the number of trajectories in $T_{s_i,p}$, where

$T_{s_i,p} = \{T \in \mathcal{T} | T = (\ldots, (s_i, entry_{t_i}, exit_{t_i}), \ldots), \quad and \ the \ temporal \ interval$
$[entry_{t_i}, exit_{t_i}] \ overlaps \ with \ period \ p\}$

For instance, considering the trajectories T_1 and T_2 crossing the sector s_2 in Fig. 4, it holds that $T_{sector_2,p} = \{T_1, T_2\}$, with $p=[10:10, 10:15]$.

The trajectories in $T_{sector_i,p}$ are defined to be *interacting trajectories* for the period p and the sector $sector_i$.

Each sector $sector_i \in S$ has a specific capacity C_{sector_i}. The aim is to resolve imbalances of sectors' demand and capacity: These are cases where $D_{sector_i,p} > C_{s_i}$, for any period p of duration Δt in H, in any $sector_i \in S$. Δt equals to the Occupancy Counting Period duration. We refer to these cases as *capacity violation* or *demand-capacity imbalance* cases, resulting to *hotspots*.

In case of capacity violation for a period p and sector $sector_i$, the interacting trajectories in $T_{sector_i,p}$ are defined as *hotspot-constituting trajectories*: one or more of these trajectories must be delayed in order to resolve the imbalance in $sector_i$.

Clearly, imposing delays to trajectories may propagate hotspots to a subsequent time period for the same and/or other sectors crossed by that trajectory: In any case, the sets of interacting trajectories in different periods and sectors may change, and thus, in case of demand-capacity imbalances, hotspot-constituting trajectories may change as well. This can be done in many ways, when different trajectories delay. Having said that, we must clarify that the only type of change in a trajectory that may be imposed by a regulation is "delay": i.e., shifting the entry and exit time for each sector by a specific amount of time. The sequence of sectors crossed is not affected.

Towards the agent-based formulation of the problem, we consider the following: Each agent A_i is specified to be the aircraft (instrument) performing a specific trajectory, in a specific date and time. Thus, we consider that agents and trajectories coincide in our case and we may interchangeably speak of agents A_i, trajectories T_i, or agents A_i executing trajectories T_i. Agents, as it will be specified, have own interests and preferences, although they are assumed collaborative, and take autonomous decisions on their delays: It must be noted that agents do not have communication and monitoring constraints given that imbalances are resolved at the planning phase, rather than during operation.

Therefore agents have to learn joint delays to be imposed to their trajectories w.r.t. the operational constraints concerning the capacity of sectors crossed by these trajectories. It must be noted that agents have conflicting preferences since they prefer to impose the smallest delay possible (preferably none) to their own trajectory, while also executing their planned trajectories safely and efficiently.

Agents with interacting trajectories are considered to be "peers" given that they have to jointly decide on their delays: The decision of one of them affects the others. This implies that agents form "neighbourhoods" of peers, taking also advantage of the inherent sparsity of the problem (e.g. a flight crossing the north part of Spain, will never interact in any direct manner with a flight crossing the southest part of the Iberian Peninsula). However, as mentioned above, these neighbourhoods have to be updated when delays are imposed to trajectories, given that trajectories that did not interact prior to any delay may result to be interacting when a delay is imposed. Thus, a dynamic update of peers' neighbourhoods is necessary according to agents' decisions.

Given an agent A_i the traffic for that agent is determined to be the trajectories of all other agents forming its neighbourhood. More specifically:

Traffic(A_i)
= $\{T_j | T_j$ *is a trajectory that interacts with the trajectory* T_i *executed by* A_i *for any specific sector crossed by* T_i *and any time period within* H $\}$
= $\cup_{(sector,\cdot,\cdot) \in T_i,p} T_{sector,p}$

A society of agents $S = (\mathcal{T}, \mathcal{A}, \mathcal{E})$ is modelled as a graph with one vertex per agent A_i in $\mathcal{A}$ and any edge (A_i, A_j) in $\mathcal{E}$ connecting agents with interacting trajectories in $\mathcal{T}$. As pointed out above, the set of edges are dynamically updated by adding new edges when new interacting pairs of trajectories appear.

$N(A_i)$ denotes the neighbourhood of agent A_i, i.e. the set of agents connected to agent $A_i \in \mathcal{A}$ including also itself: These are the peers of A_i.

The options available in the inventory of any agent A_i for contributing to the resolution of hotspots may differ between agents: These, for agent A_i are $D_i \subseteq \{0, 1, 2, ..., MaxDelay_i\}$. These are ordered by the preference of agent A_i to any such option, according to the function $\gamma(i) : D_i \rightarrow \mathbb{R}$. We do not assume that agents in $\mathcal{A} - \{A_i\}$ have any information about $\gamma(i)$: This represents the situation where airlines set own options and preferences for delays even in different own flights, depending on different circumstances. However, we expect that the order of preferences should be decreasing from 0 to $MaxDelay_i$. In this paper we ran experiments assuming that $D_i = D_j$, and thus $MaxDelay_i = MaxDelay_j$, and $\gamma(i)(d) = \gamma(j)(d)$. This assumption does not affect the generality of the proposed methods, which may be applied to any other case. However, this issue requires further investigation for agents to reach optimal solutions.

Considering two peers A_i and $A_j \in N(i) - \{A_i\}$, agents must select among the sets of available options D_i and D_j respectively, so as to increase their expected payoff w.r.t. their preferences on options, and resolve the DCB problem.

This problem specification emphasises on the following problem aspects: *(a)* Agents need to coordinate their strategies (i.e. chosen options to impose delays) to execute their trajectories jointly with others, taking into account traffic, w.r.t. their preferences and operational constraints; *(b)* agents need to explore and discover how different combinations of delays affect the joint performance of their trajectories w.r.t. the DCB process, given that the way different trajectories do interact is not known beforehand (agents do not know the interacting trajectories that emerge due to own decisions and decisions of others, and of course they do not know whether these interactions result to hotspots i.e., demand-capacity imbalances); and *(c)* agents' preferences on the options available may vary depending on the trajectory performed, and are kept private.

3   Collaborative Reinforcement Learning Methods

3.1   The MDP Framework

Using the model of collaborative multiagent MDP framework [6,11] we assume:

- The **society** of agents $S = (\mathcal{T}, \mathcal{A}, \mathcal{E})$.
- A **time step** $t = t_0, t_1, t_2, t_3, ..., t_{max}$, where $(t_{max} - t_0) = H$.
- A **local state** per agent A_i at time t, comprising state variables that correspond to (a) the delay imposed to the trajectory T_i, ranging to the sets of options assumed by A_i, and (b) the number of hotspots in which A_i is involved in (for any of the sectors and time periods). Such a state is denoted s_i^t. The **joint state** $s_{i,j}^t$ of agents A_i and A_j at time t is the tuple of the state

variables for both agents. This is generalised for any subset of agents in the society. A **global state** s^t at time t is the tuple of all agents' local states.

- The **local strategy** for agent A_i at time t, denoted by str_i^t is the action that A_i performs at that specific point: An action for any agent at any time point, in case the agent is still on ground, may be, either impose a delay or not. Thus, at each time point the agent has to take a binary decision. When the agent flies, then it just follows the trajectory. The location (i.e. sector) of that agent at any time point can be calculated by consulting its trajectory. The **joint strategy of a subset of agents** A of $\mathcal{A}$ executing their trajectories (for instance of $N(A_i)$) at time t, is a tuple of local strategies, denoted by str_A^t (e.g. $str_{N(A_i)}^t$). The set of all joint strategies for $A \subset \mathcal{A}$ is denoted $Strategy_A$. The **joint strategy** for all agents $\mathcal{A}$ at time t is denoted str^t.

- The **state transition function** gives the transition to the joint state s^{t+1} based on the joint strategy str^t taken in joint state s^t. Formally $Tr : State \times Strategy \to State$. It must be noticed that although this transition function may be deterministic in settings with perfect knowledge about society dynamics, the state transition per agent is stochastic, given that no agent has a global view of the society, of the decisions of others, while its neighbourhood gets updated. Thus no agent can predict how the joint state can be affected in the next time step. Thus, for agent A_i this transition function is actually $Tr : State_i \times Strategy_{\{A_i\}} \times State_i \to [0,1]$, denoting the transition probability $p(s_i^{t+1}|s_i^t, str_i^t)$.

- The **local reward** of agent A_i, denoted Rwd_i, is the reward that the agent gets by executing its own trajectory in a specific joint state of its peers in $N(A_i)$, thus $Traffic(A_i)$, according to the sectors' capacities, and the joint strategy of agents in $N(A_i)$. The **joint reward**, denoted by Rwd_A, for a set of peers A specifies the reward received by agents in A by executing their actions in their joint state, according to their joint strategy.

The joint reward Rwd_A for $A \subseteq \mathcal{A}$ depends on the number of hotspots occurring while the agents execute their trajectories according to their joint strategy str_A^t in their joint state s_A^t, i.e. according to their decided delays, and also according to their preferences on the chosen delays. Formally:

$$Rwd_A(s_A^t, str_A^t) = \lambda_1 * X(str_A^t, s_A^t) + \lambda_2 * D(str_A^t, s_A^t) \qquad (1)$$

where, $X(str_A^t, s_A^t)$ is equal to the total number of hotspots in which agents in A are involved while executing their joint strategy in their joint state (i.e. according to the delays decided up to t), $D(str_A^t, s_A^t) : s_A \to \mathbb{R}$, is a function aggregating the preferences of agents on their chosen delays. The parameters λ_1 and λ_2 are used for balancing between the interests of different stakeholders towards reaching an optimum solution. Currently we have set $\lambda_1 = -100$ and λ_2 is a very small number close to zero: Methods are indeed proved to be very sensitive to preferences on delays although they do favour small delays, and this requires further investigation as part of our future work.

Thus, the reward received by any agent depends on (a) the sectors' capacity and the hotspots in which they participate, and on (b) their preferences on delays while performing their trajectories jointly.

A (local) policy of an agent A_i is a function $\pi_i : State_i \rightarrow Strategy_{\{A_i\}}$ that returns local strategies for any given local state, for A_i to execute its trajectory. The objective for any agent in the society is to find an optimal policy π^* that maximises the expected discounted future return

$$V_i^*(s) = max_{\pi_i} E[\sum_{t=0}^{\infty} \delta^t Rwd_i(s_i^t, \pi_i(s_i^t))|\pi_i)] \tag{2}$$

for each state s_i, while executing its trajectory. $\delta \in [0, 1]$ is the discount factor.

This model assumes the Markov property, assuming also that rewards and transition probabilities are independent of time. Thus, the state next to state s is denoted by s' and it is independent of time.

3.2   Collaborative Q-Learning Methods

$Q-$functions, or action-value functions, represent the future discounted reward for a state s when deciding on a specific strategy str for that state and behaving optimally from then on. The optimal policy for agents in s is to jointly make the choice $argmax_c Q^*(s, str)$, maximizing expected future discounted reward.

The next paragraphs describe three collaborative reinforcement learning methods that take advantage of the problem structure (i.e. interactions among flights), considering that agents do not know the transition and reward model (model-free methods) and interact concurrently with all their peers.

Independent Reinforcement Learners (Ind-Colab-RL): The independent learners Q-learning variant proposed in [7] decomposes the global Q-function into a linear combination of local agent-dependent Q-functions. Each local Q_i is based on the local state and local strategy for agent A_i:

$$Q(s, a) = \sum_{i=1}^{|N|} Q_i(s_i, str_i)$$

Dependencies between agents, and thus the coordination graph, are defined according to the agents' society specified above. It must be pointed out that these dependencies may be updated by adding new ones while solving the problem. Each agent observes its local state variables.

A local Q_i is updated using the global temporal-difference error, the difference between the current global Q-value and the expected future discounted return for the experienced state transition, using

$$Q_i(s_i, str_i) := Q_i(s_i, str_i) +$$
$$\alpha[Rwd(s_{N(A_i)}, str_{N(A_i)}) + \delta max'_a Q(s'_i, str^*_i) - Q(s_i, str_i)] \,(3)$$

where, str^*_i is the best strategy known to the agent for the state s'_i. It must be noticed that instead of the global reward $Rwd(s, str)$ used in [7], we use the reward received by the agent, taking into account only the joint state and joint strategy of its neighbourhood.

Edge-Based Collaborative Reinforcement Learners (Ed-Colab-RL): This is a variant of the edge-based update sparse cooperative edge-based Q-learning method proposed in [8]. Given two peer agents performing their tasks, A_i and A_j, the Q−function is denoted succinctly $Q_{i,j}(s_{i,j}, str_{i,j})$, where $s_{i,j}$ with abuse of notation denotes the joint state related to the two agents, and $str_{i,j}$ denotes the joint strategy for the two agents. The sum of all these edge-specific Q−functions defines the global Q−function.

The update function in this case is as follows:

$$Q_{i,j}(s_{i,j}, str_{i,j}) = Q_{i,j}(s_{i,j}, str_{i,j}) +$$
$$\alpha\left(\frac{Rwd_i(s_i, str_i)}{N(A_i)} + \frac{Rwd_j(s_j, str_j)}{N(A_j)} + \delta Q_{i,j}(s'_{i,j}, str^*_{i,j}) - Q_{i,j}(s_{i,j}, str_{i,j})\right) \,(4)$$

where, $str^*_{i,j}$ is the best joint strategy for agents A_i and A_j and for the joint state $s'_{i,j}$. In this case this is approximated using the *max-plus message-passing algorithm* [10]. Actually, given the society of agents (i.e. the coordination graph), in order to compute the optimal joint action str^*, each agent A_i repeatedly sends a message μ_{ij} to its neighbors $A_j \in N(A_i)$. The message μ_{ij} can be regarded as a local payoff function of agent A_j and is calculated as

$$\mu_{ij}(str_j) = max_{str_i}\{Q_i(str_i) + Q_{ij}(str_i, str_j) + \sum_{k \in N(A_i)-A_j} \mu_{ki}(str_i)\}, \quad (5)$$

The local Q-function for A_i is defined as in the Ind-Colab-RL update case above (formula (3)). Agents decide on their best local strategy by computing

$$str^*_i = argmax_{str_i}(f_i(str_i) + \sum_{j \in N(A_i)} \mu_{ji}(str_i)) \quad (6)$$

Agent-Based Collaborative Reinforcement Learners (Ag-Colab-RL): This is a variant of the agent-based update sparse cooperative edge-based Q-learning method proposed in [8]. As in *Ed-Colab–RL* method, given two peer agents performing their tasks, A_i and A_j, the Q−function is denoted succinctly $Q_{i,j}(s_{i,j}, str_{i,j})$, where $s_{i,j}$ denotes the joint state related to the two agents, and $str_{i,j}$ denotes the joint strategy for the two agents. The update function is as follows:

$$Q_{i,j}(s_{i,j}, str_{i,j}) = Q_{i,j}(s_{i,j}, str_{i,j}) +$$
$$\alpha \sum_{k \in \{i,j\}} \frac{(Rwd_{i,j}(s_{i,j}, str_{i,j}) + \delta Q_k(s'_k, str^*_k) - Q_k(s_k, str_k))}{|N(A_k)|} \,(7)$$

where, str_k^* is the best strategy for agent A_k in state s_k', $k \in \{i, j\}$. Agents, compute their local Q-functions and their best local strategy as in the $Ed - Colab - RL$ method.

4   Experimental Results

We have performed a series of experiments in order to test and compare the efficiency of the three collaborative Q-learning methods to resolving the DCB problem in ATM. The efficiency is measured by means of the resulting number of hotspots, the mean delay achieved and the distribution of interacting flights in Occupancy Counting Periods – in conjunction to the number of learning periods needed for methods to compute policies. To this purpose, we create specific simulation scenarios of trajectories crossing an airspace. The scenarios are artificial, but correspond to typical and difficult cases in the real world, found in datasets provided by CRIDA, the Spanish Reference Centre for Research, Development, and Innovation in ATM. They have been used during this phase of our research in order to control the experimental settings and explore the potential of the proposed methods.

For the simulation we consider that the airspace comprises a grid of sectors, all having a specific capacity value (that could possibly differ from sector to sector). Table 1 presents the data used in producing the experimental cases and the parameter values used in all simulated runs.

Table 1. Parameter values used during the simulated experiments

Parameter	Value
Grid structure of sectors	4×4
Capacity of sectors, C	$\in [4, 10]$
Number of planes, N	100
Duration and step of occupancy counting period	6
Total time period duration H	180
Maximum delay	10

All three approaches follow an ϵ-greedy exploration strategy starting from probability 0.8, which is gradually reduced in subsequent rounds. However the *Ind-Colab-RL* differs from the other methods in that it initiates an ϵ-greedy exploitation phase for 1000 rounds with high probability, while in a subsequent phase of 1000 rounds, it does pure exploration. To evaluate the three approaches in cases of varying difficulty, we modify the *capacity* of sectors (C), and the number m of sectors that each flight crosses. Herein we report results only for the most hard cases in the grid considered, where $m \in [3, 4]$. For every capacity value $C \in [4, 10]$, we generated 50 random experimental cases. Figure 5 shows the mean value and the standard deviation of the final (after learning) number of hotspots, as well as the mean delay for all flights and for all experiments performed. According to the results and as shown in Fig. 5(a), all methods demonstrated

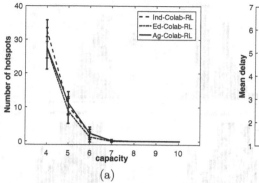
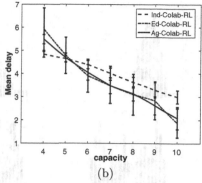

Fig. 5. Comparative results: Plots illustrate (a) the number of hotspots and (b) the mean delay estimated by each method in terms of various values of sectors' capacity (x-axis).

very similar behaviour wrt. hotspots' eradication, with $Ed - Colab - RL$ being slightly more effective compared to others: The x-axis in Fig. 5(a) shows the capacity of each sector, while y-axis shows the number of hotspots when agents' strategies converge. When the capacity of sectors was greater than or equal to 7 all methods reached the optimum policy for the hotspot criterion. However, an improvement in the 'mean delay' criterion is shown in Fig. 5(b) concerning the edge-based and the agent-based collaborative RL approaches: x-axis in this figure shows the varying capacity of each sector, and the y-axis shows the mean delay achieved by each method. $Ind - Colab - RL$ shows the worst performance, while the performance of $Ed - Colab - RL$ is similar to that of $Ag - Colab - RL$, although the later is more consistent while the capacity of sectors increases. This confirms that the proposed multi-agent formulation provides a promising framework for tackling the DCB problem.

Figure 6 illustrates an example of the received learning curves by each method, i.e. the number of hotspots and mean delay as estimated for 1000 episodes during learning (we set sector's capacity as $C = 7$ to all cases). For the Ind–$Collab$–RL method, these episodes are from the pure exploration phase.

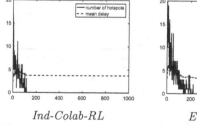
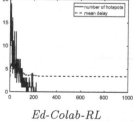
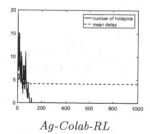

Ind-$Colab$-RL $\qquad$ Ed-$Colab$-RL $\qquad$ Ag-$Colab$-RL

Fig. 6. Learning curves received by three methods in a setting considering sectors' capacity equal to 7. The x-axis shows the number of the learning episode, while the y-axis shows the number of hotspots and mean delay achieved in each episode.

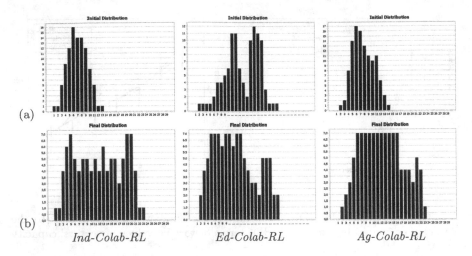

(a)

(b)

Ind-Colab-RL   Ed-Colab-RL   Ag-Colab-RL

Fig. 7. An example of the distribution of interacting flights in Occupancy Counting Periods (a) initially and (b) as produced by three methods

All methods were able to converge rapidly, achieving strategies with zero hotspots to any sector, and with flights' delay much less than the maximum acceptable delay (which was 10 in all experiments). Finally, in Fig. 7 we present an example of the distribution of hotspots (y-axis) in terms of Occupancy Counting Periods in a number of 29 non-overlapping occupancy periods, each of duration equal to 6 time instants (e.g. 6 min). This was obtained by measuring the interacting flights to a specific sector in different periods: (a) at the beginning and (b) at the end of learning. As can be seen, our schemes manage to offer strategies with significantly reduced hotspots (zero in these cases, given that demand in any occupancy period is not greater than capacity).

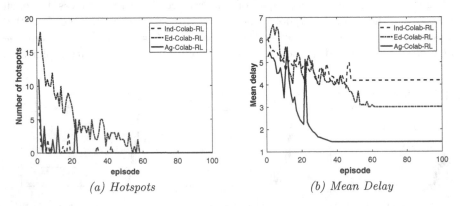

(a) Hotspots   (b) Mean Delay

Fig. 8. Learning curves received by the three methods in a setting where $N = 3000$ and sectors' capacity $C = 20$. The x-axis shows the number of the learning episode, while the y-axis shows (a) the number of hotspots and (b) the mean delay achieved in each episode.

Providing further evidence to the viability of the proposed methods, Fig. 8 shows the learning curves received by the three methods in a setting where $N = 3000$ and sectors' capacity $C = 20$, while the remaining parameters are as specified in Table 1. In that figure the x-axis shows the number of the learning episode, while the y-axis shows the number of hotspots in each episode (Fig. 8(a)) and the mean delay achieved per method (Fig. 8(b)). As it is seen there, all methods converge fast, after only 60 episodes, resolving all imbalances. Specifically, the *Ag–Colab–RL* method converges as fast as the *Ind–Colab–RL*, but in a solution where the mean delay is lower than those achieved by the other methods.

5   Related Work

Most works on agent-based modelling of the air traffic management system focus on the tactical phase, and mostly to the problem of avoiding collisions: These are mostly reactive approaches using probabilistic models [3] or geometric approaches [9]. For instance, following an agent-based approach, [2,12] propose decentralised methods for air traffic management application as well as for UAV collision avoidance. The first work proposes a negotiation approach for agents to find safe trajectories. Similarly in the second work agents, aiming to collision avoidance (tactical phase) following either an iterative p2p or a multi party collision avoidance method.

Using the Brahms multi-agent simulation framework, authors in [14] study the issues that affect the effectiveness of flow management in strategic planning. Although no decision-making or planning abilities are provided, the paper provides interesting insights for modelling the problem and addressing inefficiencies.

Closely to our aims, [1] propose multiagent reinforcement learning methods to reduce congestion through agents' local actions. Each agent may perform one of three actions: (a) setting separation between airplanes, (b) ordering ground delays or (c) performing reroutes. Agents are related to fixed points (sectors' entry points), while the hotspots are not guaranteed to be solved.

A recent work that provides Bayesian reinforcement learning (BRL) solutions for collaborative multiagent settings, is that of [13]. Like [8], the approach employs a variant of max-plus [10] for message-passing, but, crucially, it is able to extend single-agent and centralized multi-agent Bayesian RL methods [4] in collaborative settings by decomposing the coordination problem into *regional* sub-problems. In future work, we intend to explore the applicability of that paper's ideas in our problem domain.

6   Concluding Remarks

This paper investigated a collaborative reinforcement learning framework for strategic planning of flight trajectories, with the aim of minimizing total conflicts and eliminating the effect of hotspots with minimum delays. The key aspect of the proposed scheme is the formulation of the DCB problem in the Air Traffic

Management as a collaborative multiagent MDP framework where the aircrafts are treated as agents. Three multiagent RL schemes were studied, with their preliminary results being quite promising.

Our primary aim is to further extend our work in a variety of challenging issues. We intend to examine more systematically the generalization capabilities of the proposed RL-based multi-agents scheme to more complex environments and validate it in real operations.

This involves work in several interesting aspects: (a) Preparing datasets of flight plans in specific periods (e.g. days) of varying traffic. Historical data on flight plans do exist, including initial (unregulated) flight plans and their regulated versions per flight. (b) Exploiting historical data to train our methods and compute solutions using them, (c) tune/learn a reward model, and finally (d) compare delays imposed by our methods to those imposed by domain experts in real-life scenarios.

Of course the problem of resolving hotspots can be seen as a constraint optimisation problem (COP) and it is our aim to also compare the solutions produced by reinforcement learning methods to those produced by COP methods.

Another direction for future work is to introduce alternative joint Q-functions among agents taking into account geometric properties, and to exame different forms of the reward function.

Acknowledgements. This work is supported by the DART project, which has received funding from the SESAR Joint Undertaking under grant agreement No. 699299 under European Unions Horizon 2020 research and innovation programme. For more details, please see the DART project's website, http://www.dart-research.eu.

References

1. Agogino, A.K., Tumer, K.: A multiagent approach to managing air traffic flow. Auton. Agents Multi-agent Syst. **24**(1), 1–25 (2012)
2. Albaker, B.M., Rahim, N.A.: Unmanned aircraft collision avoidance system using cooperative agent-based negotiation approach. Int. J. Simul. Syst. Sci. Technol. **11**(4), 1–8 (2010)
3. Baek, K., Bang, H.: ADS-B based trajectory prediction and conflict detection for air traffic management. Int. J. Aeronaut. Space Sci. **13**(3), 377–385 (2012)
4. Chalkiadakis, G., Boutilier, C.: Coordination in multiagent reinforcement learning: a Bayesian approach. Proc. AAMAS **2003**, 709–716 (2003)
5. Eurocontrol: Air Traffic Flow and Capacity Management (ATFCM) (2011)
6. Guestrin, C.E.: Planning under uncertainty in complex structured environments. Ph.D. thesis, Stanford, CA, USA, aAI3104233 (2003)
7. Guestrin, C.G., Lagoudakis, M., Parr, R.: Coordinated reinforcement learning. In: Proceedings of the ICML-2002 The Nineteenth International Conference on Machine Learning, pp. 227–234 (2002)
8. Kok, J.R., Vlassis, N.: Collaborative multiagent reinforcement learning by payoff propagation. J. Mach. Learn. Res. **7**, 1789–1828 (2006). http://dl.acm.org/citation.cfm?id=1248547.1248612

9. Orefice, M., Di Vito, V., Corraro, F., Fasano, G., Accardo, D.: Aircraft conflict detection based on ADS-B surveillance data. In: 2014 IEEE Metrology for Aerospace (MetroAeroSpace), pp. 277–282. IEEE (2014)
10. Pearl, J.: Probabilistic Reasoning in Intelligent Systems: Networks of Plausible Inference. Morgan Kaufmann Publishers Inc., San Francisco (1988)
11. Puterman, M.L.: Markov Decision Processes: Discrete Stochastic Dynamic Programming, 1st edn. Wiley, New York (1994)
12. Sislak, D., Volf, P., Pechoucek, M.: Agent-based cooperative decentralized airplane-collision avoidance. IEEE Trans. Intell. Transp. Syst. **12**(1), 36–46 (2011)
13. Teacy, W.T.L., Chalkiadakis, G., Farinelli, A., Rogers, A., Jennings, N.R., McClean, S., Parr, G.: Decentralized Bayesian reinforcement learning for online agent collaboration. In: Proceedings of the 11th International Conference on Autonomous Agents and Multiagent Systems, AAMAS 2012, vol. 1, pp. 417–424. International Foundation for Autonomous Agents and Multiagent Systems, Richland (2012). http://dl.acm.org/citation.cfm?id=2343576.2343636
14. Wolfe, S.R., Jarvis, P.A., Enomoto, F.Y., Sierhuis, M., van Putten, B.J.: A multi-agent simulation of collaborative air traffic flow management. In: Multi-agent Systems for Traffic and Transportation Engineering, pp. 357–381. IGI Global (2009)

Indoor Localization of JADE Agents Without a Dedicated Infrastructure

Stefania Monica$^{(\boxtimes)}$ and Federico Bergenti$^{(\boxtimes)}$

Dipartimento di Scienze Matematiche, Fisiche e Informatiche,
Università degli Studi di Parma, 43124 Parma, Italy
{stefania.monica,federico.bergenti}@unipr.it

Abstract. This paper describes and compares two of the algorithms for indoor localization that are implemented in the localization add-on module for JADE. Described algorithms perform localization of agents running on smart devices in known indoor environments using only received WiFi signals from access points. First, distance estimates from access points are computed using received signal strength in routinary network discovery. Then, computed distance estimates are used to generate estimates of the position of the smart device that hosts the agent using one of described algorithms. The first algorithm, known as two-stage maximum-likelihood algorithm, is a well-known technique and it is considered a point of reference to evaluate the performance of other algorithms. The second algorithm, which has been recently introduced to overcome numerical-instability problems of classic geometric algorithms, works by turning localization into an optimization problem which is effectively solved using particle swarm optimization. In order to show the applicability of the proposed algorithms, the last part of the paper shows experimental results obtained in an illustrative indoor scenario, which is representative of envisioned applications.

1 Introduction and Motivation

Among the classic characterizations of agents, it is often said that agents are *situated entities* that execute in an environment and that act on the environment to bring about their goals. Whether the environment is physical or not is irrelevant, but agents executing in physical environments are traditionally called *robots*, while the term *software agents* is used for agents executing in nonphysical environments. Notably, such a distinction is quickly becoming obsolete because of the concrete possibilities of implementing ubiquitous and pervasive computing that *smart devices* [25] offer. Smart devices are now sufficiently powerful to easily accommodate useful software agents, and they also provide a direct contact with the physical environment that agents can use to try to achieve their goals. The link between software agents and smart devices is particularly close and it dates back to more than 20 years ago, when the *Foundation for Intelligent Physical Agents* (now *IEEE FIPA*, www.fipa.org) was established by a group

© Springer International Publishing AG 2017
J.O. Berndt et al. (Eds.): MATES 2017, LNAI 10413, pp. 256–271, 2017.
DOI: 10.1007/978-3-319-64798-2_16

of companies and research institutions that were driving the raise of ubiquitous and pervasive computing at the time. In the research landscape that FIPA contributed to create, it is worth recalling project *Lightweight and Extensible Agent Platform (LEAP)* [1,6], which was launched by the European Commission in 1999 and was led by Motorola to bring the *Java Agent and DEvelopment framework* (JADE) [2] to mobile devices with the help of Siemens, Broadcom, Telecom Italia, British Telecom, ADAC and the University of Parma. Project LEAP had a very challenging goal for the time because JADE needed to be severely scaled down to meet the constraints that mobile devices of early 2000s imposed. The objective of LEAP was finally achieved in 2001, when the results of the project were fed back to the main development line of JADE and, since then, JADE has been effectively used to host software agents on mobile devices.

Nowadays, smart devices offer adequate resources to host JADE containers with minor restrictions [5], and the challenges pushed by the use of software agents on mobile devices are now very different from those that project LEAP faced in the past. In order to fully adhere to the metaphor of *agents as situated entities*, we need to provide agents with the possibility of sensing the physical environment where they execute and of acting on the physical environment to achieve their goals. Smart devices are ideal candidates to substantiate this metaphor because they offer sophisticated on-board sensors (e.g., compass, gyroscope, and accelerometer) and actuators (e.g., high-resolution display, high-fidelity speakers and vibration motor) that can be effectively used to provide agents with a bidirectional link with the physical environment where they execute. Needless to say that the features of smart devices can be enriched using ad hoc connectivity, which enables the use of external sensors and actuators.

Besides the enormous possibilities that they offer, smart devices are still immature concerning their localization capabilities, which are essential to let agents deliver so called *location-aware services*. It is common opinion that the problem of outdoor localization can be considered (almost) solved because of technologies, such as the *Global Positioning System (GPS)*, that allow estimating the position of a device with an acceptable accuracy [8]. On the contrary, indoor localization is still an open problem and various approaches have been studied in the literature to try to solve it. The use of *Ultra-Wide Band (UWB)* technology seems very promising in this respect because it guarantees accurate and robust indoor localization [11,28]. This is the reason why the use of UWB technology for accurate indoor localization in industrial environments [17] and to provide agents with indoor localization capabilities [14] has been already investigated. However, specific smart devices were needed to run those experiments because UWB sensors were—and still are—not widely available, and a dedicated infrastructure in the environment was demanded just to support localization. In order to overcome the limitations that the need of specific devices and of a dedicated infrastructure imposed, we looked for valid alternatives to the use of UWB technology [15,16] and, in this paper, we present experimental result in this respect. This paper is about recent developments of the indoor localization capabilities of JADE agents hosted on ordinary Android devices, which use only ordinary WiFi infrastructures. In detail, in this paper we assume that an agent hosted on a smart device is interested in acquiring accurate and timely estimates of its dynamic position within a known indoor environment. In addition, we assume that a set of known WiFi *Access Points (APs)* is available in the considered environment. The basic idea of the proposed method is based on the possibility of estimating the distances between the smart device and each AP by means of WiFi signals. The smart device does not need to be connected to a WiFi network, nor does it require special access privileges, and it only relies on signals that are used to discover available networks. The power of such signals, as received from the smart device, is used to compute estimates of the distance between the smart device and each responding AP. Such estimates are then properly processed to estimate the position of the smart device, which is immediately made available to the agent. We have already discussed the architecture of the localization add-on module for JADE [14,16]. The module is open to accommodate most of the algorithms that have been proposed in the literature to solve localization problems [10,22], and in this paper we discuss and compare the performance of two algorithms that ships with the module. The first algorithm, called *Two-Stage Maximum-Likelihood (TSML)*, is a classic technique which is commonly considered a point of reference to evaluate other techniques. The second algorithm, introduced in [18] for UWB technology, and further improved in [19,21], addresses the numerical instability of TSML by turning the localization problem into an optimization problem solved using *Particle Swarm Optimization (PSO)*. Note that discussed algorithms are not necessarily limited to JADE, and they can be adopted in completely different contexts, but the current implementation assumes that agents are hosted in JADE containers.

This paper is organized as follows. The details of the range acquisition phase are explained in Sect. 2, which also fixes notation and details the two discussed algorithms. Section 3 shows experimental results obtained in a representative indoor scenario, and it compares the performance of studied algorithms. Finally, Sect. 4 concludes the paper and outlines future work.

2   Agent-Based Localization

We have recently implemented a specific add-on module for JADE to provide agents with self-localization capabilities [14,16]. A discussion of the architecture of the module, which is briefly summarized in [14], is not needed to detail expected localization performance, which is the major topic of this paper. Therefore, rather than focusing on the description of the internals of the module, in this paper we provide an in-depth description of available localization techniques together with an experimental evaluation of their performace.

2.1   Notation and Reference Scenarios

We consider scenarios where M WiFi APs are available and, in the rest of this paper, their coordinates are denoted as

$$\underline{s}_i = (x_i, y_i)^T \qquad i \in \{1, \dots, M\}. \tag{1}$$

We assume that the indoor environment is known to the agent, and, in particular, we assume that the coordinates $\underline{s_i}$ of APs are known to the agent. Note that from (1) it is evident that we consider bi-dimensional scenarios and, even if such an assumption may seem restrictive and unrealistic, the approaches discussed in this paper can be easily generalized to three-dimensional environments as shown in [20]. In addition, [16] shows a generic technique to relate a localization problem in a three-dimensional environment to a proper localization problem in a bi-dimensional environment. Finally, note that APs are assumed to be static in the environment, and this is the reason why they are often called *anchor nodes*.

The *ranging capabilities* that the smart device is requested to offer in order to support discussed algorithms concern the possibility of measuring estimates of the distances between the smart device where the agent is running, which is denoted as *Target Node (TN)* in the rest of this paper, and each one of the M APs used for localization. Such distance estimates are obtained by analyzing the average received power of WiFi signals traveling between the TN and each responding AP during routinary network discovery. According to the Friis transmission equation [11], the average received power $\bar{P}(r)$ can be expressed as a function of the distance r between a transmitter and a receiver. The explicit expression of the Friis transmission equation is

$$\bar{P}(r) = P_0 - 10\beta \log_{10} \frac{r}{r_0} \tag{2}$$

where P_0 is the known power at reference distance r_0 and β accounts for the details of the transmission. By inverting (2), the value of r as a function of $\bar{P}(r)$ can be expressed as

$$r = r_0 \cdot 10^{-\frac{\bar{P}(r)-P_0}{10\beta}}. \tag{3}$$

Hence, in order to derive an estimate of distance r between the TN and a generic AP, it is sufficient to measure the average received power of the signal traveling between them and to apply (3). Note that each range estimate can be associated with the corresponding AP and with its coordinates. Actually, communications between the TN and an AP during network discovery include the *Basic Service Set IDentification (BSSID)* of the latter, which can be used to identify the responding AP. Hence, assuming that each known BSSID can be associated with the coordinates $\underline{s_i}$ of the corresponding AP, each distance estimate can be related to the coordinates of the corresponding AP. This is a key assumption to guarantee localization capabilities, which involve proper processing of acquired range estimates and the knowledge of the coordinates of APs from which they originated. Discussed localization algorithms use only the coordinates of APs and range estimates acquired during routinary network discovery to compute estimates of the position of the TN.

We denote the true position of the TN as $\underline{u} = (x, y)^T$. We remark that $\underline{u}$ is supposed to be unknown and it is the vector to be estimated. Using this notation, the true distance between the TN and the $i-$th AP is

$$r_i = ||\underline{u} - \underline{s_i}|| \qquad i \in \{1, \ldots, M\}. \tag{4}$$

The knowledge of true distances $\{r_i\}_{i=1}^M$, together with the knowledge of the coordinates $\{\underline{s}_i\}_{i=1}^M$ of the APs, would easily determine the position of the TN because the coordinates of the TN could be found by simply intersecting the circumferences centered in $\{\underline{s}_i\}_{i=1}^M$ with radii $\{r_i\}_{i=1}^M$. Mathematically, this translates into the solution of the following system of M quadratic equations

$$
\begin{cases}
(x - x_1)^2 + (y - y_1)^2 = r_1^2 \\
\ldots \\
(x - x_M)^2 + (y - y_M)^2 = r_M^2.
\end{cases}
\tag{5}
$$

Unfortunately, since true distances $\{r_i\}_{i=1}^M$ between the TN and each AP are unknown, localization can only be performed using the following system of quadratic equations

$$
\begin{cases}
(\hat{x} - x_1)^2 + (\hat{y} - y_1)^2 = \hat{r}_1^2 \\
\ldots \\
(\hat{x} - x_M)^2 + (\hat{y} - y_M)^2 = \hat{r}_M^2,
\end{cases}
\tag{6}
$$

which is obtained from (5) by replacing the values of true distances $\{r_i\}_{i=1}^M$, with their estimates, denoted as $\{\hat{r}_i\}_{i=1}^M$. Due to errors on range estimates, the M circumferences corresponding to the equations in (6) often do not intersect in a single point and therefore a proper localization algorithm needs to be considered to find an estimate of the position of the TN, denoted as

$$
\underline{\hat{u}} = (\hat{x}, \hat{y})^T.
\tag{7}
$$

In order to derive a proper localization algorithm, let us first observe that system (6) can be re-written as

$$
\underline{1}\,\underline{\hat{u}}^T \underline{\hat{u}} + \underline{A}\,\underline{\hat{u}} = \underline{\hat{k}}
\tag{8}
$$

where $\underline{1}$ is a vector with M elements equal to 1, $\underline{\hat{k}}$ is a vector whose i−th element is $\hat{r}_i^2 - (x_i^2 + y_i^2)$, and $\underline{A}$ is the following $M \times 2$ matrix

$$
\underline{A} = -2 \begin{pmatrix}
x_1 & y_1 \\
x_2 & y_2 \\
\vdots & \vdots \\
x_M & y_M
\end{pmatrix}.
\tag{9}
$$

Algorithms to solve (8), based on least square techniques, on Taylor series expansion, and on maximum-likelihood methods, are classic topics of the literature on localization and they are described, for instance, in [26].

2.2   The TSML Localization Algorithm

The *Two-Stage Maximum-Likelihood* (*TSML*) algorithm [12] starts from the quadratic system (6), and, as suggested by its name, it is structured in two cascaded phases. In order to describe the two phases of the algorithm, a specific notation is needed. First, assuming a bi-dimensional environment, let us define the Euclidean norm of the coordinates of the i−th AP as a_i

$$a_i = ||\underline{s}_i|| = \sqrt{x_i^2 + y_i^2} \qquad i \in \{1, 2\}. \tag{10}$$

Moreover, let us define a new variable $\hat{n}$, which is related to the estimated coordinates of the TN, according to the following equation

$$\hat{n} = ||\underline{\hat{u}}||^2 = \hat{x}^2 + \hat{y}^2. \tag{11}$$

Using such a notation, system (6) can be written as

$$\underline{G}_1 \, \underline{\hat{\omega}}_1 = \underline{\hat{h}}_1 \tag{12}$$

where

$$\underline{G}_1 = -2 \begin{pmatrix} x_1 & y_1 & -1/2 \\ \vdots & \vdots & \vdots \\ x_M & y_M & -1/2 \end{pmatrix} \qquad \underline{\hat{\omega}}_1 = \begin{pmatrix} \hat{x} \\ \hat{y} \\ \hat{n} \end{pmatrix} \qquad \underline{\hat{h}}_1 = \begin{pmatrix} \hat{r}_1^2 - a_1^2 \\ \vdots \\ \hat{r}_M^2 - a_M^2 \end{pmatrix}. \tag{13}$$

Observe that system (12) is written as if it was a linear system. However, recalling (11), it is easily observed that the third component of $\underline{\hat{\omega}}_1$ is related to the first two components. This is taken into account in the second phase of the algorithm. In the first phase of the algorithm, system (12) is solved using a *Maximum-Likelihood* (*ML*) approach, so that the solution vector $\underline{\hat{\omega}}_1$ can be expressed as

$$\underline{\hat{\omega}}_1 = (\underline{G}_1^T \, \underline{W}_1 \, \underline{G}_1)^{-1} \underline{G}_1^T \, \underline{W}_1 \, \underline{\hat{h}}_1 \tag{14}$$

where $\underline{W}_1$ is a positive definite matrix. Observe that the simplest choice of $\underline{W}_1$ is the identity matrix. Another possible explicit expression of $\underline{W}_1$ is suggested in [12], and it is based on a least square approach.

Given the explicit expression of $\underline{\hat{\omega}}_1$, it is possible to advance the algorithm to the second phase, according to which another system of equations, related to (6), is derived. In detail, in order to take into account the dependence of $\hat{n}$ on the first and second components of $\underline{\hat{\omega}}_1$, we consider the following system

$$\underline{G}_2 \, \underline{\hat{\omega}}_2 = \underline{\hat{h}}_2 \tag{15}$$

where

$$\underline{G}_2 = \begin{pmatrix} 1 & 0 \\ 0 & 1 \\ 1 & 1 \end{pmatrix} \qquad \underline{\hat{\omega}}_2 = \begin{pmatrix} \hat{x}^2 \\ \hat{y}^2 \end{pmatrix} \qquad \underline{\hat{h}}_2 = \begin{pmatrix} [\underline{\hat{\omega}}_1]_1^2 \\ [\underline{\hat{\omega}}_1]_2^2 \\ [\underline{\hat{\omega}}_1]_3 \end{pmatrix}, \tag{16}$$

and $[\hat{\underline{\omega}}_1]_j$ in (16) denotes the j−th component of $\hat{\underline{\omega}}_1$. The system (15) can be solved according to the ML technique and the unknown vector can be found as

$$\hat{\underline{\omega}}_2 = (\underline{\underline{G}}_2^T \, \underline{\underline{W}}_2 \, \underline{\underline{G}}_2)^{-1} \underline{\underline{G}}_2^T \, \underline{\underline{W}}_2 \, \hat{\underline{h}}_2 \tag{17}$$

where $\underline{\underline{W}}_2$ is a positive definite matrix. As when solving (12), the simplest choice of $\underline{\underline{W}}_2$ is the identity matrix, but different choices can be considered [26]. Given the explicit expression of $\hat{\underline{\omega}}_2$, the estimate of the position of the TN is [26]

$$\hat{\underline{u}} = \underline{\underline{U}} \left[\sqrt{[\hat{\underline{\omega}}_2]_1}, \sqrt{[\hat{\underline{\omega}}_2]_2} \right]^T \tag{18}$$

where $\underline{\underline{U}} = \mathrm{diag}(\mathrm{sign}(\hat{\underline{\omega}}_1))$.

2.3 The PSO-Based Localization Algorithm

The literature proposes various algorithms to solve (8). All such algorithms may suffer from numerical instability in correspondence of peculiar configurations in space of APs, e.g., if APs are aligned [21]. In order to derive a more robust algorithm, we proposed in [21] to reformulate (8) as an optimization problem and we described a PSO-based approach to solve it, as outlined in the rest of this section. Note that the original proposal was designed to work with UWB signals, which are very robust to multipath noise. The implemented algorithm was retargeted to use WiFi signals and, besides the use of different values for the parameters of the PSO algorithm, it includes pre-filtering to mitigate multipath noise. In order to outline a fair comparison between the PSO-based algorithm and the TSML algorithm, pre-filtering is not considered in this paper.

Observe that (8) can be written as a minimization problem, according to

$$\hat{\underline{u}} = \arg\min_{\underline{u}} F(\underline{u}) \tag{19}$$

where $F(\underline{u})$ represents the *fitness function*, which is computed as

$$F(\underline{u}) = ||\hat{\underline{k}} - (\underline{1}\,\hat{\underline{u}}^T\,\hat{\underline{u}} + \underline{\underline{A}}\,\hat{\underline{u}})||. \tag{20}$$

In order to solve the minimization problem (19), we propose to use the PSO algorithm, which was introduced in [13]. According to such an algorithm, the set of potential solutions to a minimization problem can be considered as a swarm of particles whose positions and velocities are iteratively updated according to proper rules. Such rules are inspired by biological phenomena like the movements of birds in swarms. In the context of optimization problems, such rules are meant to move all particles towards the position corresponding to the optimal solution of the considered minimization problem.

In detail, the algorithm that we adopted to solve the minimization problem (19) works as follows. First, the positions of particles are randomly initialized in the *search space*, which, in our context, corresponds to the physical indoor environment where the TN and APs are situated. The initial positions are denoted as $\underline{x}^{(i)}(0)$, where $i \in \{1, \ldots, S\}$ is the index of the generic particle and S is the number of particles. Analogously, the velocity of the $i-$th particle is initialized to $\underline{v}^{(i)}(0)$. After the initialization phase, positions and velocities of all particles are updated at each iteration $t \in \mathbb{N}$ to simulate a swarm [24]. At the $t-$th iteration, the velocity of the $i-$th particle whose position is $\underline{x}^{(i)}(t)$, is updated according to the following rule [27]

$$\underline{v}^{(i)}(t+1) = \omega(t)\underline{v}^{(i)}(t) + c_1 R_1(t)(\underline{y}^{(i)}(t) - \underline{x}^{(i)}(t)) + $$
$$c_2 R_2(t)(\underline{y}(t) - \underline{x}^{(i)}(t)) \qquad i \in \{1, \ldots, S\} \tag{21}$$

where, following [9],

- $\underline{y}(t)$ is the best position globally reached so far;
- $\underline{y}^{(i)}(t)$ is the best position reached so far by the $i-$th particle;
- $\omega(t)$ is the so called *inertial factor*;
- c_1 is a positive real parameter called *cognition* parameter;
- c_2 is a positive real parameter called *social* parameter; and
- $R_1(t)$ and $R_2(t)$ are independent uniform random variables in $(0, 1)$.

From (21) it can be easily observed that the velocity of a particle at iteration $t+1$ is obtained as the sum of three addends. The first addend is related to the velocity of the particle at previous iteration t, which is weighed according to the inertial factor $\omega(t)$. The second addend is meant to move each particle towards the best position it reached so far. We remark that such a best position is the one which corresponds to the lowest value of the fitness function and, therefore, $\underline{y}^{(i)}(t)$ can be expressed as

$$\underline{y}^{(i)}(t) = \underset{\underline{z} \in X^{(i)}(t)}{\arg\min} F(\underline{z}) \qquad X^{(i)}(t) = \{\underline{x}^{(i)}(0), \ldots, \underline{x}^{(i)}(t)\}. \tag{22}$$

Finally, the third addend aims at moving each particle towards the *global best position*, namely the position which corresponds to the smallest value of the fitness function among all positions reached by any particle in the swarm [24]. Hence, $\underline{y}(t)$ is expressed as

$$\underline{y}(t) = \underset{\underline{z} \in Y(t)}{\arg\min} F(\underline{z}) \qquad Y(t) = \{\underline{y}^{(1)}(t), \ldots, \underline{y}^{(S)}(t)\}. \tag{23}$$

Typically, the inertial factor $\omega(t)$ is chosen as a decreasing function of t, in order to guarantee low dependence of the solution on the initial population and to reduce the exploration ability of the swarm as the number of iterations increases, making the method more similar to a local search in last iterations [27].

The velocities computed with (21) are used to update the positions of particles at each iteration according to the following rule

$$\underline{x}^{(i)}(t+1) = \underline{x}^{(i)}(t) + \underline{v}^{(i)}(t) \qquad i \in \{1, \ldots, S\}. \tag{24}$$

From (24) it can be observed that the position of the $i-$th particle at iteration $t+1$ is simply obtained by adding $\underline{v}^{(i)}(t)$ to its previous position.

The execution of the PSO algorithm terminates when a stopping condition is met. Possible stopping conditions are the reach of a maximum number of iterations or the reach of a satisfying value of the fitness function. Once the execution of the algorithm terminates, the solution is computed as the position of the particle in the global best position, namely the particle with the lowest value of the fitness function.

The generic PSO algorithm just outlined is used to solve the localization problem formulated in (19). In order to obtain the experimental results shown in the rest of this paper, the value of the inertial factor is set to 0.5, the values of c_1 and c_2 are set equal and they are set to 2, the size of the population S is set to 40, and the stopping condition corresponds to the reach of 50 iterations. Such values proved to be effective for localization purposes using WiFi, and they are different from values used for UWB. Illustrative experimental results concerning the performance of the proposed PSO-based algorithm are shown in next section.

3   Experimental Results

In this section, experimental results obtained using discussed algorithms, as implemented in the localization add-on module for JADE, are shown. Note that in order to make a fair comparison, discussed scenarios are not meant to emphasize how the PSO-based algorithm overcomes the well-known numerical instability of geometric algorithms like the TSML algorithm. As a representative scenario, we consider $M = 4$ APs in a square room whose sides are 4 meters long. Note that implemented algorithms can be applied with a different number of APs and, in general, an increased number of APs typically improves the performance of algorithms. The coordinates of APs expressed in meters are

$$\underline{s}_1 = (2,0)^T \qquad \underline{s}_2 = (0,2)^T$$
$$\underline{s}_3 = (4,2)^T \qquad \underline{s}_4 = (2,4)^T. \tag{25}$$

The performance of implemented algorithms are investigated with three TNs in different positions, which can be expressed in meters as

$$\underline{u}_1 = (1,1)^T \qquad \underline{u}_2 = (2,1)^T \qquad \underline{u}_3 = (2,2)^T. \tag{26}$$

The positions of TNs and of APs are shown in Fig. 1, where APs are marked with red squares and TNs are marked with blue stars. For each TN, 100 localization estimates are computed using the PSO algorithm. In the rest of this section, the j−th position estimate of a TN is denoted as

$$\hat{\underline{u}}_P^{(j)} = (\hat{x}_P^{(j)}, \hat{y}_P^{(j)}) \qquad j \in \{1, \ldots, 100\}. \tag{27}$$

The accuracy of the PSO-based algorithm is analyzed in terms of the distance between the true position $\underline{u}$ of the selected TN, which is known, and its j−th estimate $\hat{\underline{u}}_P^{(j)}$. Such a distance is

$$d_P^{(j)} = ||\hat{\underline{u}}_P^{(j)} - \underline{u}|| \qquad j \in \{1, \ldots, 100\}. \tag{28}$$

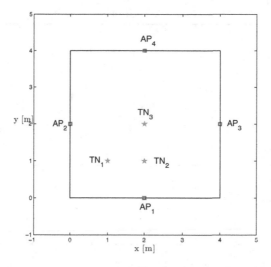

Fig. 1. The positions of four APs (red squares) and of three TNs (blue stars) are shown. The walls of the room are shown in black. (Color figure online)

Moreover, we are also interested in evaluating the average distance error of the PSO-based algorithm, denoted as $d_{\text{avg}}^{\text{PSO}}$, which can be computed as

$$d_{\text{avg}}^{\text{PSO}} = \frac{1}{100} \sum_{j=1}^{100} d_P^{(j)}. \tag{29}$$

Similarly, 100 localization estimates based on the use of the TSML algorithm are performed, and the j-th position estimate of the considered TN is

$$\hat{\underline{u}}_T^{(j)} = (\hat{x}_T^{(j)}, \hat{y}_T^{(j)}) \qquad j \in \{1, \dots, 100\}. \tag{30}$$

As done in the case of PSO-based position estimates, we are interested in evaluating the distances between the true position of the TN and the 100 position estimates obtained using the TSML algorithm

$$d_T^{(j)} = \|\hat{\underline{u}}_T^{(j)} - \underline{u}\| \qquad j \in \{1, \dots, 100\}. \tag{31}$$

Finally, the average distance error for the TSML algorithm can be computed as

$$d_{\text{avg}}^{\text{TSML}} = \frac{1}{100} \sum_{j=1}^{100} d_T^{(j)}. \tag{32}$$

Let us start by considering experimental results obtained when the TN is in position $\underline{u}_1$, which is denoted as TN_1 in Fig. 1. Range estimates from each AP are acquired and used to estimate the position of the TN according to the PSO-based algorithm. This procedure is applied 100 times, thus obtaining 100

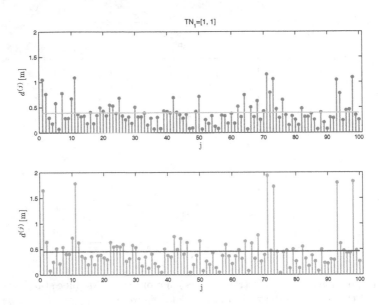

Fig. 2. The values of distance errors corresponding to 100 estimates of the position of the TN in $\underline{u}_1$ are shown when applying: the PSO-based algorithm (upper diagram), and the TSML algorithm (lower diagram). The values of average distance errors in the two cases are also shown with lines across diagrams.

position estimates $\{\underline{\hat{u}}_P^{(j)}\}_{j=1}^{100}$ for TN$_1$. Distances $\{d_P^{(j)}\}_{j=1}^{100}$ between each position estimate and the true position of the TN are evaluated according to (28). Such values are shown in the upper diagram of Fig. 2, together with the average distance error $d_{\text{avg}}^{\text{PSO}}$, which corresponds to 39 cm. From Fig. 2 it is also possible to observe that distances $\{d_P^{(j)}\}_{j=1}^{100}$ are smaller than $d_{\text{avg}}^{\text{PSO}}$ in 65% of the cases, they are larger than 1 m only 6 times (over 100), and they are always smaller than 1.2 m. According to the results in Fig. 2, the PSO-based algorithm can be considered sufficiently accurate for many reference applications (see, e.g., [7]). In order to compare the performance of the PSO-based algorithm with that of a classic algorithm, the TSML algorithm is also applied in the same scenario, leading to 100 (different) position estimates for TN$_1$, denoted as $\{\underline{\hat{u}}_T^{(j)}\}_{j=1}^{100}$. The distance between each position estimate and the true position of the TN is evaluated according to (31) and denoted as $\{d_T^{(j)}\}_{j=1}^{100}$. The lower diagram of Fig. 2 shows such values, together with the average distance error $d_{\text{avg}}^{\text{TSML}}$, which is evaluated according to (32) and it corresponds to 45 cm. The lower diagram of Fig. 2 also shows that distances $\{d_T^{(j)}\}_{j=1}^{100}$ are smaller than $d_{\text{avg}}^{\text{TSML}}$ in 62% of the cases, they are larger than 1 m only 6 times (over 100), and they are always smaller than 2 m. A comparison among upper and lower diagrams of Fig. 2 shows that position estimates obtained according to the PSO-based algorithm are often more accurate than those derived using the TSML algorithm. An accurate analysis of results shows that the PSO-based algorithm performs better than the TSML

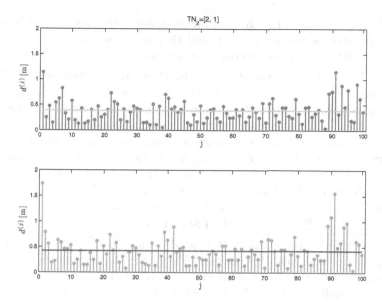

Fig. 3. The values of distance errors corresponding to 100 estimates of the position of the TN in $\underline{u}_2$ are shown when applying: the PSO-based algorithm (upper diagram) and the TSML algorithm (lower diagram). The values of average distance errors in the two cases are also shown with lines across diagrams.

algorithm in 65% of the cases. It is also possible to observe that the maximum of distances $\{d_P^{(j)}\}_{j=1}^{100}$ related to the PSO-based algorithm is 1.15 m, while the maximum of distances $\{d_T^{(j)}\}_{j=1}^{100}$ related to the TSML algorithm is 1.93 m.

Let us now consider the results obtained when the TN is positioned in the point denoted as TN_2 in Fig. 1, which is the point whose coordinates are named $\underline{u}_2$ in (26). Range estimates from each AP are acquired and they are first used to feed the PSO-based algorithm. This procedure is applied 100 times to obtain 100 position estimates $\{\underline{\hat{u}}_P^{(j)}\}_{j=1}^{100}$, which are used to evaluate the performance of the PSO-based algorithm. Distances $\{d_P^{(j)}\}_{j=1}^{100}$ corresponding to the 100 position estimates are evaluated according to (28), and they are shown in the upper diagram of Fig. 3, together with the average distance error d_{avg}^{PSO}, which corresponds to 38 cm. Observe that the average distance is very close to that obtained in the previous case. The upper diagram of Fig. 3 also shows that distances $\{d_P^{(j)}\}_{j=1}^{100}$ are smaller than d_{avg}^{PSO} in 56% of the cases, they are larger than 1 m only 2 times (over 100), and they are always smaller than 1.2 m. Such results, relative to the TN positioned in $\underline{u}_2$, confirm that the proposed PSO-based localization algorithm can be effectively applied to obtain position estimates which are accurate enough for various applications.

As done in the first scenario, let us now apply the TSML algorithm to estimate the position of TN_2. The application of the TSML algorithm is repeated 100 times, thus leading to 100 position estimates $\{\underline{\hat{u}}_T^{(j)}\}_{j=1}^{100}$ for TN_2. Distances

$\{d_T^{(j)}\}_{j=1}^{100}$ between each of such position estimates and the true position of the TN are evaluated according to (31), and they are shown in the lower diagram of Fig. 3, together with the average distance error $d_{\text{avg}}^{\text{TSML}}$, which corresponds to 43 cm. The lower diagram of Fig. 3 also shows that distances $\{d_T^{(j)}\}_{j=1}^{100}$ are smaller than $d_{\text{avg}}^{\text{TSML}}$ in 57% of the cases, they are larger than 1 m only 3 times, and they are always smaller than 2 m. From a comparison among upper and lower diagrams of Fig. 3, it is evident that the PSO-based algorithm often leads to position estimates which are more accurate than those derived using the TSML algorithm. Moreover, by properly analyzing obtained results, it is possible to observe that in 60% of the cases distance estimates obtained with the PSO-based algorithm are closer to the true position of the TN than those obtained using the TSML algorithm. It is also possible to observe that the maximum of distances $\{d_P^{(j)}\}_{j=1}^{100}$ related to the PSO-based algorithm is 1.15 m, while the maximum of the distances $\{d_T^{(j)}\}_{j=1}^{100}$ related to the TSML algorithm is 1.73 m.

Let us now consider the TN positioned in $\underline{u}_3$, which corresponds to the center of the room, as shown in Fig. 1, where it is denoted as TN$_3$. In this configuration, APs are all equidistant from the TN. First, range estimates from each AP are acquired and they are used to formulate the localization problem, which is then solved using the PSO algorithm. The same procedure is repeated 100 times, thus leading to 100 position estimates $\{\underline{\hat{u}}_P^{(j)}\}_{j=1}^{100}$ for TN$_3$. For all the 100 position estimates, distances $\{d_P^{(j)}\}_{j=1}^{100}$ are evaluated and they are shown in the upper diagram in Fig. 4. The same diagram also shows the average distance error $d_{\text{avg}}^{\text{PSO}}$, which is equal to 18 cm. Observe that $d_{\text{avg}}^{\text{PSO}}$ in this configuration is less than a half of the value obtained when performing the localization of TN$_1$ or of TN$_2$. This is due to the fact that, in this case, APs are all quite close to the TN (with a true distance of 2 m). On the contrary, when considering, for instance, the TN positioned in $\underline{u}_1$, two of the four APs are more than 3 meters far from the TN, and the larger is the distance, the less accurate are range estimates. From the upper diagram of Fig. 4 it is also possible to observe that distances $\{d_P^{(j)}\}_{j=1}^{100}$ are smaller than d_{avg} in 65% of the cases, and they are lower than 40 cm in 90% of the cases. Moreover, all $\{d^{(j)}\}_{j=1}^{100}$ are smaller than 1 m. From the results in Fig. 4, it can be concluded that the performance of the PSO-based algorithm is better than that obtained for the two previous positions of the TN.

Finally, the TSML algorithm is also applied in this scenario, obtaining 100 position estimates $\{\underline{\hat{u}}_T^{(j)}\}_{j=1}^{100}$ for TN$_3$. Distances $\{d_T^{(j)}\}_{j=1}^{100}$ between each one of such position estimates and the true position of the TN are shown in the lower diagram of Fig. 4, together with the average distance error $d_{\text{avg}}^{\text{TSML}}$, which corresponds to 20 cm. The lower diagram of Fig. 4 also shows that distances $\{d_T^{(j)}\}_{j=1}^{100}$ are smaller than $d_{\text{avg}}^{\text{TSML}}$ in 65% of the cases. A comparison among upper and lower diagrams of Fig. 4 shows that also in this last case the PSO-based algorithm is often (65% of the cases) more accurate than the TSML algorithm, even though the difference is less evident than in previous cases.

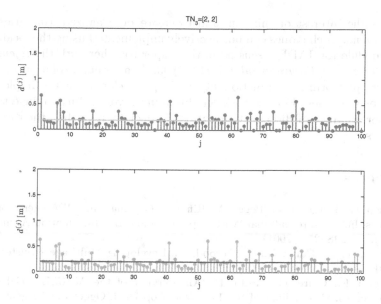

Fig. 4. The values of distance errors corresponding to 100 estimates of the position of the TN in u_3 are shown when applying: the PSO-based algorithm (upper diagram) and the TSML algorithm (lower diagram). The values of average distance errors in the two cases are also shown with lines across diagrams.

4   Conclusions

This paper discussed the performance of two localization algorithms that are included in the localization add-on module for JADE to provide agents with the possibility of acquiring dynamic estimates of their positions in known indoor environments. Such algorithms use only the WiFi signals intended to let smart devices discover available WiFi networks, as emitted from APs of the networks, which are assumed to be static and located in known positions. No dedicated infrastructure is needed to support localization, and smart devices are not even requested to be connected to a WiFi network because only network discovery messages are used. While other types of wireless technologies, such as UWB, ensure more accurate and robust localization, WiFi has the advantage of being already available in all realistic indoor scenarios. The discussed add-on module for JADE can host a number of localization algorithms, and the main contribution of the paper is to discuss and compare two algorithms that have already been implemented. Illustrative results presented in the last part of this paper show that the performance of algorithms can be considered sufficiently good for many applications. Possible envisaged applications of discussed techniques include *location-aware smart emergency applications* [23], which are typically intended for outdoor environments because they need accurate localization. In addition, another interesting application area of discussed techniques regards *location-aware games* [7], as envisioned, for instance, inside museums and exhibitions to attract the interest of children, and to create personalized itineraries using treasure hunts. Such games can be effectively implemented using the localization add-on module for JADE discussed in this paper together with the *Agent-based Multi-User Social Environment* (*AMUSE*) [3,4], a recent evolution of JADE that offers platform-level functionality to help developers in the implementation of social games. Future work on this topic involves further investigation on the performance of discussed algorithms, especially regarding their expected robustness.

References

1. Adorni, G., Bergenti, F., Poggi, A., Rimassa, G.: Enabling FIPA agents on small devices. In: 5th International Workshop on Cooperative Information Agents (CIA 2001), pp. 248–257 (2001)
2. Bellifemine, F., Caire, G., Greenwood, D.: Developing Multi-agent Systems with JADE. Wiley, Hoboken (2007)
3. Bergenti, F., Caire, G., Gotta, D.: An overview of the AMUSE social gaming platform. In: Proceedings of the 14th Workshop Dagli Oggetti agli Agenti (WOA 2013). CEUR Workshop Proceedings, vol. 1099. RWTH Aachen (2013)
4. Bergenti, F., Caire, G., Gotta, D.: Agent-based social gaming with AMUSE. In: Proceedings of 5th International Conference on Ambient Systems, Networks and Technologies (ANT 2014) and 4th International Conference on Sustainable Energy Information Technology (SEIT 2014). Procedia Computer Science, vol. 32, pp. 914–919 (2014)
5. Bergenti, F., Caire, G., Gotta, D.: Agents on the move: JADE for Android devices. In: Proceedings of the 15th Workshop Dagli Oggetti agli Agenti (WOA 2014). CEUR Workshop Proceedings, vol. 1260. RWTH Aachen (2014)
6. Bergenti, F., Poggi, A.: LEAP: a FIPA platform for handheld and mobile devices. In: 8th International Workshop on Intelligent Agents VIII: Agent Theories, Architectures, and Languages (ATAL 2001), pp. 436–446 (2001)
7. Bergenti, F., Monica, S.: Location-aware social gaming with AMUSE. In: Demazeau, Y., Ito, T., Bajo, J., Escalona, M.J. (eds.) PAAMS 2016. LNCS, vol. 9662, pp. 36–47. Springer, Cham (2016). doi:10.1007/978-3-319-39324-7_4
8. Bulusu, N., Heidemann, J., Estrin, D.: GPS-less low cost outdoor localization for very small devices. IEEE Pers. Commun. 7(5), 28–34 (2000)
9. Eberhart, R., Kennedy, J.: A new optimizer using particles swarm theory. In: Proceedings of the 6th International Symposium on Micro Machine and Human Science (MHS), Nagoya, Japan, pp. 39–43, October 1995
10. Farid, Z., Nordin, R., Ismail, M.: Recent advances in wireless indoor localization techniques and system. J. Comput. Netw. Commun. 2013, 1–12 (2013)
11. Gezici, S., Poor, H.V.: Position estimation via ultra-wide-band signals. Proc. IEEE 97(2), 386–403 (2009)
12. Ho, K.C., Lu, X., Kovavisaruch, L.: Source localization using TDOA and FDOA measurements in the presence of receiver location errors: analysis and solution. IEEE Trans. Sig. Process. 55(2), 684–696 (2007)
13. Kennedy, J., Eberhart, R.: Particle swarm optimization. In: Proceedings of the IEEE International Conference on Neural Networks (ICNN), Perth, Australia, pp. 1942–1948, November 1995

14. Monica, S., Bergenti, F.: Location-aware JADE agents in indoor scenarios. In: Proceedings of 16th Workshop Dagli Oggetti agli Agenti (WOA 2015). CEUR Workshop Proceedings, vol. 1382, pp. 103–108. RWTH Aachen (2015)
15. Monica, S., Bergenti, F.: A comparison of accurate indoor localization of static targets via WiFi and UWB ranging. In: Trends in Practical Applications of Scalable Multi-Agent Systems, the PAAMS Collection, pp. 111–123 (2016)
16. Monica, S., Bergenti, F.: Experimental evaluation of agent-based localization of smart appliances. In: Proceedings of the European Conference on Multi-Agent Systems (EUMAS), Sevilla, Spain (2016)
17. Monica, S., Ferrari, G.: Impact of the number of beacons in PSO-based auto-localization in UWB networks. In: Proceedings of the International Conference on the Applications of Evolutionary Computation (EvoApplications 2013), Vienna, Austria, pp. 42–51, April 2013
18. Monica, S., Ferrari, G.: Particle swarm optimization for auto-localization of nodes in wireless sensor networks. In: Proceedings of the 11th International Conference on Adaptive and Natural Computing Algorithms (ICANNGA 2013), Lausanne, Switzerland, pp. 456–465, April 2013
19. Monica, S., Ferrari, G.: Swarm intelligent approaches to auto-localization of nodes in static UWB networks. Appl. Soft Comput. 25, 426–434 (2014)
20. Monica, S., Ferrari, G.: A swarm intelligence approach to 3D distance-based indoor UWB localization. In: Proceedings of the International Conference on the Applications of Evolutionary Computation (EvoApplications 2015), Copenaghen, Denmark, April 2015
21. Monica, S., Ferrari, G.: A swarm based approach to real-time 3D indoor localization: experimental performance analysis. Appl. Soft Comput. 43, 489–497 (2016)
22. Pavani, T., Costa, G., Mazzotti, M., Conti, A., Dardari, D.: Experimental results on indoor localization techniques through wireless sensors network. In: Proceedings of the IEEE Vehicular Technology Conference, Melbourne, Australia, pp. 663–667, May 2006
23. Poggi, A., Bergenti, F.: Developing smart emergency applications with multi-agent systems. Int. J. E-Health Med. Commun. 1(4), 1–13 (2010)
24. Poli, R., Kennedy, J., Blackwell, T.: Particle swarm optimization. Swarm Intell. J. 1(1), 33–57 (2007)
25. Poslad, S.: Ubiquitous Computing: Smart Devices, Environments and Interactions. Wiley, Hoboken (2009)
26. Shen, G., Zetik, R., Thomä, R.S.: Performance comparison of TOA and TDOA based location estimation algorithms in LOS environment. In: Proceedings of the 5th Workshop on Positioning. Navigation and Communication (WPNC 2008), Hannover, Germany, pp. 71–78 (March (2008)
27. Shi, Y., Eberhart, R.: A modified particle swarm optimizer. In: Proceedings of the IEEE International Conference on Evolutionary Computation (ICEC), Washington, DC, pp. 69–73, July 1999
28. Zhang, J., Orlik, P.V., Sahinoglu, Z., Molisch, A.F., Kinney, P.: UWB systems for wireless sensor networks. Proc. IEEE 97(2), 313–331 (2009)

A Holonic Multi-Agent System Approach to Differential Diagnosis

Zohreh Akbari[1](✉) and Rainer Unland[1,2]

[1] Institute for Computer Science and Business Information Systems (ICB),
University of Duisburg-Essen, Essen, Germany
{zohreh.akbari, rainer.unland}@icb.uni-due.de
[2] Department of Information Systems, Poznan University of Economics,
Poznan, Poland

Abstract. Medical diagnosis has always been a crucial and sophisticated matter, and despite its remarkable progresses, a reliable, cost-efficient, and fast computer-based medical diagnosis is still a challenge. There are two main types of computerized medical diagnosis systems: knowledge-based and non-knowledge-based systems. While the challenge of scalability and maintainability are the main shortcomings of the first group, the fact that the non-knowledge-based systems cannot explain the reasons for their conclusions makes them less appealing too. Moreover, even the most advanced systems fail to help the user in providing the right input. This work discusses the feasibility of the use of Holonic Multi-Agent Systems (HMASs) to tackle this problem, by performing differential diagnosis (DDx), that can improve diagnostic accuracy, and moreover guide the user in providing a more comprehensive input. The Holonic Medical Diagnosis System (HMDS), as a Multi-Agent System (MAS), offers the necessary reliability and scalability. By using Machine Learning (ML) techniques, it can also be self-adaptable to new findings. Furthermore, since it aims to perform DDx and tends to present the most likely diagnoses, the reasoning behind its output is also always implicitly recognizable. While the HMAS approach to DDx is the practical contribution of this work, the introduction of the ML techniques that support its functionality and dynamics is its theoretical contribution. Swarm Q-learning, as an off-policy reinforcement learning, is shown to be a perfect solution to this problem, and the Holonic-Q-learning technique is proposed, which can in general also be applied to any HMAS.

Keywords: Holonic Multi-Agent System (HMAS) · Medical Diagnosis System (MDS) · Reinforcement Learning (RL) · Self-organization · Swarm Q-learning

1 Introduction

Since 1950s, computer scientists have aimed to support and improve the health care system. Clinical Decision Support Systems (CDSSs) link health observations with health knowledge to influence health choices by clinicians for improved health care[1]. Some comprehensive overviews on the CDSSs have been presented in [1, 2, 3].

---

[1] Definition proposed by Robert Hayward of the Centre for Health Evidence.

© Springer International Publishing AG 2017
J.O. Berndt et al. (Eds.): MATES 2017, LNAI 10413, pp. 272–290, 2017.
DOI: 10.1007/978-3-319-64798-2_17

There are two main types of CDSSs [1]: Knowledge-based and Non-knowledge-based. Contemporary knowledge-based CDSSs have their roots in early expert systems and attempt to replicate the logic and reasoning of a human decision maker, reaching firm decisions based on existing knowledge [3]. Opposed to this group, non-knowledge-based CDSSs use a form of Artificial Intelligence (AI) called Machine Learning (ML), which allows computers to learn from experiences and identify patterns in the clinical data [1]. Such systems may be based on neural networks, genetic algorithms, support vector machines, decision trees, or any other ML technology, which learns to recognize patterns in data sets in a case-by-case proceeding [4].

Since the current ML based CDSSs cannot explain the reasons for their conclusions, most clinicians do not use them directly, for reliability and accountability reasons [1]. The most remarkable non-knowledge-based CDSSs are based on neural networks and genetic algorithms [1]. The problems with neural networks include selecting the best topology, preventing overtraining and undertraining, and determining the training cases. The complexity of such problems also grows with the size of the neural networks. Regarding the genetic algorithm based CDSSs, again the complexity is a big challenge. Moreover, the low rate of convergence and the lack of guarantee of finding the global maxima make such approaches less appealing. The scalability and maintainability of knowledge based CDSSs, i.e. expert systems, has always been a challenging issue as well; since an extension of the rule-bases can cause serious problems as the overall semantics and behavior of the rule base may get out of control. Therefore, a reliable and easy scalable CDSS is needed that is capable of learning in order to self-adapt to new findings, and can furthermore explain its reasoning. This work discusses the feasibility of the use of MASs to tackle this problem. This paradigm, with its distributed architecture, is a promising solution to the shortcomings of the old methods, and offers much more flexibility, adaptability and scalability. Although already a number of attempts in applying MASs to CDSSs can be found in literature (Sect. 1.2), this work suggests a completely new approach, i.e. the usage of HMASs (Sect. 2) in order to perform Differential Diagnosis (DDx). In medicine, a DDx is the distinguishing of a particular disease or condition from others presenting similar symptoms [5], which leads to more accurate diagnoses [6]. This systematic method is used to identify the presence of a disease entity where multiple alternatives are possible, and tries to gather enough evidence and supporting information to shrink the probability of the other candidates. This is very critical, since a misdiagnosis may lead to delay in the correct diagnosis, as well as exposure to inappropriate medication that can lead to serious irrecoverable effects.

This work, in fact, concentrates on a specific type of CDSS, namely Diagnostic Decision Support Systems (DDSSs) [2], that are developed to calculate an ordered list of potential diagnosis for given signs and symptoms. Available systems, including the state of the art (Sect. 1.2), mainly focus on finding the perfect link between the given input and their health knowledge. However, prior to this process there should be a precise method to guide the user in providing the right, all-encompassing input. This is similar to what a physician does when listening to a patient. (S)he would carefully listen to the symptoms explained by the patient, considers some potential diagnoses and then tries to gather enough evidence and supporting information to shrink the probability of the other candidates by questioning some signs and symptoms that might have been simply ignored by the patient, or requesting the patient to undertake some medical examinations. This process is called the History and Physical examination (H&P) and is a critical component of a patient encounter in which information relevant to a present complaint is obtained, by asking questions about family and personal medical history and the organ systems examined in as great detail as necessary to manage the present condition or evaluate–workup–the patient [7]. As the first step in the encounter with a patient, H&P can narrow down the DDx list to a few possibilities based on the patient data, i.e. the symptoms, the signs, and the medical history. The results of executive physicals, e.g. laboratory and radiographic findings could then help to narrow down this list even more. As the shortage of medical doctors is worsening in the recent years, roles such as Physician Assistant (PA) and Nurse Practitioner (NP) have been introduced in order to ease the problem. PAs and NPs are qualified to perform the H&P step, diagnose medical problems and carry out necessary treatments mainly under the supervision of a physician. Undertaking the H&P step, they would help the doctors to be able to see more patients in a certain period of time, as they would just need to review and asses the already prepared H&P report.

Although PAs and NPs are able to compensate for the shortage of doctors to some extent, they don't solve the problem completely. Both groups require a special formal degree of education and years of experience; and moreover there is also never enough number of PAs and NPs available. This is where AI could help. In fact, a system capable of undertaking the H&P step, could save the physician time or even guide less experienced nurses in performing this step. This system should be able to gather the patient data and suggest some possibilities accordingly. Of course, special knowledge and experience is needed to perform the H&P successfully, and here again DDx concerns could keep the whole process focused. In fact, irrelevant questions and tests should be ignored and every single piece of information should be used in order to narrow down the possibilities. This study will show how a HMAS approach can simply guide the system to perform this process based on DDx concerns.

The Holonic Medical Diagnosis System (HMDS) suggested in this work is based on MASs and, hence, clearly offers the necessary reliability and scalability in CDSSs. The possibility of applying ML techniques to MAS also makes it self-adaptable to new findings. Furthermore, since it aims to perform DDx and tends to present the most likely diagnoses as the result, the reasoning behind the output of the system is also always implicitly visible for verification and control purposes of human beings.

1.1   Research Questions

As mentioned above, this research applies the advantages of HMASs to the field of medical diagnosis. In order to take full advantage of the most attractive aspect of these systems, i.e. the dynamics that such systems offer, these capabilities need to be supported by suitable ML techniques. Hence, in fact, the development of the HMDS, which is capable of performing DDx, is the practical contribution of this work. On the other hand, the introduction of ML techniques that support the functionality of this system is the conceptual/theoretical contribution of this work.

1.2   The State of the Art

According to the research questions, the state of the art of both medical diagnosis systems and ML techniques for the HMASs will be covered in this section.

The State of the Art of the Medical Diagnosis Systems. This section tends to study the IBM Watson (as the most powerful AI based system capable of performing medical diagnosis), the Isabel (as the best known DDx generator), and the multi-agent based MDSs.

IBM Watson. Watson is a cognitive computer system developed by IBM [8] that has the capability of understanding natural language. Along with the advantages, the usage of Watson has also some disadvantages [8] such as: high switching costs, long integration time, and time and effort-consuming learning phase. Several application areas have been considered for Watson, including the healthcare. From the technical point of view, Watson searches a large knowledge base, generates potential hypotheses, and then initiates another search to collect evidence that supports them. Although Watson is very powerful in performing this action, this process doesn't necessarily guarantee that it will conduct a DDx or guide the user to perform a focused H&P. So it is always possible that the final strong deduction is based on some incomplete input. And even if the system decides on a DDx (i.e., finds some relevant articles), this simple conclusion might be the result of too many unnecessary operations.

Isabel. Isabel is a web based CDSS that facilitates diagnostic reminders and DDx [9, 10]. It is actually a knowledge-based system consisting of a knowledge base and an inference engine, implemented using a commercially available software, Autonomy [11], which utilizes Bayesian inference and Shannon's principles of information theory to generate pattern matching algorithms in order to enable sophisticated concept extraction from documents [10]. A systematic review and meta-analysis of DDx generators was conducted in [12] and according to this study, Isabel was associated with the highest rates of diagnosis retrieval. However, as stated in [13] Isabel is still too slow and its accuracy drops significantly if only limited information is available [14]. As Isabel fails to guide the user in performing a focused H&P, using this system it is not infrequent to face the problem of limited information and hence poor accuracy.

Multi-agent Based MDSs. A survey on multi-agent based MDSs has been presented in (Salem et al. [15]), and some notable multi-agent based MDSs are introduced in [16–19]. These systems, in fact, combine the MAS technology with the earlier paradigms and design neural network agents, expert system agents, and data mining agents. Available multi-agent based MDSs are limited to some research works and are still not in practical use. Following shortcomings can be mentioned for these systems:

1. The introduction of the neural network agents, expert system agents, and data mining agents in these CDSSs has just slightly reduced the complexity problem and hence increased the scalability and adaptability of the systems, however, each agent is still facing the same old problems. Furthermore, keeping the agents simple enough, i.e. limited to small group of diseases, the number of agents will increase, and here again the interaction between the agents will be an issue.

2. In these systems the MASs are just used to break down the problem into some simpler ones, but the mechanism which derives the final diagnosis from the agents' outputs is not using the maximum potential of the MASs.
3. Despite the learning abilities offered by MASs, there has never been a serious attempt with this regard in multi-agent based MDSs, and most of the work is just limited to a description of the architecture of the systems.
4. As is the case with Watson and Isabel, a focused H&P is here again missing.

The State of the Art of the ML Techniques for the HMASs. This section concentrates on the most remarkable Multi-Agent Learning (MAL) techniques, which have been designed for the HMASs, together with their drawbacks:

1. **Holonic MAL Based on Artificial Immune System** [20]: This work presents an adaptive agent architecture for HMASs with a learning mechanism, which is based on artificial immune systems. The affinity between two holons can be calculated only if they both react to the same problem. Therefore, the convergence rate is relatively very low. Furthermore, the affinity is calculated based on the rewards, however, in many systems such as in HMDS, this factor can be measured separately and improve the accuracy.
2. **Holonic MAL Based on Reinforcement Learning (RL)** [21]: This work presents a RL method for HMASs, however, it is originally designed for the purpose of distributed problem solving and does not cover all the aspects of self-organization. Furthermore, the convergence of the proposed learning method has not been proven for all environments.

2   Holonic Multi-Agent Systems (HMASs)

The concept of agent-oriented programming was first introduced by Shoham in 1990 [22]. An agent is a computer system that is situated in some environment, and that is capable of autonomous action in this environment in order to meet its delegated objectives [23]. A MAS consists of a collections of individual agents, and its capability is an emergent functionality that surpasses some of the capabilities of each of these agents [24]. An interesting overview of MAS architectures is presented in [25]. This section concentrates on one of the well-known MAS architectures, the HMAS.

2.1   An Introduction to the HMAS Paradigm

The field of MAS is a part of Distributed Artificial Intelligence (DAI) in the sense that a MAS lends itself naturally to distributed problem solving, where each agent has the characteristics of a distinct problem solver for a specific task. Many distributed problems exhibit a recursive structure: an agent that solves the overall problem may have a similar structure as the agents for the sub-problems, thus they should be structured recursively. More generally, an agent that appears as a single entity to the outside world may in fact be composed of many sub-agents and conversely, many sub-agents may decide that it is advantageous to join into the coherent structure of a super-agent and, thus, act as a single entity. Agents consisting of sub-agents with the same inherent structure are called holonic agents [24].

The term holon was originally introduced in 1967 by Koestler [26] in order to name recursive and self-similar structures in biological and sociological entities. According to [26], a holon is a natural or artificial structure that consists of several holons as sub-structures. In contrast to sub-structures in Koestler's framework, in HMASs all entities are restricted to agents [24]. A holonic agent of a well-defined software architecture may join several other holonic agents to form a super-holon; this group of agents, i.e. sub-holons, now act as if it were a single holonic agent with the same software architecture [24]. Depending on the level of observation, a holon can in fact be seen as an organization of holons or as an autonomous atomic entity, i.e. it is a whole-part construct, composed of other holons, but it is, at the same time, a component of a higher level holon [27]. This duality is called the Janus Effect, in reference to the two faces of a holon.

The organizational structure of a holonic society, or holarchy, offers advantages that the monolithic design of most technical artifacts lack: They are robust in the face of external and internal disturbances and damages, they are efficient in their use of resources, and they can adapt to environment changes [24]. In fact, HMAS architecture confines the environment and accordingly the responsibility of the agents in different levels of holarchy. This will reduce the complexity of the system, ease the changes and hence speed up the convergence rate. Obviously, all these advantages do not mean that HMAS architecture is more effective than the other architectures introduces for MASs, but specifically for the domains it is meant for. As stated in [24, 25] domains suitable for holonic agents should involve actions that are recursively decomposable, exhibit hierarchical structures, and include cooperative elements.

One of the most attractive characteristics of HMASs is the self-organization capability. Self-organization is the autonomous continuous arrangement of the parts of a system in such a way that best matches its objectives. This requires the holons to be able to merge with other holons according to the compatibility they have to work together [27]. ML techniques should be applied to this aspect of the HMASs in order to guaranty its improvement. A generic framework for HMASs is presented in [27], containing a generic engine that can guide the self-organization process. This research will refine this engine in order to match the objectives of the HMDS.

2.2 A Generic Framework for Holonic Systems Modelling

This section aims to introduce the generic framework for HMAS modelling presented in [27] that is not limited to any specific architecture or domain, and attempts to cover all the aspects of a HMAS. It should be noted that this framework is not going to be used as a modelling framework, but rather as a framework to consider all the aspects of a HMAS. Furthermore, the self-organization engine, proposed by this framework, can be used as a generic guideline to conduct the learning process in the HMDS.

The Important Aspects of a Holonic MAS. According to the framework the three important aspects of a Holonic MAS are:

1. **Holon Structure and Management:** A super-holon is an entity in its own right, but it is composed by its members. This part of the framework considers how the members organize and manage the super-holon.
2. **Goal-Dependent Interactions:** Super-holons are created with an objective and to fulfill certain tasks. To achieve these goals/tasks, the members must interact and coordinate their actions. The framework also offers means to model these aspects of the super-holons' functioning.
3. **Dynamics:** Dynamics are inherent characteristics of MAS. The framework considers in particular two of the most attractive characteristics of Holonic MAS: Merging (Creating and Joining a super-holon) and Self-Organization.

A Satisfaction/Affinity Based Self-organization Engine for HMASs. The second component of the framework provides a generic engine that guides the holons in their merging process. This engine is based on the roles suggested by the framework: Head, Part, Multi-Part and Stand-Alone. The Head is the representative of the group. The Part is played by those holons belonging to only one super-holon and Multi-Part by those shared by more than one super-holon. The Stand-Alone represents, how non-members are seen by an existing holon. The framework defines a set of possible transitions between these roles, that represent the likely evolution of an entity inside its super-holon. Adding conditions to these transitions can provide a guide to this evolution. The framework proposes a specialization of the generic engine based on the affinity and satisfaction between holons. The affinity measures, according to the application's objectives, the compatibility of two holons to work together toward a shared objective, and the satisfaction measures the progress of the holon toward the accomplishment of its current goal. The transition conditions should always be refined to match the application's objective and merging criteria.

3 Holonic Medical Diagnosis System (HMDS)

The HMDS, first introduced in [28–30], is a HMAS, consisting of medical experts (holons). This structure is applied to this system in a way that allows the system to perform DDx. The following sections will describe the HMDS covering all the different aspects of the HMASs mentioned in Sect. 2.2.

3.1   The Architecture of the HMDS

In general, a medical diagnosis system may either rely on highly smart deliberative agents as one extreme or on a large set of comparatively simple (reactive) agents as the other extreme. The first means that agents need to fully understand at least their area of expertise and need to have at least a basic understanding of the real world. This means that agents need to rely on a deep-going knowledge and deduction model that usually requires intensive computing power. The other extreme, which is chosen here, is to keep agents extremely simple and to get the smartness out of the smart and sophisticated interplay of extremely large amounts of simple agents as it is realized by swarm intelligence-based systems. The HMDS as a HMAS realizes an improved version of the second approach. It consists of two types of agents: comparatively simple Disease Representative Agents (DRA) as the fundament of the system on the lowest level and more sophisticated Disease Specialist Agents (DSA) as decision makers on the higher levels of the system (Fig. 1).

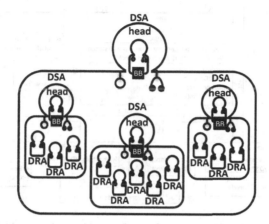

Fig. 1. DRAs and DSAs in HMDS (BB: Blackboard)

DRAs are atomic agents, thus, are not further decomposable and form the leaves of the holarchy. Each DRA is an expert on a specific disease or even only on a different appearance of it. It maintains a pattern store that contains the Disease Description Pattern (DDP) – an array of possible signs, symptoms, and test results. Thus, in order to join the diagnosis process, these agents only need to perform some kind of pattern matching (i.e., calculating their Euclidean distance to the diagnosis request description pattern). DSAs are holons consisting of numbers of DRAs and/or DSAs that rely on similar sets of symptoms; i.e., represent similar diseases. This encapsulation, in fact, enables the implementation of the DDx. DSAs can deal with a more or less broad domain of instances of related diseases. The higher they are in the holarchy the more general and broader their knowledge needs to be. A DSA on a higher level is assumed to cover a superset of all sets of diseases that are represented by all its body agents on the next lower level, however, on a more abstract level. For each DSA, a head is defined for its lifetime, representing its members by providing the common interface to the outside of the holon, i.e., to the next higher level in the holarchy.

The class diagram in Fig. 2 visualizes the different types of agents, their operations (methods), and their relations. *HMDSAgent* classifier is the generalization of all of the agents in the system. Of course, these agents will also implement some different interfaces, however, they will all extend the *HMDSAgent*. As discussed already, there are two types of agents in the HMDS, i.e., DRAs and the DSAs. Each DSA is represented by a head. This head will not be chosen from the available members, but will be created for the lifetime of the holon, based on agent cloning (for more information on agent cloning please refer to [31–33]). Agent cloning can be a comprehensive

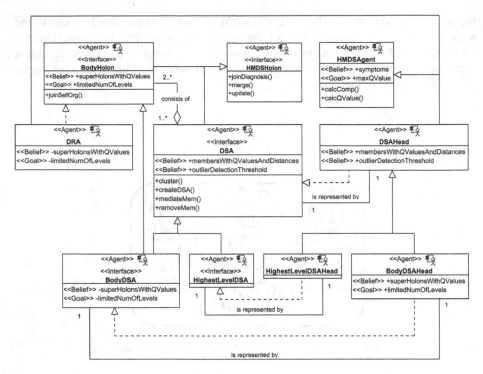

Fig. 2. AUML class diagram for HMDS

approach to the problem of local agent overhead, and since the agents may leave their super-holons, it can reduce the complexity of the system. The fact, that heads have same functionalities and their creation is merely needed when a new super-holon is being formed within an existing super-holon, indicates how agent cloning is a perfect solution to the mentioned problems. For this purpose, each head is capable of cloning, i.e., creating a copy of its code, and passing the relevant information to the new agent.

The holarchy has one root, in fact a DSA, which will play the role of the common and exclusive interface to the outside world for the complete holarchy. Due to its self-organization ability the system can start with this DSA, take all the DRAs as its members, and then let the DSAs form automatically. Although this process is based on the affinity and satisfaction, and at the beginning no information about the satisfaction factor is available, it is still possible to initially form the DSAs based on the affinity, i.e., the similarity between them. For this reason, the mentioned DSA accepts the initial description of the diseases in form of DRAs, as its members, clusters them, and defines for each of the clusters (i.e. super-holons) a head. This is repeated recursively until no further clustering is necessary[2]. This step is not mandatory but can be performed once

---

[2] The Density-Based Spatial Clustering of Applications with Noise (DBSCAN) [56] is one of the best algorithms for this issue. In [57] a simple and effective method for automatically detecting the input parameter of DBSCAN is presented, which helps best to deal with complicated data such as diseases.

as the system is being defined and accelerate the self-organization. Later on, the system can still refine its architecture using its self-organization technique.

The communication between agents is solely done via the blackboard of each DSA. More information about blackboard systems is presented in [34, 35]. According to their types, agents in HMDS also need to save a subset of the following data in their memory: Respective symptoms, Super-holons and their corresponding Q-Values (see Sect. 4.2), Sub-holons and their corresponding Q-Values, Diagnosis request, Intermediate results of the diagnosis process. In addition, the members of the super-holons need to have access to some of the data kept by their super-holons, and even share some information with the other members of their super-holons. With this regard, the super-holon's functionalities can best be supported by blackboard systems.

3.2 The Functionality of the HMDS

In principle, the proposed system works as follows: When a request for a medical diagnosis is sent to the HMDS it is actually received by the head of this holarchy (as explained already above). This head receives the request as a specific combination of signs, symptoms and medical test results and places it as an array on its blackboard. Each agent of the system which has knowledge of this blackboard, i.e. any member of this super-holon, can read the messages on this blackboard. A DRA's reaction to a request message is to send back its similarity to the request. However, based on the provided information a DSA may decide that it wants to try to join the diagnosis process or not. This will actually control the data flow in the holarchy. The decision is made based on some simple statistical information about the DSA's members. The head knows its distance to each of its members. So, it just calculates its distance to the request and in case the request is not an outlier, the head will decide to join the diagnosis process. This means that it will read all the information from the blackboard of its head and will place it on its own blackboard. Then the same process starts again and repeats recursively until the request reaches the final level of the holarchy.

Results obtained by participating agents now flow the other way round from bottom to the top of the holarchy. On their way up the results are sorted according to their similarity. More precisely, each agent will send its final results, suggestions and questions to its super-holon including: the top diagnoses together with all the signs, symptoms or test results that are relevant from the agent's point of view. This implies that originally not provided relevant information may be requested from the user in a second step. In fact, according to the DDx, the system may suggest the user to provide more information or undertake specific medical tests to improve diagnostic accuracy.

A simplified example will be given here in order to demonstrate the system functionality. Suppose a system of 20 diseases, and 40 different entries for the DDP. This will form a 20×40 matrix, whose entries are real numbers between 0 and 1, indicating the frequency of the characteristics under consideration in the DDP for each of the diseases. The diagnosis request will be considered in form of an array with 40 entries, in which the chief complain, the claimed symptoms and the general signs will be saved. The corresponding entries are set to 1 and the rest of the entries will be set to 0.5 as a neutral entry. For the simplicity reasons suppose that after clustering the disease number 1 to 10 have formed DSA1, disease number 11 to 16 have formed DSA2, and disease number 17 to 20 have formed DSA3.

In this example, the first diagnosis request contains the following signs and symptoms: $E_6, E_{11}, E_{18}, E_{20}, E_{32}, E_{33}, E_{39}, E_{40}$. As this entry is no outlier to the system's members, it will be placed on its blackboard. All the members will then check if they can provide any solutions and as seen in Fig. 3, DRA1 and DRA2 pass their most possible diagnoses and the items under question to their head. The head will then put them in order, extract the most possible ones and their corresponding questions. Following this stage, the user should try to provide the answers to the given questions, i.e. the second input. In this example E_{12}, E_{23}, and E_{37} are present and hence set to 1 and the rest of the questioned items are set to 0. After receiving this input the system is able to provide a more precise diagnosis (see Fig. 4). The system actually narrows down the items to be checked (in this case from 32 to 15). In real systems with many different tests under consideration this difference can be of eminent importance.

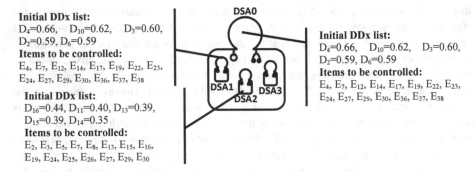

Initial DDx list:
$D_4=0.66$, $D_{10}=0.62$, $D_3=0.60$,
$D_2=0.59$, $D_6=0.59$
Items to be controlled:
E_4, E_7, E_{12}, E_{14}, E_{17}, E_{19}, E_{22}, E_{23},
E_{24}, E_{27}, E_{29}, E_{30}, E_{36}, E_{37}, E_{38}

Initial DDx list:
$D_{16}=0.44$, $D_{11}=0.40$, $D_{13}=0.39$,
$D_{15}=0.39$, $D_{14}=0.35$
Items to be controlled:
E_2, E_3, E_5, E_7, E_8, E_{13}, E_{15}, E_{16},
E_{19}, E_{24}, E_{25}, E_{26}, E_{27}, E_{29}, E_{30}

Initial DDx list:
$D_4=0.66$, $D_{10}=0.62$, $D_3=0.60$,
$D_2=0.59$, $D_6=0.59$
Items to be controlled:
E_4, E_7, E_{12}, E_{14}, E_{17}, E_{19}, E_{22}, E_{23},
E_{24}, E_{27}, E_{29}, E_{30}, E_{36}, E_{37}, E_{38}

Fig. 3. Initial DDx list based on the first input (D: Disease/E: Element of the DDP)

Revised DDx list:
$D_3=0.84$, $D_4=0.72$, $D_{10}=0.58$,
$D_1=0.58$, $D_2=0.55$

Fig. 4. Revised DDx list based on the second input

3.3   The Self-organization in the HMDS

In the self-organization process of HMDS, the agents decide on their actions, i.e. to leave, stay in or join a super-holon, according to the similarity between their symptoms and some learned values (c.f. Sect. 4). In general, the decision making idea is based on some statistical techniques for outlier detection, called the empirical rule [36], i.e. an agent may decide to join a holon if it's not an outlier to its members, and may decide to leave its super-holon in the opposite case.

4 Reinforcement Learning (RL) in HMASs

In HMDS, the holarchy is keeping track of the best decisions made by the system. This process needs to be supported by some suitable ML techniques. Considering the nature of the problem, the absence of desired input/output pairs, and the accessibility of a dynamic environment, RL is the best match for the problem. Many different RL techniques can be found in literature from which the best fitting one for the system is to be chosen and adapted to the requirements; i.e., in order to apply RL to the problem, it is first essential to model it in a way that the algorithms can be applied. For this reason, the Markov Decision Processes (MDPs) framework [37, 38] is used [39].

Since RL algorithms do not assume a given model for the MDP, one of the key issues while using them is that learners need to explore the environment in order to discover the effects of their actions. This problem is usually known as exploitation-exploration trade-off. Two basic ways exist to address this question. On-policy methods estimate values of the policy that is currently being used and attempt to improve on this policy. In contrast, in off-policy methods the agent uses a behavior function or control function, which differs from the goal policy that is being learned. In this case the process is often divided in a learning phase during which the optimal policy is learned, and a control phase during which it is used for control [40]. An advantage of this separation is that the estimation policy may be deterministic (e.g. greedy), while the behavior policy can continue to sample all possible actions [41].

Table 1 lists a number of notable RL techniques. QL method, as an off-policy technique, is an excellent candidate for the realization of the RL in the HMDS, and this is also the case for most of the Multi-Agent RL (MARL) methods [49]. In fact, even though among the mentioned RL techniques QL tends to converge a bit slower, it has the capability to continue learning while changing policies and is more flexible if alternative routes appear. This is only the case with off-policy methods, where even if an agent changes its policy, the system is still able to use what it has learnt so far. Since HMDS is a self-organizing system, consisting of several autonomous agents that may have different policies and may even change their policies constantly, it is clear

Table 1. A number of notable RL techniques

RL technique	Policy	Year	Reference
Actor-Critic (AC)	On-policy	1983	[42]
Temporal Difference (TD)	On-policy	1988	[43]
Q-Learning (QL)	Off-policy	1989	[44]
R-learning	Off-policy	1993	[45]
State-Action-Reward-State-Action (SARSA)	On-policy	1994	[46]
Actor Critic Learning Automaton (ACLA)	On-policy	2007	[47]
QV(λ)-learning	On-policy	2007	[47]
Monte Carlo (MC) for RL	On-policy	2008	[48]

that the usage of an off-policy technique is here essential. It should be noted that R-learning is a variant of QL and also an off-policy technique, however, specifically for non-discounted, non-episodic problems, and hence not suitable for the HMDS.

4.1 Q-Learning for Agent-Based Systems

A significant number of researches on learning in agent-based systems use RL. The algorithms can be divided into three different classes: single-agent RL, multi-agent RL (a combination of Game Theory and RL), and swarm RL (a combination of Swarm Intelligence and RL). A comprehensive overview of single and multi-agent RL is presented in [49]. Rather than developing complex behaviors for single individuals, swarm intelligence-based RL investigates the emerging (intelligent) behavior of a group of simple individuals that achieve complex behavior through their interactions. Similar to single-agent RL, in swarm RL state transition functions are described by a single agent's action. On the other hand, similar to MARL, swarm RL recognizes other agents' actions, however, solely implicitly by considering their effects.

Most swarm RL algorithms are based on Ant Colony Optimization (ACO) and pheromones: Ant-Q [50], Pheromone-QL (Phe-Q) [51], Swarm RL based on ACO [52]. These techniques are all designed based on QL algorithms, however, applying them to the self-organization of a HMAS has the following disadvantages: (1) In an ant colony the ants will follow the pheromones because of their strength and not the type of food they can expect at the end. In HMDS the latter plays a role, since the agents, that are experts in special disease or group of similar diseases, are just interested in the trails matching their specialty, (2) Most swarm RL algorithms consider a constant value as the reward for each action, however, this value can indicate the satisfaction in the HMDS and should be calculated each time the action is chosen.

4.2 Holonic-Q-Learning (HQL)

In holonic-QL, the Q-value is in fact measuring how good it is for a holon to be a member (i.e. sub-holon) of another holon. In this case, the states are the existing holons $\{h_i\}$ and action h_i indicates becoming a sub-holon of holon i.

$$Q_t(sub(h), h) \leftarrow (1 - \alpha_t)Q_{t-1}(sub(h), h) + \alpha_t(R_t(sub(h), h) + \gamma \underset{Q_{t-1}(h, \sup(h))}{\operatorname{argmax}} (Q_{t-1}(h, \sup(h)).Aff(sub(h), \sup(h)))) \tag{1}$$

where, $\alpha_t = \frac{1}{1 + visits_t(sub(h), h)}$, $\gamma \in [0, 1)$ is the discount factor, and $Aff(sub(h), h) = 1 - \frac{d(sub(h), h)}{\max d(sub(h), h)}$. The reward is actually calculated by the head of a super-holon. For this reason, each of the sub-holons will calculate their similarity, i.e. affinity, to the final diagnosis. Then all the members with close affinity values will be awarded with the highest affinity value reported by the sub-holons. Any possible sub-holon with an affinity value that is an outlier to the sub-holons' affinity values will not receive a reward. The head/super-holon will be rewarded by its own super-holon.

Convergence of the HQL. In order to prove the convergence of the HQL, an approach similar to the one used for QL in [53] is followed here, which uses a theorem on random iterative processes convergence [54, 55].

Theorem 1. A random iterative process $\Delta_{n+1}(x) = (1 - \alpha_n(x))\Delta_n(x) + \beta_n(x)F_n(x)$ converges to zero w.p.1 if (i) The state space is finite, (ii) $\sum_n \alpha_n(x) = \infty$, $\sum_n \alpha_n^2(x) < \infty$, $\sum_n \beta_n(x) = \infty$, $\sum_n \beta_n^2(x) < \infty$, and $E\{\beta_n(x)|P_n\} \le E\{\alpha_n(x)|P_n\}$ uniformly w.p.1, (iii) $\|E\{F_n(x)|P_n\}\|_w < \gamma\|\Delta_n\|_w$, where $\gamma \in (0,1)$, and (iv) $Var\{F_n(x)|P_n\} \le C(1 + \|\Delta_n\|_w)^2$, where C is some constant.

Here $P_n = \{\Delta_n, \Delta_{n-1}, \ldots, F_{n-1}, \ldots, \alpha_{n-1}, \ldots, \beta_{n-1}, \ldots\}$ stands for the past at step n. $F_n(x)$, $\alpha_n(x)$, and $\beta_n(x)$ are allowed to depend on the past insofar as the above conditions remain valid. The notation $\|.\|_w$ refers to some weighted maximum norm.

Proof. See [55].

Theorem 2. Given a finite $MDP(H, A, T, R, \gamma)$, the HQL algorithm, given by the update rule (1) Converges w.p.1 to the optimal Holonic Q-function if (i) The state and action spaces are finite, (ii) $\sum_t \alpha_t(s,a) = \infty$ and $\sum_t \alpha_t^2(s,a) < \infty$ uniformly w.p.1, (iii) $Var\{R(s_t, a_t)\}$ is bounded, and (iv) $2\gamma \le \gamma' < 1, \gamma.\max \Delta Q \ge 1$.

In order to prove Theorem 2, it is first essential to show that the optimal Holonic-Q-function, i.e. Q^*, is a fixed point of a contraction[3] operator H, defined as:

$$(Hq)(sub(h), h) = \sum_{h \in H} T(sub(h), h) \left[R_t(sub(h), h). \right.$$

$$\left. + \gamma \underset{q(h, \sup(h))}{\text{argmax}} \; q(h, \sup(h)).Aff(sub(h), \sup(h)) \right]$$

This operator is a contraction in the sup-norm, i.e.

$$\|Hq_1 - Hq_2\|_\infty \le \gamma'\|q_1 - q_2\|_\infty \tag{2}$$

This inequality can be proven as follows:

---

[3] A mapping $T : X \to X$ is a contraction on a metric space (X, d), if there exists a constant c, with $0 \le c < 1$, such that $d(T(x), T(y)) \le c.d(x, y)$ for all $x, y \in X$ [58].

$$\|Hq_1 - Hq_2\|_\infty = \max_{h_i,h_j}\left|\sum_{h_j\in H} T(h_i,h_j)\left[R_1(h_i,h_j)\right.\right.$$

$$\left.\left. + \gamma \operatorname*{argmax}_{q_1(h_j,h_k)} q_1(h_j,h_k).Aff(h_i,h_k) - R_2(h_i,h_j) - \gamma \operatorname*{argmax}_{q_2(h_j,h_k)} q_2(h_j,h_k).Aff(h_i,h_k)\right]\right|$$

$$\le \max_{h_i,h_j}\left|\sum_{h_j\in H} T(h_i,h_j)[\max \Delta R + \gamma \max \Delta q]\right| \le \max_{h_i,h_j}\sum_{h_j\in H} T(h_i,h_j)|2\gamma \max \Delta q|$$

$$\le \max_{h_i,h_j}\gamma'\sum_{h_j\in H} T(h_i,h_j)\|q_1 - q_2\|_\infty = \gamma'\|q_1 - q_2\|_\infty.$$

Proof of Theorem 2. Subtracting from both sides of the HQL update rule the quantity $Q^*(sub(h),h)$ and letting $\Delta_t(sub(h),h) = Q_t(sub(h),h) - Q^*(sub(h),h)$, yields:

$$\Delta_{t+1}(sub(h),h) = (1 - \alpha_t)\Delta_t(sub(h),h) + \alpha_t[R_t(sub(h),h)$$
$$+ \gamma \operatorname*{argmax}_{Q_{t-1}(h,\sup(h))} (Q_{t-1}(h,\sup(h)).Aff(sub(h),\sup(h))) - Q^*(sub(h),h)]$$

The algorithm can be seen to have the form of the process in Theorem 1 with $\beta_n = \alpha_n$. In order to verify that $F_t(sub(h),h)$ has the required properties, the third condition is considered here first. Since $Q^* = HQ^*$, $\mathbb{E}[F_t(sub(h),h)|P_t] = (HQ_t)(sub(h),h) - Q^*(sub(h),h) = (HQ_t)(sub(h),h) - HQ^*(sub(h),h)$. It is now immediate from (2) that $\|\mathbb{E}[F_t(sub(h),h)|P_t]\|_\infty \le \gamma\|Q_t - Q^*\|_\infty = \gamma\|\Delta_t\|_\infty$.
Finally,
$$Var[F_t(sub(h),h)|P_t] =$$

$$\mathbb{E}\left[\left(R_t(sub(h),h) + \gamma \operatorname*{argmax}_{Q_{t-1}(h,\sup(h))} (Q_{t-1}(h,\sup(h)).Aff(sub(h),\sup(h)))\right.\right.$$

$$\left.\left. - Q^*(sub(h),h) - (HQ_t)(sub(h),h) + Q^*(sub(h),h))^2\right] = \mathbb{E}[(R_t(sub(h),h)\right.$$

$$\left. + \gamma \operatorname*{argmax}_{Q_{t-1}(h,\sup(h))} (Q_{t-1}(h,\sup(h)).Aff(sub(h),\sup(h))) - (HQ_t)(sub(h),h))^2\right]$$

$$= Var\left[R_t(sub(h),h) + \gamma \operatorname*{argmax}_{Q_{t-1}(h,\sup(h))} (Q_{t-1}(h,\sup(h)).Aff(sub(h),\sup(h)))|P_t\right]$$

which due to the fact that R is bounded, verifies $Var[F_t(sub(h),h)|P_t] \le C\left(1 + \|\Delta_t\|_w^2\right)$

For some constant C. Then, by Theorem 1, Δ_t converges to zero w.p.1. i.e. Q_t converges to Q^* w.p.1. In order to assure the convergence of the HQL the learning step should be repeated until $\max \Delta Q \ge \frac{1}{\gamma}$.

5 Conclusion

The first step to a successful diagnosis is a focused H&P, that can narrow down the DDx list to a few possibilities. This paper discussed the feasibility of the usage of the HMAS paradigm for this reason and proposes the HMDS. Additionally, also some ML techniques were suggested that support the functionality and the dynamics of this holonic system. Swarm QL, as an off-policy RL, is argued to be a good solution to this problem, and the HQL technique is introduced, which can in general also be applied to the self-organization of any HMAS. The convergence of this method is also proved based on a well-known theorem on the convergence of the random iterative processes. The implementation of the system is now in progress and future work will include the complete implementation and validation of the system. The development process is being carried out with the help of a MAS platform, Janus, that is fully implemented in Java and provides a default implementation of holons using an organizational perspective. The programming language being used is the SARL agent-oriented programming language that supports HMASs and is fully interoperable with Java.

Acknowledgement. The authors gratefully acknowledge the informative and encouraging discussions with Dr. Farzad Fakouri, MD on the medical aspects of the project, and would like to express appreciation and gratitude for his knowledgeable insight and expertise, that greatly assisted the research.

References

1. Berner, E.: Clinical Decision Support Systems. Springer, New York (2016)
2. Berner, S.E.: Clinical Decision Support Systems: State of the Art. AHRQ Publication No. 09-0069-EF. Agency for Healthcare Research and Quality (2009)
3. Alther, M., Reddy, C.: Clinical Decision Support Systems, Chap. 19. In: Healthcare Data Analytics, pp. 625–656. Chapman and Hall/CRC (2015)
4. Miner, L., Bolding, P., Hilbe, J., Goldstein, M., Hill, T., Nisbet, R., Walton, N., Miner, G.: Practical Predictive Analytics and Decisioning Systems for Medicine: Informatics Accuracy and Cost-Effectiveness for Healthcare Administration and Delivery Including Medical Research. Academic Press, Cambridge (2014)
5. Merriam-Webster: Differential Diagnosis. https://www.merriam-webster.com/dictionary/differential%20diagnosis. Accessed 15 June 2017
6. Maude, J.: Differential diagnosis: the key to reducing diagnosis error, measuring diagnosis and a mechanism to reduce healthcare costs. Diagnosis 1(1), 107–109 (2014)
7. Segen, J.: Concise Dictionary of Modern Medicine. McGraw-Hill, New York (2006)
8. IBM WATSON. http://ibmwatson237.weebly.com/. Accessed 15 June 2017
9. Fisher, H., Tomlinson, A., Ramnarayan, P., Britto, J.: ISABEL: support with clinical decision making. Pediatr. Nurs. 15(7), 34–35 (2003)
10. Ramnarayan, P., Kulkarni, G., T., Britto, J.: ISABEL: a novel Internet-delivered clinical decision support system. In: Current perspectives in healthcare computing, pp. 245–256 (2004)

11. Autonomy Corporation plc: Autonomy Technology Overview (Autonomy Whitepaper). https://db.bme.hu/~gajdos/2012adatb2/4.%20eloadas%20MBC-Autonomy%20doc.pdf. Accessed 15 June 2017

12. Riches, N., Panagioti, M., Alam, R., Cheraghi-Sohi, S., Campbell, S., Esmail, A., Bower, P.: The effectiveness of electronic differential diagnoses (DDX) generators: a systematic review and meta-analysis. PLoS ONE **11**(3), e0148991 (2016)

13. Yuan, M.: Watson and healthcare: how natural language processing and semantic search could revolutionize clinical decision support. https://www.ibm.com/developerworks/library/os-ind-watson/. Accessed 15 June 2017

14. Graber, M.L., Mathew, A.: Performance of a web-based clinical diagnosis support system for internists. J. Gen. Intern. Med. **23**(1), 37–40 (2008)

15. Salem, H., Attiya, G., El-Fishawy, N.: A survey of multi-agent based intelligent decision support system for medical classification problems. Int. J. Comput. Appl. **123**(10), 20–25 (2015)

16. Klüver, C., Klüver, J., Unland, R.: A medical diagnosis system based on MAS technology and neural networks. In: BPSC. LNI, vol. 147, pp. 179–191 (2009)

17. Iantovics, B.: Agent-based medical diagnosis systems. Comput. Inf. **27**, 593–625 (2008)

18. Chao, S., Wong, F.: A multi-agent learning paradigm for medical data mining diagnostic workbench. In: Cao, L. (ed.) Data Mining and Multi-agent Integration, pp. 177–186. Springer, Boston, MA (2009). doi:10.1007/978-1-4419-0522-2_12

19. Arsene, O., Dumitrache, I., Mihu, I.: Expert system for medicine diagnosis using software agents. Exp. Syst. Appl. **42**(4), 1825–1834 (2015)

20. Hilarie, V., Koukam, A., Rodrigue, S.: An adaptive agent architecture for holonic multiagent system. ACM TAAS **3**(1), 1–24 (2008)

21. Abdoos, M., Mozayani, N., Bazzan, A.: Towards reinforcement learning for holonic multi-agent systems. Intell. Data Anal. **19**(2), 211–232 (2015)

22. Shoham, Y.: Agent-oriented programming. Technical report STAN-CS-90-1335. Stanford University (1990)

23. Wooldridge, M.: Chapter 2: Intelligent agents. In: An Introduction to MultiAgent Systems. Wiley (2009)

24. Gerber, C., Siekmann, J., Vierke, G.: Holonic multi-agent systems. Technical report DFKI-RR-99-03. German Research Centre for Artificial Intelligence (1999)

25. Lavendelis, E., Grundspenkis, J.: Open holonic multi-agent architecture for intelligent tutoring system development. In: Proceedings of IADIS International Conference on Intelligent Systems and Agents (2008)

26. Koestler, A.: The Ghost in the Machine. Hutchinson, Paris (1967)

27. Rodriguez, S.: From analysis to design of holonic multi-agent systems: a framework, methodological guidelines and applications, Ph.D. thesis. University of Technology of Belfort-Montbéliard (2005)

28. Unland, R.: A holonic multi-agent system for robust, flexible, and reliable medical diagnosis. In: Meersman, R., Tari, Z. (eds.) OTM 2003. LNCS, vol. 2889, pp. 1017–1030. Springer, Heidelberg (2003). doi:10.1007/978-3-540-39962-9_97

29. Unland, R., Ulieru, M.: Swarm intelligence and the holonic paradigm: a promising symbiosis for a medical diagnostic system. In: Khosla, R., Howlett, R.J., Jain, L.C. (eds.) KES 2005. LNCS, vol. 3682, pp. 154–160. Springer, Heidelberg (2005). doi:10.1007/11552451_21

30. Ulieru, M., Unland, R.: A stigmergic approach to medical diagnosis. In: Proceedings of the 2nd International Workshop on Multi-Agent Systems for Medicine and Computational Biology, pp. 87–103 (2006)

31. Shehory, O., Sycara, K., Chalasani, P., Jha, S.: Agent cloning: an approach to agnt mobility and resource allocation. IEEE Commun. Mag. **36**(7), 58–67 (1998)

32. Ye, D.: Self-organisation in multi-agent systems: theory and applications. Ph.D. thesis. University of Wollongong (2013)
33. Schwaiger, A., Stahmer, B.: Probabilistic holons for efficient agent-based data mining and simulation. In: Mařík, V., Brennan, R.W., Pěchouček, M. (eds.) HoloMAS 2005. LNCS, vol. 3593, pp. 50–63. Springer, Heidelberg (2005). doi:10.1007/11537847_5
34. Corkill, D.: Blackboard systems. AI Exp. 6(9), 40–47 (1991)
35. Corkill, D.: Collaborating software: blackboard and multi-agent systems and the future. In: Proceedings of the International Lisp Conference (2003)
36. Black, K.: Business Statistics: For Contemporary Decision Making, 7th edn. Wiley, Hoboken (2011)
37. Bellman, R.: A Markovian Decision Process. J. Math. Mech. 6(5), 679–684 (1957)
38. Puterman, M.: Markov Decision Processes: Diecrete Stochastic Dynamic. Wiley, New York (1994)
39. van Hasselt, H.: Insights in Reonforcment Learning. Wöhrmann Print Service, Zutphen (2011)
40. Vrancx, P.: Decentralised reinforcement learning in markov games. Ph.D. thesis, Vrije Universiteit Brussel (2010)
41. Sutton, R., Barto, A.: Reinforcement Learning: An Introduction. MIT Press, Cambridge (1998)
42. Barto, A., Sutton, R., Anderson, C.: Neuronlike adaptive elements that can solve difficult learning control problems. IEEE Trans. Syst. Man Cybern. SMC-13, 834–846 (1983)
43. Sutton, R.: Learning to predict by the methods of temporal differences. Mach. Learn. 3, 9–44 (1988)
44. Watkins, C.: Learning from delayed rewards. Ph.D. thesis. Cambridge University (1989)
45. Schwartz, A.: A reinforcement learning method for maximizing undiscounted rewards. In: Proceedings of the 10th International Conference on Machine Learning, pp. 298–305 (1993)
46. Rummery, G.A., Niranjan, M · On-Line Q-Learning Using Connectionist Systems. Cambridge University Engineering Department, Cambridge (1994)
47. Wiering, M., van Hasselt, H.: Two novel on-policy reinforcement learning algortihms based on TD(λ)-methods. In: Approximate Dynamic Programming and Reinforcement Learning, ADPRL 2007 (2007)
48. Hoffman, M., Jasra, A.: Trans-dimensional MCMC for Bayesian policy learning. Neural Inf. Process. Syst. 20, 1–8 (2008)
49. Buşoniu, L., Babuška, R., Schutter, B.: Multi-agent reinforcement learning: an overview. In: Srinivasan, D., Jain, L.C. (eds.) Innovations in Multi-Agent Systems and Applications - 1. Studies in Computational Intelligence, vol. 310, pp. 183–221. Springer, Berlin, Heidelberg (2010)
50. Gambardella, L., Dorigo, M.: Ant-Q: a reinforcement learning approach to the traveling salesman problem. In: Proceedings of ML-95, 12th International Conference on Machine Learning, pp. 252–260 (1995)
51. Monekosso, N., Remagnino, P.: Phe-Q: a pheromone based Q-learning. In: Stumptner, M., Corbett, D., Brooks, M. (eds.) AI 2001. LNCS, vol. 2256, pp. 345–355. Springer, Heidelberg (2001). doi:10.1007/3-540-45656-2_30
52. Iima, H., Kuroe, Y., Matsuda, S.: Swarm reinforcement learning method based on ant colony optimization. In: 2010 IEEE International Conference on Systems Man and Cybernetics (SMC), pp. 1726–1733 (2010)
53. Melo, F.: Convergence of Q-learning: a simple proof. institute of systems and robotics. Technical Report, pp. 1–4 (2001)

54. Jaakkola, T., Jordan, M., Singh, S.: On the convergence of stochastic iterative dynamic programming algorithms. Massachusetts Institute of Technology, Artificial Intelligence Laboratory, A.I. Memo No. 1441 (1993)
55. Jaakkola, T., Jordan, M., Singh, S.: On the convergence of stochastic iterative dynamic programming algorithms. Neural Comput. **6**(6), 1185–1201 (1994)
56. Ester, M., Kriegel, H.-P., Sander, J., Xu, X.: A density-based algorithm for discovering clusters in large spatial databases with noise. In Simoudis, E., Han, J., Fayyad, U. (eds.) Proceedings of the 2nd International Conference on Knowledge Discoverey and Data Mining (KDD-96), pp. 226–231 (1996)
57. Akbari, Z., Unland, R.: Automated determination of the input parameter of DBSCAN based on outlier detection. In: Iliadis, L., Maglogiannis, I. (eds.) AIAI 2016. IAICT, vol. 475, pp. 280–291. Springer, Cham (2016). doi:10.1007/978-3-319-44944-9_24
58. Hunter, J., Nachtergaele, B.: Applied Analysis. World Scientific Publishing, Singapore (2001)

Author Index

Printed in the United States
By Bookmasters